Telling Identities

Telling Identities

The Californio *testimonios*

Rosaura Sánchez

University of Minnesota Press

Minneapolis

London

The author and publisher gratefully acknowledge permission from the Bancroft Library of the University of California at Berkeley to print material from its collection of manuscripts and manuscript dictations.

Extracts from *testimonios* reproduced on the cover include (*clockwise from upper left*) María Angustias de la Guerra Ord, *Ocurrencias en California*. 1878. (BANC MSS C-D 134); Mariano Guadalupe Vallejo, *Recuerdos históricos y personales tocante a la Alta California*. 1874, 5:17 (BANC MSS C-D 21); Agustín Escobar, "La campaña de '46 contra los americanos en California, 1877." In Carlos Hijar, Eulalia Pérez, and Agustín Escobar, *Three Memoirs of Mexican California*, Berkeley: Friends of the Bancroft Library, 1988, 112 and 115.

Published by the University of Minnesota Press
111 Third Avenue South, Suite 290, Minneapolis, MN 55401-2520
Printed in the United States of America on acid-free paper

Library of Congress Cataloging-in-Publication Data
Sánchez, Rosaura.
    Telling identities: the Californio testimonios / Rosaura Sánchez.
      p.   cm.
    Includes bibliographical references and index.
    ISBN 0-8166-2558-1 (HC)
    ISBN 0-8166-2559-X (PB)
    1. California — History — To 1846 — Sources. 2. Mexican Americans — California — History — 19th century — Sources. I. Title.
    F864.S235 1995
    979.4'0046872 — dc20   94-36503

To A. R. Sánchez (1904–1974)
and Frances Arteaga Sánchez

Contents

Preface

> Only that historian will have the gift of fanning the spark
> of hope in the past who is firmly convinced that even the
> dead will not be safe from the enemy if he wins.
>
> Walter Benjamin

In the decade of the 1870s the conquered Californios were living in occupied land, looking back on their past in Alta California with both nostalgia and resentment. The U.S. invasion and its aftermath had left them dispossessed and marginalized. Their loss was further compounded by the demeaning representation of Californios given in various historical accounts, as much by hegemonic historians as by visitors, sailors, merchants, and early Anglo pioneers. It was these, for the most part disparaging, accounts that the Californios felt the need to counter by offering a reconstruction of their history from their own vantage point. In the 1870s, however, publication in mainstream venues was not accessible to an impoverished population that, although once dominant in the territory, now saw itself outnumbered and disempowered.

In that same decade the Californios were asked by agents of Hubert Howe Bancroft, a rich San Francisco book dealer and publisher, to narrate their recollections of their past in Alta California as part of a research project seeking to assemble all available information and documentation on California history. A good number of older Californios—about sixty-two—agreed to dictate their reminiscences to Bancroft's agents. Some agreed to short interviews; others dictated more extensive memoirs and made use of their own writings, correspondence, and documents. These elicited dictations, or testimonials (as they are called in this study), represent an effort on the part of this subaltern population to counter hegemonic historiography, to construct a collective identity, and to reposition and recenter themselves textually at a time when the physical and social spaces from which they could operate had become increasingly circumscribed.

The reconstruction of life in Alta California before 1846 necessarily looks back on difference, on the particularity of the population and on "the way it used to be" before invasion and the capitalist restructuring of California had brought deep and widespread sociospatial and geopolitical changes to this former Mexican territory, in the process displacing the Californio collectivity as if all that was solid had, in fact, melted into air. For those who lost everything, especially their lands, the resentment ran deep; others faced the situation with resignation and with nostalgia for the past; still others tried to accommodate to the new society. The perspectives in these testimonials are multiple and contradictory, for they emerge from complex sets of residual, emergent, and, in more than a few instances, still current ideological discourses generated by a series of social conditions that are still with us today and that continue to problematize the politics of ethnic identity.

A great deal has been written by historians and political scientists alike on the Spanish and Mexican periods of California history; yet although the mediated narratives produced by Californios have often been consulted by scholars, there is no analysis of the testimonials themselves as historical and literary texts nor has there been a reading of their cognitive mapping of local and global social spaces and social practices. Except for work on some of these texts as autobiographies, these narratives have as yet gone unexamined as sites of political struggle for representation, and unexplored in terms of the discursive construction of collective identity in the textual disjunctures produced by overlapping, interconnecting, and colliding discourses.

This book sets out, first of all, to recover and examine texts long relegated to what we might term the dustbin of literature and history, and second, to engage in a reconstruction of our own conflictive past and its contradictions, political struggles that speak to us as present-day Chicanos. Rooted in a cultural politics, the study considers cultural production as inseparable from structural and agential relations and for that reason takes on and examines the issue of representation by a subaltern population within the context of relations of production, social restructuring, and collective agency. This study of subaltern texts is thus necessarily concerned with politics of identity construction and with the recognition that the bones of "our dead" have too long lain cluttered in the mausoleum of "the enemy," and that without examining the Californios' contradictory countering of dominant regimes of representation embedded in these texts we will not be able to "fan the spark of hope" in our own construction of a new politics of representation.

This study focuses on close to thirty testimonials narrated primarily in Spanish by Californios in the 1870s for the Bancroft project, as well as on additional narratives, diaries, letters, and documents from the nineteenth century. Most of this material has never been published and is accessible only in its original handwritten form or on microfilm at the Bancroft Library, housed at the University of California at Berkeley. Difficulties in accessing and decoding these nineteenth-century manuscripts perhaps also explain why these texts have not before received the attention that they merit.

The book is divided into seven chapters and narrated in the plural "we" in recognition of the collective efforts that lie behind all cultural production, including that of the "Californio" dead, and all the theorists, cultural critics, and historians whose work has been tapped for this study. A genre like the *testimonio* in which literary and nonliterary, popular and elite, historical and fictional discourses overlap and intersect also requires an interdisciplinary methodology. For this reason, this analysis draws from several disciplinary areas that deal with issues of ideology, subjectivity, nationalism, racism, ethnicity, gender, feudalism, colonialism, neocolonialism, capitalism, and especially Marxist theory. All of these theoretical discourses have enabled the construction of a space of engagement and analysis wherein these testimonials can be viewed as representational spaces and as ideological fields for discursive struggle. In so doing we assume an ideological approach that allows for both a macrostructural and microstructural, historical and literary decoding of these texts.

The first chapter of this study reads the testimonial as a macrotext and as a genre of mediated narratives and distinguishes it from autobiography. After addressing the implications of the dependent mode of testimonial production, the chapter goes on to provide specific details on the Bancroft historiographic project while focusing on the politics of representation of the Californios involved. The chapter concludes with a delineation of the theoretical and analytical instruments mobilized for this study, in particular the notions of agency, subjectivity, social space, and discursive formations that underpin our disarticulation of Californio identities.

In chapter 2 we begin to explore the mission as the dominant social space of Alta California during the Spanish colonial period and as a religious and economic institution inscribed in testimonial configurations as a heterotopic site. Of special interest are the discourses of caste, social order, and culture, which are central to representations of Indians, missionaries, soldiers, and settlers during the Spanish phase of colonization, as well as the strategies of repression and discipline mobilized to maintain that social order.

Chapter 3 maps the restructuring of Alta California after Mexican independence by focusing on the strategic appropriation of the discursive framework — liberalism — by the emergent class of *rancheros* and on their positioning in relation to the secularization of the mission, the dispossession of the Indians, and the privatization of the land. The representation of the Híjar-Padrés colonization project in particular serves to provide an overview of the various perspectives and counterdiscourses on secularization and allows us to examine the manipulation of liberal discourses called upon to legitimate the political and economic practices of what would become the dominant class in Alta California.

Chapter 4 focuses on the dominant social spaces after secularization (the *ranchos* and *haciendas*) and on the new landed class of *rancheros* and *hacendados*. Like chapter 3, it continues to trace Californio subjection and exploitation of the Indians as well as native resistance against displacement and occupation. The mininarrative of the Indian raid at Rancho Jamul is shown to reconfigure social antagonisms and to work out allegorically what are perceived as threats to the Californio nation.

Chapter 5 examines the restructuring of sexual politics in Alta California after Mexican independence through a reading of several mininarratives provided in a number of the testimonials that deal with Californio women, from both before and after 1821, whose life stories took on legendary proportions. These episodes, rewritten as allegories, transcode and rework relations between Alta California and outsiders, especially foreign merchants, by establishing women as links to the Californio "family." What interests us here particularly is the recombination of discourses of gender, class, and nation for a reconstruction of two phases of California history that trigger a reconfiguration of social spaces and a concomitant reordering of gender roles.

Chapter 6 foregrounds protonationalism in Alta California and traces the liminal spaces generated in the interstices of colliding social spaces and agencies after Mexican independence and the restructuring of the territory. These new sites are bound up with interconnecting discourses of nation, region, and political orientation that serve to rechart what is a failed Californio attempt at national independence and to resituate M. G. Vallejo's constructed meeting of prominent Californios to assess their options on the eve of U.S. invasion. The chapter concludes with a reassessment of these competing discursive formations and a mapping of the diverse political positions among Californios before 1846.

The last chapter evokes the disjuncture produced by antagonistic social relations after 1848. To residual counterdiscourses are added emergent discourses for a new politics of representation. It is here, in the mediated narratives, that the Californios collectively generate new discourses of ethnicity, new constructs of identity as a marginalized, disempowered, and dispossessed ethnic minority. The final chapter in M. G. Vallejo's testimonial, an essay that summarizes the resentment and frustrations of these Californios, as well as Coronel's discussion of banditry and racism in the mining camps of the gold rush era, serves to frame comments on these issues by other Californios and to map out new sites of struggle.

This is a study of discourses of the subaltern, the Californios, who, acutely aware of their displacement, felt compelled to speak, to engage in cultural struggle, not as an end in itself, but as a strategy toward repositioning themselves collectively. Unlike Edward Bellamy, who looked forward into the past, we argue that only by looking back into the future do we become aware of the need to measure our own present in terms of the past. The subaltern can speak and do in these texts have a voice that needs to be heard.

I would especially like to acknowledge my indebtedness to Beatrice Pita, who helped me track down the many manuscripts available at the Bancroft Library, the Huntington Library, the San Diego Library, and the San Diego Historical Society Library, and with whom I have discussed the various aspects of this work. I am grateful for all her comments, suggestions, and support. Special thanks are in order to Carlos Blanco Aguinaga, who first introduced me to Marxist analysis and whose comments and suggestions on the manuscript have been greatly appreciated. I would like to acknowledge and thank Biodun Iginla, Elizabeth Stomberg, and Laura Westlund for all their help, as well as the press readers for their comments on the manuscript. I would also like to recognize the assistance provided by Bonnie Hardwick, head of the manuscript division at the Bancroft Library. I would be remiss if

I failed to thank my colleagues, students, and friends Angie Chabram, Rosa Linda Fregoso, and Margarita Barceló for their moral support throughout the various stages of this project. Finally, I would also like to thank all those whose names appear in the text, notes, and references. Without this textual dialogue, this book would not have been possible.

La Jolla, California, 1994

Testimonials as Dependent Production

No dudo de que [la generación venidera] coincidirá
conmigo cuando afirmo que en despecho del tratado de
Guadalupe Hidalgo los norteamericanos trataron a los
californios como pueblo conquistado y no como
ciudadanos que ingresaron voluntariamente a formar parte
de la gran familia [estadounidense].

M. G. Vallejo

In the decade of the 1870s approximately sixty-two old Californios who
participated in Bancroft's historiographic project began mapping their
imaginary sense of position within a conquered terrain no longer recov-
erable except in memory. Through their dictated narratives, which function as early sites of ideological struggle, these Californios not only reconstruct their past and retrospectively narrate the nation, but map a
new geopolitical cartography,[1] a liminal ethnic space produced as much
by their particular history as by U.S. expansionism.[2] Having lost their
"homeland" and the political and economic power to regain their former social status, the narrators turn to representational spaces, wherein
the past, the land, and political power can be discursively reasserted.
This narrative space, produced some thirty years after the major restructuring of 1846 that brought new antagonisms and tensions, is necessarily contradictory as it encompasses cultural, economic, and political spaces that overlap, collide, and trigger slippage and shifting from
one space to another, producing ambivalence and finally, in the interstices, a new liminal space, the space of ethnicity. Through these cultural practices the Californios, displaced both spatially and agencially,

attempt to recover agency and to construct and recenter a precarious collective subjectivity.

If, as Jameson (1991: 410) suggests, cognitive mapping is a modernist strategy, then California in the 1870s is ready for a new cartography, for it is precisely at a liminal point of passage from market to monopoly capital. The restructuring of the territory, initiated after the U.S. invasion of California in 1846 and the absorption of the population into a capitalist social formation, had been accelerated by the admittance of California as a state in the Union (1850) and the gold rush (1848–59), the latter stimulating a rapid increase in population. By 1879, with a population of close to a million, California with its vast agricultural potential and its burgeoning manufacturing, mining, and transportation enterprises faced not only a "deepening of class divisions, growing social conflict, periodic depression, and widespread poverty,"[3] fully in keeping with that faced by the rest of the industrialized United States, but mass political movements against the powerful railroad monopoly as well.

During this decade of restructuring but evidencing political resistance, the Californios, marginalized, proletarianized, and pauperized, attempt, by constructing their own concrete difference or particularity, to map their way through alienating social relations and to bridge the gap between their positioning within a racist class structure and their previous positioning as the dominant class within semifeudal Alta California society. This cognitive mapping or represented consciousness (Jameson, 1991: 418) is constituted by a variety of ideological discourses, both residual and emergent, which we propose to analyze in this work by focusing on the overlapping, disjunctive, and intersecting social spaces reconstructed in these Californio narratives.

In several of the testimonials dictated for the Hubert Howe Bancroft historiographic project, the space of defeat and the subaltern status of the Californios are traced as much to invasion and conquest as to a series of textual practices, beginning with the Treaty of Guadalupe-Hidalgo, signed in 1848 to end the war between Mexico and the United States. This treaty forced upon the native population of California a sociospatial choice: to move to Mexico or stay in their homeland, in the California territory, ostensibly as citizens of the United States and enjoying "all the rights of citizens of the United States according to the principles of the Constitution."[4] But the text soon became the basis for complaints of deception; it was said to have misrepresented its claims and under false pretenses enticed Californios to join the Union, only to facilitate their real defeat, their loss of private property. This became apparent three years later, when the Land Commission was established by Congress in 1851 to rule on the validity of all Spanish and Mexican titles. The treaty in effect turned out to be a map of dislocation. By 1875, when the testimonials were being narrated for Bancroft, it had become clear that the Californios, who previously had dominated political and economic spaces in the territory, were now, as the Texas Mexican Juan Nepomuceno Seguín had so aptly put it in 1858 and Mariano Guadalupe Vallejo repeated in 1875, "foreigners" in their native land.[5]

This sense of being "social exiles" and decentered, the outrage, resentment, and disillusionment at being displaced by others within their own terrain, constitutes the sociospatial dominant mapped in the nineteenth-century Californio testimonials we will explore in this study. It is in fact the Californios' sense of marginalization and awareness of themselves as early victims of U.S. gunboat diplomacy that make these testimonials, silenced for over a hundred years, a revealing collection of texts that speak to us today by means of strategies of resentment, accommodation, resignation, and contestation. The resentment inscribed in these texts allows for a reconstruction of territorial and genealogical nationalism, that is, for an assertion of "the autonomous identity of a national culture"[6] repressed since 1846. The testimonials narrate the nation and wage a defense of the territory through text. But these discourses of resentment are intersected by strategies of evident accommodation as well, that appeal to dominant society for justice, reconciliation, and a recognition of the Californios as the intellectual and political equals of the "Americans," revealing thereby an attempt to reconcile difference (the particularity of the Californios) with identity (a shared universality with U.S. bourgeois society).[7] Yet the very narration of these mediated testimonials, while bearing witness to discourses of resignation, also signals a strategic retreat to discursive spaces, marking off spaces of representation as sites of political struggle, as sites for a "war of position."[8]

In accepting to speak through mediated narration there is an implicit concession to hegemonic ideological production in the very midst, ironically, of countering hegemonic policies toward Californios and contesting dominant historiography as well as the discourses of rival Californio and Mexican sectors. These contradictions must be examined in relation to the time axes that intersect, for while the majority of the testimonials in question do not primarily focus on the period of dispossession, still this post-1846 period of land loss and cultural-political displacement intrudes at every turn in the process of reconstruction of the past. These time shifts, like shifts in discursive strategies and in positioning, need to be examined in the context of a double restructuring, one initiated after Mexican independence and recalled as favorable to the emergent *ranchero* class, and the second, after 1847, represented as disastrous for all Californios, even for those who following the U.S. invasion had envisioned increased modernization and greater economic gain for themselves. Taken as a whole, Californio testimonials, then, constitute the discourses of the subaltern, voiced here by a minority population that by the 1870s was painfully aware of its displacement—social, linguistic, and political—and its marginal status as an ethnic minority, and that, moreover, was afforded little or no opportunity to be heard or read by the powers-that-be, except through the mediation of hegemonic voices.

Discourses of marginality are always contradictory, produced as they are by outsiders who are very much within, that is, very much insiders as well, although ex-centric, decentered by dominant social relations. It is of course important to stress that the Californios' sense of marginality and alienation springs from a material alienation, concretely from alienated space (*enajenado* in Spanish, that is, made *ajeno*, made the property of another), and from the concomitant loss of power, a loss of agency. This loss of agency is not, however, a matter of individual "identity crisis" of the type typically addressed in autobiographies, in terms of "shifting and conflicting models of self,"[9] for here the individual continues to see himself or herself positioned within the Californio collectivity. Despite critical changes in property relations and political power, all of which admittedly play a significant role in the construction of identity, several other discourses (those of language loyalty, religion, culture, family, national origin, and, last but not least, a shared history, a memory of an imagined territorial community and a shared oppression) continue to interpellate them as Californios while at the same time combining disjunctively with hegemonic discourses to produce a new inchoate identity, one no longer based on territorial-nationalism but rather grounded on a strong sense of ethnic identity. Old and poverty-stricken, as a rule, with no space of their own to claim after loss of their land, and often Spanish monolinguals, the Californios, for the most part, see the new political order as antagonistic to their interests. Their ties are to the past, their attachment to a lost sense of territoriality, to a previous common experience of history in which they played a useful and important role. It is at this juncture that the Californios agree to the politics of mediated representation and to an overall attempt to relocate and recenter the displaced collectivity textually through a reconstruction—from their own vantage point—of their former spatial and temporal configuration; in so doing, the narrators propose to carve out a new space, a new territory for themselves in dominant historiography, which had until then offered a pejorative account of California history within the dominant racist historical perspective.

Through these testimonials the Californios seek to project a new "political culture"[10] of ethnic dimensions, as much for themselves as for future generations. As M. G. Vallejo notes in a letter to Juan Bautista Alvarado on March 17, 1876, after the latter finally agrees to participate in Bancroft's historiographic project, they have a "sacred duty" to the homeland (Alta California) in which they were born and to all those of their "race" who founded it. The discourses of nation and race/ethnicity are here clearly interpellating a collective identity, the "We, the Californios" who share a common origin, who are the descendants of the founders of the nation of Alta California. In the name of the old political community, the "historical nation"[11] now an ethnic collectivity, Vallejo makes his individual appeal to Alvarado:

> No one better than you ... could rise to the occasion in this difficult
> task of relating events that have been distorted by mercenary or upstart
> writers to the discredit and detriment of the native sons of this
> privileged land. They have vilified us, treating us as half-barbarians
> and [disparaged us with] other degrading epithets; it was necessary to
> counter their lies, proving the opposite with the truth that no one is or
> will be able to disprove.

Here, memory of an earlier territorially based protonationalism and individual links to that collective construct of a Californio homeland confer an urgency and obligation to counter this last form of deterritorialization by hegemonic historians; it is crucial that Californios provide their own constructs of identity, their own reconstruction of California history, proffer their views and ideological discourses for all posterity, lest the younger generations have no idea of who they are. It is perceived as an ever more urgent task, for many of the Californios who had participated in governing the Mexican territory or had held important political, military, and economic positions had died by the time Bancroft initiated his project, and those alive were by and large in ill health and impoverished. Vallejo himself was then sixty-eight years old and his nephew Alvarado only a year younger. The uncle had been making his case for participating in Bancroft's project for two years, since 1874, when he began dictating his memoirs to Bancroft's assistant, Enrique Cerruti. Vallejo's insistence had focused even then on the need for a corrective representation, one with a different narrative and ideological perspective that countered hegemonic views produced "either out of malice or ignorance" (MGV, letter to Alvarado, August 24, 1874).

These testimonials are thus historical and literary contestations of contemporary nineteenth-century historiography, which often portrayed the Californios as lazy, cowardly, and incompetent.[12] In countering hegemonic discourses legitimating the U.S. invasion and providing denigrating and essentialist analyses of Californio society, the narrators assert their right to centeredness and claim it—if not in the historical reality of the rapidly developing California of the 1870s, at least in texts dealing with the preinvasion period of California history. As signifying subjects, they narrate their own invasion, colonization, and domination of Alta California from 1769 to 1846, from their own perspective. Yet, despite their affiliation with the Californio collectivity, no idyllic homogeneous community is constructed in these narratives; instead, there is strong evidence of dissidence, internecine conflict, and group fragmentation throughout the testimonials, cleavages giving rise to discourses of disavowal and disclaimers for particular territorial policies and discourses. Additional disjunctures are generated between discourses justifying and legitimating specific social practices and those condemning them; vacillations between ideological positions often permeate the same testimonial, especially in relation to the slaughter and exploitation of the Indian population. It follows, then, that what interests us primarily in this study is an analysis of ideological discourses and specifically a consideration of the intersecting ideological frameworks that serve to contain and structure constructs of identity in relation to given social spaces. A reading of these texts thus requires unraveling a complex network of discourses, separating antagonistic discursive frameworks, distinguishing between contradictory ideological positions, all the while trying to bear in mind the whole dynamic of history. The mode of textual production reveals the narrators' limited power of representation and explains their willingness to enter Bancroft's heterotopia of time accumulation—his library—in anticipation of a future retrieval and recovery of their discourses through these testimonials.

Genre: Autobiography and Testimonial

The genre of testimonials or *testimonios* has attracted a great deal of attention during the past two decades, particularly within Latin American literature with the publication of numerous testimonials by Latin

American revolutionary figures, including *guerrilleros* from Nicaragua and El Salvador, victims of torture from Argentina and Chile, labor activists such as the Bolivian Domitila Barrios de Chungara, peasant leaders like the Honduran Elvia Alvarado, and Indian leaders, including the Nobel Prize winner Rigoberta Menchú from Guatemala. This genre is not new; links have been established with colonial *crónicas* of Spanish conquerors, explorers, and missionaries and with nineteenth-century memoirs of military campaigns, as well as with ethnographic life histories like those by Oscar Lewis on Mexican and Puerto Rican families.[13] But although sixteenth-century chronicles of the conquest, like that of Díaz del Castillo, and *relaciones*, like that of Las Casas, involve a similar enterprise of textualizing lived experience, those texts are not testimonials, for they are self-generated narratives, as are diaries and various types of travel literature. Nor are testimonials reformulated texts, rewritten from the perspective of the anthropologist or writer, as in the case of *Cinco familias* by Lewis or *Hasta no verte Jesús mío* by Elena Poniatowska.[14] Interest in defining *testimonios* as a separate genre came with the Cuban revolution in 1959 and the Bay of Pigs invasion three years later, two events that generated a number of testimonials and led Casa de las Américas in Cuba to establish a literary prize in 1970 for this type of narrative and to distinguish between various categories of *testimonios*, from self-generated accounts of critical political moments to mediated narratives by a subaltern person interviewed by an outsider (generally a professional who subsequently organizes, edits, and revises the interview to produce a full-length manuscript, often for publication in a First World country). The latter has gained wider recognition, particularly with the publication of Menchú's testimonial focusing on the cultural oppression and class exploitation of the Quiché in Guatemala.[15] It is, in fact, only the mediated type of *testimonio* that we are classifying as "testimonial" and analyzing in this study.

Recent interest in "postcolonial" literature and subaltern studies, along with a centering of popular culture in cultural studies, has undoubtedly created a climate within literary studies for the institutionalization of these noncanonical texts.[16] Some theorists see testimonials as a postmodernist genre, ostensibly because the testimonial implies a rejection of modernist parameters[17] or because it grants a voice to the marginalized or peripheral while jarring or overlapping with a variety of conventional generic boundaries.[18] In this age of information technology, with its attendant compression of time and space, rampant consumerism, and multinational/transnational capitalism,[19] it is the cannibalization of a premodernist genre produced with late capitalist technology (tape recorders, camcorders, and so on) for commodification and sale on a world market by multinational publishers that best exemplifies the expansion of capital into even the most peripheral areas and signals most clearly the heterogeneous nature of cultural production in the Third World today. In earlier periods testimonials were merely resources to be tapped as one of many raw material ingredients involved in literary industries; today the raw material itself, as it were, is "packaged" and commodified.

Distinguishing "testimonials" from "autobiographies" is important, for the two are not synonymous, although testimonials contain autobiographical elements within them.[20] Recent interest in ethnic, women's, and immigrant autobiographies within American literature has led critics to redefine the genre in an effort to determine its parameters (Eakin, 3–19). Although there is no consensus as to the genre's formal attributes, in general it is held that an autobiography offers a self-generated/ agential discursive construction of "self" within particular social spaces. This agency, this awareness of the singularity of self,[21] and the structural capacity to construct a "self" textually, that is, to textualize the various discourses structuring this identity, clearly defines and constitutes an autobiography. Collaborative efforts of the type generated under "sponsorship of members of the dominant culture" (Eakin, 7) would not then enter within this definition of autobiography, as their production is mediated and filtered through a second, more powerful agency, that of the interviewer/editor. In these cases the narrating voice is othered in terms of production as well as at the discursive level. In its very production the mediated testimonial introduces a disjuncture, a doubling, a split voice, an overlay of subaltern and hegemonic narrative spaces, perceptible in its dual modality: oral and written. Narrating agency in texts of this nature is thus not simply that of the speaking subject but also that of the editing and writing subject. Krupat's analysis of different constructs of subjectivity within autobiography, for example, makes a distinction between "Indian autobiography" and "the autobiography by an Indian" and in so doing pinpoints the problem.[22] For us, only the latter, the texts by Indians themselves, the "self-written lives," are autobiographies. Mediated texts, like the testimonials we will discuss, are not (by this definition) autobiographies, though they might harbor autobiographical elements within. In addition to being mediated, testimonials interpellate not an individual subjectivity but a collective identity, a "We" engaged in political struggle within a diversity of social spaces. Cultural, class, and political differentials and slippages between the various social spaces allow for an ambivalent and contingent identification within the texts but all are part of the process of narrating the nation, the culture, the collectivity. In the Californio testimonials, the autobiographical element is evident in the narrators' interest in representing their own participation as public figures within the larger historical scheme, objectifying themselves and the entire collectivity in the process of reconstructing the past but assuming agency collectively in the act of narrating.

In fact, the narrators' participation as individuals within private or intimate spaces is a focus largely absent from these testimonials. In these reconstructed spaces, cultural and political identification calls for an exclusion of intimate and personal sites, except when the space is emptied of intimacy and either ridiculed or totally idealized, as in the case of Vallejo's public farewell in verse to his bride as he marches off into battle right after their marriage. That this episode probably never took place is not really the point;[23] what is clear is that the genre is oriented toward the public and the collective to the extent that even editorial insistence on anecdotal, preferably humorous, asides (MGV, 1:324) can only generate a romantic simulacrum. Most of the narrators of these testimonials provide only a few perfunctory details about their origin, parentage, place of residence, time of immigration if not native Californios, and, if a women, occupation of husband, all in response to questions the interviewers raise.[24] It is the public domain—their social and historical role, their occupation, their participation in some political event, their political policies (if in positions of power), their regional conflicts—and the lives of others that are the focus of these testimonials. The narrators see themselves as subject to criticism on the part of other Californios if they dwell on themselves exclusively, for there is an understanding and consensus that the enterprise is not individual but collective. Vallejo, for example, who had been accused of trying to influence Bancroft's historical perspective,[25] felt it incumbent upon himself, when he turned over his manuscript, to have his letter to Bancroft, together with Bancroft's response, published in a Spanish-language newspaper of San Francisco, to make clear to his fellow Californios that his history was not an attempt at self-aggrandizement, as they all suspected:

> Though I held, during many years, a prominent position in California, I deemed it proper to mention my acts only when I could not possibly avoid it.[26]

Vallejo's letter addresses not only Bancroft but the Californios as well to assure them that his historical account is a collective enterprise that includes the reports and testimonials of others and provides what he considers an impartial account of the social practices of his fellow Californios. Its publication in *La Voz del Nuevo Mundo* is in effect an attempt to bring the collectivity together and end its polarization by regional and other political differences and to allay any anxieties about his representation of them. He has not, Vallejo writes, focused on "personal disputes and petty [political] differences among my countrymen in the early times" (Bancroft, 1890: 440) nor has he stressed differences with the Anglos, "because I have no wish to contribute to the revival of any national, religious or personal prejudice; and it is no part of my plan either to flatter friends or abuse enemies" (443). It is in some measure a gesture that invites other Californios to contribute their own accounts and to correct his own, if necessary. The important thing in the process, in the final analysis, is "the good name of my native land, the memory of our efforts in the service of civilization and progress" (*La Voz*).

As illustrated by this particular case, the Californio testimonials, though narrated from a first-person "I" perspective, focus primarily on the collectivity, with the "We, the national community" at the forefront in the narratives, as Bancroft recognized when he thanked Vallejo for a testimonial that was inclusive:

> I note with pleasure your evident appreciation of the true historical
> spirit, which no longer ignores the masses to describe the
> commonplace acts of rulers. This appreciation is clearly shown in the
> vivid pictures you present of life among all classes. Rich and poor,
> official and private, secular and religious, *padre, hacendado* and humble
> *ranchero*; aristocrat and plebeian—all appear to the view as they lived
> and acted in the primitive pre-gringo times. (Bancroft, 1890: 442)

All Californios, however, do not get "equal time" in these testimonials. The nonpropertied classes and what Bancroft calls the plebeian "humble *ranchero*" are largely absent or mentioned only in passing. Significantly, the Indians are very visible as the Other of the Californios, especially in reference to the earlier periods, although acculturated Indians constitute a very small percentage of those interviewed. In every case, representation follows the ideological perspectives of dominant segments of the Californio population, perspectives often at odds with those of other factions, given regional and social divisions of Californio society.

Another point of divergence that needs to be addressed is that (unlike the testimonials that John Beverley discusses) the Californio narratives are not part of print culture, as they have not, with the exception of a handful, been published. They are accessible to the public, albeit an exclusive minority made up primarily of academics, students, and other researchers, at the archives of the Bancroft Library at the University of California at Berkeley. In this sense they are not unlike numerous out-of-print literary collections that exist only in special collections. The notion of "oral histories" is also not quite appropriate in an analysis of these Californio testimonials, for, though orally produced and retaining to some degree a constructed "oral" narrative style, the testimonials do not reproduce speech, existing as they do only in transcribed and extensively edited form. These Californio informants, unlike most informants for oral anthropological interviews, are almost all literate, a few in fact autodidacts or educated, for most of the narrators were members of the dominant families in Alta California or their allies. M. G. Vallejo kept an official diary and had undertaken writing his own history until his 895-page text was consumed in a fire that destroyed his Sonoma home in 1867 (MGV documents, 597). Vallejo also prepared an outline for several of his friends to follow, as is evident in a letter from Vallejo to Alvarado providing a long list of major events and issues that he and other Californios should address. Alvarado subsequently also prepared an extensive (241 pages) preliminary draft of topics and chapter divisions on his own and later, like Vallejo, acceded to dictate his own text to Cerruti. In neither case, however, did Cerruti simply serve as an amanuensis, as we shall see.

Beverley, in his "Anatomía del testimonio," has described the mediated *testimonio* in terms of five general characteristics. It is (a) a first-person narration of a marginalized individual (either illiterate or without access to means of publication) (b) who witnesses or participates in some significant historical experience (armed struggle, labor organizing, imprisonment, and so on). There is (c) a certain urgency in narrating events and/or denouncing certain conditions (given the state of repression, poverty, exploitation, armed struggle, and so forth) and (d) the perspective is always collective and marginal. The *testimonio* is (e) the collaborative product of an informant and a professional interviewer (for example, a writer, ethnographer, or reporter) who records the interview, then transcribes and compiles it. What distinguishes a *testimonio* from an autobiography, according to Beverley, is its collective perspective and dependent status, which stands in sharp contrast to the autonomous individual "I" perspective of the narrator of an autobiography (Beverley, 1987: 8).

Although in general we agree with Beverley's analysis, we find the urgency of the *testimonio* to be contingent, as he does in his second essay on the topic.[27] The *testimonio* is usually narrated at a critical distance from the primary events that are being reconstructed rather than in the midst of an event itself, as is the case in narratives of guerrilla campaigns. As a rule the interviewer's agenda is being pursued, rather than any "urgency" on the part of the interviewee, and this agenda determines the interview and eventual publication. Clearly there is always the possibility of manipulating the informant's testimony, for, in this mode of cultural reproduction, the interviewer authorizes the project; it is the interviewer who controls the interview and the technologies, not only through the types of questions posed but, more specifically, in the transcription, revision, editing, and organization of the recorded narration. Of course the interviewer generally represents the only means for transmission that the informant has, and for this reason, as Beverley (1987: 15) notes, if there is any manipulation, it must be seen as mutual. This is especially the case when the informant has a pressing need to elicit the support of the "outside world"; but in fact the informant usually does not seek out the interviewer and may have no idea of the possible repercussions and extension of a published testimonial, as apparently occurred with Menchú. Yet once given the chance to "testify," the informant seizes the representational space. In the case of the Californios, it is precisely the potential mutual manipulation that leads them to accede to the interview initiated by Bancroft's agents, but in view of the fact that it is Bancroft who controls the concrete texts and their particular use, the subaltern have only limited power to subvert the interview and editorial procedure or the text's distribution and circulation, at least in these specifically nineteenth-century cases. The narrators can attempt to manipulate the discourses by assuming a dual tactic of concession to and questioning of the social order and its dominant discourses and by appropriating, in the act of narrating, this representational terrain for themselves as a historically positioned collectivity. Through these textual exchanges, then, the collectivity reconstructs its cultural practices at a moment when no other mainstream avenues are open to it for the construction of national and ethnic identities.

Three additional characteristics of the *testimonio* that are implicit in Beverley's definition need to be considered further. First, testimonials are narratives of identification. In all testimonials, the subaltern seizes the liminal space of mediated representation to "write" or narrate identity. In view of the subaltern's separation from hegemonic means of reproduction, the testimonial is the subaltern's site for constructing collective identity or identities, be it in terms of class, gender, culture, or nation, within hegemonic spaces. Second, testimonials are counternar-

ratives, heterotopic representational spaces that stand against hegemonic representations of social movements or collectivities. This contestatory function is implicit in Beverley's description of the *testimonio*
as a genre used to denounce conditions of oppression, but missing in
this formulation is a recognition of the narrator's active and conscious
effort to counter other representations that either exclude or misrepre-
sent the collectivity. Contrary to Sommer's position ("Testimonials, on
the other hand, never put the referentiality of language into question"),
testimonials, by contesting hegemonic texts, do indeed problematize
referentiality and posit the constructedness of history.[28] For what matters to the narrators is not so much the details or intensity of suffering, but rather the denunciation of repression through its strategic reconstruction. Third, testimonials represent a shift of the struggle to a
war of position; testimonials are sites of protracted struggle (Gramsci,
233), launched often from exile or outside the immediate battlefront,
such as beyond the mines of Bolivia or the Quiché villages of Guatemala.
For the Californios, conquered and dispossessed as they were by 1875,
social exiles within their own homeland, the testimonials are spaces
for resistance, refutation, and disavowal, counterspaces for recentering collective subjectivity. These three supplemental functions constitute the testimonial's capacity for cognitive mapping and point to the
importance of cultural production as rejoinders in a "war of position."

These various definitions of the genre could be reformulated in
terms of three levels that we will designate as (1) the level of oral interaction and narration; (2) the level of transcription, edition, and publication; and (3) the level of the narrative. Within the level of interaction, analysis must necessarily consider the context of exchange and
the interlocutors involved in the dialogue. The interviewer's mediation is consolidated at the second level in the process of transcribing,
editing, and, in the case of the Californio testimonials, commenting on
the text. The third level, which is the primary concern of this work, is
the end product, the literary text that the interviewer in editing and
revising converts into both "a text" and "literary" (Beverley, 1991: 16).
It is at the narrative level that the first two, constituting the level of
production, are inscribed. To analyze the constructs of identity produced within this narrative space, we must first consider the implications of what dependent textual production is.

The collaborative effort at the level of production of these testimonials is what allows us to speak of a mediated text, for testimonials are
always elicited narratives. This designation, however, fails to capture the
uneven power relations between the oral producer of the testimonial

and the transcribing interviewer. In her work on "subaltern studies" Gayatri Chakravorty Spivak notes that in oral histories of Third World women that have surfaced since the 1960s "through the dominant mediation of an investigator or fieldworker," there has been a concerted effort to "efface or at least minimize the role of the investigator."[29] She finds that in what might be termed an artificial process of constructing the subordinate Other as subject, the subordinate is in fact objectified. Thus, "in the context of colonial production, the subaltern has no history and cannot speak."[30] Given the context of invasion and conquest in California, the subordinate Californios are in a similar situation and, in part, are objectified as objects of analysis; nevertheless, the Californio community does reconstruct a set of identities, that is, contingent and variable collective subjectivities, in the act of representation. In the process of narrating the testimonial, in the very act of appropriating representational spaces, the subaltern does recover some degree of agency. Our search in scrutinizing these Californio testimonials is not, moreover, for any essential "voice" of the Californio subaltern, nor do we seek to find "a pure form of consciousness" of the subaltern (Spivak, 1988: 286), but rather we endeavor to focus analysis on the network of ideological discourses within these texts, multiple, contradictory, and mediated as they are. Through them the subaltern collectivity speaks, neither always hegemonically nor subversively, but always, through a continual realignment of discourses, in search of both voice and audience.

Production of the Testimonial

The Californio testimonials are collaborative productions by an informant-narrator and an interviewer for a specific historiographic project. The testimonials are above all social practices, both discursive and nondiscursive, and require a historical interpretation. It is important to consider not only the immediate domain and conditions of interaction but the larger context of the decade of the 1870s in California, which brought a number of fundamental material and political transformations, if we are to understand the strategies of containment at work in the production of this type of text. During this period of rapid economic growth a wealthy book dealer and cultural entrepreneur named Hubert Howe Bancroft embarked upon historiographic research for what was to be a moneymaking enterprise for his publishing company. If we are to fully grasp the importance of these unpublished documents, not as foundational narratives in Chicano literature but as representational sites, as a strategic clearing within which our earliest constructs of ethnic identity emerge, we will need to review at least briefly some pertinent issues and background practices underpinning the production of these texts.

According to Benedict Anderson, national consciousness owes a great deal not only to capitalism but to the development of rapid communication in a national language.[31] Print communication was nonexistent in Alta California until the decade of the 1830s; the only written texts produced in the territory until then were the handwritten letters, diaries, official notices, proclamations, and documents of governors, *presidio* commanders, other officers, merchants, other literate Californios, and missionaries, especially the latter, who were among the best-educated men in the territory. For reasons economic, political, and cultural in nature, the print market did not develop locally prior to 1847; in fact, until very late in the Mexican period, all printed matter was brought over by ship from Mexico, Europe, or the U.S. East Coast. In an area where the total population of colonists never exceeded seven thousand,[32] it must be remembered that a large percentage of the early Californio population was illiterate and only a small percentage of the mission Indians could read. As Antonio Franco Coronel explains in his testimonial, literacy in California, as elsewhere, was gendered, with few women trained to read and write (Coronel, 227). Second-generation Californios, the native sons and daughters, children of the original soldiers and craftsmen, would become literate, thanks to the basics offered at the *presidios* by older literate soldiers and in the *pueblos* by literate women and men, or, in the case of the children of the affluent, through the experience of studying abroad in Mexican or Sandwich Island schools.

To understand the implication of this lack of print media in pre-1846 California, we need to consider briefly and summarily the historical context during the late eighteenth and early nineteenth centuries. In speaking of California before 1846 we are always discussing a local precapitalist economy integrated into an international capitalist market through the agency of a handful of merchant capitalists; the contradictions that derive from such a system of production are evident at every level, including that of cultural production. The Spanish period (1769–1821) marks a slow colonization of the territory, and only during the Mexican period (1822–46), also relatively short and conflictive, does a printing press make an appearance. Without a significant literate population and no newspapers for the literate segments, it would seem that discourses of national identity would have been hard to disseminate.

How then did communication among the Californios take place? How could they "imagine" themselves to be part of a community? Communication among the various *pueblos, presidios,* and missions extending from San Diego to Monterey and north to San Francisco and Sonoma was difficult at first but not a serious problem in Alta California after 1822, thanks to increased trade and fast horses.

Except for two very brief periods, the California territory had no ships of its own to travel up and down the coast or to San Blas and the Sandwich Islands, although there were small sailboats and rowboats for short-distance travel. Fresh horses were always available at strategic distances, enabling communication to take place fairly fast from Monterey to San Diego. Mail riders carried letters, proclamations, and official documents, all handwritten unless the material was printed in Mexico;[33] this information was circulated throughout the *pueblos,* missions, and *presidios,* and generally posted on mission doors or the doors of public halls. Communication between the two regions via the dominant families of California, the maintenance of a tight mission network, and the more regular arrival, after 1825, of ships seeking to trade for hides and tallow in San Diego, San Pedro, Santa Barbara, and Monterey kept the settlements informed not only of events and social changes in Mexico but also of a host of internal problems, conspiracies, and events throughout the California territory.

The first printing press that came to California, in 1833, a Ramage printer, was in operation by 1834 and served to print a number of announcements, a governor's proclamation, grammar and religious texts, and books of remedies,[34] but no newspaper would be produced on that old Ramage press until 1846, after the invasion of California.[35] This lack of access to the vehicles of information perhaps contributed to maintaining local enclaves of power and reinforced regional divisions among the colonists, although, given particular political, economic, and regional interests, it is possible that these rifts would not have disappeared even with the availability of print media, as indeed they did not even after invasion and admission into the Union (Olin, 21–22).

Bancroft as Cultural Entrepreneur

The testimonials or "dictations," as Bancroft called them, of the early California settlers need to be examined in relation to the mode of literary production that brings a small marginalized national minority under the microscope of the Bancroft historical and publishing laboratory. The process itself of document collection and ethnographic interviews tells us a great deal about this type of text. This entire cultural under-taking was initiated by an enterprising young bookseller who made a fortune in the book and stationery business after coming west to Cali-fornia. The Bancroft building on Market Street in San Francisco was known for its printing, bookbindery, and publishing, and for the sale of books, stationery, school supplies, and sheet music.[36] Reproduction of cultural technologies was thus Bancroft's primary interest.

In the process of collecting material for the publication of a Pacific Coast Handbook, in essence a guidebook for the "opening" of Califor-nia, Bancroft became a collector of books and other materials relating to California and the West, particularly the Southwest. As his collection grew—it would one day number sixty thousand volumes (Caughey, 67)—so too did his interest in expanding his original focus. He now incorporated materials on the Americas (especially Mexico and Cen-tral America), books, libraries, newspaper collections, manuscripts, pam-phlets, and even scrapbooks, which he acquired not only in the United States but throughout Europe, envisioning a historiographic project of ambitious proportions. This collection would eventually be sold to the Regents of the University of California and be housed at the Uni-versity of California Library at Berkeley. In his *Literary Industries* (a re-vealing title in itself), Bancroft describes his own collection as "incom-parable" (214).

Research was not the only motivating force for the capitalist pub-lisher who controlled the technologies of production; clearly, with his resources, he could write, publish, and distribute any textual com-modity, including histories. He first embarked on the classification of his vast collection,[37] using various ad hoc methods, and eventually ini-tiated what would be the first cooperative method of authorship of var-ious volumes of history on the native races, Central America, Mexico, California, the Northwest, Texas and the North Mexican States, Ari-zona, New Mexico, Nevada, Colorado and Wyoming, Utah, Oregon, Washington, Idaho and Montana, Alaska, and British Columbia. A num-ber of writers, none of them historians by training, would be hired to use the materials in Bancroft's collection for the writing of these vol-umes in what resembled a literary assembly line with its strict division of labor and mass production techniques. All of the works, however, would be published under Bancroft's name; he assumed that because he was paying for the writers' labor he could lay claim to their work as his own. Profit as much as knowledge guided Bancroft's research and publication effort, despite his claims to have done it for personal gratification and out of a love of literature (Bancroft, 1912: 325).

As part of the historiographic undertaking on California, which required the collection, examination, and copying of official documents, letters, interviews, notes, manuscripts, and so forth, Bancroft ordered two of his agents to secure the dictations of Californios and other "pioneers" who were to serve as "resources," raw material to be extracted and exploited for publication and profit. The entire historiographic project was thus a capitalist undertaking of a cultural sort, a commercial as well as a literary venture (as his book title *Literary Industries* suggests), but comparable only in part to his publication of *Chronicles*, to which he sold subscriptions to underwrite the project.[38] This fee system was not employed in the writing of his histories (Caughey, 322), yet reports of Bancroft's having the subjects of his *Chronicles* pay by the inch for their biographies would in the end stigmatize his other works as well. There is, of course, no such thing as "pure research," not today, not then, but Bancroft's method of writing on the basis of paid subscriptions was too blatantly compromised, and his method of collective production of the histories without acknowledging the authors or collaborators (Caughey, 268) provoked "savage diatribes" from the likes of Ambrose Bierce, writing for the *San Francisco Examiner*, especially after the real authors of the volumes on the Northwest (Frances Fuller Victor) and of the volumes on California (Henry L. Oak) publicly voiced their indignation and claimed authorship rights. Criticism would detract substantially from the works' acceptance, as they were often dismissed in toto for that very reason, and also for being written by individuals who were not trained as historians. Today, although not considered the best of histories, the Bancroft works are deemed invaluable repositories of information (Caughey, 277). The incorporation of ethnographic and testimonial material in the process of "history-making" and the collaborative production make these histories unique for their time.

Bancroft's cooperative method meant in effect the conversion of historiographic production into an industry with division and stratification of labor and the use of both skilled and semiskilled workers. The procedure after the dictations had been conducted, "written out," and turned in to the Bancroft Library was as follows: the contributions of informants or raw data were often first copied, then classified by the library assistants; copious notes were taken, assembled, and turned over to the writers who incorporated the data into their work (Bancroft, 1890: 565–66). Once worked on cooperatively or by one or two assistants, one individual then became primarily responsible for the final product. The perspective assumed by the "historian" in the case of the volumes on California was, as Bancroft insists, that of a liberal concerned with "a spirit of fairness" (Bancroft, 22:461). Critics charged that the histories reflected Bancroft's "biased" opinions, which he inculcated in his assistants (Caughey, 275).

The questioning of authorship would lead to additional works by Bancroft (*Literary Industries* and *Retrospection*) to explain and justify the process of writing and describe the involvement of certain individuals. Two of the latter, Enrique Cerruti and Thomas Savage, are of special interest to this work, for both men would participate in the collection of data and manuscripts from the Californios and early Anglo settlers in Alta California, serving as the second voice in the dual narration of testimonials. Savage, of New England ancestry, was born in Havana, Cuba, where he worked at the U.S. consulate for twenty-one years (Bancroft, 1890: 255–56) before going to Central America and later to California, where he was hired by Bancroft. As a native Spanish speaker he was in charge of copying and abstracting Spanish documents from the provincial California archives, mission records, the U.S. Land Office, and the archives of the archbishop; he was likewise consulted about all translations from Spanish manuscripts.

Enrique Cerruti, whose literary activities we can follow in his *Ramblings in California*, was an Italian by birth and expert in Italian, French, and Spanish. He had been a U.S. consul in Colombia and fancied himself a soldier and a friend of General Melgarejo, deposed dictator of Bolivia. Cerruti traveled to Valparaíso, Chile, from Bolivia and later to the United States; afterward he went south to Mexico, across the Isthmus of Tehuantepec, and back north to San Francisco. A man given to boasting and flattery, according to Bancroft, he was, however, able to gain the confidence of several Californios, among them Mariano Guadalupe Vallejo. Thanks to Cerruti's intervention Vallejo contributed his manuscript collection and finally his history to the Bancroft collection. In 1876 Cerruti committed suicide after losing heavily on the stock market (Bancroft, 1890: 444). Had he not been Bancroft's agent, it is unlikely that Vallejo and others would ever have consented to dictate their recollections and testimonials. Bancroft acknowledges as much in *Literary Industries*, where he recalls his contact with Cerruti, noting his significant contributions and his own fondness for him. In a period of two years Cerruti was able to collect, copy, and record material that no one else had managed to acquire (Bancroft, 1890: 373).

The interviews or "dictations" of Californios and early Anglo settlers (the "pioneers") conducted by Cerruti and Savage were only a small part of the material collected by Bancroft, who was interested in acquiring or copying as many official documents and letters as he could from the Spanish-Mexican periods. In his notes on bibliography of California history, Bancroft refers to 160 dictations taken by reporters of the personal reminiscences of individuals from all walks of life, half of them Californios, including twenty-four men who had occupied prominent public positions in the north and in the south. Eleven of those interviewed were women (Bancroft, 1:55). In addition to these dictations, Bancroft acquired more than five hundred other manuscripts, including diaries, journals, reports by military and religious officials, regulations, *expedientes,* and the like (Caughey, 189), as well as narratives provided by both men and women of Californio origin for the Bancroft Library but not dictated or written expressly for the historical project.

In the case of prominent individuals, Bancroft himself determined that efforts were to be made to establish contact with them. Former Commander General Mariano Guadalupe Vallejo was Bancroft's primary target in Sonoma but he also asked Cerruti to induce the general's brother, Major Salvador Vallejo, to dictate a history of early days. The major resisted at first, but eventually Cerruti won him over with offers of good conversation, cigars, and whiskey. In Sonoma Cerruti also became personally acquainted with a number of older Californios, whom he treated to drinks and then asked for interviews, for it was, he said, his duty "to interview every old settler living in the country; the words 'old settlers' included every white man that had settled in California prior to 1850, and every native Californian upwards of sixty years of age" (Cerruti, 7). Once Cerruti had won over Vallejo, the old Californio general[39] himself would present Cerruti to his friends in Monterey, San Jose, and San Francisco for interviews. In the south, Savage followed a similar procedure, assisted by a number of Californio and Mexican men trained to take dictations.

Bancroft's "Spirit of Fairness"

The scandal at the Bancroft House prompted by claims of unrecognized authorship and the biography-by-subscription bids was not yet part of history when the Californios were interviewed. In his approach to them, Bancroft would argue later, his only motive was knowledge, and his purpose was "to write a complete, accurate, and impartial history of California" (1890: 443). Until then, he says, there had been only an incomplete history of California; those travelers, merchants, and missionaries who had written on California provided only faulty and fragmentary information:

All these sketches were superficial and incomplete; many were grossly inaccurate; not a few were written with the intent, or at least willingness, to deceive, in the interest of party, clique or section. The official records of the Anglo-American invasion and conquest were more complete and accurate, but presented only one side where it were best to have both. (Bancroft, 1890: 441)

Contemporary efforts to write this history were equally superficial, according to Bancroft, for they lacked the requisite resources. The wealthy Bancroft could either buy or have copied all of the necessary documentation and published references, and thus he would scoff at the pretensions of others less endowed financially, if not intellectually, to duplicate his historiographic efforts (1890: 596–98).

Bancroft's exhaustive search for material on Alta California and his willingness to pay his agents to travel throughout the state to acquire the Californio dictations and copy materials are related not only to his capital but also to his concept of historiography. His works reveal an empiricist historian who repudiates theory and concentrates on providing the objective "facts," as he himself indicates in relation to his work on *Native Races*: "I dealt in facts, gathered from new fields and conveniently arranged" (1890: 312). Theories, he states, are dispensable: "In all my work I was determined to keep upon firm ground, to avoid meaningless and even technical terms, to avoid theories, speculations, and superstitions of every kind, and to deal only in facts" (1890: 298). Empirical historiography or antiquarianism, as Jameson indicates, seeks to subvert folk, popular, or theological visions of history.[40] What Bancroft was subverting or rejecting, beyond transcendental notions of historiography[41] and theological interpretations by missionaries, can be adduced from his own reflections on all aspects of his literary-historical production, works written undoubtedly in an effort to legitimate the process and counter critics' reviews and attacks. He saw first the need to consider a variety of texts, rather than simply those written or published by merchants (like Robinson), visiting foreigners (like de Mofras), and missionaries (like Palou) or friends of missionaries. But he still retained the notion of the historian as judge who, once data were collected, with up to a hundred different versions of what had occurred at any one historic moment, determined "the truth" (1890: 611). Bancroft's history of California is interesting in its inclusion, often through footnoting, of divergent views on an episode and remarks on the diversity of positions, although these are always followed by an "authorized" version of the event.

Bancroft was clearly aware that the history of Alta California was not of much interest to some historians who "before 1846 see nothing but the acts of a few *padres* and 'greasers,' of which nobody cares to hear" (1890: 599). Given his antiquarian approach and his desire to demystify the past, he saw himself as a pioneer, blazing a trail through unknown country and discovering the natives to be "subjects" with a history of their own to be told:

> Indeed, at the time of beginning my work the popular idea of a history of California dated in reality from the coming of the Americans. All before that was shadowy, if not, indeed, mythologic. At all events it was generally supposed to be something no one knew much about, and the little that could be ascertained was not worth the writing or the reading. The *hijos del país* were regarded as being nothing, as having done nothing, as being able to communicate nothing, and would not tell of themselves or of the past if they could; so that at this period of my investigation a white man who had come to the country in 1846 or in 1848 was a magazine of historical information. (1890: 619)

To his credit Bancroft acknowledged the need to provide the Californio perspective in a history of California; for this ideal "balanced" perspective Bancroft needed Californio sources. Not one to shrink from flattery himself, upon receiving M. G. Vallejo's manuscript Bancroft thanked him for providing the missing link,

> a history of Spanish and Mexican California, including the Anglo-American invasion, written from a Hispano-American standpoint, by a native Californian of culture, prominent among and respected by his countrymen, possessed of sound judgment, a liberal spirit, an enthusiastic love for his subject, and appreciation of its importance. These qualifications, General, you have long been known to possess in a high degree, and more fully than any other living man could have done have you supplied the pressing need to which I have alluded. (Letter to Vallejo, reprinted in Bancroft, 1890: 441–42)

Ample evidence indicates that in these and other flattering remarks Bancroft simply acceded to protocol, although he was at the same time anxious to get his hands on the manuscript. Not all those approached by Bancroft, however, whether Anglo or Californio, were as generous with their time as Vallejo, nor did they see Bancroft's interest as purely historical and driven by nothing more than a love for "pure investigation and an unbiased recording of the truth" (1890: 373). These suspicious would-be informants who were more perceptive of Bancroft's interest in using them and who sought to profit from his venture are dismissed by Bancroft as opportunistic, as "those mercenary minds, who could see nothing but money in it, who having documents or knowledge of historical events would not part with their information but for a price" (1890: 374). Bancroft would argue that those who had common sense or were patriotic did not seek compensation for their testimonials,

> but I had to do with individuals possessed of neither sense nor patriotism, common or uncommon. I had to do with men in whose eyes a dollar was so large that they could not see beyond it; in whose eyes money was not alone the chief good, but the only good; whose dim intelligence ran in channels so muddy that no sunlight could penetrate them. (1890: 374)

Among those who placed no trust in his words were several Californios, who viewed his efforts with suspicion:

> The Hispano-Californians particularly, many of them had been so abused, so swindled, so robbed by their pretended friends, by unprincipled Yankee lawyers and scheming adventurers, that they did not know whom to trust and were suspicious of everybody. (1890: 375)

Knowing that their manuscripts and dictations had a market value, some Californios were unwilling to provide their time without compensation, but Bancroft was unwilling to provide any reward or wages for their contributions. He did not view with disfavor inviting the interviewees or informants to a treat or drink during the interview session, however. Savage indicates, for example, that when he interviewed Narciso Botello in San Diego, he found him reduced to poverty and residing at the *rancho* of a friend, for which reason he offered "a reasonable pecuniary compensation to meet his expenses" (see Botello, introduction). Informants such as Alvarado and Manuel Castro, aware of the profit that Bancroft would glean from these texts, tried to gain some compensation and succeeded only minimally. Alvarado only consented to dictate his history, in view of Cerruti's unwillingness to spend time in San Pablo, on condition that Bancroft pay his room and board at a hotel in San Francisco: "I had told Alvarado plainly that I would not pay him for his information; indeed he never asked me to do so. He would accept nothing in direct payment but he was determined to make the most of it indirectly" (Bancroft, 1890: 412). Alvarado would also request that his son be employed by Bancroft at his bookstore; he was hired but he did not last long, because Alvarado was not pleased with his assignment as errand boy. Manuel Castro began dictating and at the same time borrowing money from Bancroft. The related anecdote is quite telling: at one point Castro went so far as to pawn his documents for an unspecified amount, but his papers eventually fell into the hands of the Bancroft Library when he left them with Felipe Fierro, the editor of *La Voz del Nuevo Mundo*. Even his dictation was copied unbeknownst to him: "Several years later he endeavored to obtain money from me on the remnants and was surprised to learn that his *papeles* had no longer a market value" (Bancroft, 1890: 426). Bancroft thus acknowledges his commerce with these cultural commodities, this raw material, that was to serve for his literary industries.

Aside from the small compensation offered for food or drink (and only in Alvarado's case for lodging), why did a number of Californio men and women, even those like Fierro, who was not an old Californio, agree to assist or participate in the project and consent to being interviewed? The texts themselves reveal three reasons: representation, outreach, and struggle. Despite the limits placed on agency in mediated testimonials that were not to be published, there is implicit in the Californios' acquiescence to be interviewed a desire to be able to manipulate the process as insurance against oblivion. Californios like Vallejo and Alvarado saw themselves collectively and individually in danger of being misrepresented, forgotten, or marginalized historically by mainstream historians who had no idea of the issues and antagonisms that had led to the various revolts and contestation of Mexican authority, nor did they have any interest in making the particular roles of the Californios known to posterity. For the Californio narrators, figuring in history, in a version that took their perspective into account and had the possibility of gaining acceptance, unlike anything that they, the conquered minority, might produce, was in the last instance more important and more realistic than aspiring to see their own work in print (letter by Vallejo, *La Voz del Nuevo Mundo*, January 30, 1875). In the best of cases, a favorable representation and at least recognition for the Californios as objects of knowledge were what was at stake. Speaking through the Yankee Bancroft, however, implied a concession to the dominant historiography that had so blatantly sought to degrade and dismiss them up until then. The testimonials were thus at times made with a certain trepidation and entered upon with caution and second thoughts, as the novelist María Amparo Ruiz de Burton would tell Bancroft in a letter:

> The fact of it is (and a very serious fact which you as a conscientious historian must not omit) that "the natives" with the loss of all their property and their prestige ... allow themselves to be swept away to "oblivion" by the furious avalanche let loose upon them by the hand of the Anglo-Americans, the pitiless Anglo-American! So, we must not

blame the disheartened Californians if they do not rise to the importance of appreciating your work, and you, without resentment for their unambitious indifference, which is the result of their misfortune, must speak kindly of them. You can afford it. And being an American you can say many things that the American people would perhaps not accept from a foreigner. (Ruiz de Burton Carta, July 15, 1878)

The reconstruction of the cause and effect behind the fall of the Californios would be taken up by Ruiz de Burton, who in her 1885 novel *The Squatter and the Don* would not hesitate to place the blame for the Californios' misfortunes squarely on U.S. government policies.[42] The Californios, however, did not for the most part have her English language skills and by 1875 were much older than she and totally impoverished. As a marginalized, dispossessed, and disempowered minority, the Californios had come to believe that anything they said would carry little weight and find no acceptance from the American public, as Vallejo, reiterating Ruiz de Burton's words, indicated to Bancroft in his letter accompanying his finished manuscript:

Your work will be accepted by the world, which already knows you for a trustworthy writer, as a reliable and complete history of my native land. Mine, however favorably received, would perhaps be looked upon as giving on many points, only M. G. Vallejo's version.[43]

Even Vallejo, who had a very high opinion of himself, considered and finally rejected the idea of having his own manuscript published and came to see advantages in a history "authorized" by Bancroft.[44] When he was approached by several Californios who suggested that he have his manuscript published in its entirety and independently, Vallejo expressed his willingness to relinquish his pen to a higher authority, as Cerruti explains:

The general, who has a good share of sound sense, told those persons that he would be highly pleased to be quoted in your great work, as your history would be in future ages the great authority on Californian matters, while the history written by him would not carry an equal weight of conviction. (Cerruti, quoted in Bancroft, 1890: 421)

Undoubtedly Bancroft quoted Cerruti to show that Vallejo was fully aware that he would not be published in toto:

It was in April 1874 that Cerruti began writing in Spanish the *Historia de California*, dictated by M. G. Vallejo. It was understood from the first that this history was for my sole use, not to be printed unless I should so elect, and this was not at all probable. It was to be used by me in writing my history as other chief authorities were used. (Bancroft, 1890: 396)

Clearly Vallejo came to feel that the Californios' identity and history as a people were in danger of being erased and obliterated, along
with everything else that they had once possessed. It was important
for the Californios to lay aside whatever misgivings they had about
their own past action and role if they were to figure in history as a collectivity and as individuals. After all, no one was perfect (MGV, letter
to Alvarado, August 24, 1874). Their story, their own version of their
history had to be written, and now Bancroft offered an opportunity
they could not disdain. The project implied a mutual dependence, for
though the book dealer might have the economic power, theirs was
the intimate knowledge of the past. Failure to reconstruct their identity and their emplacement within the history of California had already
made their conquest and marginality doubly difficult to bear, but now
textuality offered a way out of the shroud of invisibility that threatened to engulf them forever (MGV documents, 591). To seize the opportunity at hand called for accepting Bancroft as their interpretive
Other, as their redeemer, who could make their past intelligible to the
world.[45] Immortality through representation was an expensive proposition, and they were penniless, but through Bancroft's agency they
could set down and transmit their testimony, at least partially, and enter textual history as Californios. Needless to say, they would in fact
enter, piecemeal and fragmented, through the back door, as it were;
for the most part their contributions would ultimately remain in the
recesses of the Bancroft Library stacks.

In the longer, more comprehensive testimonials, like those of M. G.
Vallejo and Alvarado, there is ample evidence that the addressee is
not exclusively Bancroft, that Bancroft is only a short-term conduit,
and that, in the long run, the narrators hope to be able to reach out
more directly to a broader audience. Resignation to mediated representation is thus offset by expectations of broader dissemination of
their work through Bancroft's intermediation. This goal is especially
evident in both Alvarado's and Vallejo's testimonials wherein they
address their Mexican readers, their fellow Californio readers, their
Anglo-American readers, historians in general, and even future readers, their descendants. Implicit in this writing as well is the anticipation that their work will one day see publication and that *their* version
of California history, what is admittedly their own reconstruction of
their past as a nation, will be read, recognized, and accepted within a few
years (Alvarado, 4:248). A product of his own century, Vallejo appears
initially to posit likewise a "truth" —a Californio version of history—

that has not been heard; but he is undoubtedly conscious that in historiography there are various "truths" and that representation is a form of coercion as well, in view of the distortion of Californio history and the defamation of Californios in dominant historiography. To his mind, it is crucially important that he and Alvarado join forces to provide their own history of their homeland and that their versions or reconstructions coincide:

> You can be sure that if, as I expect, our manuscripts on the history of California coincide, no one will be foolhardy enough (least of all the dead) to question our versions. (MGV, letter to Alvarado, March 17, 1876)

Vallejo's words suggest that he sees his manuscript and those of other Californios as arenas for struggle in the cultural sphere. Thus rather than a naive antiquarian position (Jameson, 1988: 152) that assumes a "truth" to be narrated in opposition to other versions of history, there is a consciousness of the constructedness of history and a keen desire to struggle through narration, to deploy their own reconstruction of history and identity as weapons to be wielded in the contest. It is in effect a battle, a game, of constructions, as important for the future as for the present, for the reconstruction of the past is also linked to the Californios' survival in the 1870s. Given an alienating society and a subaltern positionality, interpellation of a residual identity or even of an emergent ethnic identity is difficult without a network of discourses from the past. There is in Vallejo's words a call for a collective effort to reconstruct the discourses of California during its previous two stages of development, as only these can interpellate the Californios as subjects. This perspective goes far in explaining his indefatigable efforts in assisting Cerruti and Bancroft in the collection of documents and in setting up introductions to a number of individuals.

Like Vallejo, Alvarado sees the testimonials as a representational countersite providing opportunities for disavowals and contestation, especially in view of the inaccessibility of the English-language media. In February 1876 the *San Francisco Chronicle* ran an article previously published in the *Philadelphia Times* dealing with John Augustus Sutter, an early pioneer in Alta California who aided the Bear Flag filibusters against Mexican California in 1846 and whose testimonial was the basis of the newspaper story. Alvarado, former governor of Alta California and the official who had granted Sutter over forty-eight thousand acres in what is now Sacramento, considered the published text to be full of lies and subsequently sought to publish a response in the *Chronicle*. The editor refused to grant him space, arguing that because the text was reprinted and had not originated in the newspaper, the *Chronicle* was not in any way obliged to publish a response (Alvarado, 4:238). Countering hegemonic discourses within mainstream media was to prove an almost impossible task for Californios, given social, political, and linguistic constraints. Alvarado's extensive response to Sutter's declarations would ultimately be included in his five-volume testimonial narrated for the Bancroft historiographic project — but this too would never be published. It is clear that the subaltern had, even then, a voice, but aside from Spanish-language newspapers, there were few, if any, hegemonic channels for transmission of these contestatory discourses. Little did Alvarado and Vallejo know that their narratives, as well as those of other fellow Californios, would, with few exceptions, lie buried and unpublished in the stacks of the Bancroft Library over a hundred years later.

Bancroft's history would, in the end, not "save them," as Vallejo had hoped, for despite his "charitable," sometimes romantic, and patronizing view of the Californios as a people, the would-be historian was no redeemer and more often than not had nothing but contempt for the Californios' opinions. In a war of position, then, one does not turn over one's weapons to the enemy for safekeeping, unless, perhaps, it is the only way of ensuring their storage and survival. Bancroft indicates that he did not feel bound to the Californios' views simply because they had deigned to entrust to him their testimonials or documents:

> I never hoped to please Californians; I never thought it possible to satisfy them, never wrote to satisfy them, or, indeed, any other class or person. And I used to say to General Vallejo: "You being a reasonable man will understand, and will, I hope, believe that I have aimed to do your people justice. But they will not as a class think so. I claim to have no prejudices as regards the Hispano-Californians, or if I have they are all in their favor. Yet you will agree with me that they have their faults, in common with Englishmen, Americans and all men." (1890: 397)

In Bancroft's history the testimonials would be atomized and reduced to footnotes or often unattributed sources. Although he bases his history on these accounts as much as on official documentation, letters, and other texts, he leaves the reader with the idea that the Californios' versions of events are not always to be trusted, for they often exaggerate, invent, lie, and fantasize. Bancroft of course failed to consider the testimonials as literature and saw them only as potential sources of information to be mined in the measure that they corroborated his own perspective on the Californios and on California history. At the same time, given Bancroft's continuation to a certain extent of nineteenth-century historiography's propensity to dwell on "character analysis" and "great men" and to provide ethnocentric assessments of societies, it is not surprising that he too focuses primarily on the leaders of the Californios, both living and deceased, and views them as flawed, weak, incompetent, cowardly, and given to drink. Bancroft's comments on Alvarado provide a good example of his sarcasm and condescending attitude toward all Californios:

> In common with all his countrymen he fancied he had been badly abused, had been tricked and robbed of millions of dollars which he had never possessed, and of hundreds of leagues of land which he had neglected to secure to himself. To the accursed Yankee were to be attributed all his follies and failures, all his defects of character, all the mistakes of his life. (1890: 408)

In one swift stroke Bancroft dismisses thirty years of American occupation of California lands and discredits all complaints against the U.S. invaders, but in so doing he also enables us to note not only his ethnocentrism and disdain for the Californios but what we can term the microstructural approach at work throughout his cooperative historical accounts. His focus is always on local developments and key individuals in California rather than on the underlying dynamics of Spanish or Mexican policies (Caughey, 199); moreover, he fails to consider global political and economic relations as well as the mode of production and class structure of Mexican society. As in any study characterized by methodological individualism that explains history in terms of the attributes of particular individuals,[46] outcomes likewise blamed on flawed leadership are here to be remedied by an infusion of new "Anglo" blood.

So run the thoughts of this hegemonist, who despite his critique of the U.S. war with Mexico, which he recognizes was not "just and honorable," enjoys admitting that it has been quite "profitable, giving us the California country, the garden of the world" (Bancroft, 1912: 15). His racist and ethnocentric views in relation to other non-European peoples, including Native Americans, African Americans, Asians, Filipinos, and Latin Americans in general are made quite explicit in his later work (1912: 370–71). In this, Bancroft is typical of other mainstream historians of the nineteenth century. As Weinberg demonstrates in his *Manifest Destiny*, the century produced numerous ethnocentric discourses legitimating expansionism and imperialist action across to the Pacific coast as well as in Mexico, Central America, and the Caribbean. Even filibustering activity by Americans was said by President Buchanan to be in accord to "natural laws which had long determined the relations of unequal races."[47] Part and parcel of the jingoistic discourses of "Manifest Destiny," which naturalized U.S. occupation of lands said to be fated to become a part of the "American family of States,"[48] were those describing the conquered as inferior, inept, and in need of regeneration (Weinberg, 169). The work of Farnham, characterized even by Bancroft as "worthless trash" and as "a tissue of falsehoods"[49] is nevertheless a good example of the kind of representation of the subaltern faced by Californios in the decade of the 1870s when they narrated their testimonials:

> In a word, the Californians are an imbecile, pusillanimous, race of men, and unfit to control the destinies of that beautiful country. (Farnham, 139)

Numerous texts like Farnham's were written before and after 1846 describing conditions and events in California and providing a portrayal of the Californios as a lazy, thieving, superstitious, Catholic population that presumed to own hundreds of thousands of fertile acres, which any red-blooded American knew ought, by divine right, to belong to Americans. By the end of the nineteenth century, however, a few historians and writers, like Royce, presented their own critiques of "Manifest Destiny" and "land hungry" Americans who had despoiled a population through conquest, litigation, squattering, and robbery, but these critical accounts were always the exception.[50]

The Californios interviewed by Savage and Cerruti were well aware of distorted portrayals of Californio history circulating in published accounts and even in local newspapers. Their fate with Bancroft would not be much better, however, for despite his paternalistic praise for some of them, especially those of Spanish origin, his positivistic approach to history situating non-Europeans on a lower rung of development led to an essentialist portrayal of all Californios. In particular, he had little regard for mestizos, said to be "a wild, turbulent humanity characterized by ignorance and fanaticism." He argued that dictatorial rule in Mexico was the only viable road open to Porfirio Díaz because a nation of mestizos was not, like the Anglo Americans, predisposed toward democratic institutions (1912: 292). Of course the Mexican population in California, especially new immigrant professionals editing newspapers, often shared the same pro-Díaz perspective and praised the dictator for his "law and order" policies (Neri, 198).

A man with little tolerance for people of color and the working class, except in the measure that they were useful and exploitable, Bancroft also applauds U.S. intervention in the affairs of other nations, including Cuba, Panama, Nicaragua, and the Philippines (1912: 524); opposes the right of labor to go on strike (1912: 382); and in general defends the interests of his own class. Bancroft's bourgeois discourses further corroborate the image of a Yankee entrepreneur bent on defending an empire not on the basis of moral strength, like Royce, but on the basis of economic and military might. Ironically, it is to this same imperialist, Eurocentric, antiunion, racist publisher to whom we owe the existence of a number of testimonials still held in manuscript form in the stacks of the Bancroft Library. That they were never published independently is undoubtedly linked to Bancroft's opinion that the views expressed in the testimonials carried little weight and had even less marketability. More important, the marginalization of these texts and their exploitation as raw materials speak loudly and clearly to the relations of production and the Californios' structural capacity and lack of agency by the 1870s, more than twenty years after invasion.

Why, with a few exceptions, these manuscripts have never been published since then is of course the more serious question. In the past few decades the Friends of the Bancroft Library and the Historical Society of Southern California have in fact published a few of the "dictations," including several by California pioneers, that is, Anglo settlers. The majority of the testimonials remain in their original state, handwritten manuscripts to which only the privileged have access. The Californios have of course not fared any better in the hands of contemporary historians, although their testimonials have been used as primary sources for many historiographic essays. Most telling is the fact that many historians, like Bancroft, have used the Californios' statements without attributing their words to individuals, as if they had become a mass of indistinguishable voices, there for the taking in what can only be termed discursive pillage and plunder. Salvador Vallejo's statement on the use of Indian labor is quoted almost verbatim in McWilliams's history of California but attributed to an anonymous Californio *ranchero*.[51] It was this type of violence of representation that the testimonials sought to counter, but ironically in the end would authorize by acceding to mediated narration.

Mediated Narratives

> Men make their own history, but they do not make it just as
> they please, they do not make it under circumstances
> chosen by themselves but under circumstances directly
> encountered, given and transmitted from the past. The
> tradition of all the dead generations weighs like a
> nightmare on the brain of the living. And just when they
> seem engaged in revolutionizing themselves and things, in
> creating something that has never yet existed, precisely in
> such periods of revolutionary crisis they anxiously conjure
> up the spirits of the past.
>
> Karl Marx

In these testimonials men and women reconstruct their own history,
but they do not reconstruct it just as they please, but under circumstances directly encountered at the moment of production. It is the
mediated and dependent nature of these testimonials that calls for a
certain wariness and special attention to contradictions within these
texts, for it is evident that the narrators cannot be as forthright and
outspoken as they might be if they were in positions of dominance;
they cannot express their resentment as candidly as they might if they
were on equal footing in the historiographic undertaking. The Californios find themselves feeling like guests who have overstayed their
welcome in a land that was once theirs. They must be cautious about
what they say if they are to be considered as authoritative sources on
California history, a history that they themselves made, if not as they
would have liked. The task faced in deciphering the testimonials is, in
part, to gauge the disjunctures in the testimonials by situating the texts
within the site of production and focusing on contradictions between
texts and between discourses within the same text. Disarticulating lay-
ers of text also requires examining discursive practices in relation to
other texts, be they other testimonials, letters, histories, diaries, fiction
or poetry, and other documents, both U.S. and Mexican, for purposes
of identifying discursive shifts and ideological maneuverings, in order to understand what is being countered. The gaps, the disjunctures,
are important because what is not said directly is often implied or
coded in a different way; what is said is moreover often subsequently
refuted. The testimonials are thus heterodiscursive and dialogical.

In these textual interstices the testimonial's particular mode of production becomes crucial. It is important, then, to recall that the Californio testimonials are "collaborative" narratives embodying uneven

power relations. The interviewer in his role as transcribing or writing subject, as agent of the editorial enterprise, has a great deal of control, not only of the final version of the narrative but of the direction of the narration itself, although at any given moment the narrator may deviate from established guidelines. In most of the narratives the question/answer format is not immediately visible, so the testimonial deceptively appears as one continuous narration, spontaneously narrated, without prompting or pauses. The topics too appear to have originated with the narrator. (Only in two of the dictations considered here, that of Dorotea Valdez and Rosalía de Leese, have the questions been maintained in the transcription; the topics raised with Coronel are obvious from the subheadings.) As in any kind of production, the control of technologies, of the means of production, tells us much about the social structure and about the place of Californios within late-nineteenth-century California. The dominant position of the capitalist cultural entrepreneur initiating the entire project and his technical staff of interviewers, editors, and writers becomes clear when we look not only at the final product and format of the texts but at technical aspects of the production level that allow the transcribing interviewer to cross out sentences, include his own comments in parenthesis, modify the language,[52] translate the original Spanish text,[53] and impede editing of the original text.[54] In some cases the narrators reject the interviewers' total authority and attempt to control the procedures themselves (as did M. G. Vallejo, who would tear up what had been written if he was not satisfied), but the informants generally, if grudgingly, acquiesce to Bancroft's method.

The implications of these relations of production are clear: the mediated narrations are involved in a concession to hegemonic ideological reproduction. The fact that they are solicited narrations, that the active agency is not that of the informant but rather that of the agent of the Bancroft House, that they exist given the initiative of Bancroft who pays Cerruti and Savage to find the Californios, to interview them and transcribe their narration, reveals the commodification of cultural production and the appropriation of discursive labor to be compensated only with historiographic representation. By narrating under these conditions, the Californios consent, however resentfully, to being represented by the Other, by the (usurping) enemy, and end up abdicating discursive agency, to a certain extent, by placing their counterdiscourses in the hands of a literary "industrialist." In such circumstances, contestatory action requires particular strategies revealed in the text's contradictions, enigmatic statements, and inexact repetitions

of earlier statements and gaps, elements that Cerruti noted and attributed to the narrators' ignorance:

> Justice imperiously demands that none should gainsay my claim to a
> certain amount of praise for the fidelity with which I have reported in
> their own words, conversations held with ignorant persons dwelling in
> different parts of the state. A few contradictions may also be discovered
> but they are explained by the fact that Mr. Hubert Bancroft had given
> me instructions to "note down" every word said by native Californians;
> and as they held different opinions, entertained views at variance with
> each other, could not with any show of reason be expected to coincide
> in the manner of judging of persons and creeds. (Cerruti, 109)

Thus, despite some editorial intervention, Bancroft's agents did not
interfere with all narrative techniques, though in their marginal and
parenthetical annotations the interviewers did not hesitate to question
or mock what was being said. We need to consider these logical and
rhetorical strategies in our analysis of what is, for all intents and purposes, a literary text.

The Californio testimonial is examined here as a literary and historical narrative, as a product of this disjuncture, as a genre produced
during a period of flux, conflict, and alienation, within which distinctions between history and fiction readily collapse. Neither a binary
distinction between history and fiction nor the notion that texts can be
classified in terms of truth value or in terms of their representational
fidelity to reality has a place in an analysis that regards all texts as discursive and ideological. Texts do not mirror reality, but "reality" is always already discursively embedded in any text, in its enabling and
constraining effect. As texts and as social practices, narratives are always in constant interaction with other discursive and nondiscursive
practices. We do not need texts to prove the existence of the world,
but we do need them for knowledge and interaction in the world, both
past and present,[55] as they are sites for ideological contestation—at
times the only site available for struggle within hegemonic spaces, as
the Californio narratives hold forth.

The testimonial's literariness, as Beverley indicates, is first evident
in its written form, for the interviewer-editor and, in some cases, the
narrator-editor have shaped the narration, eliminating its orality and
allowing for a flowing narrative style without the usual pauses, repetitions, and faltering of oral discourse. In this sense, much like historical romances, these are readerly texts, multiform in style and heterodiscursive. Given the multiplicity of discourses at work, we propose

examining the testimonials not only in terms of constructs of identity and agency but also, more importantly, collectively, as a macrotext, as a collective dialogical narrative with a variety of narrators, a variety of narrative perspectives, and a variety of elite and popular, literary and nonliterary forms of discourse, for, like a novel, these testimonials are heterodiscursive, and as likely to offer classical references to Roman history or Greek literature as to incorporate popular ditties. These multivalent discourses can be classified not only sociospatially and ideologically but also generically. As will become evident, the testimonials include romantic discourses idealizing the past as much as satirical discourses denouncing past social practices and leaders. They incorporate communal legends that function allegorically and popular diatribes in verse that refer to regional and national antagonisms. Some chapters of the longer testimonials are essays on specific issues. Poetry, popular ballads, short stories, picaresque episodes, humorous anecdotes, sketches, manifestos, letters, legal documents, and newspaper articles are also included. Of special importance are the testimonial micronarratives incorporated within each testimonial, several of them marked by discourses of gender and nation. The macrotextual nature of the testimonials is evident not only in their cross-referentiality, with the inclusion at times of parts of the testimonials of others, but in the multipositional focus on the same episodes, revealing in some of the narratives not only a variety of perspectives but meaningful gaps as well. Vallejo's testimonial offers numerous examples of the intertextual nature of these testimonials, as his extensive narrative includes accounts by Alvarado and Teresa Guerra de Hartnell (these accounts form part of their own testimonials as well); a manifesto by Governor Figueroa (quoted by a number of Californios in their testimonials); a sermon by one of the missionaries (Friar Vicente Francisco Sarría), said to rival any of Beecher's sermons (MGV, 4:50); copies of letters by Vallejo and other officials; short stories (including a gothic tale by Luis Castillo Negrete); ballads and other poetry by several Californio and Mexican poets; newspaper articles; speeches read before the Mexican Congress and reports of Mexican Congressional committees; *pasquines* (anonymous notes placed in public areas); and humorous anecdotes told by other Californios or Indians. Significant too is the fact that the mediated words of the Indians appear not only in Vallejo's but in several of the testimonials. In addition to this multiplicity of generic discourses, which constitute the macrotext's generic discontinuities,[56] the testimonials make use of a diversity of discursive styles (sarcastic, sentimental, ironic, humorous, and so on) that allows the narrators to convey their resentment, cynicism, frustration, disdain, antagonisms, nostalgia, and resignation. At times they contain "fantasms and dreams" as well.

The multiplicity of intersecting, overlapping, and colliding discourses in the text implies that all discourses bear traces of other discourses and of the social spaces to which they are linked. In effect the testimonial itself is a representational space within which a complex of discourses, social sites, and positionalities are reconstructed. The narration of everyday activities within these social spaces often serves allegorically as a comment on political, caste, and class relations and on antagonisms between rival groups and factions. At another level, these testimonials function not only as socially symbolic acts to resolve conflict but as sites of struggle for the power of representation. As sites of contention, sites for the construction of identity, for a recentering of collective subjectivity, for contestation of dominant representations of Californios, these narratives are necessarily concerned with the politics of representation. Whose reconstruction of the past survives becomes a polemical issue within the Californio community itself. We have stressed that the testimonials reveal that there is no single political vision among Californios, given their multiple affiliations, nor is there any essential identity, in view of the number of communities within the Californio collectivity, yet there is a dominant construct in the testimonials of native Californios: the discourse of nation. This nation-space is generated in the very vacillation in positioning, in the shifts from one social space to another, from one identity to another, from one political perspective to another, producing a layered identity, a construct that overlaps with spaces of family, religion, caste, class, and region, and that embodies an ensemble of social relations. This reconstructed nation-space jars with lived experience, with defeat in 1846 and with social relations of the 1870s. Out of this disjuncture, out of the contradictions between a reconstructed past and a constructed present, arises a new liminal space, a zone of engagement, the space of ethnicity.

The Problematic of Constructions and Reconstructions

> Memory is crucial to identity.
>
> Perry Anderson

When we argue that history and memory are crucial to the construction of ethnic and national spaces, we are positing history both as textually transmitted knowledge and as nondiscursive practices that, as Jameson (1988: 150) reminds us, are accessible to us only in reconstructed form. History, however, is never merely the reconstructed past ("time arrested"); it is also ongoing social reality ("time passing").[57] The fact that the temporal/spatial is apprehended through discourse does not negate its existence; to put it in Bhaskar's words, reality "can only be known, not shown, to exist" (82). Perhaps Prigogine and Stengers sum it up best when they indicate that "whatever we call reality, it is revealed to us only through the active construction in which we participate."[58] It is this construction of past and present, of social space and collective identity that the Californios offer in their testimonials.

Unlike history, which is both discursive and nondiscursive, identity is a wholly discursive phenomenon, a representation generated reflexively and collectively within concrete historical, social, and spatial conditions. As such it is always multiple and variable, necessarily contingent and contradictory. A consideration of identity as a historically determined construct, as a sociodiscursive product, requires a framework that will allow us to explore not only shifts in positionality in relation to structural location and to different social spaces — the territory, the mission, the *rancho*, the *ranchería*, the territorial administration, and the region — but also identification with various collectivities and agencies as well. For a framework that posits an ensemble of social relations embodied in discourses and social spaces, we have looked to the Marxist (and sometimes post-Marxist) proposals put forth by Mouzelis, Callinicos, Therborn, Lefebvre, Jameson, and others, and developed a composite Marxist model for the analysis of discourses and social spaces.

To speak of a Marxist discursive analysis might appear to be a contradiction in terms, given that those favoring discourse analysis are often described in relation to the "linguistic fallacy"[59] or the "epistemic fallacy" (the "definition of being in terms of knowledge"; Bhaskar, 181). Both "fallacies" reductively assume that outside of the discursive realm there is no conceivable "reality." A Marxist, however, always foregrounds material reality and cannot therefore reduce everything to epistemological issues or textuality. Yet, admittedly, any analysis of literary and historical texts is always an analysis of a multiplicity of discourses, as Bakhtin indicated long ago. Bakhtin also noted the textual nature of all disciplinary research: "Where there is no text, there is no object of study, and no object of thought either."[60] The same notion appears in Prigogine and Stengers, who suggest that "the reality studied by physics is also a mental construct; it is not merely given." They add, "on all levels reality implies an essential element of conceptualization" (Prigogine and Stengers, 225–26). Theoretical discursive practices no doubt play a central role in research, for theory or "language," as Prigogine and Stengers have said, determines the questions being asked and therefore the partial responses found—partial, of course, because "each language can express only part of reality" (Prigogine and Stengers, 225). Marx himself recognized and stressed the importance of theoretical discourses when he differentiated men from animals by their capacity to generate constructs:

> What distinguishes the worst architect from the best of bees is this, that the architect raises his structure in imagination before he erects it in reality. At the end of every labour-process, we get a result that already existed in the imagination of the labourer at its commencement.[61]

What characterizes the human species, then, appears to be the capacity to produce discursive constructs, imaginary constructs—and, especially germane to the texts studied here, not only in anticipation, but in retrospect. No one denies this discursive competence; the problem lies at another level, that of representation. The pitfall, as some critics see it, is assuming a direct correlation between theoretical discourses and concrete reality, that is, the notion that the nondiscursive is the object of knowledge.[62]

Perhaps it goes without saying that the reduction of all theoretical foci to textuality is "the research dominant" of much of this so-called postmodernist period. Granted that texts or discourses do not mimetically reflect objective reality and that any conceptualization about the world involves discursive practices that can only examine objects of discourse, yet we must acknowledge that reality is not reducible to our knowledge or experience of it. In the end, this "reality," which is only contingently related to our experience of it, that is, only "contingently, partially and locally humanized" (Bhaskar, 182), can only be posited on the basis of cognitive claims about conditions that would be necessary for the production of particular practices and discourses. To avoid conceptual reductionism ("that concepts are not only necessary for, but exhaustive of, social life"; Bhaskar, 185), Bhaskar proposes that we view reality in terms of both a conceptual and a material dimension, thus acknowledging "the historicity, relativity and essential transformability of all our knowledge" and the historicity of all discursive constructs (Bhaskar, 155, 174, 177).

Like Bhaskar, in this study we always assume a material social reality, consisting of historically determined structures, social relations, and practices, all of which constitute the always-already social context on which human agency is dependent for its reproduction or transformation. Discursive formations, which enable our knowledge of reality, always play a role in the transformation of reality, for at this level ideological struggle takes place. The testimonials themselves serve to clarify the relation between the discursive and the nondiscursive in their engagement with existing and prior political and social practices. Although carried out at a discursive level, this engagement reveals a dialogical relation between different levels of social practices generated within economic, political, and cultural domains that condition the existence of various discursive formations at play in these nineteenth-century texts.[63] In this study, discursive formations are seen not generically but ideologically and sociospatially, both in relation to structural location and agential position. Discursive formations function in effect like ideological frameworks, and are the basis for the construction of identity, or, more specifically, identities, for nineteenth-century Californios identify along a number of interconnecting axes, all sites of ideological discourses that challenge, resist, and sometimes conform to dominant regimes of representation.[64]

Discursive formations linked to particular structural sites, practices, and agencies or collectivities are what "position" individuals, and it is the shifting from one ideological framework to another, the slippages and sliding from one social space to another, that allows for multipositionality and for what Goffman calls "footing," shifts in positionality according to social space, topic, or function of the discourse.[65] In the Californio testimonials, as in any dialogue, these shifts occur in relation to social space and agencies (collectivities) with which the narrators identify. The social sites and collectivities with which we will be concerned in this work are those of class, caste, family, nation, region, gender, party, and religion, all of which will be analyzed discursively, that is, as constructs, but in dialogical relation to both discursive and nondiscursive social practices in the process of political and economic transformation. The fact that the figuration of social practices takes place during a period of restructuring in California contributes to the variability of antagonistic discourses, both emergent and residual, in these testimonials and to shifts in positionality and sliding from one ideological framework to another. The testimonials are consequently marked by a myriad of contradictions, the result of being grounded in different and competing ideological frameworks. In these testimonials, ambivalence and vacillation occur principally, but not exclusively, between feudal-colonial (religious) discursive formations and liberal-rationalist (secular) discourses, but also between discourses of nation, caste, class, and gender.

Structure, Agency, and Identity

A discussion of the "social reality" of the Californio population requires an analytic instrument that allows for an accounting of the structural constraints and capacities that position this population within the social formation and enable or limit its agency as constructed within the literary text. Accounting for the relation between structure, agency, and identity is bound up with a discursive approach. Here we will consider the analysis suggested by Therborn, who, following Althusser, views subject identity as the product of discursive interpellation. Therborn's analysis leads us to view discourses as social and ideological practices generated within particular historical material sites in articulation with other discourses and overdetermined by the dominant social relations of that particular historical moment.[66]

What is lacking in Therborn's formulation is a distinction between agency and subjectivity in view of his reduction of agency to what Callinicos terms "an ideological illusion."[67] In his critique of the collapsing of these categories, Callinicos states that, for Therborn,

> social actors are not agents, able to pursue their own goals, but are rather social constructs, the passive bearers of social relations which, it is true, may involve contradictions between the processes of subjection and qualifications but of which the actors themselves are also mere effects. (128)

The crux of the problem is the relation between agency and structure, both of which, as Perry Anderson rightfully indicates, are central to Marxist analysis today.

Callinicos engages this question by positing all human beings as "agents, conscious agents moved by beliefs and desires" (148). Agents are said to derive their "structural capacities" from their position within the relations of production, but these structural relations do not in and of themselves determine agents' beliefs and desires, though they do determine access to particular resources necessary for action (235–36). Callinicos presents us with a problem: the invocation of "beliefs and desires" as some kind of human universal that must be studied outside of structural constraints. The attribution of "causal powers" to individuals on the basis of their capacities for consciously reflecting on and altering not merely their actions but also their thoughts disregards the undeniable historical contingency of "beliefs and desires." The problem perhaps arises given the reduction of structures to economic structures and the limiting of structural position to class location. Although Callinicos questions Giddens's notion that "actors have interests by virtue of their membership [in] particular groups, communities, classes, etc." (Callinicos, 129), it is, we would suggest, precisely as members of collectivities capable of assuming various sites and positions that individuals have agency.

These issues, central to the analysis of the Californio testimonials, are addressed to a certain extent by Mouzelis in his analysis of the social formation and in his notion of agency as collective, rather than individual. To avoid automatically viewing political and cultural phenomena in exclusively economic terms, Mouzelis suggests looking at society as an ongoing construction.[68] Mouzelis further proposes to conceptualize the social formation in terms of three major spheres of production: economic, political, and cultural (80), each of which is constituted by specific technologies (forces), processes, or institutional arrangements. Each level represents a means of production or domination, the appropriation and control of which generates power relations or antagonisms between various collective actors or agencies (for example, between missionaries and *rancheros*). Antagonistic relations within the economic sphere (exploiter/exploited) are akin to those within the political level (dominant/dominated). Within each division there are thus particular forces and relations to the means of production or domination. Correlative ideological discourses are also generated at every level, enabling the reproduction, adaptation, and/or transformation of that sphere.

Within the social totality, these three spheres, linked, overdetermined, and structured in dominance, determine the *structural capacities* of agencies, that is to say, "the powers an agent has in virtue of his or her position within the relations of production" (Callinicos, 235). Social actors are, however, defined not only in terms of their structural location, that is, their relationship to the means of economic, political, and cultural production, but also by their collective capacity to create, appropriate, and control economic, political, and cultural technologies (Mouzelis, 56). Collective actors are thus both products and re-producers or transformers (Bhaskar, 76) of their social world. Only macroagents, not individuals, are capable of constituting and transforming social orders, and then only in relation to structural conditions that, as Giddens suggests, both enable as well as constrain (cited in Callinicos, 235). Macroactors or macroagencies can be analyzed therefore not only in terms of their various structural locations and capacities, but also in terms of their social practices and their "collective awareness of common interests" (Mouzelis, 61), a crucial notion at the core of the testimonials. This formulation provides Mouzelis with what he terms a balanced agency-system approach and enables a consideration of macrolevel structures as well as of macroactors or macroagencies within a "position-practice system" (62, 63).

In *Capital* Marx also deals with macroagents, indicating that "individuals are dealt with ... only in so far as they are the personifications of economic categories, the bearers of particular class-relations and interests" (1:10). In fact individuals are bearers of a variety of social relations generated within different social sites, that is, different agential and structural spaces. Individual structurally positioned agents, then, whether consciously or unconsciously, act as positioned representatives of an ensemble of collectivities, all individuals being members or representatives of several collectivities or agencies simultaneously. It bears recalling that only as part of a collectivity does one become individuated.[69] Not all collectivities are structural institutions or organizations, however. Our definition of "collectivities" does not specifically follow Mouzelis's or Callinicos's schemes, but it incorporates notions from both as it attempts to account for positionality within a variety of collectivities distinguished by race, nation, region, order (military/religious), and so on.

Mouzelis restricts his concept of macroactors/agency or collectivity to refer to organized agencies or institutions, like "business corporations, political parties, trade unions, governmental agencies," all of which he sees as "decision-making entit[ies]" (63). For Mouzelis, then, agencies are akin to apparatuses, institutions, or organizations, whether state, cultural, or economic. Within Californio society, if we follow Mouzelis's analysis, the missionaries, the *presidio* troops, and the administrative apparatuses of the territory could all be considered agencies, in light of their capacity as organized entities for decision making and action. Agency, however, needs to be posited outside particular structures if it is to be analyzed as other than epiphenomenal, and beyond the parameters of organized units, that is, if "imagined communities" (B. Anderson, 15) are to be considered. Here the distinction established by Callinicos between agency and system is crucial, as is his distinction between individual and collective agency. Thus, while viewing agency as a given (134), Callinicos sees collective agency as dependent on collective action and identity:

> A collectivity exists where persons coordinate their actions because they believe themselves to have a common identity. (135)

This formulation requires that the collectivity go beyond awareness of common interests to a consciousness and construction of a shared identity and coordinated collective action. Within this definition, "classes may, but need not be, collectivities" (136). What Callinicos's analysis suggests is that collectivities can include both structured organizations and nonstructured collectivities, that is, *imagined communities* that do not necessarily "emerge from the recognition of pre-existing social relationships" but instead "create a social relationship" (136). An "imagined community," like that of nation or ethnicity, is in fact a discursively constructed collectivity, not necessarily defined by structural position, although in effect all collectivities are constituted by an ensemble of social relations rather than by only one. Identification with a collectivity on the basis of nation, race, ethnicity, gender, sexuality, or some other constructed (i.e., cultural) attribute does not preclude members from forming part of other collectivities as well. No one is a member of only one community, but rather of several simultaneously, as is clear in an analysis of collectivities in pre- and postinvasion California. Agencies or collectivities are historically determined and necessarily vary from one mode of production to another or even from one phase of the mode of production to another. Characterized by positions of power (insider/outsider, central/marginal, majority/minority) and evincing cleavages within them as well, collectivities in Alta California will be involved in a series of conflicts and struggles that are the product of economic and political antagonisms.

In this study, we will focus primarily on collectivities and on structural location. Individuals will be seen to be characterized by their multipositionality, occupying particular positions within the three spheres of the social formation and within various agencies or collectivities. In this sense, structure and agency are implicated, in concrete historical and spatial terms, as the sites or domains within which are generated a multiplicity of discourses, all serving to construct identity. It follows that individual action is always enabled or constrained by structural capacities and concomitantly by identification with specific agencies. The articulation between structural position and agency, the combination of constraints and power generated within cultural and structural closures, leads to particular political positions and constructs of identity. An individual is thus necessarily an ensemble of structural and cultural positions; we will be looking at discursive constructions of identity and of Californio history as ideological reconstructions conditioned by structural location and position within collectivities. The discursive practices generated within these nineteenth-century testimonials constitute an ideological field in which individuals from particular classes or collectivities either become conscious of their oppression, exploitation and dispossession and participate in contestatory[70] (both discursive and nondiscursive) action or alternatively legitimate and justify existing or even previous structural relations and their own positions and practices within the system. Ideological discourses are produced at every level of the social formation, within every social space, within every collectivity, and although these are invariably impacted by or competing with hegemonic discourses, subordination and disempowerment can generate discourses with contestatory potential. This is central to our argument that the Californio testimonials must be taken as discursive sites, as zones of engagement, wherein contestation of hegemonic discourses is embedded.

The capacity of hegemonic frameworks to absorb all contestation, however, requires noting the importance of alternative discursive frameworks. Here the model of hegemony as presented by Gramsci provides interesting insights despite the fact that we cannot speak of hegemony in precapitalist Alta California.[71] Gramsci's framework for examining the alliances of classes or fractions of classes to form a historical bloc, his consideration of domination through consensus as well as coercion, his work in what Hall calls "the ideological field,"[72] and his discussion of a "war of position" as a strategy when a "war of maneuver" is not possible (Gramsci, 233) are important for a study of postinvasion California of the 1870s when the narrators are reconstructing their past, and also for a deconstruction of nationalism and racism. Gramsci's analysis also forces us to come to terms with the ideological snares set by dominant cultural agencies in an attempt to ensure that all arguments are conceived within previously established frameworks, wherein even counterarguments in the end often affirm the very structures that ensure the subordination of particular classes or groups.[73] These strategies of containment (Jameson, 1981: 210) serve to contain dissent within hegemonic frameworks, even as they ostensibly give voice to that selfsame dissent. Yet although dominant ideologies permeate all representation, counterhegemonic discourses may be generated within residual and emergent discursive formations, that is, within discursive disjunctures produced by intersecting and overlapping discourses. Californios wield these alternative frameworks in their "war of position" in the testimonials.

Social Spaces and Identity

Any analysis of ideological discourses during a particular historical period must bear in mind the sociospatial dimensions within which they are contained. Every society, Lefebvre indicates, creates and organizes "its own space," a productive social space that in turn can give rise to other spaces. Social spaces could be said to have a generative capacity and, like all social elements, to be dynamic and ever capable of change. Because social spaces are historically specific products, each mode of production produces, occupies, and reproduces space in a certain way. Thus, sociospatial changes, both before and after 1846, accompany changes in the social structures. And given the spatialization of relations of production, the dissolution of a social space necessarily implies the transformation of sociospatial relations.[74] For this reason, a study of the configuration of space within any historical period provides important insights into its social formation. As previously suggested and modifying to some degree the useful focus offered by Lefebvre on the production of social space, we conceive of the Californio testimonials themselves as representational spaces within which are represented or reconstructed a number of social spaces and sociospatial practices from both the semifeudal and post-1846 capitalist periods of nineteenth-century California. If social space always embodies class relations as well as an ensemble of other social relations,[75] a consideration of socially constructed space is thus always already a spatialization of agential and structural relations. Consequently, in any discussion of identity or subjectivity we are always considering sociospatial positionality.

In the testimonials, the appropriation and domination of social space is the crucial problematic for the Californios, who by the time they are narrating their testimonials no longer occupy dominant social spaces or actively produce them. As a result of this separation, they find themselves in the 1870s reduced to marginal spaces and to dependent cultural representation. One might argue, however, that in 1846 their historical situation was akin to that of the Irish in that it encompassed two overlapping social spaces, that of the First World and that of a conquered Third World nation.[76] Much like the Irish in this respect, the Californios went from an early post-1846 phase as an internal colony with a colonized elite to a second phase as a proletarianized and impoverished national minority. Faced with additional overlapping, now of ethnic and class social spaces, the Californios by 1876 are in a position to look back and observe that historically the domination of social spaces has been their greatest challenge and their appropriation of religious-economic spaces (the disestablishment of the mission system) their greatest triumph, one Alvarado (1:208) finds comparable to the colonization of California in 1769.

In the representation of social spaces, like in all representation, space is often subject to being either idealized or reified (Lefebvre, 27–30), as is evident in the fetishism of space, that is, the consideration of space as a thing in and of itself and not as an embodiment of social relations. Any social space, Lefebvre reminds us, "contains and dissimulates social relationships" (83). Spatial representations are thus ideological and can function to conceal and mask particular social relations. Figuration of the mission is a prime example; it contains and dissimulates social relationships that several of the Californio narrators are quick to disarticulate. Other social spaces will also serve in the Californio narratives to contain and conceal property relations, social stratification, military abuse, political differences, cultural domination, and sexual politics. These spatial practices or strategies of containment and configuration will prove useful in our analysis of the reconstructed social spaces of Alta California within the testimonials.

Space itself serves as a trope in these testimonials. Decoding these spatial tropes, especially the configuration of space as vertically and horizontally structured sites, reveals Californio perspectives on social stratification in Alta California and makes evident the relation between the disposition of space and property relations. Extension and hierarchy enable as well a consideration of power relations between center and periphery, global and local, state and territory, colonial power and colony, dominant and dominated, interior and exterior, private and public domains. Additionally, sociospatial configurations point to strategies of inclusion-exclusion, domination and subordination operating within the reconstructed sites. Notably useful are Lefebvre's and Foucault's designations of utopias, isotopias, and heterotopias,[77] which allow us to consider spaces that oppose, complement, or resemble one another, as is the case with the mission, the *ranchos,* and the territory of California itself.

Generally speaking, the social spaces within which identity is constructed are viewed in these testimonials in relation to geographical, demographic, and political concerns. Often these take precedence over relations of production that inevitably underlie a number of decisions made in relation to secularization of the missions and immigration policies in the Californias under Mexican rule. The impact of geography and demography on settlement and economic development, as well as on the mode of security and political structure, is often the primary explanation offered by the Californios for the limited advancement in the development of the productive forces and for failure to resist the U.S. invasion of 1846 successfully. Similarly, a reconstruction of geopolitical considerations and externally directed interventions either on the part of gentile Indians or foreigners is offered by the Californios to

explain the patterns of *pueblo*/mission/*rancho* relations, regional dissensions, and the weakness and at times outright incompetence of political authority.

Other spatial considerations are also crucial in this study. The primary spatial division is that separating the remote and peripheral territory from central Mexico, where the political power of the state is
concentrated. Spatiality also enters in a distinction opposing native
Californios to incoming settlers from Mexico. The spatial division of
production that separates castes and classes is likewise basic to all the
chapters, as is the spatial and political division between north and
south, shaped by the numerical superiority of the south and by the
control of the market by the north. All of these geopolitical conditions
are seen by the Californios to have constrained their agency and ill
equipped them to face the onslaught of invasion.

Macrotext

In view of the heterogeneity of the Californio population and the rifts
between its members, this study will not focus on any individual text
but will approach the testimonials as a whole, as a macrotext, in order
to foreground and analyze intra-Californio dialogues on, for example,
the missions, the Indian neophytes, the Hijar-Padrés colonization project, the arrival of foreign merchants, the Californios' struggle for independence, and the subsequent invasion by U.S. forces. The fragmentation of the collectivity, the Californio class and caste structure,
the place of women and Indians within this patriarchal society, and
the political dissension within the territory most interest us. In each
case, social spaces are in contention and what is at stake for the Californios is nothing less than the power to represent themselves from a
particular ideological position. These sociospatial conflicts generated
by regional factionalism, national animosities between Mexicans and
Californios, class antagonisms, and political divisions lead to textual
density and contradictions.

The various testimonials are consequently neither uniform nor homogeneous. Rather, they are contradictory, heterogeneous, and inconsistent in their attempts to counter hegemonic representations that do
not coincide with their vantage point. The sociospatial positioning is
thus multiple, sometimes territorial, sometimes national or regional,
sometimes caste-bound, sometimes partisan, sometimes familial. As the
testimonials progress largely chronologically, the operative constructs
change as well; the dominant sociospatial construct at the beginning —

caste—will have been replaced by the 1870s by that of ethnicity. There is thus in the testimonials a continual severing, realignment, and reconstruction of identity, of political interests, of ideological discourses, and of social space.

The narrators of these testimonials, although narrating "from below" in the 1870s, by then positioned within dominated spaces as a subaltern collectivity (Spivak, 1988: 283), are, however, representative of the elite classes of Alta California before 1846; this disjuncture leads to the emergent identity of ethnic nationalism constructed in the testimonials. Most of the interviewees are either members of the ruling families of Mexican California, like the Lugos, Vallejos, de la Guerras, Alvarados, and Picos, or situated within what could be termed middle-management positions and allied to the dominant power, as, for example, the two mission housekeepers Apolinaria Lorenzana and Eulalia Pérez.[78] Because the "history" harvested and amassed by Bancroft was selectively collected, it could hardly be considered representative of the Californio population as a whole, nor was it in the 1870s—given the numerous Mexican immigrants during the gold rush period—representative of the population of Mexican origin in the state. The informants do represent a diversity of positions within the upper and middle strata in Alta California society, be they soldiers or officers, governors or commander generals, *pueblo* mayors (*alcaldes*) or secretaries, mission housekeepers or administrators, merchants, wives of *rancheros* and merchants, wives of political officials, first- and second-generation (native-born) Californios, *rancheros*, or *hacendados*. Bancroft and his agents evidently contacted the most "noteworthy" individuals. The lower stratum from the pre-1846 period is conspicuously absent at the level of narration, although a few assimilated Indians were briefly interviewed as well as a handful of post-1846 Mexican immigrant laborers. We cannot therefore speak of a homogeneous population or even of a heterogeneous selection of informants, even in light of the ideological differences evidenced in the testimonials.

In the chapters that follow we will examine these overlapping spaces in about thirty testimonials, as well as in several other nineteenth-century texts by Californios (see the list of testimonial references at the end of the book). Some of the testimonials are voluminous (over one thousand handwritten pages); most are forty to fifty pages long; a few are quite short (six pages).[79] Most of these texts have to date never been published and remain in the original handwritten Spanish version; a few have been translated. Although references are primarily to the original text, if the testimonials have been published and translated, we will cite the published text except in cases where there are discrepancies with original Spanish versions.[80] Though this is not an all-inclusive list of the Californio *testimonios* available at the Bancroft Library, the testimonials to be discussed represent some of the most important ones in the collection as they are the most comprehensive and are reflective of the ideological diversity within Alta California society. Also referred to in this study are narratives concerned with the same period that were produced independently. Several short dictations included in Cerruti's *Ramblings in California* are dealt with, as are diaries by soldiers during the Spanish period and speeches read before the Mexican Congress and the California legislature. Other documents, including official and personal letters, financial statements, legal and political texts (treaties, laws, and regulations), as well as hegemonic histories of the United States, Mexico, and California and other accounts of travels through California in the nineteenth century form part of the ideological discourses to be analyzed here, for any study of counterdiscourses necessarily implies a consideration of the discourses and constructs being countered.

The testimonials are dialogical and heterodiscursive texts that position the Californios in relation to particular agential and structural sites. The texts' juggling of both residual and emergent discourses and their continual slippage from one social site to another explain the multiple collective perspectives in the narratives. What we propose to carry out is an analysis of discourses of caste, class, nation, region, political persuasion, religion, and gender in order to survey and explore the ideological constructions and the production of those liminal sites of nation and ethnicity from a position of marginality and disempowerment. In documenting the story of conquest, land loss, and subordination, the testimonials, despite mediation, tell an important story of a struggle for representational space, a struggle through cultural practices that continues still.

2

The Mission as Heterotopia

Creo que no andaba equívoco el gran jefe indio Succaro,
que decía que los cristianos no le daban lugar a escoger
entre Cristo y la muerte.

M. G. Vallejo

Alta California was considered a penal colony even as late as the 1820s, a land of savages fit only for convicts and ex-convicts (Alvarado, 2:120). When the Hijar-Padrés colonists, including men, women, and children, left Mexico City in caravans to come to California in 1834, their neighbors cried and tried to dissuade them from going to a place where they would all meet certain death at the hands of the Indians (Coronel, 6). Three hundred years before, however, California had been portrayed in fantastic tales as a geographical utopia, a land of fantasy, the door to earthly paradise.[1] Since 1492 the Americas as a whole had inspired many utopian representations; the Jesuit Guaraní reservations of Paraguay, for example, were classified by Montesquieu "as one of the grand Utopian designs."[2] The Franciscan missionaries in Mexico had shared a similar "eschatological hope" for a divine consummation of an ideal religious society and an idyllic Indian world in the Américas—a Utopia to be preserved by missionary zeal (Góngora, 232).

But like all utopias, this imaginary one had no real location, for Alta California after 1769 was far from utopian; it was a heterogeneous space, an area of multiple complex sites defined by sets of social relations.[3] One site within California, however, was linked to all the other sites and yet outside of all places; one site was a heterotopia, as it contained, countered, inverted, and represented all the other sites (Foucault, 1986: 24). This site was a heterotopia of crisis and deviation; it was like Foucault's mirror, a "sort of mixed, joint experience" (Foucault, 1986: 24–25), both imaginary and placeless, like the mirror, like any utopia, but simultaneously a countersite, a real site countering the mirror image. This heterotopia was the mission. It countered the missionaries' utopia and served for them instead as a heterotopia of compensation. In its mirror image it was the "sacred" place where starving Indians found warm clothing and food, but was as well a penal colony, the dystopia from which it was practically impossible for the Indians to escape. For the Californios too it constituted a heterotopia, for it juxtaposed, in one space, several incompatible sites (Foucault, 1986: 25): it was both a religious and commercial realm, as much a place of worship as bank, market, ranch, and prison. It was a heterotopia slightly out of sync in historical time, for it was established in California by the Spanish Crown only a few years before the end of Spanish dominion in the Americas, only a few years before the restructuring of space throughout Latin America.

Between 1769 and 1823, twenty-one missions were established in Alta California, each one as much an instrument of coercion as a sacred space for the Franciscan friars, who set out to form a monastic society of Indian *pueblos* inside these *reducciones,* one separating the neophytes from the *gente de razón.* Under the direction and control of a patriarchal and paternalistic order of missionaries, the neophytes in effect lost their freedom of movement. The very spatial configuration of the mission, built always a bit distant from the *presidio,* functioned as a strategy of containment and allowed for spatial mechanisms of control.

A visitor to mission reproductions of today, or to any convent in Latin America for that matter, is first impressed by the fortress-style enclosure that opens up to several cell-like compartments around a central garden area. Everything inside—the thick walls, the numerous locks, even the walled cemetery—speaks of closure, of retreat and order, of regimented existence. The spatial arrangement of the mission is hierarchically organized, with the chapel's high ceiling and bell tower as the highest points within the structure. In some cases, as in the Santa Barbara mission, the main sanctuary has a smaller chapel to the side that opens up to the altar; here the distinguished families, the *gente de razón,* could sit and hear the sermon without commingling with the Indians in the temple. Inherent in the structuring of mission space is a strong sense of place and rank. Despite the simplicity of the architecture, a definite hierarchical configuration of the grounds evidences the labor and care of many hands. These self-sufficient establishments with their spartan cubicles, orchards, vineyards, vegetable gardens, wells, separate quarters for different industries, and stocks for punishment were yesterday's Indian reservations.

The mission enclosure served as much to contain the Indians as to exclude most of the Californios (primarily soldiers and their families), who penetrated the walls only at the invitation of the missionaries. Within the garrisons there were chapels, not always willingly serviced by the missionaries, who did not feel that serving as priests to the lay populaton was their obligation. Even the *presidio* soldiers assigned to guard the mission lived in quarters outside the mission walls. These quarters marked spatially divisions between the separate orders: the military order often in conflict with and subordinated to the religious order, as Palou indicates.[4] It was clearly a conflict over power, over who determined what missions were to be built or rebuilt and when, who controlled the soldiers stationed at each mission, and who controlled the "temporalities" of the mission, and thereby the economy of the territory. The soldiers who guarded the missionaries were in effect under the supervision of the missionaries because their salaries were routed through the mission for payment (MGV,1:80). If the soldiers had their firearms and horses, the missionaries had a powerful ideological weapon: excommunication, which generally guaranteed acquiescence from the soldiers (MGV, 1:346; Palou, 98). With Mexican independence in 1821, however, the balance of power begins to shift and by the decade of the 1830s the sons of the original soldiers emerge as a powerful class that will secularize the missions and markedly change property relations in Alta California. With the dismantling of the religious spaces will also come the dissolution of the *presidios,* both replaced by civil structures and militias.

After the U.S. invasion in 1846 the missions were abandoned and left to deteriorate until the early part of the twentieth century, when they began to be reconstructed and restored as "historical" tourist sites. They stand now as pastiches of nineteenth-century missions with adjoining tourist shops selling postcards, candles, maps, books on the missions, and religious artifacts. The few reconstructed rooms with staged effects of mission life that are open to public view are cordoned off, a mission spectacle in the form of congealed space that one can examine from a distance. Unreconstructed or concealed are the forbidden places, like the *monjerios* where the neophyte women were locked up at night. At the time of the narration of the Californio testimonials, the simulacrums had not yet been set up, although romantic depictions of the missions by local artists were already beginning to appear.[5] To see behind and beyond the simulacrum, we need to examine the testimonials carefully, for in these discursive reconstructions of the Californio past, much like in the reconstituted missions of today, spaces overlap and interconnect in such a way that it is sometimes difficult to penetrate beyond the outer walls of defenses, be they discursive or architectonic.

The establishment of the missions in Alta California involved a transfer or transposition of semifeudal social spaces to the territory in order to ensure control over the northern Spanish frontier. Spatial discourses thus assume center stage, for, far from being a limited enclosure, the mission proved to be amoeba-like in its capacity to expand, increase its power, and absorb all the coastal lands of Alta California. It transformed the ecology and cultural geography, changing the Indians' local habitat and displacing them culturally as well. Its multispatial dimensions — cultural, political, and economic — perhaps help to explain why intersecting and overlapping discourses on the missions in these testimonials are highly contradictory. The testimonials are thus sites of contention that represent competing discursive frameworks generating discourses both condemning the mission's exploitative nature and defending it on the basis of its purported evangelical and civilizing function. At the same time there is in these narratives an evident desire to respond to published accounts of particular mission practices. In order to understand why and in what fashion these perspectives are at odds with each other as well as the social practices creating, sustaining, and containing these discourses, we will need to review briefly the colonial period in Nueva España, particularly social relations before and after Mexican independence, for property relations in Alta California were a continuation and transformation of social relations in New Spain and, later, in the Mexican state.

Reducciones, encomiendas, and haciendas

To understand the developments in Alta California in the nineteenth century requires at least a cursory review of the more salient traits of the colonial enterprise in the New World in order to situate the spatial and discursive sites in play. After a bloody conquest that led to the massacre and enslavement of thousands of Indians throughout the Americas, colonization faced a sociospatial problematic. To ensure the Crown's effective control of the new territories, the Spanish monarchy first attempted to maintain a despotic-tributary system by claiming all the lands as its own and all the indigenous populations as royal subjects. This early policy allowed the communal Indians to continue in usufructuary possession of their land and in control of production; only surplus production or tribute was controlled by the Crown's administrators. The Indians thus retained their social organization and a relative freedom within the community, that is, within localized spaces.[6]

To continue the exploitation of communal labor, however, the Crown created new spaces, new sociospatial sites for the reproduction of these social relations. These *congregaciones* or *reducciones* of Indians removed from their lands and brought together to form new reservations or *resguardos* enabled the Crown to form new *pueblos*, within which it could institute new sites of production (Semo, 70). The consequences of this economic system led to a spatial struggle between the Crown and the conquerors/colonists, who were of course opposed to this spatial configuration and made demands on the Crown for recognition and reward for their risk-taking and service. Thus the despotic-tributary system supported by the king and the church was short-lived, replaced fairly rapidly by a new sociospatial site, the *encomienda*, the dominant mode of production of the sixteenth century. The *encomienda* is seen by Semo as equivalent to the feudal manor and as a transitional phase that would begin to be replaced during the seventeenth century by the *hacienda* system. By the eighteenth century, private property and the vast feudal *latifundios* had become the dominant mode of production (Semo, 98). Indians, previously forcibly relocated to work in given tasks (mining, public works, agriculture, and the like) as a result of a system of *repartimiento* (distribution of labor to different sites) or a system of leasing, would become subservient to a patriarchal family within a new worksite, the *hacienda* (Semo, 219, 225, 227). At these autarkic sites tied to a local market economy, the Indians or even mestizos and poor Spanish peons were legally free but in practice their movement was controlled by the *hacendado* on the basis of debts incurred. They did not own the means of production nor did they possess the land like the communal Indians. They were the producers, but the *hacendado* owned the land, the tools, and the animals, and controlled surplus production. These patriarchal practices that provided the peons with no more than subsistence would in turn give rise to discourses of subordination, servitude, and ultimately resentment, as would become quite evident near the end of the nineteenth century with the uprisings of both Indians and other landless peasants.

This spatial and economic division of the Spanish colony is key for understanding the social formation in Alta California. The entire colonization project in Alta California at the end of the eighteenth century would signal an attempt to return to an earlier phase of production, with the institution of *reducciones* and a despotic mode of production within the missions. At a moment when the *hacienda* was the dominant mode of production in Mexico, Alta California after 1769 would be returning to a communal form of forced labor. Only later, under Mexican rule, would the *rancho* and *hacienda* become the dominant spaces of production in Alta California after secularization of the missions; *repartimiento* or leasing of Indian labor would occur here as well. Constructs of dispossession, enslavement, and extermination of the Indians are central in the testimonials of the Californios, framing their own subsequent policies toward "emancipated" neophytes and serving to constitute their identities as *gente de razón* during the earlier Spanish period of Alta California.

Constructs of Social Order and Caste

Identity is established in difference—cultural, economic, and political—and through complex strategies of identification. Although these three differentials constitute an integral part of a historicopolitical template of nationalist discourses, each at any historical point can also mobilize what Hobsbawm calls "certain variants of feelings of collective belonging."[7] During the first phase of settlement, caste and social order (politicomilitary versus ecclesioeconomic) as constituted within specific social spaces (the mission and the *presidio*) are the primary discourses interpellating collective identity. At a time when Alta California is an outpost in the northernmost frontier of the Spanish colony in North America, established to forestall encroachment by Russia, Britain, and the United States, both social spaces serve to ensure Spanish possession of the land and to create a sense of collective objectives. Thus in Alta California, both the ecclesiastical agents (the missionaries) and the military forces (the soldiers and officers) identify as agents for the Spanish Crown, which had, since 1508, gained the right of patronage over the church. Although both function as mutually dependent spaces of security, the Californio testimonials also bear witness to the historical antagonism played out between civil-military and ecclesiastical authorities in Alta California during the mission period. From the start there was friction between the Franciscan missionaries sent to establish mission stations and the military garrisons chartered to defend the military frontier. The conflicts first concerned decision-making power (for example, determinations as to when and where a mission would be built or rebuilt), but later revolved around issues of economic power, territorial jurisdiction, contact with the neophytes, command of the mission guards, land grants to retired soldiers, and the establishment of *pueblos*.

Yet both were also interdependent spaces of violence: the soldiers during the Spanish period served principally as the coercive and repressive arms of the missionaries in their dealings with the native population.

The two dominant social spaces during the Spanish period, mission and *presidio*, reproduced and were products of despotic and caste relations. Caste in Alta California functioned as a social practice for strategic inclusion and exclusion of particular segments of the population. To say caste is to say racism, an institutionalized practice that discriminates on the basis of race, ethnicity, or culture, and postulates the superiority of one group in relation to others. Racial and cultural distinctions were an integral part of Spanish colonialism just as formerly they had played an important role in the *Reconquista* of the Peninsula and in the Inquisition's persecution of Arabs and Jews,[8] despite the extensive *mestizaje* as a result of intermarriage with these Semitic groups in Spain. In Spanish colonies in America the semifeudal social formation was dependent on a caste system that spatialized society hierarchically in relation to caste classification. Caste is of course determined by birth, and within the Spanish colonies a variety of categories distinguished up to fifty-two different ethnic types, cataloging varied combinations of Spanish, Indian, and Black.[9] The motivation at the center of this social stratification was an attempt to keep the Indians in a servile condition by separating the castes, restricting their movement, and attaching them compulsorily to a *pueblo* or *estancia* (Góngora, 157). In colonial Mexico (Nueva España), growing miscegenation would eventually erode strict "dividing lines between castes" on the basis of racial combinations (Góngora, 156) and allow for geographical mobility. Racist practices on the basis of ethnicity and class, however, would continue long after independence and even to the present day.

In Alta California, the discourses of caste and the notion of "purity" of blood came with the colonists and continued to hold sway throughout the Mexican period, as is very much in evidence in the testimonials. In practice, given the degrees of *mestizaje* of the settlers, caste stratification served primarily to distinguish and exclude unacculturated Indians from particular circles, for clearly the acculturation and relocation of the Indians often blurred these dividing lines. Among the early settlers and soldiers coming from Nueva España to Alta California were, in addition to the mestizos, a large number of acculturated Indians, Blacks, and mulattoes as well as a few criollos and Spaniards.[10] Information on caste based on mission records, census reports, and other official documents provides a general idea of the ethnic and national composition, as well as the occupations, of the earliest settlers, many of whom were related by blood and marriage.[11] In addition to the Fernandino missionaries (the Franciscans sent from San Fernando College in Mexico, most of them originally from Spain), those coming during the first thirty years were for the most part poor soldiers with their families. A handful of contracted artisans and ex-convicts also accompanied the expeditions, many of whom returned to Mexico as soon as their contracts or sentences were over.[12] Several of the single soldiers who came with the early expeditions married Indian women in California, although most of the soldiers were either already married or proved willing to wait until settlers' daughters were grown enough to marry. Intermarriage among the settlers would create an even larger network of family relations than before. These colonists of various castes were known as *gente de razón* (Zalvidea, 238), a category defined on the basis of culture (*los de razón*, that is, those "endowed with reason"), rather than on the basis of race, ancestry, and color. The classification included all missionaries, *presidio* soldiers, and settlers, be they mestizos, mulattoes, Blacks, Christian Indians, criollos, or Spaniards.

Given the multiethnic composition of the colonizers subsumed within the *gente de razón* category, it is evident that the old colonial multiple caste distinctions are in fact inoperative in California. With the simplification of social categories and concentration on one central opposition, that between *gente de razón* and local Indians, caste discourses shift into new cultural, rather than racial, spaces and serve primarily to distinguish the presumed "bearers of civilization" from the "heathen" and "uncivilized." Culture clearly functions here as a "permeable" closure including and excluding particular groups. The term "Indian" itself is contingent upon spatiality, culture/religion, and language. Acculturated Indians with a trade, like Pacomio, residing within non-Indian sites much like the earliest Indian colonists and military scouts in Alta California, become part of the collectivity of *gente de razón*. Those Indians acculturated to some extent and with a Hispanic name but who continue to reside in the *rancherías* or within Indian settlements (like those around Los Angeles in 1836) are still designated as Indians; this is the case with some caciques, like Chief Juan Antonio from Jurupa (Lugo, 208). This distinction (Indian versus non-Indian), the fundamental antagonism within early California society, is the linchpin around which discourses of identity are articulated.

The othering of the Indians, both neophyte and gentile, perceived by the Californios as culturally, linguistically, and ethnically different, serves therefore not only to mask the fact that a large percentage of the original colonists as well as later arrivals from Mexico shared the same Indian blood but more significantly to legitimate the conquest and exploitation of the Indians on the basis of a racial and cultural superiority. Caste distinctions are thus nothing more than a form of "culturalist" racism (Balibar, 24), a colonial practice not based on strictly racialist considerations, especially given ongoing miscegenation, but used to "justify" the racism of extermination and of oppression or exploitation.[13]

Caste nevertheless persists as a powerful discourse that serves the earliest colonists for a construction of difference and leads José de Jesús Vallejo to confuse deliberately the cultural construct *gente de razón* with that of racial differences:

> I shall begin by saying that in New California the descendants of Europeans and of white Mexicans were called *de razón*; this term was used to distinguish them from mulattoes, *chinos* [mixture of Indian and mulatto], *zambos* [mixture of Black and Indian], and Indians. (JJV, 7–8)

Racist practices faced by the Californios after 1846 may perhaps account for this tendency among the testimonial narrators to cloak themselves with a mantle of European superiority and to identify as Spanish rather than as Mexican (not unlike "Hispanics" of today), aware as they were that Mexicans and mestizos were always described derogatorily as a "mongrel" race, unfit for U.S. citizenship.[14] It is not surprising then to find them collaborating in the construction of romantic portrayals of the Californio "pastoral" period that allude to aristocratic men and women of Spanish origin leading a life of bliss in an "Arcadia." Guadalupe Vallejo, nephew of M. G. Vallejo, makes mention only of "Spanish ancestors" in his "Ranch and Mission Days in Alta California." As in some romantic tales in which all the ladies are fair and all the gentlemen light-complexioned, some of the testimonial narrators also relish describing the governors or *comandantes-generales* of California as fair-skinned gentlemen, except perhaps for rogues like Governor Victoria, nicknamed "the Negro of Acapulco" (Machado, 26; JJV, 110). The more liberal Californios, like M. G. Vallejo and Alvarado, are careful to document Victoria's despotism.[15] Those appreciating his promissionary stance stress his dark features, handsome eyes, and splendid military bearing (Ord, 1956: 20–23). Phenotype also appears to have played an important role among the principal families of the territory, especially regarding marriage; many men of these families had illegitimate children with Indian or mestizo women, but they did not often marry them. Intermarriage with neophyte Indian women was not unheard of, however, especially during the earlier phase of settlement.[16]

Several published studies documenting the *mestizaje* of the majority of the early settlers have sought to counter these idealized representations of Californios as "Spanish" colonists, a construct still popular in local lore.[17] Discursively, however, identity in these testimonials is not on the basis of *mestizaje*. What predominates is a territorial-Eurocentric construct, especially among the dominant classes in Alta California, on the basis of Spanish origin but native to the Americas. The term "criollo," prevalent throughout Latin America, does not appear in these narratives, but the construct is assumed and functions principally at the level of phenotype; thus those of fair skin consider themselves Hispanic, whether their parents were of Spanish origin or not (Pérez, 1). The claim to Spanish descent is documented by Salvador Vallejo when he includes in his testimonial a copy of the Spanish Inquisition's report confirming his father Ignacio Vallejo's "limpieza de sangre" (family purity of blood). The novelist Ruiz de Burton, in her written testimonial about her grandfather José Manuel Ruiz, commander of Loreto in Baja California, also traces her own Spanish roots, as well as those of several Californio families, to Castilla La Vieja (Savage documents, 2:133). This underlying construct of *criollismo* functions as a construct of identity rather than difference, that is, as an attempt to appear on the same racial plane with the Yankee invaders, as if national origin and race could be wielded as a strategic discourse to combat racist representations of the conquered Californios as half-civilized Indians (MGV, letter to Alvarado, August 24, 1874). After Mexican independence another spatial/cultural construct would become dominant, that of *hijos del país*, a term that does not include native Indians, but rather only second-generation *gente de razón*, native sons and daughters of the Californio colonists.

Although caste categories were made juridically obsolete after Mexican independence, which emancipated the Indians and granted them citizenship, and despite the mass *mestizaje* in Alta California, residual discourses of caste, that is, cultural racism, continued to intersect Californio discourses and to emerge in intra-Californio relations. Racial slurs are in fact one of the ideological discourses used to underscore many denunciations or condemnations in these testimonials. Alvarado (4:81–82), for example, speaks of the mestizo Gil Ibarra, a native of San Diego, as "a chocolate-colored Indian," a remark undoubtedly brandished because Ibarra was a partisan of the South against Alvarado. Likewise the ex-convicts forming part of the military detachment accompanying Governor Micheltorena are called *cholos*, because, says Alvarado (3:1), they are mestizos. The same disdain for mestizos and

Indians is expressed by Vallejo in his comments filled with contempt for the Zacatecan missionaries sent to take over positions left by the elderly Fernandino Spanish friars. These Mexican friars, said to be corrupt and lascivious, are described as "color de chocolate" (MGV, 4:71). Even Vallejo's son is appalled by this clearly pejorative remark, as he indicates in an attached note. Thus, in an area where most of the population is mestizo, slurs on the basis of phenotype are invoked for the most part by the elite as a discursive strategy to invalidate the opinions of others. If that opinion is valued, however, as in the case of Governor Figueroa, said to be mestizo and "proud of his Indian blood,"[18] then race or caste is considered irrelevant. The racism of these Californios is especially obvious in their frequent racist comments about Blacks, evident, for instance, in M. G. Vallejo's insulting descriptions.[19]

To summarize: the testimonials offer a social distinction of caste and culture designated by the opposition: *gente de razón* versus *indios.* This polar distinction is bound up with discourses of spatiality and religion, both serving to differentiate the Indian population further as mission Indians (neophytes) or nonmission Indians. Those that have not been Christianized and have stayed beyond the reaches of the mission are the gentiles, a term evoking the notion not only of "heathen" but also of the excluded, the nonchosen. If we consider that "gentiles" is synonymous with *bárbaros infieles,* then it becomes clear that the terms refer as much to religious conversion as to civilization and acculturation. The basic distinction for the Indian population neophytes versus gentiles in effect serves as a basis for organizing social spaces in Alta California.

Even these categories can be broken down. As several of the testimonials attest, mission Indians often succeeded in breaking away and rejoining the gentiles. Runaway neophytes are called *cimarrones* (maroons), the term used in the Caribbean for runaway slaves. This plurality of categories corresponds to a variety of relations and situations. Thus neophyte Indians staying at the mission are classified according to years of service and conversion, much as the distinction in Spain between new and old converts. The *catecúmenos* are the newly arrived Indians in the process of being baptized and indoctrinated. The older Indian converts or old Christians, perhaps even second generation, are termed neophytes. In every case, of course, identification is imposed by the Californios and missionaries, on the basis of their colonial configuration of the territory. Even gentile Indians are further subdivided according to their relations with Californios. The friendly gentiles are those trading with the Californios or living on the *ranchos* and *haciendas* as servants, tenant farmers paid with part of the harvest, or quasi-wage workers or peons who are housed, clothed, and paid in kind. They are distinguished from the hostile Indians who repel incursions of the Californios into their territories and who often team up with *cimarrones* to raid the mission *ranchos* or other *haciendas*. The diversity of distinctions notwithstanding, the crucial and ultimately most important social difference between Indians and *gente de razón* is that determined by relations of production, or, in Brenner's reformulation, property relations, that is, what distinguishes the Indians as producers from the *gente de razón* as exploiters.[20] The ultimately dominant political discourses in post-1822 Alta California, of the liberal/secularist orientation, would seek to legitimate not the restructuring of these semifeudal property relations but rather their continuance.

Heterotopic Mission Spaces in Alta California

The mission as a countersite that challenged the Indian *rancherías* in Alta California is evident in the earliest missionary documents, like the memoirs of Palou, and throughout the testimonials of the Californios. As we shall see in chapter 3, the mission was also the social space that countered and thwarted the land tenancy aspirations of the native Californios. This cultural-religious institution was at the same time to be the Spanish Crown's most effective means of ensuring its geographical sovereignty in the northernmost frontier and of attaining and maintaining outright subjection and control of the Indian population. The overriding goal of the Crown in chartering the missions was to exert effective control over the territory and resist encroachments by foreign forces. Both Vallejo and Alvarado begin their memoirs recalling the political considerations that led José de Gálvez, the Spanish Visitor General who was alarmed in 1768 over the penetration of Russian trappers and soldiers in the north, to work out a plan for the establishment of colonies in Alta California (MGV, 1:30–31; Alvarado, 1:17–18). The few missions instituted in Baja California since 1697 were, only a year after the expulsion of the Jesuits in 1767, in ruins. After visiting the peninsula Gálvez transferred the missions to the Franciscan order and determined that the Franciscans would go north to establish and administer the missions in Alta California. Two missionaries were to be assigned to each mission and paid a stipend by the government from its Pious Fund.[21] All necessary implements as well as livestock and grain were to be provided. Artisans, sailors, and

Indian families from Baja California were to accompany the missionaries, and a military detachment was to protect the *comitiva*.

For the Crown, the colonization of Alta California was strictly a political enterprise despite the fact that the principal agents were missionaries who had their own—though not unrelated—agenda. Years later, after Mexican independence, even Californios who contested Mexican sovereignty in the California territory were still accepting of religious arguments that justified the displacement and reduction of Indians to the missions for the sake of conversion, although by then the notion of the New World as a mission field had been superseded by subsequent political constructs. When California was first colonized by Spain in 1769, the operating principle was no longer one defending conquest and the use of force for the sake of conversion of the natives and the extension of the Catholic monarchy, but rather a much more pragmatic and juridical one that viewed the right of dominion on the basis of occupation and international law (Góngora, 60, 66).[22] Yet even while recognizing the importance of occupation and settlement of the territory as a means of staving off Russian encroachment, most Californios continued to hold to the notion of a religious and civilizing mission. Some of the Californio testimonials even reconstruct the missionaries as benevolent and self-sacrificing friars, even in the face of their own descriptions of the immense wealth generated at the missions and their acknowledgment of coerced Indian labor. Notwithstanding a number of contradictory constructs, all the testimonials do recognize that the mission was the site of power that controlled the economy and influenced political appointments and decision making between 1769 and 1833, and, to a much lesser extent, thereafter.

The missionaries' appropriation of land in Alta California involved a restructuring of Indian space and a displacement of the Indians. Even in those cases where the Indians remained in the same general geographical areas, the site was transformed. It was an entirely different place with a changed ecology; new forms of production; new plants, crops, animals, and trees; new diseases, weapons, tools, clothing, and foodstuff; and a new culture. In erecting their twenty-one missions, the early Spanish missionaries had chosen their mission sites wisely, as the Junta de Fomento established by President Victoria in 1825 recognized many years later, for "the villages of the heathen [were] the very places which they as the experienced masters of the land had selected, because of convenience and nearness to the rivers and springs, to be their places of meeting and habitation" (Junta, 300). This geographical dislocation and transformation would ultimately lead to the extermination of the Indians. According to the Californios, there were six hundred thousand Indians in California in 1769 (MGV, 1:335).. McWilliams estimates that there were approximately thirty thousand Indians in 1769 and only 1,250 by 1910, with the survival rate higher among gentile Indians, that is, among those who kept their distance from Western civilization.[23]

The indictment of the missions that we do find in the testimonials is tellingly not on the basis of the extermination of the Indians, but rather grounded in their control of the means of production, that is, their possession of the prime coastal lands and their control of the Indian labor force. Economic control also meant political control, even though the military officer appointed as governor was ostensibly in charge of civil and military affairs in the territory. The mission's overriding power was evident in that any disagreement between the head of the missionaries and the governor was always arbitrated in Nueva España by the head of the San Fernando College of Franciscans and the Viceroy, who, more often than not, ruled in favor of the missionaries, the Crown's most important political instrument in the occupation of the northern frontier, Alta California (Palou, 150). From their vantage point, the Californios' indictment of the mission, broached from a "natural rights" perspective, would censure the missionaries' power on the basis of the Indians' involuntary servitude and the institution's failure to acculturate them, casting the missionaries in this liberal critique as agents of oppression and obscurantism. But there is as well, often within the same narrative, a defense of the missionaries, whether on the basis of the mission's productivity or on the basis of their civilizing efforts toward a backward heathen society, a defense that competes with the more severe assessment of the mission. It is not surprising that the texts should reveal these contradictory assessments, for in both defending and attacking the mission system these Californios not only are venting their resentment against hegemonic historical accounts of their history but are also engaged in either justifying their collaboration with the missionaries or expressing their disidentification with what had come to be seen as a retrograde institution.

What McWilliams describes as "picturesque charnel houses" (29) were *reducciones* or *resguardos* established by the missionaries for as many as two to three thousand, or as few as two hundred, neophytes, depending on the size and location of the mission.[24] The organization of labor within the mission was not based on a precolonial communal model that the Crown sought to maintain, as in Mexico, but was rather a despotic model brought from outside the area and imposed by the missionaries. The California Indians were not an agrarian society like the Aztecs; they had a primitive mode of production and were for the most part hunters, gatherers, and fishermen. The missionaries, as representatives of the Crown entrusted with this land, in effect created new Indian *pueblos,* often from several tribes, wherein they functioned as the despots in direct control of the means of production (land, seeds, livestock, tools, and implements) and the surplus production.[25]

The mission, then, was more than a political instrumental space for the control of the Indian population and occupation of the land. It was also a site for production and reproduction of particular social relations. Within this despotic system the mission Indians (neophytes) had no freedom of movement and although they were the ostensible communal "possessors" of the mission lands, they had no direct access to the means of production (Brenner, 1986: 28) — only through the missionaries and their supervisory staff. As producers the neophytes were not a free labor force; extraeconomic coercion was in fact required to keep them at the mission and sometimes even to bring them there. The neophytes were for all practical purposes much like slaves: they were not free to leave, and the missionaries, though not the de jure owners of the land, exerted de facto control over the extraction of surplus from the lands they occupied and the labor of the Indians.[26] For the exploiters, the mission served as a precapitalist site for a primitive accumulation of capital, making the mission the wealthiest institution in Alta California and an obstacle standing in the way of the creation of private landed estates. With the secularization of the mission after Mexican independence would come not a transition to capitalist relations of production but rather the establishment of semifeudal *haciendas* and *ranchos,* parallel to those dominant in Mexico at the time. Economically and politically, the mission was averse to the interests of the majority of the Californios although, politically, the mission system had a number of allies among conservative Californios. Culturally, the mission continued to generate the religious and caste discourses with which the Californios identified.

These contradictory relations lead to a series of inconsistencies in the representation of the mission throughout the testimonials. As a heterotopia, a social site within which a variety of spaces are subsumed as well as countered, the mission encompasses a variety of competing spatial and social functions that resist one-sided reconstruction. Constructs of the missions thus vary from a recognition of its success as a political and religious enterprise to a condemnation of its enslavement of the Indians. Missions, sites of both civilization and exploitation, are mapped in the testimonials around the following configuration: penal colony (dystopia) + business (enterprise) + religion (cultural institution) + imaginary (utopia). These multiple spatial attributes are discussed in the rest of this chapter, as well as the Californios' positioning with respect to this heterotopic space.

Lefebvre's description of heterotopias as "mutually repellent spaces"[27] speaks to this diversity of social sites and antagonisms realized in constructs of the missions. In the early period the crucial and much-debated opposition is that between the mission and the *rancherías* of the gentile Indians. The *rancherías* out in the wilderness are viewed as the spaces of difference, the spaces of barbarism, in opposition to the mission, the space constructed as a site of civilization.

Mission ◄─────► **Indian** *rancherías*
+ civilization   + barbarism
+ order   + chaos, disorder

A second antagonism found in a number of the testimonials is that of the mission as an enslaving social site, an enclosure in opposition to the open lands beyond the reach of the mission and the soldiers: the wilderness.

Mission ◄─────► **Wilderness**
+ enslaving   + freedom

At times "civilization" for the Indians seems to M. G. Vallejo to be an achievement worth the price of freedom. Here paternalistic and positivistic frameworks conceal the coercive nature of these civilizing strategies and instead sanction them for enabling a demonstration of the Indians' capacity to appropriate new ideological discourses and be regenerated (MGV, 1:93). At other times Vallejo recognizes that these discourses of civilization served only to legitimate an oppressive situation that the Indians found intolerable and that many resisted. The testimonials are full of references to Indian resistance and counterattacks. The Indians, who greatly resented their loss of freedom and the forced conversion exacted from them by missionaries with their crosses and soldiers with their lances, were not remiss in voicing their discontent ironically, as Vallejo reveals in the following appropriation of Chief Succaro's words to put forth his own criticism of the mission system:

> I don't think the great Indian Chief Succaro was off the mark when he said that the Christians offered him no choice at all when they asked him to choose between Christ and death. (MGV, 1:17)

Even in this romanticized notion of the freedom-loving "noble savage" — in need, however, of civilization — there is an acknowledgment of coercion by both mission and *presidio*.

That this forced "civilization" is limited and limiting becomes clear when Vallejo expresses regret that the missionaries failed to inculcate principles of individual freedom in their neophytes (MGV, 1:93). An opposition is thus posited in the text between a notion of the natural liberty of individuals and the liberal notion of what Blackburn calls "negative freedom," the right to be free from the state's interference.[28] The latter, Vallejo insinuates, is a construct that has to be acquired but was not made accessible to the Indians, whereas they had previously enjoyed a natural freedom found in the wild. Vallejo does not seem willing to recognize that an awareness of rights would have run counter to the ideological aims of the mission and consequently was a programmed gap.

Californios were thus not blind to the despotic system imposed on the Indians within monastic life. In one passage (MGV, 1:348–49), Vallejo offers in a nutshell a concise summary of constructs common in the liberal Californios' representation of mission life: exploitation of the Indians (forced labor through coercion), oppression (excessive cruelty of the missionaries toward the Indians and excessive labor demands), enslavement (neophytes as unfree labor), cultural alienation (interdiction of their communal practices), monastic rigidity (no comforts), ideological and material manipulation (creation of consumer desires), and resistance (escape from the mission). Yet even anticlerical Californios like Vallejo are willing to set aside their critiques and praise the missionaries' dedication to the project of Christianization as well as their effectiveness in organizing an Indian labor force, reducing hostilities, and opening up an area to new colonists. The mission's practical function as a civilizing, pacifying, disciplining, productive institution thus overrides all criticism of the mission as an enslaving, coercive, abusive apparatus of the Crown. During the 1840s Vallejo himself would advocate that new missions be established in the northern frontier, but by that time the missionaries whose lands and properties had been secularized were no longer interested in a new "civilizing project" under the auspices of a liberal secular state.

Throughout his extensive testimonial, M. G. Vallejo is ever conscious of his U.S. reader. He makes clear that whatever problems there were with the mission method of domination, it was always preferable to what the United States had tried in its relations with the Indians, a policy that had led to numerous Indian uprisings (MGV, 1:18). This suggestion that the mission system was a plan of "pacification" of the Indians much preferred over the method of removal and extermination practiced by the United States conveniently forgets to mention the decimation of the California Indians in the process.

Some Californios reject these polemical representations and, on the basis of equally positivistic reasoning, assume a pseudoscientific, condescending perspective, viewing the Indians, for example, as inhabitants of another time, a time whose era had elapsed. Those who assigned the Indians to an earlier stage of development, like Platón Vallejo, did not blame the missionaries for what they could not possibly have accomplished. In his testimonial reconstructing life in Sonoma, Platón Vallejo is also concerned with countering negative representations of the missions and missionaries. Troubled by his own father's anticlericalism, the son of M. G. Vallejo attempts to dismantle his father's critique through a reconstruction of the missionaries as saintly men with vision who, if they failed in civilizing the Indians, succeeded in developing agricultural production:

> The padres introduced the vine, the olive, the citrus fruits, the fig, and the various stoned and seeded fruit trees, demonstrating their singular adaptability for the soil and climate. They grew great crops of wheat and barley, paving the way for another great industry. They introduced the alfalfa plant, the economic value of which was not recognized till later on. They were the acknowledged founders of irrigation. They built up a considerable foreign trade. Everything they did indicated rare foresight and efficiency. Yet because they failed to completely civilize the Indian, many writers call them impractical dreamers and failures. (P. Vallejo, 23)

Platón Vallejo views the missions as the nucleus for the later development of capitalism, forgetting the major restructuring (as regards private land tenancy) that was necessary with secularization, given the mission's control of most of the coastal lands, the limitation of production primarily for local consumption, the system of despotic labor relations, and limited trade. Unwilling to analyze the mission mode of production, Platón Vallejo dismisses out of hand all critiques of a failed mission system as "idle trash" and attributes any failure to the Indians' essentially retrograde nature:

> They could not change in one or two generations the ingrown habits of thought and action backed by the ancestry of countless generations. They were never able to make the Indian see the advantage and necessity of systematic work. (24)

This notion of the Indians as a backward society is frequent in Alvarado's testimonial as well (Alvarado, 2:19), but Platón Vallejo takes a more developmental view and considers barbarism to be a universal evolutionary stage, difficult to eradicate. Not even the Europeans, he says, had managed to eliminate barbarism in Europe within one century (24). Like primitive Europeans, the Indians are at a lower level of development. They are children of nature, underdeveloped:

> The fathers were not to blame because they failed to tame the California Indians nor should we blame the Indian because he refused to be tamed, because he returned to nature like a boy let loose from school (25)

From a positivistic analysis of stages of development, Platón Vallejo returns to a discussion of the Indians' mental habits, their social practices, and their ability to subsist without farming. The Indians, he insists, despised agriculture ("their pet aversion was work") and had to be persuaded to do anything. These were all seemingly insurmountable obstacles that the heroic missionaries had overcome. Nevertheless, the younger Vallejo finally has to recognize that despite their attributed deficiencies, many Indians had become bilingual and literate, and had demonstrated a talent for music and art (24).

In minimizing the import of Indian labor, Platón Vallejo merely repeats the missionaries' own views of the Indians' lack of inclination toward work (Zalvidea, 239). Curiously, the more he insists, the more Platón Vallejo deconstructs his own argument against the Indians' lack of productive drive. He claims that they had an aversion to systematic work, but states that they had built everything at the missions. The Indians' nature, he says, was to chat and dance, yet they were capable of learning what Californios could learn in school. The Franciscan missionaries may have brought the seeds, but all the cultivation, harvesting, and working the land had been done by the Indians. Platón Vallejo could not deny what Indian labor had accomplished, but he was incapable or unwilling to reassess the mission as an exploitative system that had dominated the Indians and contributed to their extermination. If the Indian had disappeared, Platón Vallejo the physician says there was a scientific explanation: the cause was an epidemic of smallpox that "swept the native *rancherías* in 1837–39, killing tens of thousands," an epidemic aggravated by their bathing in the *temescales* (the Indian saunas) when they were stricken. For Platón Vallejo the apologist, the missions had had nothing to do with it:

Most writers, as I have said, lay all the blame on the mission fathers. The Indians, they claim, learned nothing by their contact with the White Man to help them in a fight for civilized existence. (29)

What the good doctor neglects to see is that more than a biological phenomenon, disease as an invading force assumes the form of racism when its devastating impact is reduced to particular social spheres. Epidemics have historically accompanied conquest, for armies always harbor and disseminate disease, as Blackburn explains:

The deaths occasioned by epidemics among alien people in the wake of wars and conquest greatly exceeded those incurred on the battlefields. (61)

The extermination of the Indians can thus be viewed at one level as a result of a horrible epidemic that originated in the Russian settlement and was brought back by a Californio (Fernández, 48), but at another as a direct consequence of conquest and colonialism. The smallpox epidemic that would kill thousands of Suysunes thus assumes sociospatial form and devastates the gentile Indians within their sites, for none of them was vaccinated like the Californios and some mission Indians. Estimates of the number of deaths vary between forty thousand and one hundred thousand Indians (Fernández, 48). Alvarado (4:164) mentions that the disease would reach all the way to the south, although fewer cases were reported there. In an epoch in which immunization was available, colonial racism must be considered as a contributing factor in the spread of smallpox as well as of other serious contagious diseases, including measles and venereal disease. Epidemics were not the only factor in the extinction of the major part of the Indian population, however; removal of the Indians from their lands, excessive work, malnutrition, abuse, and warfare with the *gente de razón* all contributed to the annihilation of the Indians. In fact, all contact with the *gente de razón* proved deadly to the native peoples.

The lack of inoculation of the gentile Indians curiously does not trouble the physician Platón Vallejo, who spoke the Suysun language and sought to preserve that culture's myths and stories. In the last instance, for him as for many Californios, the colonization, the forced service of the Indians, and the military expeditions against Indian communities resisting efforts at "civilization" — all of these measures and practices had been necessary and unavoidable. These testimonials are full of refutations and disclaimers. No one assumes any blame.

Alvarado (4:55–56) will even have the effrontery to say that he did more for the Indians than he should have. Liberal rhetoric about the individual rights of the Indians does little to screen out discourses of racism. Alvarado, the most severe critic of the missionaries, in the end appropriates the racist discourses of Americans who justified the removal of the Indians from their lands on the basis of their lack of interest in farming. His disdain for the Indians, grounded on their not caring for sheep or cattle or tilling the soil, leads Alvarado to undermine the significance of the disappearance of the Indian: "Alta California suffered no great loss with the disappearance of two to three thousand Indians" (4:166). With these words, Alvarado was of course implicitly challenging any American to brand him a brazen racist or fool, for had not the Americans justified removing the Indians from their soil precisely because they did not farm it, and had they not exterminated them when they refused to leave? Even when the Cherokee did become farmers in Georgia, had they not been dispossessed and removed anyway?[29] Alvarado, who resented the U.S. invasion of California, is not averse to using the invaders' own racist discourses to justify social and political practices that had led to the extermination of an entire Indian society in California under his own rule.

The Californios' representation of the Indian as indolent, ignorant, and reluctant to work is doubly ironic, not only because the Indians had carried out all the work–had, in fact, constructed all that there was in Alta California before 1846 — but also because in 1875 the criticism of indolence and derogatory portrayals were being proffered against people of Mexican origin in the United States and especially against Californios. Yet, in reference to Indians in the testimonials, this is a recurring construct, an attempt to demonstrate Californio superiority by constructing the Other, the Indians, as inferior. José de Jesús Vallejo calls upon the same stereotypical portrayal of the Indians in his testimonial. He claims that he knew the Indians well; he had grown up with them and could attest that they were more "addicted to indolence than to work" (JJV, 39). Fortunately, despite the overt intention to denigrate the Indians as a race, this is not the only construct of the Indians to be found in these testimonials.

In what follows we will examine in more detail the various conflicting ideological discourses and constructs of the missions, the missionaries, and the Indian population, and the constant realignment of these discursive practices in the testimonials. The missionaries, the government, and the Indians are constructed as three important agencies that clash and compete and that will be challenged by an emergent class of landowners. In supporting and opposing, in aligning and severing relations with particular social groups, the Californios construct their own identities vis-à-vis the other collectivities.

Space and Order: Inside the Mission

From the perspective of the Californios, the missionaries arrived in California in 1769 to find a land of plenty but without order, a nonagrarian population that had no notion of private property, only of possession. M. G. Vallejo recalls that the Suysuns of northern California considered all the land in the north to be theirs; it was fertile, with an abundance of acorns, wild lettuce, oats, wild onions, and many other edible plants as well as deer, fish, and other game animals, all there for the sustenance of thousands of Indians. The construct of an Indian Eden is subsequently dismantled by Vallejo's introduction of the notion of disorder in the idyllic order. He explains that the land was full of warring savages, fierce at times like the Satiyomís, who were a constant threat to the other Indian tribes (MGV, 4:63). Alvarado (4:59) likewise diminishes his admiration for these brave Indians by coupling his praise with racist remarks about how little they valued life and how governed they were by their instincts and cunning. Like other Californios, Alvarado tends to essentialize the Indians and to disidentify with those he considers bloodthirsty barbarians,[30] but in his construct of Indian disorderly conduct there is also an underlying indictment of "civilization" and its attendant vices, all too willingly attributed to Indian character flaws in a prime example of "blaming the victim" (4:60–61).

Alvarado's tendency to imply that the Indians were "stupid" is a distinction, that he shares with U.S. historians like Hittell, who in his history of California refers to the Indians in terms akin to those he would later use to describe the Californios:

> On account of their [the Indians'] low grade on the scale of humanity ...
> and therefore almost as degraded as any human being on the face of
> the earth, they can hardly be described as divided into distinct tribes ...
> All were equally stupid and brutish. Some exceptions from these
> general remarks must be made ... but in general they resembled mere
> omnivorous animals without government or laws.[31]

Thus Hittell also constructs an indigenous space of disorder. The Californios, however, saw their own arrival, and especially that of the missionaries, as the establishment of order in a primitive paradise first populated by brave but fierce and backward Indians; even the Indians were immigrants, as Vallejo emphasizes.[32] We see a similar attitude put forth in Coronel's *testimonio*:

> It is most odd to see those priests, without more backing than four or five Californios acting as so-called soldiers (for they scarcely could be termed such) ruling over a good number of neophytes all in an orderly fashion and without encountering the least insubordination from them. (216)

Although Coronel here waxes romantic about the power of the missionaries over their docile flock, he also recognizes that the maintenance of order among the many by the few relied on strategies of fragmentation and division, highlighted when he focuses on the very spatial organization of the missions, geared principally toward production and the extraction of labor. The mission itself was divided into several sites forming what could be termed cubicles within the larger enclosure for a spatial enforcement of power (Coronel, 213). Spatial divisions within the mission facilitated the imposition of constraints and rules; space itself was repressive, for its configuration determined the social hierarchy within. Only the missionaries' rooms looked out beyond the mission walls; every other site sat within the enclosure and had an inward perspective that identified the inner cells as part of the mission whole. The front of the mission with the missionary's room next to the chapel dominated the lateral and back rooms, which constituted the work and storage areas.

The order imposed by the mission went beyond the distribution of space; it also called for the allocation of workers to various sites at particular times as part of different crews, some working within the square in crafts and arts, some beyond the mission walls as agricultural workers, cowboys, shepherds, and hunters. The labor power of the Indians was inscribed in every site of the mission and even beyond—in the *ranchos,* the *presidios,* and the *pueblos.* The fields, grazing lands, corrals, carpentry shops, tanneries, forges, wineries, and cheese factories were all the work domains of Indians. Within the "domestic space" of the missions, where the neophyte Indians were housed, fed, clothed, and hospitalized, where they worked the looms, carded the wool, sewed, made soap, and cooked, there were also *gente de razón:* craftsworkers, supervisors, and housekeepers in charge of management. The revealing *testimonios* of two Californio women, Eulalia Pérez and Apolinaria Lorenzana, who played a key role in the administration of the mission industries in their roles as housekeepers and supervisors, allow us to view the mission space from within and to penetrate as well the space occupied by the managerial class of Californios that accommodated to missionary interests with which they identified.

This supervisory class also included mestizo and criollo Californios who served as foremen of the mission crews and its extramural ranches; the missions alleged that they needed vast acreage for grazing their livestock and claimed lands far beyond those surrounding the mission proper. Lorenzana recalls that there were three foremen at the San Diego mission: one in charge of the mission ranch at El Cajón, one at Santa Isabel, and one at the mission itself. The mission at San Luis Rey had four *ranchos* under its jurisdiction in what is now Riverside County as well as ranches at Pala, Temécula, and San José, as the testimonial of Pío Pico informs us. Because of their intimate contact with the institution, both before and after secularization, the testimonials of Lorenzana, Pérez, Pico, and José de Jesús Vallejo are crucial for understanding the day-to-day details of mission operations. Additional insights and critiques come from the work of Coronel, Ord, Alvarado, and M. G. Vallejo, both supporters and antagonists of the mission system.

The various constructs provided in these Californio *testimonios*, often from a microstructural perspective, allow us to reconstruct the larger picture: a colonial entity policed by the missionaries, within which, as Alvarado points out, the Indians were coerced into subservience:

> Though many might take issue with it, I have no problem in saying that the Ferdinand fathers educated the Indians in the same fashion that one would raise a beast of burden: they were interested only in training them to serve and, isolated exceptional cases aside, this was the only training that these ministers of the Merciful Lord provided to the neophytes. (4:61)

In this sardonic critique, Alvarado appears to share the views of the French navigator La Pérouse, who, when visiting the California missions in 1786, expressed concern that the neophytes were not learning to be self-reliant and independent. Yet the Frenchman also held the opinion that the Indians were childlike, irrational, and only receptive to a stimulus-response type training:

> I know also that reasoning has almost no weight with them, that it is absolutely necessary to strike their senses, and that corporal punishment with recompense of double rations has been so far the only means adopted by their legislators.[33]

Alvarado, though often falling back on racist and essentialist portrayals of the Indians, also recognized, like Vallejo, that the Indians, if

given the appropriate training, could learn to read and write like anyone else (as several in fact did), but they were being trained to remain
ignorant. The missionaries, Alvarado says, but for isolated cases, taught
the Indians nothing except rote prayers in Latin, which they failed to
understand (1:51–52). Similar concerns were expressed by Coronel,
who, on thinking back on the situation of the Indians after securitiza-
tion, acknowledged that they had been poorly prepared by the missionaries for emancipation:

> That was perhaps the result of the instruction given to the Indians,
> who were never trained so that they could be self-governing or self-
> sufficient. They were always treated as if they were minors and
> constantly kept at work. (225)

Teaching the Indians only to serve may have been a point of contention for Alvarado and Coronel, but for most of the Californios interviewed by Savage and Cerruti, the missionaries were nothing but a
great civilizing force. Carlos Carrillo, the California representative to
the Mexican Congress and the first native Californio to have one of
his speeches, "Exposición sobre el Fondo Piadoso," printed (Bancroft,
1964: 83),[34] defended the mission system for its civilizing efforts, its
"reduction of many thousands of gentiles who had been converted from
savage wandering vagabonds into established families and useful workers in agriculture and the arts, and into men capable of social relationships" (Carrillo, 4). In this speech Carrillo presented the opinion of his
friend Guerra y Noriega, but made it seem as if all Californios were of
one opinion with respect to the missionaries, said to be "objects of veneration and respect" (Carrillo, 6), and the missions, described as the
only means for subduing the "savages," for maintaining the territories, and even for stimulating further settlement of unoccupied lands.
The use of forced Indian labor was for Carrillo simply a civilizing act
rather than one of colonialism and exploitation (Carrillo, 10).

Thus for some Californios the institution of the mission system was
a civilizing process and for others a means of ensuring the Indians' ignorance and servitude, which in the end guaranteed their consent to
their own exploitation. These ideological differences with respect to
the mission are linked of course to social, economic, and political interests, which we will examine in subsequent chapters. Mission strategies for keeping the Indians subservient and obedient were further
buttressed by the regimented schedule that the neophytes followed at
the mission. And here the Californios' testimonials provide a range of
discourses on order, discipline, and paternalism, all called upon as dis-

courses of legitimation of the mission system and of the Californios' acquiescence or complicity in maintaining it, and all, in the final analysis, discourses that would serve historians as the basis for their designation of the missions as "charnel houses."

The Regimentation of Everyday Life

A policy of deliberately spatialized regimentation was the missionaries' best disciplinary strategy for curtailing and containing any attempts by the Indians to question their subordination. Each everyday practice was strategic in that it guaranteed collective participation by small groups and acquiescence as well as developing the nonalienating aspect of familiarity, for the routine varied but little. Given their participation in implementing mechanisms of control, it is not surprising that neither Pérez nor Lorenzana questions the sunrise-to-sundown schedule of work forced on the Indians. Instead, like other Californios of both genders, they applaud the level of organization and efficiency and delight in describing the daily routine of a well-run mission. Both women dwell on a diversity of domestic practices, and Lorenzana provides information on work carried out in the fields as well. These comments are important because each of these two testimonials offers not only a woman's view of this patriarchal institution but also an insider's perspective on mission spatial practices. Most of the testimonials by Californio men and women present outsiders' views of the mission, not the perspective of those privy to the inner workings of what was undoubtedly a formidable productive machine.

Pérez's testimonial focuses on the "domestic space" within the San Gabriel mission, the wealthiest of the chain of twenty-one missions. She emphasizes her role as housekeeper and dwells on the character of the priests with whom she was in close contact. Her descriptions of this autarkic institution with its division of labor, housing, and storage provide valuable information on the mission as an economic unit, on the social hierarchy established within the mission, and on her position within these relations of power. In this mission that produced its own grains, vegetables, fruit, meat, cloth, clothing, and leather goods, Pérez supervised all the domestic industries within the mission walls and controlled the distribution of goods and foodstuffs from the storehouse to the troops and Californio servants as well as to the married neophytes living in the *rancherías*. For the neophytes living at mission quarters she supervised the *pozolera* (the kitchen for Indian meals) and the separate kitchen facilities that prepared the friars' table.

Lorenzana had similar duties at the San Diego mission. She supervised the housekeeper (*el llavero*) as well as the Indian workers and the storekeeper; she oversaw the distribution of rations; and she served as nurse and teacher. Both women's testimonials reconstruct the order established by the missionaries to control the neophyte community of producers involved in subsistence production for themselves and their exploiters. Indian labor did, however, generate a substantial surplus, especially at the larger missions like San Gabriel. The fact that the production — farming, and sheep and cattle raising — was labor intensive and that all mission household goods, clothing, and foodstuffs were elaborated at the mission itself, affords us an idea of the daily schedule imposed by the productive apparatus of the mission. Mechanisms of discipline include repetitive operations, timed activities, and minimal nutrition, all of which are detailed in the re-creation of mission life offered by several of the testimonials.

In their texts, the two women provide constructs of the mission as a site of industriousness, with everyone busy at their assigned task and within a designated space. In their detailed breakdown of spatial distinctions and divisions, they demonstrate that spatial practices, as Lefebvre (358) indicates, regulate life, and that time itself is spatially divided. The spatialization of daily life with workers shifting from spaces of rest and consumption of food to spaces of labor is also manipulated as a narrative strategy to heighten the sense of mission organization and order while at the same time minimizing the degree of exploitation within the mission. Both Lorenzana and Pérez go to great lengths to detail the regimented daily schedule set up at the mission and underscore that the neophytes were fed three times a day and given rest breaks. Neither woman comments on the portions provided, nor are they overly concerned about the food's lack of variety or its nutritional value, or about the fact that hard labor in the mission fields required substantial meals. Their descriptions of what was served — barley or corn gruel and grain-based stews with an occasional piece of meat — allow the reader to note the meager diet of the Indians. Pérez's detailed account of her preparation of delicacies and a variety of dishes for the missionaries at the San Gabriel mission is striking in comparison, yet her reconstruction of the sumptuous fare prepared for the missionaries does not elicit from Pérez any remark on the obvious differences in diet. What does come through in these narratives is the fact that the two women were linked to the power structure, for they both relish describing their positions of trust and the authority they exercised over the Indians. Clearly the missionaries entrusted them with a number of responsibilities in which they acted as the friars' agents, supervising a variety of tasks performed by Indian men and women.

Neither Pérez's nor Lorenzana's testimonial gives any indication on whether particular tasks were always restricted to a particular gender. Housekeeper Pérez recalls being in charge of distributing the materials used in the leather shops and carpentry shops and of overseeing the work in the winery, olive oil mill, and soap-making factory, but, beyond a description of the master craftsmen as male, except for seamstresses, there is no other mention of whether assignments were gendered or whether women also participated in all the activities she supervised. Tasks requiring hard labor are enumerated in Lorenzana's testimonial, but without a description of the work process itself there is no way of determining the gender of the hundreds of individuals involved in farming, ranching, crafts, domestic labor, and other arts (Lorenzana, 10). Unlike Lorenzana and Pérez, Coronel describes the participation of Indian women in domestic as well as nondomestic tasks, like harvesting, the cleaning of seedbeds, and the carrying of heavy loads, revealing that some labor was not gender-bound:

> Indian women were also employed in the harvesting and cleaning of seeds, in the grape harvest and in the preparation of wool, cleaning and spinning, and at times as hod carriers for the factories and roof tile-making shops, especially the single Indian women who were kept in constant labor. (222)

Lugo too recalls the use of Indian women for heavy fieldwork, given their numerical superiority (226).

The method for organizing and controlling the work of the Indians within this despotic mission system is "simple control"[35] exercised personally by the foreman, supervisor, or missionary. Some testimonials go into detail as to the types of incentives, threats, bullying, and force used to ensure production; others try to justify the use of these methods by describing tasks that required little exertion. The tight discipline necessary in the missions is explained by José de Jesús Vallejo as an antidote to laziness. But, he claims, the missionaries countered this natural tendency with the assignment of short rather than long tasks. In his reconstruction, J. J. Vallejo projects a paternalistic missionary who cajoled his workers into completing their tasks and then rewarded additional work with candy, clothes, pictures, or some other articles; at the same time Vallejo remarks that no Indian could return to his or her *ranchería* or the mission until the task had been completed (JJV, 39). The extraction of surplus labor from manual laborers who provided subsistence for thousands would seem to require not a slow-paced workday, as the missionaries and some Californios alleged, but, as previously suggested by M. G. Vallejo, a grueling work schedule.[36] Coronel also suggests a heavy schedule in his reconstruction of the daily work assignments: the regimented spatialization of the day with the ringing of bells to mark the end of one activity and the beginning of another; the division of the workers into various crews, each with its overseer; and the various craft shops within the mission walls.

The supervision of Indian women involved in domestic industries was the responsibility of women like Lorenzana and Pérez, who like other managers were also required to serve at times as experts in some craft. Thus Pérez and Lorenzana, both seamstresses, taught the Indian girls to sew the clothing for all the neophytes. In San Diego the Indian women did all the sewing, but at San Gabriel Pérez and her daughters were involved in the sewing of the fancier items for the church and for the cowboys, sometimes in conjunction with other Californio women from the *pueblo* who were hired on as extra help. The organization of space with separate work sites—one for the production of specialty items and one for the production of coarse clothing—again manifests the class and caste relations of the period. Thus clothing was a sign of social rank and served as an incentive to contain worker resistance. In general, the Indian women wore skirts and *rebozos*, and most of the Indian men had a loincloth, a shirt, and a blanket, all produced by Indian labor on the mission grounds. Favored Indian workers within the mission became *vaqueros de silla;* they were allowed to ride a horse with a saddle and were rewarded with garments like those worn by the Californios. Acculturation through consumption of more elaborate clothing items was a reward for good performance, because the other Indian cowboys rode bareback and wore only loincloths (Pérez, 11). Clothing differences and special privileges served as a strategy to divide the Indian community established within the mission.

Spatialization of activities, the regimentation of the labor process, and rewards for good work and acquiescence are only some of the methods of control in the missions reconstructed in these testimonials. There were of course more blatant forms of coercion and more subtle forms of ideological domination that ensured the missionaries' control of the neophyte Indians, and these too are discussed by the Californios in their narratives.

Ideological and Coercive Strategies

In addition to being a political space ensuring the Crown's occupation and domination of Alta California and a space of Indian production, the mission was also a cultural space, a religious space, a superstructural space generating ideological discourses and strategies to maintain the Indian producers subordinated and acquiescent. Like all heterogeneous spaces subsuming a variety of spaces, this heterotopia underpins and in fact presupposes other spaces, among them the space of military violence: the *presidio* or garrison, of which there were four (San Diego, Santa Barbara, Monterey, and San Francisco) and later a fifth in Sonoma (MGV, 1:120), with never more than five hundred soldiers in the entire territory (MGV, 1:336). These spaces of security and violence allowed the mission to accomplish its multiple functions.

The first generation of settlers coming with the missionaries to Alta California was made up primarily of soldiers with their families. They were sometimes accompanied by contracted craftsmen, political prisoners, exiles, rebel priests, and even convicts or field laborers forcibly drafted and placed on a ship to California. Many of the testimonials, narrated by soldiers or their descendants, express a high regard for the courage and daring of the California soldiers that kept the "heathen" at bay and protected the missions and *pueblos*.[37] Rarely, however, do the testimonials focus on the acts of violence or carnage carried out by the soldiers. The exception here is Alvarado's testimonial, wherein he describes in some detail the bloody scene at the military attack of Estanislao's estacada (2:66), a massacre for which the missionaries and Hittell blamed the young officer M. G. Vallejo.[38]

Although the primary task of the *presidio* soldiers was to protect the missions, *presidios*, and *pueblos* from attack by hostile tribes, a role stressed by the military M. G. Vallejo, they also served as mission troops, ensuring that Indians attracted to the missions remained there, and that those who tried to flee were returned and punished, a role for the most part avoided by Vallejo in his testimonial. In diaries and reports by soldiers and officers during the Spanish period, the troops' function as a police force for the missionaries is quite clear. The diary of José María Estudillo about his visit in 1819 to the Indian villages in the area of Los Tulares in search of escaped neophytes provides a good description of military practices on behalf of the missions' interests. Unable to keep all the neophytes under surveillance, the missionaries would inform the governor of those neophytes in flight from the mission; the governor in turn would send troops to bring them back in fetters or kill them if they resisted.[39] Indians attracted to the mission and Christianized could not therefore leave without permission once they had agreed to become mission neophytes. They had to carry passports when away from the mission site; those permitted to go to the hills to collect acorns, piñons, and other seeds or nuts that they liked did so only under supervision (Lugo, 225). This lack of freedom of movement was felt by the Indians to be especially odious and unbearable, as made clear by the Licatiut warrior Marín, friend of Quintín, captured and imprisoned in the San Francisco *presidio*. There he was visited by a missionary from the Dolores mission who came to talk him into bringing his tribe to join the mission community. Marín is said to have answered that the Indians were accustomed to being free in the wilderness like deer, and not in the mission like horses harnessed to carriages.[40] Alvarado's reconstruction of Marín's broken Spanish allows him to acknowledge Marín's awareness that the sedentary existence offered by the missionary was a form of imprisonment. Marín, Alvarado acknowledges, was not foolish enough to fall for the discourse of salvation, and neither of course was he (Alvarado, 1:95).

Coercion thus plays a significant role in the establishment of these mission communities, but in view of the small number of soldiers accompanying the missionaries and settlers, the troops could not have been the only effective method for subduing thousands of Indians and keeping them under mission control; moreover, as Coronel (38) recalls, often the men at the *presidios* were not even trained soldiers. The primary inducement for Indian consent to their subordination, then, was material. The Indians were attracted to the mission centers with offers of food, clothing, and shelter, incentives that drew them away from their Indian communities while at the same time isolating them from the community of *gente de razón*. This spatial separation, this racist division, was also a means of maintaining mission control. José de Jesús Vallejo recalls that the missionaries always took possession of all the land that surrounded the site where the mission was to be established, purportedly not out of a desire to increase their possessions but to "safeguard" the neophytes, that is, to create a *cordon sanitaire* around the mission to keep the neophytes from harm and contamination (JJV, 26). In so doing the Franciscan missionaries sought to reintroduce the sixteenth-century notion of separate societies, one Indian and one non-Indian. In effect this interest in establishing a separate Indian republic in Alta California was the missionaries' rationale for claiming hundreds of miles in the environs and being averse to ceding mission lands for Californio *pueblos*. The procedure was simple. First the mission had to attract a large number of Indians with gifts of clothing and blankets, and then persuade them to stay within the mission confines. Once it became evident that some of the Indians left as soon as they received their gifts, the clothing was provided only after the Indians had learned to recite certain prayers by rote. The attraction of clothing and food and a desire to improve their social condition, rather than any spiritual conversion, brought the Indians to the mission, Vallejo argues, and for that reason more came during periods of drought (JJV, 27).

José de Jesús Vallejo's analysis disarticulates any romantic notion of appealing to the Indians on religious grounds. Once basic needs for subsistence and warm clothing were satisfied, a second strategy came into play to retain them in the *reducciones* (MGV, 2:106). Ideological strategies, as J. J. Vallejo explains, were especially effective. In no small measure, he argues, the spectacle of the church rites and the ostentatious performative allure of the missionaries was what kept the Indians convinced of the friars' superiority. Culture thus played an important role in the pacification and control of the Indian population (JJV, 30–31). The Californios who perceived this function of religion applauded the missionaries' astuteness in using their religious paraphernalia as a visual strategy of containment that allowed for the domination of Alta California without the degree of bloodshed that would otherwise have been requisite. For this reason, Vallejo suggests that historians should not censure the missionaries for their good wine, servants, fine carriages and horses, and comfortable quarters: all were necessary parts of the simulacrum (JJV, 31). In his apparent defense of the missionaries' use of fine boots prohibited by their order, Vallejo will summon up the rhetorical argument of the nonexistence of roads and the need to break paths with machetes every time one went out (JJV, 32). His tongue-in-cheek praise is at bottom an implicit censure of missionaries known worldwide for their veneration of poverty yet living in relative opulence in Alta California. The missionaries were obviously willing to bend the rules whenever it suited them; the ends were construed to justify the means.

Within the mission itself, ecclesiastical ceremony thus played an important role in keeping the Indians submissive, as did religious practices. Even the Californios were not exempt from the religious tyranny of the missionaries. M. G. Vallejo recalled the forced recitation of Ripalda's *Catechism*, a "monstrous code of fanaticism" and superstition and his utter disgust with it (MGV, 4:186–87). All the missionaries, Vallejo argues, calling them "false apostles of a religion of peace, humility and kindness," sought to reduce intelligence to stupor by requiring that the Californios read a book whose sole objective was to ensure "the imbecility of the people" (MGV, 4:187).

The resentment of the liberal Californios toward the missionaries for maintaining them in ignorance is transcoded as the younger generation's impatience and biting critique of the ideological manipulation of the Indians. Liberal-rationalist discourses condemning the missionaries for their enslavement of the Indians (MGV, 1:368) thus also serve as a protest against their own religious brainwashing in the days of their youth. When Vallejo accuses the missionaries of keeping the Indians "in a state of humiliating tutelage" given their fear of knowledge in the hands of the Indians ("an educated Indian would have been king"), he is, by implication, speaking of the Californios as well, who were for the most part illiterate (MGV, 4:194–95). Class, Vallejo insists, is also a cultural distinction; to deprive a people of education is to keep them unaware of their subordination and unable to overthrow their oppressors. Vallejo, who tries to be discreet in his testimonial and takes great pains to avoid sounding anticlerical, has in one sitting linked power and knowledge and made the missionaries' repressive mechanisms the fundamental problem in California, affecting Indians as well as Californios, a state of domination that both were unable to overthrow. According to Vallejo, the Mexican period only exacerbated these conditions, and this state of affairs disappeared only with the American occupation, after which Californios and the few surviving Indians were reduced to a mere transaction, commodities bought and transferred like rams by what he terms the "stepmother" Mexico. The trope of a dysfunctional family could serve here to describe the shared lot of all the inhabitants of Alta California — Indian and non-Indian alike — abandoned by their cruel stepmother and dominated, abused, and reduced to ignorance and superstition by their missionary fathers. What particularly irked M. G. Vallejo was to think that it would be the invaders, and not the Californios, who would introduce public secular instruction. Of course Vallejo conveniently disregards relations of production and the dispossession of the Indians and Californio complicity in the process by focusing on culture alone in his attacks.

Whatever the cultural strategies of domination, coercion was never abandoned as a strategy of subjection. The walls of the mission as much as the soldiers served to contain the neophytes. The Indians who were proselytized and brought to the mission were tied to it almost as bonded servants. They were not serfs in the strict sense of the word, but they had no control over their labor power or over the means of production

(Cohen, 13). For all practical purposes they were enslaved, except that of course they were not *property* of the mission or of the church. They could not be sold, but their labor could be leased, to the *presidios* or townspeople, for example, and their wages went to the mission coffers (Lugo, 226). Thus, once they accepted being fed, sheltered, and dressed they lost their autonomy and freedom of movement. Consonant with these repressive dictates, single Indians were quartered at the mission and were locked up at night. Married Indians fared little better; they were allowed to return to their *rancherías* on mission lands in the evenings but had to report to work every morning. For the Indians who were baptized, then, the mission became a prison of sorts, even for those allowed to sleep outside its walls. Once on appropriated mission lands, often their former space, they were always under mission jurisdiction and subject to its dictates.

Neophytes who chose to escape tried to rejoin the company of gentiles, non-Christian Indians who lived beyond the pale of the mission. Escapees, termed *cimarrones*, were always hunted down; once caught, they were punished with beatings, stockades, and imprisonment, all forms of punishment practiced as early as 1786 when La Pérouse and his ship visited Monterey and the San Carlos mission. Although impressed with the missionaries' zeal, he also remarked in his journal account of the trip the treatment of the Indians, which he compared to that suffered by Black slaves on Santo Domingo plantations (Bancroft, 1885–86, 1:437). Similar information is provided in the testimonials of Lorenzana, Pérez, Pico, and Alvarado (see, for example, Lorenzana, 12). Like any slave plantation, the mission was well equipped with various technologies for an entire regime of physical punishment for Indians who failed to report for work or were delinquent in some way (theft, neglect of duties, and so on). Corporal punishment and the fear of it served to keep the neophytes in line. Both Lorenzana and Pérez describe the punishments inflicted upon delinquent Indians: stockades, imprisonment, shackles, the *corma* (a kind of hobble), and flogging.

In more serious cases, the neophytes were turned over to the corporal in charge of the mission guard or even to the *presidio* commander for punishment. Alvarado (1:89) provides a more detailed construct of punishment for runaway neophytes (including up to one hundred lashes, chains, weights, food deprivation, and isolation), even more severe if a secondary accusation was involved, such as robbery or a malicious act. Especially denigrating was the punishment of flogging, as Alvarado makes clear. Yet these discourses of discipline and punishment do not, as one might expect, form the basis for a Californio attack on the mission system. Lest anyone think that he was opposed to the use of the whip, Alvarado adds:

> Perhaps my readers will think the mission fathers cruel, but I, who knew the Indian races and lived amongst them since 1810, forgive them for having resorted to those means [whippings] in order to govern and civilize the Indians, for this punishment was the only one they feared and only by means of the whip and the lash could the friars induce respect and obedience amongst the Indians and it was by means of strong doses of whippings that major infractions were avoided. (1:96–97)

No, Alvarado could not very well attack the use of coercive practices subsequently employed during his administration at secularized missions and even on privately held Californio ranches. Perhaps for this reason, the use of these coercive practices by mission administrators is generally glossed over or ignored in the testimonials of those connected with the missions. Only Pico acknowledges that he arbitrarily had an Indian put in shackles and whipped when he was the administrator of the secularized San Luis Rey mission (91). Like the rest, Alvarado resorts to discourses of civilization, order, and discipline to attempt to justify the brutal punishment imposed on the Indians who sought to resist and escape from their enslavement. Undoubtedly the blood of the Indians was on every Californio's hands; Alvarado could not condemn the missionaries for treating the Indians as they did, for the Californio caste was complicit in the entire enterprise.

Discipline, order, the lash, stocks, and imprisonment are all coercive strategies used to contain the resistance of the Indians, as are a rigid work schedule and ideological manipulation, but as in all colonial structures, one additional strategy is employed to enslave the Indians: the Indians themselves. The construct of the Indian as a willing instrument of coercion is taken for granted in these testimonials. Even the soldiers who go after the escaped *cimarrones* describe being led by the *caporales,* Indian scouts and trusted neophytes originally from the *rancherías* who act as interpreters and agents for the missionaries and soldiers. At the mission, the top supervisory Californio "managers" always have Indian assistants who help to control the hundreds and sometimes thousands of Indians (Lugo, 226). Thus within the mission, the missionaries follow strategies of the battlefield, what Vallejo, describing his fight for survival in the northern frontier, calls his strategy of "divide and conquer" (MGV, 3:89). By establishing an internal policing agency made up of Indian neophytes, the missionaries in effect fomented internal division. Alvarado best describes the intent and functioning as follows:

For the local internal governance [of the mission] the missionaries had
organized a policing force composed of the elder neophytes who had
been there longest, were married, had families, and were considered
morally upright; these were given the title of *alcaldes* (mayors) and had
the faith and trust of the missionaries, were protected and instructed by
them in the duties entrusted to them [which included] the constant
observation and vigilance of all actions and conversations carried out
by the other neophytes, reporting and warning anyone that committed
some infraction or was remiss in the execution of the communal duties
assigned to them or in any way failed to carry out the padres' orders.
This police or spy network was also charged with reporting if anyone
had become seriously ill. (1:85)

As in a traditional colonial model, the missionaries created an elite
within the mission to police their own and to serve as intermediaries
for control of the labor force. In most missions the Indians went through
the formality of electing their overseers, but in fact the *alcalde* was chosen by the missionaries, who did not think the Indians capable of self-
government (Bancroft, 1885–86, 1:585). It is this division of the Indians
from within, this fifth column created from within their ranks, that
Alvarado blames for their inability to counter the Spanish domination. Had the Indians united, he insists, their numerical superiority
would have made them unconquerable (2:68). Consequently, the construct of internal dissension is central to these testimonials. As in so
many other instances, here too the Indians serve as a displaced trope
for the Californios themselves, also rendered weak by dissension, as
we shall see in chapter 6.

The testimonials thus provide an interesting overview of disciplinary practices in the heterotopic space of the mission. Several levels of
policing and control — within the Indian collective (the *alcalde*, the *matrona*), within the mission itself (the mission guard and the missionaries), and outside the mission walls (the foremen, soldiers, and *presidio*
commander) — served to maintain the missionaries' power and ensure
Indian production for the subsistence of all, the Californios included.
The missionaries, recognizing that the disciplinary apparatus would
not be necessary if the Indians consented to their own subordination,
found their best strategy to be the indoctrination of the Indians when
they were very young. The physical confinement of the younger Indians, that is, their separation from their parents and families, was the
missionaries' master plan for acculturation and the destruction of the
Indian culture. Both Pérez and Lorenzana mention the sleeping quarters of the young neophytes and the fact that an Indian woman called

matrona or *madre abadesa* (mother superior) was in charge of the young women's quarters, the *monjerío* (nunnery). An *alcalde* was in charge of the young men's quarters, called the *tayunque* (Alvarado, 1:86). Single neophytes were locked up at night within these quarters, and the key was handed over to the missionaries. This confinement, which guaranteed an audience for proselytizing and Christianizing, was justified paternalistically as sexual protection of the young people, particularly though not exclusively the young girls.[41] Protection from sexual assault was considered a necessary and desirable practice and supported by most Californios. Several testimonials make a point of reporting the death of a Californio killed defending three neophyte girls from rape by Indian raiders (MGV, 3:379). But in daily practice most Californio men, at one time or another, took neophyte women as concubines, as did several missionaries (MGV, 4:96).

The discourses of conversion and protection thus paradoxically serve to legitimate kidnapping practices; girls as young as seven or eight years old, according to Pérez (fourteen or fifteen years, according to Pío Pico), were taken from their parents and brought up at the missions until they married. Lorenzana and Pérez find nothing repugnant in these practices. Instead, they too assume paternalistic discourses in their account of the surveillance of young Indian girls, looked after by the *matronas*, who accompanied them when they bathed or worked and ensured their attention to the weaving, carding, or spinning (Lorenzana, 8). At night there was a roll call to determine if each and every boy and girl who worked outside the mission walls had returned to the mission. If a girl were found missing, her mother was brought to the mission and punished, and the daughter was locked up in the nunnery. The *monjerío* is presented in these testimonials as a space of security rather than as a cell within a penal colony. But in indicating that the girl was "locked up," Pérez (17) confirms the function of the nunnery as a prison cell. Although several of the testimonials refer to these practices and to the configuration of space within the mission, none describes the interior of the Indians' sleeping quarters; the filthy conditions, open sewers, and poor ventilation are totally left out of these accounts.[42]

These spatial strategies of confinement to the mission were imposed on single men and women, but married couples, though restricted to mission lands, lived outside mission walls at the *rancherías*, their Indian villages. In their narratives, the Californios often speak of "going among the Indians" (Pico, 99), but there is no description of the Indians' huts, gentile or neophyte, in these testimonials. Even the *diario* of

Estudillo provides only a distant general view of *jacales*, huts made of reeds and branches, and *rancherías* that housed over a thousand people each. The space of the other is thus blurred in these texts, and the Indians' agency, as we shall see in chapters 4 and 5, is always represented as a hostile force invading the spaces appropriated by Californios. Foreigners visiting California, however, like Simpson and La Pérouse, often include descriptions of destitute Indians living in wretched conditions and subject to all kinds of diseases. Simpson's description of a Suysun village is a good example:

> They are badly clothed, badly lodged, and badly fed. As to clothing, they are pretty nearly in a state of nature; as to lodging, their hovels are made of boughs wattled with bulrushes in the form of bee-hives, with a hole in the top for a chimney, and with two holes at the bottom toward the northwest and the southeast, so as to enable the poor creatures, by closing them in turns, to exclude both the prevailing winds.[43]

The degradation of the Indians constructed in Simpson's account is an Englishman's indictment of the Californios rather than the expression of any particular concern for the Indians, but it does pinpoint a glaring absence in these testimonials. Did Cerruti and Savage never ask about the Indians' huts, or had the Californios no interest in making their close contact with the Indians known? Lorenzana obviously had ample contact with the gentile Indians that worked on her *ranchos*, as did Vallejo, who was constantly taking his visitors to Suysun festivities and celebrations at the *ranchería*. Yet in Vallejo's five volumes there is no description of Chief Solano's home, a site he must have visited many times. Nor is there any description of the *rancherías* in the testimonial of Salvador Vallejo, who lived and worked closely with the Indians in the northern frontier for many years (he does describe Indian torture and defense techniques in detail; S. Vallejo, 88, 92). Coronel (110) recalls seeking shelter at the hut of an Indian when he was fleeing from Kearny's troops, but again the space, *el jacal*, is not described. It is perhaps to avoid being linked to a people they considered racially inferior as much as to avoid being blamed for the conditions of the *rancherías* that the Indians' domestic space is always fading in the background. Yet the Indians' territorial space, their land, is constantly foregrounded, a construct that the Californios will both manipulate and try to disarticulate during secularization, as we shall see in the next chapter.

In addition to forced labor and corporal punishment, the neophytes at the missions faced other life-threatening problems that the Californios discuss without assuming any degree of responsibility. In these testimonials the discourses of disease are routinely disassociated from discourses of conquest and colonization; disease is naturalized, presented as either the fault of the patient or the fault of some individual said to have introduced the disease, but never the responsibility of the Californio collectivity. Epidemics and disease have always historically accompanied warfare and invasions. In California mere contact with the invaders was deadly to the Indians and confinement in the mission meant a more rapid spread of contagious diseases. As Platón Vallejo recalls, a smallpox epidemic could wreak demographic havoc and wipe out thousands of Indians, as it did in Northern California in the late 1830s, but more insidious diseases, measles and venereal disease, were in evidence from the onset. The problem is discussed in passing by Lorenzana, who as a nurse at the San Diego mission saw a number of Indian women at the mission hospital suffering from syphilis:

> The diseases suffered by the Indian women aside from the ordinary headaches and simple fevers were those of syphilis and body sores. Married women living at their *rancherías* who worked outside of the mission acquired these illnesses despite the efforts made by the fathers and overseers so that they would not act shamefully and deal with any nonmission people. (7)

According to Lorenzana, the married neophyte women living outside the mission walls in their *rancherías* acquired these venereal diseases from contact with men from outside the mission, that is, with other Indians, soldiers, and townsmen. The *desórdenes* (shameful acts) are seen to be on the part of the women rather than the acts of men, who in all likelihood raped them.

In her testimonial, Lorenzana, a woman who supervised the mission hospital and worked closely with the Indian women, makes no mention of Indian abortion, suicide, or infanticide as strategies to combat rape or put an end to forced labor. In his romantic idealization of Californio times, the third-generation Guadalupe Vallejo, nephew of M. G. Vallejo, does afford us a glimpse of the type of sadistic punishment that could be inflicted upon Indian women whose children, for one reason or another, died, thus betraying a social practice among Indian women that was clearly punished by the missionaries uninterested in Indian birth control. His general account of women's neglect could very well have been an instance of abortion or infanticide, as in the case of Indian women resisting enslavement in Mexico (Semo, 78). Guadalupe Vallejo describes the customary punishment as follows:

In several cases where an Indian woman was so slovenly and
neglectful of her infant that it died, she was punished by being
compelled to carry in her arms in church, and at all meals and public
assemblies, a log of wood about the size of a nine-month-old child. This
was a very effectual punishment, for the Indian women are naturally
most affectionate creatures, and in every case they soon began to suffer
greatly, and others with them, so that once a whole Indian village
begged the father in charge to forgive the poor woman. (8)

Despite these and other sadistic methods of discipline, neither Lorenzana nor Pérez has anything negative to say about the mission system
or about the missionaries; both women are concerned with presenting
a positive description. Pérez, after mentioning the types of punishments
common at the mission, quickly makes clear that at San Gabriel the
friars were very considerate, whatever else they might have done elsewhere (20). In fact, she saw them as substitute parents and even married one of the missionaries' friends, Lieutenant Juan Mariné, a Catalonian widower with a family, simply to please the missionaries (13).
The missionaries gave Pérez land for a *rancho* and an orchard. Thus,
strong economic incentives for accommodating to mission practices
existed among Californios as among Indians.

As women working within a paternalistic and male-dominated institution, the two housekeepers express no dissatisfaction with their
own subordinate position. On the contrary, they enjoy stressing their
particular role of power in relation to the Indians and their nurturing
role in relation not to the neophytes but to the most important figures
in the area, the missionaries. Despite this skewed representation, obvious contradictions and gaps in the two women's narratives call for
a different reading of the mission, not so much as a "civilizing" and
"Christianizing" site but as a marketplace, a place of industry and
commerce.

The Mission as Monopoly and Bank

In addition to the construct of a monastic heterotopia, of the mission
as a penal colony for Indians, there is a competing construct in these
testimonials: the mission as a business enterprise. This economic construct is shown to be antagonistic to the interests of Californios, who
(in retrospect, of course) question practices of land tenancy dominant
in the territory before 1821. In effect the testimonials seek to demonstrate why it was necessary to secularize the mission, and to this purpose they provide information on the mission's wealth and power.

At first dependent on supplies sent from San Blas, the missions were by the 1780s able to provide not only for their needs and those of the soldiers at the *presidios* and their families but also for transport vessels. By 1800 the missions were doing very well trading hides, tallow, otter pelts, and supplies in exchange, generally, for imported articles and sometimes for currency. The representation of the mission as a wealthy institution with caches of gold is frequent in these testimonials. Pérez, for example, comments on the gold pieces stored in hides or buried under the missionaries' room floors or storeroom planks. She recalls as well the story about Father Antonio Peyri, formerly at the San Luis Rey mission, who is said to have left California in 1832 with a satchel of gold. María Angustias de la Guerra de Ord, however, whose father, Captain José de la Guerra y Noriega was the *síndico* (banker and accountant) for the missions, dismisses these allegations as unfounded, although she does recall that missions such as that of San Miguel were very rich (Ord, 1956: 31): "They were full of goods, grain, etc., and also had a goodly sum of money belonging to the mission." But she immediately counters the statement by adding that "transactions with traders were always goods for goods" and that there was "but little money in the country" (32–33). As to missionaries leaving the country with money upon secularization, Ord insists that those who left took only enough to secure their passage, remembering that most of the missionaries died in California. Peyri, the missionary from San Luis, is said to have taken his *sínodos* amounting to three thousand pesos, not a small sum for the time, to pay for travel expenses for the "two or three little Indians" that he took to Rome (Ord, 1956: 33). Ord is also quick to explain that when the missionaries died, they had nothing left in their accounts, as her father their treasurer could attest. Ord's testimonial provides the conservative position of several wealthy families closely allied to the missionaries, who, though not dominant in the territory, were powerful in their particular regions.

The missions' wealth was of course evident to all (except perhaps the daughter of the missionaries' treasurer). M. G. Vallejo, in discussing the debts of the Mexican government to the California missions, indicates that the missions were wealthy enough to grant loans (which were admittedly never repaid) for about seven hundred thousand pesos. Each missionary head was like a governor (MGV, 2:131). The power of these missionary heads, Vallejo says, came not only from control of the land and other means of production but from their control of trade. Neither Lorenzana nor Pérez, however, discusses the role the mission played in the contraband trade of hides and tallow. Only Ord recognizes that "the missions at certain times of the year had slaughtering on a grand scale for hides and tallow with which they purchased from the ships materials in which to dress their neophytes" (1956: 32). We do know from Pérez's and Lorenzana's *testimonios* that the Indians' few items of clothing were made at the mission. Trade, then, was generally not for goods to be consumed by the Indians, but primarily for luxury supplies for the missionaries and Californios and for capital accumulation. The mission later sold its acquisitions to the *presidio* and to *pueblo* residents, just as it did the goods produced locally.

Although trade with foreign vessels was not legal in California during the early period under Spanish mercantilist economic policies that required the colonies to trade only with Spain, the missions as early as 1786 were authorized to trade otter pelts for quicksilver needed for mining from Asian ships. The missions, clearly the economic centers in California, were the sole agents authorized to transact with the Indians for pelts to be sold for the Crown. Though this trade was subsequently officially eliminated, the missions continued to trade otter pelts, tallow, hides, grain, and even hemp. After 1810, mission trade with foreign ships increased to the point where Guerra y Noriega was asked to handle the financial affairs of the missions, as Ord confirms; by then the missions held a veritable monopoly on agricultural goods and other necessary products like blankets, soap, and ground wheat (Alvarado, 1:115). Given the distance from Mexico and the lack of trade with other nations, the missionaries were able, from the beginning, to monopolize all local trade, as Alvarado (1:115) recalls. They had been recalcitrant at first to increase their agricultural production to meet the needs of the soldiers and their families, arguing that increased productivity should serve to bring in larger numbers of neophytes; the *pueblo* of San José had been established in order to meet the specific needs of the soldiers and their families (Palou, 166). In practice, however, the mission continued to serve as the local trading post and the little the townspeople had was traded to the missions for foodstuff and other articles. The mission businessmen, recalls Alvarado, had no real competition,

> for they were such good businessmen that no one could compete with them, and in truth who on the outside would have been able to compete with a wool cloth merchant who acquired the wool for free, the buildings for free, the workers and salesmen for free? And if to this one added that relatives of these cared for the sheep, cut the firewood, made the cloth, and sold the blankets, and provided for all the peons

and workshop staff at the missions, kept without cost to the merchants, it is abundantly clear that the mission friars did not have before them as hard a task as some have proffered in their books where they are praised to the heavens. (1:115)

Alvarado notes sarcastically that he too could do better even than U.S. businessmen if he were in business with a low overhead, no labor costs, no cost for materials, no rent to be paid:

I too would agree to compete at an advantage with the Americans in any branch of industry if I were given thirty thousand workers duty-bound to obey my every command, free of charge and under no obligation to provide for their upkeep; and this, all told, is the source of the substantial wealth that the missionary fathers accumulated in my homeland; if indeed they brought with them a few baskets of dates and dry figs, they also reaped for their order the profits of more than fifty years' worth of the sweat and labor of nearly fifty thousand Indians. (1:116)

Alvarado here recognizes that the forced extraction of Indian labor, not any baskets of seeds brought by the missionaries, had produced the wealth of the missions. To reduce labor costs to the bare minimum of subsistence was to extract a great deal of surplus labor for the mission. The surplus produced by the workers' "slave" labor allowed for a chain of mission storehouses and enabled the missionaries to trade at first at a local level with the townspeople, but later with trading vessels (Alvarado, 1:117). Its participation in this contraband trade increased its capital, largely in the form of cattle and goods, for it was primarily involved in bartering, exchanging goods for promises of additional goods, but also willing to accept payment in gold. The mission would consequently come to serve as the financial establishment for the territory, lending money to governors, officers, and individuals from the *pueblos,* as Vallejo recalled.

The financial situation in Alta California became increasingly untenable for the Californios, who during the Spanish period were largely dependent on their soldiers' salaries and, if *pueblo* residents, on their vegetable gardens as well. Most of the coastal lands were controlled by the missionaries, who were wary of any attempts to establish *pueblos* in their vicinities. From the beginning of the colonization of California, the Spanish viceroy had authorized military officers and later governors to distribute land to worthy individuals interested in agriculture or livestock, but few land grants were made during this period — only *pueblo* lots in San José, established in 1777, and a few years later, in 1781, in Los Angeles. Alvarado (1:80) recalls that these *pueblo* lands —

two hundred square *varas*—went to veteran soldiers as a reward for having completed their term of service.[44]

As in a feudal manor the townspeople shared communal lands for grazing livestock and used their two hundred square *varas* for a house and garden. Alvarado recalls that in addition to the retired soldiers and their families, new colonists in the *pueblos* included craftsworkers brought to the missions under contract to instruct the neophytes in the production of diverse crafts. Once an Indian had been trained who could then take charge and train others, the new arrival would settle in one of the new *pueblos*, or, more often return to Mexico (Alvarado, 1:80–81). The land assigned each individual did not, in this particular context, constitute private ownership, as the land could be forfeited if the settler did not comply with the regulations on use of the land (Fages, 219), but in practice it functioned for all intents and purposes as private property. These *pueblo* lots were relatively small and did not meet the private property expectations of those wanting and needing considerably more.

As time went on additional grants of *pueblo* lands were made, but despite some immigration from Sonora, Sinaloa, and other parts of northern and western Mexico, the *pueblo* populations remained relatively small. Consumer needs continued to be met at the missions, especially when no ships arrived from San Blas and all that was available was what the mission produced. The missions profited in this trade with the *pobladores* (townspeople) as they could set the price on what they sold. When the soldiers' salaries stopped coming, as happened often during and after the wars for independence, the *pobladores* had to trade their own garden products at prices set by the missionaries or go into debt for the articles they needed (Alvarado, 1:117). The resentment of the Californios toward the missions is evident, as is their desire to set the stage for what was to come: secularization of the missions. Their grievances go beyond the mission's controlling of the marketplace and are centered primarily on their being cut off from the means of production, the land. Territorial space thus becomes the most often constructed issue separating missionaries and Californios. Boundary disputes would increase with encroachment of *pueblo* cattle on mission lands and with the granting of land after 1775 to a few retired soldiers for private *ranchos* (MGV, 1:88). By 1795 Governor Diego Borica was contesting the policy of land concessions because it meant using lands claimed by the missions for new Indian converts (Bancroft, 1885–86, 1:611). But between 1806 and 1814 the more liberal Governor José Joaquín Arrillaga began to make concessions of large tracts of land

(MGV, 1:99). Thereafter the problems Borica had foreseen between *ranchos* and *rancherías* would fast become critical as more and more *rancho* grants were awarded.[45]

The construct of the mission as business corporation stands in sharp contrast and offsets the construct of the mission as a utopian site for an imaginary idyllic monastic order. Both constructs compete with the two positing the mission as a penal colony and as a site for converting and civilizing the Indians. The four constructs allow the narrating Californios to assume and shift position according to the specific issue at hand and according to class and political perspectives. To disidentify with the Indians, the Californios see the missionaries as benevolent men intent on civilizing the backward and stupid Indians. To disidentify with the missionaries, the Californios focus on the mission as a prison for the enslavement of the Indians. To justify their own secularization policies, they focus on the mission as a business enterprise that profited at the expense of both the Californios and the Indians. Some Californios, like Alvarado, assume all three positions at different points.

The mission as heterotopia of discipline and control is a dominant construct within these testimonials, a layered construct, a social space constituted by discourses of order, protection, civilization, and Christianization as much as by discourses of enslavement, oppression, exploitation, and alienation. The articulation of each construct implies its opposite. If within the space of the mission there is order, outside its boundaries there is only barbarism. That the order is despotically achieved (and maintained) is not at all absent from the texts, whereas discourses of condemnation are all too easily buried under layer upon layer of justifications alluding to the savagery and ignorance of the Indians and their need for civilization.

These various constructs of the mission heterotopia thus imply particular constructs of the Indians as well. The primitive world of the Indian is seen as in need of the kind of order that only *gente de razón* can provide. The construct of the naive Indian serves both to indict the missionaries for taking advantage of the Indians as well as to justify the policies that will be adopted when the new generation of Californios comes to power. The construct of the fierce Indians justifies the harsh military policies adopted by Californios and missionaries alike against those that rebelled and did not consent to missionization. The construct of the Indians as forced labor despotically used by the missionaries would in turn be wielded to explain the wealth of the missionaries and to discredit them as friars true to the precepts of their order, while at the same time setting the stage for the discourses of liberation that would be manipulated by the Californios to gain control of mission lands after Mexican independence.

A by-product of the tension produced by the spatial dominance of the mission is a sense of peripheral location among the Californios. Thus the mission enclosure, by excluding the Californios from the powerful monastic realm, also fostered new spatial identities and gave rise to a new construct of secular space, the site of the Californio "family." Ubiquitous in all of these testimonials are the discourses of kinship that, like those of caste, serve to cement links between Californios all the way from San Diego to San Francisco, creating a permeable and ever-encompassing social space that includes not only those related by blood and marriage but, figuratively, all *gente de razón* residents of Alta California.[46] The space of "family" this becomes synonymous with that of community and ultimately serves symbolically to contain the "nation." It is a patriarchal family, stratified much like the patriarchal mission family, which it will eventually replace.

This "imagined Californio community" or "family" builds on other types of ties beyond kinship, other bonds that function to include and exclude, like *compadrazgos* or *padrino-madrinazgos,* friendships, officer/soldier relations, even employment affiliations or partisan loyalties, all relations linking individuals not related by blood or marriage. Regional affiliation between Indian chiefs and Californios also extends "family" ties beyond kinship. All of these links are sociospatially determined and in many cases prove to be stronger than blood ties.[47] This wide array of social relations is discursively mapped out in the testimonials and constitutive of this broader construct of family, coextensive to the whole of the California population of *gente de razón* . In fact, it becomes a trope for both territorial nationalism and dissension to the point that narrators continually lament the fragmentation of the "Californio family" (MGV, 1:295; 2:229). Ultimately, as these testimonials bear out, identity is structured by many different discourses, including those of kinship, friendship, caste, region, political orientation, class, military service, and gender. All of these discourses will overlap and collide with new liberal-rationalist discourses coming to Alta California after Mexican independence that assail the mission system.

3

Theoretical Disjunctures and Discourses of Liberalism

> Pues ya en 1832 la juventud llena de ideas liberales,
> bajo ningún pretexto, podía prestarse a tributar
> homenajes a personas que fundaban sus derechos
> en rancios pergaminos o bien en los antecedentes
> gloriosos de sus antepasados.
>
> M. G. Vallejo

With the arrival in 1825 of José María Echeandía, the first governor appointed by the newly independent Mexican state, the youth of Alta California, the Young Turks as it were, who would become the emergent class of the territory and who were then hungry for news of the world and new ideas, were granted an opportunity to imagine a new society upon being invited to participate in discussions on the latest ideological framework stirring debate in the Mexican capital: liberalism. Echeandía's notions of republicanism and individual liberty clashed with feudal discourses of aristocracy, especially with long-held tenets of birthright and "blood" as the determining factors of an individual's standing, which had held sway among particular Californio families. For this reason these young men would thereafter be especially incensed at the airs of one Santiago Argüello, brother of the ex-interim governor Luis Argüello and considered to be exceptionally haughty and conceited. To bring him down a few notches, Alvarado, Vallejo, Pío Pico, and others would avenge themselves by playing a trick on him and in so doing reveal their acquisition of the constructs of free competition and the individual's right to choose, both posited within classical liberalism.[1] At the beginning of the century, according to M. G. Vallejo, few Californios had access to these constructs (MGV, 2:176), but by 1830 these new concepts of the rights of individuals had reached the California territory and were beginning to put into question the very foundations on which men like Argüello based their ostensible superiority:

> Young men full of liberal ideas were, under no circumstances, willing to pay homage to individuals who based their rights on rancid parchments or on the glorious deeds of their ancestors. (MGV, 2:176)

Thus although the territory was still quasi-feudal, the arrival of a new framework positing property rights and individual liberty took root among a sector of the population ready for social change. The breakdown of the old order was set in motion, thanks in no small measure to Echeandía and his introduction of discourses of liberalism, secularism, and constitutionalism. (It goes without saying that only men at that time would be interpellated by these new discourses.) Constrained by their own mode of production and social conditions, the Californios would fail to extend liberalism beyond the notion of "liberty to have your own property,"[2] that is, beyond a defense of economic liberty. This defense of private property would not, however, entail rejecting local semifeudal relations of production, as we shall see in chapter 4, nor would the notion of political freedom imply liberal democracy, for freedom of choice did not extend to all the population of Alta California. As in Mexico, liberalism here would be "aristocratic."[3]

During the nineteenth century (1830–80), called the period of classical liberalism and the "era of triumphant bourgeois liberalism,[4] liberal ideological discourses were seen to frame a number of important European social, economic, and political constructs: free trade, modernization and progress (read capitalist economic development), the separation of civil and property powers, political rights, and nation-building. The tendency in this type of analysis of the universalist ideals of the Enlightenment, as Mouffe points out, is to conflate democracy and liberalism, that is, to draw no distinction between political liberalism and economic liberalism.[5] The two discourses were in fact not confused in Mexico, where the major exponents of constitutional liberalism, men like José María Luis Mora, recoiled from notions of popular sovereignty and egalitarianism.[6] The distinction between liberalism and democracy is crucial in understanding what occurred during the 1830s and 1840s in Alta California, but so too is an assessment of the role that theoretical discourses play in social change.

The universal status that this epistemological framework has been granted is of course traceable to global power relations and the Eurocentric orientation of political writings. As a consequence liberalism has been posited as the epistemic foundation for all subsequent moderniza-tion and nationalist movements in the Third World.[7] Behind this foun-dationalism based on the historical conjuncture of liberal-rationalist discourses and technological and economic advances lies what Chat-terjee terms an "epistemic fallacy."[8] In Chatterjee's words, the fallacy is the notion that "the means to the domination of the world" (15) is knowledge. This essentialism allows Western society to divide the world into prescientific and scientific and in turn to posit the "superi-ority of the European people" (16). If the world of theoretical discourses, as Chatterjee explains, is always an ambiguous interdiscursive ideo-logical field where notions are inexact, there is then no direct correla-tion between nationalism and particular European frameworks, for all nations construct their theories and directions in the disjunctures and slippages resulting from colliding and overlapping discourses, that is, in discursively constructed antagonisms (Mouffe, 1988: 95):

> It is in the shifts, slides, discontinuities, the unintended moves, what is supposed as much as what is asserted, that one can get a sense of this complex movement . . . And it is by examining the jagged edges that we can find clues to an understanding of the political relevance today of the ideological history of nationalism. (Chatterjee, vii)

These slippages are not simply instabilities or excesses in meaning but rather historically produced ideological gaps that arise out of economic and political imbalances and contradictions. Theoretical discourses in and of themselves do not produce change, for in every case nondis-cursive conditions also have to be favorable for such a transformation to occur, but as framing technologies in the field of ideology they serve both to contain and enable social struggle by constructing social an-tagonism discursively (Mouffe, 1988: 95). It is never a matter of impos-ing an already made paradigm, however, for in the formulation of a framework that speaks to the particular problematic of a people, col-lective agents are necessarily discursively positioned within a theoret-ical or ideological field in which there is always the competition of intersecting discursive formations. Ideological discourses in effect struc-ture, frame, and shape, as well as legitimate, political thought, claims, and action, as we shall see in exploring the Californios' discussion of the project of Alta California's secularization.

Alta California may have been perceived by the Spanish and later the Mexicans as a penal colony where ex-convicts and undesirables were sent, but it would also be an ideological field, a place of political exper-imentation for both Mexican conservatives and liberals, a laboratory wherein ideological claims and historical possibilities could be played out. Here, as we have seen in chapter 2, the missionaries tried to create a utopian land of Indian *pueblos* dominated by missionaries and kept distant from *gente de razón*. Liberals saw California as a place to put into effect their liberal policies and begin the process of secularization and appropriation of mission lands, reforms that liberals envisaged already for Mexico, where the church was the largest landowner and wealthiest corporation. The conservatives saw California as a place for Spain to dominate again and plotted with the missionaries to instate a monarch in an independent California. Only the liberal plot to create private property would have a measure of success in California; here, as in Mexico, liberal discourses would be primarily linked to economic liberty and private property rather than to a defense of equality, for the caste system was still operative and the subordination of Indians crucial for the mode of production.

The orientation toward economic liberalism in Alta California is a result of the specific historical conditions of the territory. It was very much a dualistic society divided first along caste/cultural lines, second between propertied (missionaries) and nonpropertied (Californios) classes, and third along political/national lines. The native sons of California, the second generation, were feeling very much like a colony of Mexico and resenting it. Their ties were not to the newly independent and at times anarchic Mexican state, which most had never visited, but to their own Californian space, the territory, land that they did not by and large own as control of the coastal areas was largely in the hands of the missionaries. The appropriation of this monastic property became their primary focus. Their goal of privatization required political control of Alta California in order to displace a social space dominated by despotic relations of production with a space preserving semifeudal relations, a space that, as in Mexico, allowed for the creation of large landed estates for cattle raising, ranches like the ones the missions possessed but that were now to be held privately and worked by Indian peons. In Alta California liberalism meant economic liberty, the right to own large expanses of land then controlled by a religious corporation.

In this chapter, we will explore the discursive construction of this land antagonism, the ambiguities and discontinuities within the Californio/ Mexican ideological field, and the particular discursive and nondiscursive practices that emerged and led to the liberal experiment in Alta California. Throughout this chapter, we keep Brenner's analysis of the shift from feudalism to capitalism in mind. Rather than focusing on geopolitical and trade factors in studying this process of transition, Brenner posits that neither depopulation, declines in productivity, development of technology, nor developments in the sphere of exchange and circulation alone can explain this shift in mode of production. It is in fact a political question, a question of the class struggle between contending forces, i.e., landlords and serfs. Thus property relations (his term for relations of production) are shown to determine the economic course of society.[9] The shift that we will discuss here and in the next chapter is not as marked as that treated by Brenner in his analysis of the crisis of late European feudalism,[10] for we are basically still dealing with the same mode of production, but secularization does signal a change from a despotic phase of feudal production (wherein a religious corporation controls the land and works it with an unfree labor force that has no control over the means of production) to a more typical Latin American semifeudal system of *latifundismo* with privately held *ranchos* and *haciendas*. Property relations or relations of production will not change for most of the producers, the Indian labor force, but they do change at the top for the largely landless sons of the *presidio* soldiers who act to gain their own land, cattle, and horses. The liberal experiment in Alta California will mean property rights for this emergent class.

We will look more closely at the changes or lack of substantive changes in relations of production in the next chapter, but what concerns us here is the instrumental use of the liberal discursive framework within the testimonials to justify, in the process of narrating the past, the changes effected in the decade of the 1830s. Equally important is the reconstructed formulation of these ideological discourses in Alta California, with details on how these liberal discourses both constrained and enabled the second generation of Californios to subvert the Mexican secularization plan in order to gain local control of the means of production, that is, the land that would all too soon be wrested from them with invasion. It will be in the process of backing one interpretation of the liberal framework in opposition to another that the outcome of secularization in Alta California will be decided.

Recent studies on liberalism in Latin America are increasingly recognizing the importance of studying the disjunctures produced by competing ideological discourses. Instead of focusing on an empirical relation between a European liberal-rationalist paradigm and particular nineteenth-century nationalist and modernizing movements, these new essays posit no universal model but rather fuzzy and ambiguous frameworks constituted by the overlapping and interconnected liberal and nonliberal discursive practices of that period.[11] But even in Europe, as Hobsbawm makes clear, "we encounter, in nineteenth-century liberal discourse, a surprising degree of intellectual vagueness." In practice, he says, "much of the liberal theory of nations emerges only, as it were, on the margins of the discourse of liberal writers" (1990: 24). Similar inconsistencies are traced by Appleby in a study of liberalism and republicanism in the United States.[12] In Latin America as well liberal discourses would play a vague peripheral role in the wars for independence, struggles in great measure between competing factions of the criollo and Spanish aristocracy that cannot be truly considered nationalist movements if we follow Hobsbawm's analysis (1992: 10). Nor were these bourgeois revolutions; the creation of a Mexican territorial state, far from producing an economic and social transformation, served in part to buttress the dominant position of the *terrateniente* (landowning) ruling class and a semifeudal mode of production.

The liberal framework would assume an important role only after the establishment of the independent Latin American nation-states. Some aspects of this liberal ideology—notably in regard to free trade—played a key part in movements of independence, but other liberal-democratic tenets, including modernization, political rights, nationalism, and separation of powers, would not become part of the ideological dialogue until after independence. Conditions were not ripe, it seems, for a total social transformation, only for ending colonial domination, though even here there was no consensus. Before independence, given the Spanish mercantilist economy, free trade, important to Mexico City merchants, had not been a stimulus for a transformation of the colonial structure; in fact, as Stein and Stein argue, "many of the colonial elite hoped to maintain allegiance to embattled Spain while enjoying the right to trade directly with all Europe and the United States."[13] Some segments of the elite even wanted the embattled King Ferdinand VII to flee French invasion and come to Mexico to reign there. The wars of independence in Latin America could perhaps be said to be examples of what Gramsci calls a "passive revolution,"[14] whereby, as Chatterjee explains, "it was possible to preserve the political and economic position of the old feudal classes, to avoid agrarian reform and, especially, to avoid the popular masses going through a period of political experience such as occurred in France in the years of Jacobinism, in 1831 and in 1848" (30).

Given these contradictory conditions, one could argue that just as the formation of states is prior to the making of nations (Hobsbawm, 1990: 10), in Latin America the creation of territorial states would be necessary to enable liberal-rationalist discourses to come to the fore in order to compete actively with feudal and religious discourses. And when they did, they would not signal the implantation of foreign frameworks in Latin America, for they would be molded and adapted to fit the social context of the Americas and compromised as well in their competition and interconnection with and concessions to other discursive formations. Nor would these fuzzy liberal-rationalist discourses, wielded primarily after independence, necessarily assume the status of counterdiscourses, manipulated as they often were as much to legitimize the existing social order as to serve the political interests of an emergent class. Yet these shifts and slippages within the ideological field would be crucial during the first fifty years after Mexican independence and would accompany a period of violence, instability, civil strife, and a great deal of political vacillation between liberal and conservative positions.

In Alta California the "passive revolution" would come after Mexican independence and bypass major social transformations, with only minor economic and political changes. It was linked not to an emergent bourgeois class but to an emergent elite, the native sons and would-be *rancheros* who, given their access to liberal-rationalist discourses, would be able to manipulate these discourses in the process of abolishing the missionary model of production in order to establish themselves as the dominant class. The economic and political contradictions would be too many and the colliding ideological discourses too antagonistic to allow for cohesive nationalist identity and the formation of a separate nation-state, as we shall see in chapter 6. Nevertheless, these liberal discourses would serve to shape the liberal program of secularization of mission lands and even to legitimate the Californios' preservation of the semifeudal political and economic order.

Liberal-Rationalist Framework

The discourses of liberalism in nineteenth-century Latin America were always contradictory and imprecise, explains González Stephan in her historiographic study of Latin American liberalism (36). The long history of colonialism, the semifeudal structure of society, and the fact that liberal discourses were accessible only to the criollo elite and *letrados,* antagonistic as much to egalitarianism as to ecclesiastical privileges, perhaps best explain the ideological inconsistency. As "aristocratic" discourses, Latin American liberalism did not address conditions of marginalization, dispossession, and neglect affecting the majority of the population. Struggles for equality, as Mouffe explains, require democratic discourses for a construction of antagonisms and definition of the enemy. Without them, elitist liberal-rationalist discourses could only go so far in deconstructing "the theological-political-cosmological vision" (Mouffe, 1988: 95) dominant in Latin America after independence. The liberal framework did set the stage for the construction of antagonisms and for future popular struggles in the process of interpellating some subjects as equals and some as subordinates.

As in the case of foundationalist arguments tracing all nationalist movements to a classical liberal-rationalist framework, essentialist notions of Latin American liberalism and conservatism have traditionally ignored the ambiguity, discontinuities, and contradictions of the ideological field. At the level of the specific political problematic, Latin American liberals of the nineteenth century have been traditionally represented as federalists and republicans; they are said to have favored economic liberalism that promoted modernization and progress over political liberalism. In fact, historically some supported liberal platforms advocating public education, popular suffrage, and the abolition of slavery, as well as individual liberty and free trade (González Stephan, 53–56), while others supported a constitutional liberalism that guaranteed equality and freedoms for the few (Hale, 76–78). Given their rational, secular, and civil concept of society, liberals, for the most part, opposed the privileges of the upper clergy and military and favored the secularization and distribution of church properties as well as of communal Indian lands, but generally there was no opposition to religious intolerance or efforts to separate church and state. In some countries, such as Argentina, liberal policies sanctioned wars to exterminate the Indians and promoted European immigration in order to "whiten" the population. In practice, as González Stephan (46) indicates, there was sometimes little difference between those bandying about the label of "liberal" and those calling themselves "conservatives." Liberals, as Hale demonstrates, often vacillated between supporting liberal issues (as when it came to the appropriation and distribution of church property and the promotion of secular education) and adopting conservative positions (for example, in relation to voting rights and Indian rights). The liberal-rationalist framework was often quite compromised by religious, racist, classist, and partisan discourses, all of which explain the vacillations and contradictions of liberal writers throughout Latin America and in Alta California as well.

The moment of arrival of these liberal-rationalist discourses in Latin America is of course difficult to determine given the interdiscursive nature of the ideological field, permeable by any and all discourses. In the late eighteenth and early nineteenth centuries, as before, Latin America not only received a number of immigrants and visitors but also saw members of its ruling class travel abroad. At the same time, in France, the United States, and Spain, the writings of Locke, Rousseau, Montesquieu, Bentham, Burke, and later Constant were dominating the political field. In the case of Mexico, the import of much of the liberal ideological framework has been traced, in part, to the liberal Spanish Constitution of 1812, the reform legislation of the Cortes of Cádiz, the work of the Spaniard Gaspar Melchor Jovellanos, and, initially at least, the Masonic lodges, associations that would play an important political function in nineteenth-century politics. By attracting intellectuals, military officers, politicians, professionals, businessmen, and others, these Masonic lodges would serve as sites of dissemination of liberal discourses and as sites of agency, for they would facilitate the organization of what in time would be the first political parties in Mexico. These secret male organizations would incorporate a whole spectrum of political tendencies and be viewed with suspicion as responsible for introducing alien frameworks (British, French, and American) and aiding imperialist designs on Mexican territory.[15]

Masonic lodges in Latin America played a role similar to that of New England Puritan ministers and churches in the early part of American independence by way of their "jeremiads" or political sermons.[16] If in New England theology was wedded to politics (Bercovitch, 1978: xiv), in Latin America Freemasonry was wedded to politics. Masonic lodges were first established in Spain in 1767 during the reign of Carlos III (1759–88),[17] a period of "Enlightened despotism," which, though eclectic in trying to "preserve an internal balance between traditionalism and modernity" and though in no way a threat to royal authority,[18] brought many reforms, including the expulsion of the Jesuits from Spain and Latin America, a slight reduction in the powers of the Inquisition, and the colonization of Alta California.[19] Liberal-rationalist concepts of modernity, nationalism, social contract, scientific research, historical analysis, and even natural law would circulate during this period (Góngora, 177–87, 196), despite little or no economic changes in the Spanish peninsula (Vilar, 51–52). In Latin America, Spanish Enlightened despotism would bring more than new discursive constructs; it would introduce bureaucratic changes and more methodical practices in fiscal and military matters, and less willingness to consider criollo opinion or appointments—all policies to which the criollos would be hostile (Góngora, 175–76), thus setting the stage for colonial insurrection.

The Constitution of 1812 promulgated several years later by the liberal Spanish Cortes of 1810–13 (organized during the Spanish war against the Napoleonic invasion of 1808–13), although issued from a position of political authority without input from popular resistance (Vilar, 55), would become an important political document in Latin America, particularly its policies related to Indian citizenship, secularization of Church lands, and its suppression of the Inquisition (Vilar, 57). Upon the abolition of the Cortes and their political program with the return of King Ferdinand VII in 1814, a new period of intolerance and persecution of those espousing anticlerical, antifeudal, scientific, and rationalist positions would set in. The return of the Inquisition, abolished by Napoleon upon invasion in 1808, would lead to emigration of a number of liberals and Masons to the Americas (Zalce y Rodríguez, 28).

The Spanish Masons established the first Mexican Masonic lodges, called, as in Spain, *escocesas*. The lodges were not, despite the name, connected to the worldwide Scottish Rite, but were in fact of French origin (Zalce y Rodríguez, 51, 71). These first lodges were made up of well-to-do criollos and prominent *mexicanos,* including Don Guadalupe Victoria, an insurgent who had fought for independence and became the first president of the newly established republic of Mexico.[20] In Jalapa in 1822–23, Victoria was instrumental in leading a number of members out of that lodge in order to establish a new one founded on strongly nationalist, and virulently anticlerical and anti-Spanish, tenets (Zalce y Rodríguez, 57–58). Out of this second organization and out of the existing *logia escocesa* would come incentives for the formation in 1825 of the Rito de York. Among the members of the first York lodges were several men who would play important political roles during the next thirty years, including General Guadalupe Victoria, General Vicente Guerrero, Lorenzo de Zavala, and Miguel Ramos Arizpe. The two Masonic lodges would become associations of the dominant classes of *terratenientes,* merchants, military officers, and *letrados* (the intellectuals). While the *escoceses* were generally conservative, pro-Spanish, pro-church, and procentralist factions, the *yorkinos* were more likely federalist liberals, often, like Zavala and Guerrero, linked to urban and rural middle classes and very anti-Spanish, as was made clear when *yorkinos* pushed in 1829 for the expulsion of the Spaniards from Mexico.[21] There were continual shifts in affiliation and ideological position; the *escocés* José María Luis Mora, for example, moved on to become the leading exponent of liberalism.[22]

The issues in Mexico during this period were of course not Masonic in nature but rather political and economic, and these lodges assumed a number of important political roles and functions. Mejía Zúñiga (116) explains that in view of a strong military and clerical presence, the Masonic lodges filled a vacuum of political parties. The *rito escocés*, for example, controlled by aristocratic landowners, upper clergymen, and heads of military branches, proposed General Manuel Gómez Pedraza as the candidate for president in 1828 in opposition to the *yorkino* General Vicente Guerrero. During the first thirty years after Mexican independence, a period of anarchy and transition marked by conflicts between republicans and monarchists and between liberals and the upper clergy, the Masonic lodges created social spaces for organization and ideological struggle. In particular, Freemasonry created a space for consensus among aristocratic liberals on the need to remove the major fetters for the economic development of Mexico: church mortmain property and the feudal system that nurtured it. From here liberals would go on to form what they called "the party of progress."[23] Mora, a statesman and professor of humanities at the Colegio de San Idelfonso, argued that the church should be a mystical rather than a political corporation (Escobar Valenzuela, 198, 202) and laid the foundation for what subsequent liberals would consider the need to destroy the economic power of the church (Mejía Zúñiga, 122). Implicit in Mora's arguments against the church as a privileged propertied corporation was the secularization of mission lands in Alta California and the rest of Mexico, but also the abolition of Indian communal property.[24]

Subsequent restructuring by the Masonic lodges led to new rites and alliances, but the major ideological cleavage between conservatives and liberals continued to be embodied in the two factions of the *escoceses* and the *yorkinos*. The situation would be further complicated by the appearance on the Masonic scene of two foreign officials: the British minister H. G. Ward and the U.S. ambassador Joel R. Poinsett, both representatives of their respective government's economic and political interests in Mexico (Mejía Zúñiga, 116). Ward, who had come to determine prospects for British commercial investments, would become involved with the *rito escocés* and Poinsett with the liberal *yorkinos* (Mejía Zúñiga, 119). For Mejía Zúñiga and other Mexican historians, the influence and participation of Poinsett and Ward in the establishment of these Masonic lodges was a clear indication of foreign intervention in the affairs of the Mexican nation. The influence of the American ambassador on national politics began to be a point of contention: he was credited with having a hand in designing the federalist system; was said to be behind the separation of the Central American nations from

Mexico, as well as the North American settlements in Texas; and later was said to have masterminded the traitorous action of Lorenzo de Zavala, a *yorkino* who participated in the secession of Texas from Mexico and later became the first vice president of the Texas Republic (Bazant, 52).

As a consequence of a revolt against Victoria and given the presence of a number of *escoceses* in Congress, in 1828 the Mexican Congress passed a law outlawing secret associations. Those participating in clandestine meetings would, for a first offense, lose their civic rights for a period of two years; the second time, they would be exiled to either Alta or Baja California for two years, with each case of recidivism adding years in the Californias or in exile (Zalce y Rodríguez, 85–86). This law, which in effect led to mutual persecution by the *logias*, also confirms the Californios' allegation that the Mexican government saw Alta California as little more than a penal colony.

The period between 1824 and 1855 is characterized by a series of military revolts headed primarily by Santa Anna, first against Iturbide (1822), later against Gómez Pedraza (1828) to install Guerrero as president, and later still against Bustamante (1832), who had revolted against Guerrero in 1829 and subsequently had him executed. In 1833, Santa Anna and Gómez Farías came to power as liberals, but in 1834 Santa Anna expelled Gómez Farías and in 1835 he declared Mexico a centralist republic—a flip-flop proving once again that the military was ready to support the dominant economic power, the church. This declaration of a centralist government would provoke the reaction of a number of states and territories that supported the 1824 federalist constitution (including Alta California, as we shall see in chapter 6).[25] The narrative of anarchy common in histories dealing with this period focuses on frequent changes of personnel at the level of the presidency, with Santa Anna making intermittent reappearances until finally in 1855 he relinquished the presidency for the last time. In reality, Mexico saw little political change during the Santa Anna decades, with power securely in the grip of the conservative oligarchy in 1846 when Mexico was invaded by the United States.

The one proponent of liberalism during this chaotic period is Gómez Farías, elected vice president in 1833 with the then-*yorkino* Santa Anna as president. Shortly after assuming office, Santa Anna decides to take a leave, and Gómez Farías is left in charge for a brief ten months. During this time he initiates a number of liberal policies that anticipate the liberal program implemented about twenty-five years later by Pres-

ident Benito Juárez. Gómez Farías's liberal program will include freedom of expression, removal of the obligation to pay tithes, abolition
of clerical and military privileges, secularization of all civil contracts
(including marriage), elimination of the church's monopoly on education, release from binding monastic vows, abolition of the death penalty
for all but premeditated murder, and the guarantee of what was termed
"national integrity" through the establishment of colonies of Mexicans
throughout the Mexican territory (Escobar Valenzuela, 41–42; Bazant,
49). This latter proposal would mark a turning point in the direction
taken by political events in California, as it would lead to the creation
of the Hijar-Padrés Colonization Project, which took approximately
three hundred settlers (men, women, and children) to California in
1834. The arrival of this colony in Alta California would bring a number of liberal issues to the fore, provide an excellent opportunity for
textualizing liberal arguments in favor of secularization, and create
the conditions that would foster an incipient California nationalism.
We are particularly interested in the Californios' reading of this period of political conflict in Mexico and in their recognition of themselves as a separate national collectivity with the agential capacity to
take political action vis-à-vis what they saw as a colonization that compromised their position of dominance in the territory.

Alta California

Alta California was a crucible for liberal experimentation, especially
during the short presidency of Gómez Farías. But throughout the period from 1822 to 1846, what becomes clear is that the political cur-
rents and contradictions prevalent in Mexico were transplanted and
took root in California. As in the state of Zacatecas, the leading Californios were federalists (or "federachos," as Micheltorena's troops called
them) and highly influenced by the dominant liberal-rationalist thinking of the time, current then in the competing Masonic rites established in Mexico. Like the Mexican *escoceses* and *yorkinos*, these Californios vacillated when class and territorial interests intervened. What
else would make a federalist like Alvarado praise a conservative centralist like Bustamante while rejecting the liberal policies of federalist
Gómez Farías to colonize Alta California, or make the liberal, federalist,
and quite possibly Masonic Vallejo go against his liberal mentor Padrés?
Considering the political conflicts in Mexico and the fuzzy ideological
field, it is not surprising that economic and political interests should

in the final analysis tip the balance in California too. More than a liberal experiment, California would become almost a parodic rendition of the Mexican republic: heterogeneous, factionalized, semifeudal, racist, and marked by dissensions, shifting alliances and fragmentation of the national family, with frequent *pronunciamientos,* mock battles, and subsequent reconciliations.

In California the rise of liberal and nationalist discourses, that is, the concept of California as a nation, as *la patria* and of its native sons as *hijos del país,* comes at a moment of restructuring, during the transition from one political structure (Spain) to another (independent Mexico) and from one phase of a quasi-feudal economy to another. The liberal-rationalist framework would not accompany a total economic transformation, perhaps because the material conditions for capitalist relations of production had not yet matured, perhaps because the emergent agency—the *rancheros*—was satisfied with semifeudal property relations once becoming a landed class. The only other agency capable of transforming property relations, the Indian population, was slowly being decimated and (as we shall see in chapter 4) not then capable of a massive revolt against feudal relations of production. Liberal discourses are nevertheless the dominant framework in the Californio testimonials, serving as the ideological underpinnings, justifying revolts against appointed Mexican governors, shaping arguments for a failed attempt to declare Alta California a free and sovereign nation, and, most important, setting down the groundwork for the complex task of the secularization of the mission lands.

In order to understand the role of a liberal framework in this restructuring, we need briefly to recall the power relations within the earlier Spanish period in Alta California (1769–1822) in terms of the two contending forces vying for dominance: the Franciscan order and the military order. At the level of production, the slavelike laboring class, the Indians, is from the beginning caught between competing modes of production: the primitive mode of the non-neophyte Indians who continue to hunt, fish, and gather in the areas surrounding their *rancherías,* especially in the northern and eastern parts of the territory, and the quasi-feudal/quasi-despotic mode at work at the mission. A crucial shift in land tenancy in the 1830s will bring a concomitant shift in the power struggle, from missionaries in contention with the military to missionaries in contention with would-be *rancheros* and *hacendados,* the second generation of Californios, sons of the landless *presidio* soldiers who until recently had been the coercive arm of the missionaries.

Agents of Liberalism in Alta California

Agency as a product of liberal discourses and class consciousness is an important construct in several of the testimonials. Especially interesting in these narratives is the reconstruction of the process of politicization of the emergent class, its acquisition of an ideological framework, its collective construction of class and national antagonisms, and its willingness to take action against those perceived as antagonistic to the group's economic interests. In the final analysis, the vacillation of this emergent class of *rancheros* between various positions within the ideological field is one of the most noteworthy aspects of these testimonials.

The liberal framework was for the most part absent in Alta California until the arrival of the first Mexican governor, although the last interim Spanish governor, José Darío Argüello (who served briefly before the last Spanish governor), was said to be a "military man of liberal ideas that loved Alta California as a second homeland" (MGV, 1:119). The last Spanish governor, Pablo Vicente Solá (1815–22), a supporter of the liberal Spanish Constitution of 1812, was also said to be a man of "liberal principles" (MGV, 1:140), and very much interested in education, allowing the outstanding schoolboys, including Alvarado and M. G. Vallejo, to use his library and read the gazettes from Mexico, the liberal Spanish Constitution, and *Don Quijote* (MGV, 1:128–30). Despite this brief introduction to alternative discourses, the dominant ideological framework before 1822 in California was, by and large, of an orthodox religious and feudal nature.

The encounter of a liberal and protonationalist consciousness in Alta California was facilitated by three key individuals, all *yorkinos*, liberals, and federalists: José María Echeandía, José María Padrés, and José Figueroa. They would be instrumental in introducing the discourses of liberalism to the emergent class of young but property-less native Californios.[26]

Echeandía came to California in 1825 as the first appointed governor after Mexican independence. A lieutenant colonel in the corps of engineers and a *yorkino* appointed by a fellow Mason, President Victoria, Echeandía would have a tremendous impact on the youth of Monterey and San Diego. José de Jesús Vallejo, ten years older than his brother M. G. Vallejo, recalls that the younger generation was quite impressed with Echeandía, who offered the young Californios challenging new discourses; the older Vallejo, however, considered the governor a capricious despot, despite his education, generosity, and bravery

(JJV, 107), on the grounds of his interference at the wedding of the San Diegan Josefa Carrillo and the foreigner Henry Fitch (JJV, 108), a telling anecdote to be discussed in chapter 5.

Governor Echeandía carried out his educative mission through the creation of study groups that met at night at his residence. M. G. Vallejo recalls in his manuscript (2:164) that the governor focused on the Enlightenment in these sessions, on the importance of education for all people—be they legitimate or illegitimate children, *culto* or *inculto*, Indian or *gente de razón*. The methods were those of the Masonic lodges, but whether the young men Mariano Guadalupe Vallejo, Juan Bautista Alvarado, Juan Alvírez, José Castro, Joaquín de la Torre, or Salvador Vallejo ever became Masons is not clear. Undoubtedly M. G. Vallejo and J. B. Alvarado were deeply affected by this introduction to a new framework wholly antagonistic to the dominant ideas promulgated by the missionaries. The illiteracy of the better part of the population and the inaccessibility of books in the territory made the arrival of Echeandía, and his willingness to teach, an even more eventful moment in the education of what was to be the Californio elite. Alvarado (2:147) is clear on what Echeandía accomplished: he had instilled "the true principles of republicanism and liberty" in the California youth.

Echeandía served as governor immediately after Mexico's independence and the establishment of the Mexican republic once Iturbide, the would-be emperor, had been overthrown. It was a period opening up to liberal expectations about the future. Of particular importance to liberals in Mexico were the Spanish Constitution of 1812 (which had recognized the Indians as equal citizens, as would the Mexican Constitution of 1824) and the Spanish Cortes law in 1813 calling for the secularization of all the missions after ten years of having been established. The liberal Cortes had also decreed that the missionaries were to become parish priests, and the land was to be distributed as private property first to the Indians and then to other persons. Given the Mexican nation's civil disturbances after independence, these recommendations would not be officially adopted by the Mexican Congress but would figure prominently in all subsequent plans for secularization, notably those prepared by the Junta de Fomento de Californias, appointed by President Victoria in 1825.[27] During the next three years this commission would produce a number of proposals for the secularization of mission lands, the conversion of missions to parishes, and the distribution of mission lands to Indians, to Californio and Mexican settlers, and to soldiers and convicts. In the end the secularization act of 1833 would be approved but not Gómez Farías's 1833 colonization bill, for the Mexican Congress was too caught up with internal strife to attend to the affairs of Alta California.[28] The Junta's impact on California would nonetheless be evident in Echeandía's call for Indian emancipation in 1826 and 1828, and in the secularization act introduced by the governor in 1831 and modified in 1832, all of which would follow the Junta's recommendations (see Junta de Fomento de Californias). Although the Fomento reports were not in the public realm until 1827 (Reynolds, 289), M. G. Vallejo uses the Junta's published decrees when he has Echeandía speak in his testimonial.

To say that Echeandía's ideological framework was totally antagonistic to that of the missionaries is an understatement; still, it found a receptive audience among some of the young men who appreciated the governor's willingness to discuss ideas and instruct them. The missionaries, as far as Alvarado was concerned, were elitist and sought to withhold information, making it accessible only to the few:

> I have always been opposed to the doctrines that indirectly advocate that enlightenment is the patrimony of the few and ignorance eternally the lot of the majority of mortals. (2:41)

The governor's study groups also propitiated an analysis of Alta California, and here the youth were especially attentive. Echeandía made them aware of the slavelike conditions under which the missionaries kept the neophyte Indians, but, more important, he made them aware of property relations. The wealth of the missions, he said, belongs to the Indians "who with their personal labor had accumulated it" (MGV, 2:109). He further argued that the land occupied by the missions did not legally belong to the missionaries, though they held usufructuary rights (MGV, 2:107). In keeping with the liberal Spanish Cortes, and long before Mora, Echeandía challenged the right of the missions to this property despite the fact that the Mexican government had made it clear in its colonization law of 1824 that only vacant lands not the property of individuals, corporations, or *pueblos* could be settled (MGV, 2:108). But was it fair, Echeandía asked, that twenty-one missions should possess all the fertile lands of the peninsula while "more than a thousand families of *gente de razón* did not possess more than what the missionaries were kindly willing to allow them" (MGV, 2:107)? Echeandía had touched a chord, making it abundantly clear to the younger generation of Californios that *their* property would, must, come from the mission lands. Alvarado and Vallejo insist that it would be thanks to Echeandía that they were eventually able to say that California was free, having shaken the missionaries' domination.[29] Liberal-rationalist ideas were thus empowering and enlightening; these young men were now able to question what they saw as not only their own brainwashing but also that of the Indians. They agreed with Echeandía that the missionaries had not opened the Indians' eyes to their political rights as free men, even though Mexican independence had made them citizens. The missionaries, Alvarado (2:166) recalls, profited from the Indians' ignorance, for it allowed the missionaries to use the Indians as if they were beasts of burden or even slaves from Africa.

It was of course the Indians' emancipation, not the Californios' intellectual emancipation, that deeply disturbed the missionaries who participated in a campaign against Echeandía for his speaking to the Indians about their rights. Angustias de la Guerra de Ord, a devout Catholic whose father was the treasurer and ally of the missionaries, best expresses the missionaries' concerns when she recalls Echeandía's introduction of republican ideas and liberal policies as dangerous:

> He was a man of advanced ideas, enthusiastic and a lover of republican liberty. Certainly he put these ideas into practice; in fact, he had been sent to California to implant the new regime. Echeandía made the Indians of the mission know that they also were free and citizens. This produced a harmful effect in the Indian mind. They began to demand the practice of these rights. (Ord, 1956: 25)

Echeandía's plan in 1826 to allow mission Indians to petition to leave the mission and his proposal in 1828 to create Indian *pueblos*, with both Indian and non-Indian settlers, at the sites where the missions stood would be strenuously opposed by the missionaries and their allies. According to de la Guerra de Ord, after hearing of these plans the Indians no longer were willing to obey the missionaries "with their accustomed submission" (Ord, 1956: 25), as children should, and this was reason enough to cause alarm.

Equally pro-missionary and anti-Echeandía are the comments published by Robinson, Gleason, and de Mofras, all "in the pay of the clergy" according to Alvarado (3:208). Vallejo was adamant about the bias and ignorance of these foreigners' reports that tried to undermine the reputation of Echeandía, to his mind a warrior who had dared to counter the missionaries' self-serving policies (MGV, 2:112). Especially intolerant of Robinson's portrayal of Echeandía, Vallejo explains Robinson's calumny of this liberal man: Robinson was the son-in-law of the treasurer of the missions and he was a merchant whose business dealings with the missionaries colored his thinking and were responsible for his biases (MGV, 1:51).

Robinson undoubtedly shares the views of Friar Antonio Peyri, who regretted revolutionary changes "among a people where anarchy and confusion so generally prevailed and who, at the time, were totally unprepared for and incapable of self-government."[30] This of course has historically been the colonialist position on independence movements of the Third World, for imperialists never see the colonized as capable of self-determination. In writing their testimonials Vallejo and Alvarado were fully aware of Robinson's unfavorable portrayal of Californios, especially of the men. What Robinson said of the people of San José in his published account is typical:

> The men are generally indolent and addicted to many vices, caring little for the welfare of their children, who, like themselves, grow up unworthy members of society. (73)

His attitude is ethnocentric and classist, looking down on the "rude Californians" who do not know the difference between sauce and soup (131). However indolent, unworthy, and given to vices he may have found the men, the women he found beautiful and known for their "chastity, industrious habits, and correct deportment" (73). Perhaps his marriage to a native daughter of California explains his willingness to make exceptions and cast the Californio women as more tractable subjects for interaction. (The testimonials' reconstruction of this and other intermarriages will be discussed in chapter 5.)

In his work, Robinson describes Echeandía as the individual who by initiating the secularization of the missions placed them "in danger of immediate subversion and ruin. Through the encouragement of Echeandía, vice of all kinds had become prevalent, and the poor misguided Indians saw in the terms *libre* and *independente* [sic] a sort of license for the indulgence of every passion" (97). Robinson was of course concerned that the source of hides, tallow, and pelts would disappear if the Indians "abandoned their labor" (97) and refused to produce for the missionaries. For this reason alone he obviously perceived the Indians' emancipation as only leading to chaos. Echeandía's plan to form *pueblos* at each mission was equally alarming, although this proposal was never approved by the Mexican Congress. At Echeandía's departure from California, Robinson remarks: "What a scourge he had been to California! What an instigator of vice!... The seeds of dishonor sown by him will never be extirpated so long as there remains a Mission to rob or a treasury to plunder!" (141). Clearly, foreign merchants who profited greatly in their exclusive dealings with the missionaries for tallow and hides saw no problem trading for surplus extracted from what for all intents and purposes was slave labor. As Dana recalls in his memoirs, a California hide was worth two or three times what was paid for it in goods on the capitalist market:

> Their hides ... which they value at two dollars in money, they barter for something which costs seventy-five cents in Boston; and buy shoes (as like as not made of their own hides, which have been carried twice round Cape Horn) at three and four dollars, and "chicken-skin boots" at fifteen dollars a pair.[31]

Alvarado too assures us in his text that Hartnell made a profit of 600 percent off the hides (2:74). Undoubtedly California was a good business for the foreign traders, and they had a vested interest in the continuance of the status quo.

The other purveyor of liberal-rationalist ideas was José María Padrés, who first came to Alta California in 1830 as assistant inspector of the troops after serving in Baja California as lieutenant of the corps of engineers and as first secretary and later *subjefe político* at Loreto after Echeandía's departure. There, it was said, he had threatened to flog a priest who had taken the wife of an Indian chief as his concubine (Alvarado, 2:174). In California he would also serve as inspector of customs and participate in formulating Echeandía's plan for secularization of the missions. He too was a member of the *yorkino* faction (Alvarado, 2:174) and considered a troublemaker and an enemy by the missionaries, who were aware that he had played a prominent role in the preparation of a law in Congress exiling all Spaniards (Hutchinson, 136). Guerra de Ord, as might be expected, remembers him as an "ultraradical" man "with very liberal ideas" (Ord, 1956: 22). Coronel, whose family had known Padrés for many years and would accompany him to California in 1834, remembers him as a liberal and a republican, much like his commander Echeandía, for which reason he was strongly disliked by the conservative pro-missionary faction and by the monarchist missionaries (Coronel, 2). In a letter to Vice President Bustamante in 1831, Friar Durán indicated that he suspected Padrés of organizing Masons in California (letter quoted in Hutchinson, 145), but the national government did not remove Padrés despite accusations from the next governor, Manuel Victoria, who was seen by the Californios as an ally of the missionaries and the conservative sector in California. In 1831 Padrés was deported by Victoria for professing and inculcating "dangerous doctrines that were a threat to the tranquillity of the country" (MGV, 2:261). Victoria himself would be deposed at the end of that year.

While he was in California, Padrés, like Echeandía, served as mentor to a number of young Californios, among them M. G. Vallejo, Alvarado, Joaquín Ortega, and Antonio María Osio (Alvarado, 2:172–73). Alvarado (3:28) recalls that Padrés and the young Vallejo had been close friends, and both Alvarado's and Vallejo's testimonials speak of Padrés as the leader of their circle (MGV, 2:260, 265). Alvarado in fact calls his uncle Vallejo "Padrés's pupil" (3:28–29). Padrés offered them an analysis of the mission system and made known to them the findings of the Junta de Fomento of 1825, quoted by Vallejo in his memoirs (MGV, 2:259). Padrés also made them aware of political liberalism and stressed the point that the neophyte Indians were no better than slaves:

> The way in which we treat the neophytes is more akin to that of a slaveholder than to that of a good Christian who educates those considered worthy of being brought up to the level of our civilization. (MGV, 2:260)

After three centuries of colonialism the status of the Indians continued to be a polemical issue in Mexico despite the fact that the Mexican Constitution of 1824 had recognized them as citizens. Mexican society did not construct them as equals and continued to see them as uncivilized subordinates, incapable of rising to the level of the *gente de razón*. By maintaining a racist/caste closure that conveniently excluded the indigenous population from all spheres of power, the Mexicans and Californios alike ensured the Indians' subordination and exploitation as the laboring class. Now, however, the young second-generation Californios were willing to consider "the oppression of the Indian" as a construct that might justify dismantling the mission system and in so doing promote their own incipient political aspirations:

> Of course the young men allied themselves with the bold preacher of doctrines that were in harmony with our own progressive and philanthropic outlook. (MGV, 2:261)

When Padrés was ordered out of California, he promised to return with orders to secularize the missions and, significantly, to place several young Californios as administrators of the missions:

> He had assured his young friends that he would return with the authority to secularize the missions, which he had promised to place under the management of several young Californios, whose moral and material support he said he considered indispensable to carry out his project. (Alvarado, 3:29)

Padrés indeed returned to California with the Hijar-Padrés colonization project in 1834, as director of the colony and as inspector of the
troops, but despite his close ties to the younger generation, especially
Vallejo and Juan Bandini, he found little support for his plans.

Through contact with Echeandía, Padrés, visitors like the German
merchant Henry Virmond from Acapulco, and others who regularly
visited California for trade and brought news (and sometimes newspapers) of the political and economic conflicts in Mexico, the Californio youth became aware of political affairs in Mexico City and the
rest of the country, especially with regard to the Masonic lodges. Alvarado, Salvador Vallejo, José Fernández, José de Jesús Vallejo, and M.
G. Vallejo all refer concretely to the Masonic affiliation of their mentors. "Los Californios de erudición," as M. G. Vallejo called his elite
group (MGV, 3:57), knew of antagonisms between *yorkinos* and *escoceses*, between liberals and conservatives, between republicans and monarchists. Although much influenced by these three *yorkinos*, by 1875
Vallejo is, in retrospect, ready to condemn the manipulation of these
Masonic groups by imperialist forces and to blame the lodges for
political strife in the Mexican republic (MGV, 2:54). Despite the distance of Alta California from the Mexican capital, M. G. Vallejo's comments reveal an awareness of foreign intervention in Mexican affairs
through both Masonic lodges. His liberalism and republicanism are
equally evident in his aversion to the support given by the missionaries and the *escoceses* to plans to install a European monarch on Moc-
tezuma's throne (MGV, 3:280). Also implicit here is the notion that
these political cleavages are to be blamed for the country's failure to
modernize.

Not all Californios were federalists, liberals, and republicans. The
center of reactionary thought was Santa Barbara, which, as Alvarado
recalls, was dominated by Guerra y Noriega, a Spaniard by origin, and
he, by the missionaries: "that *pueblo* [Santa Barbara] was dominated by
Captain Noriega, who in turn was a protégé of the friars" (Alvarado,
2:219). Guerra y Noriega always referred to Vallejo as the "heretic,"
even though Vallejo argued that he had never been an enemy of the
clergy (MGV, 3:407, 412). No one, of course, believed him. But in addition to a few conservative resident Californios, especially at the highest military levels, there were always a number of Mexican officers
and administrators in the territory, most of whom spent only short periods of time in California. They came accompanying the governors
and were often conservative and pro-missionary. The perception of
both conservative and liberal non-Californios as potential usurpers and

rivals in the struggle for economic and political power would eventually lead to a fragmentation of liberals along "national" lines.

The emergence of these liberal-rationalist discourses has to be linked, however, not only to collective and personal interaction with these Masonic mentors but to interpellation by print literature as well. Throughout Alta California illiteracy was the norm and not the exception, there were no public schools, and until 1834 there was a lack of varied reading material, yet nonetheless among the literate population a collective sense developed of being federalists, liberals, and republicans. This "imagined community" was constructed in conditions unfavorable to discourses countering theological-political notions of people's place in the world. The little schooling provided for boys at the *presidios* by older soldiers who themselves were ill-prepared and could offer no more than catechism and the basics, was really not conducive to the construction of this identity (Alvarado, 4). The situation for girls was worse. If lucky, they were sent to women like Apolinaria Lorenzana for catechism, basic reading and writing, and sewing lessons (Lorenzana, 5). She had learned to read at a Mexican orphanage before coming to Alta California, where she taught herself to write (Lorenzana, 4). So resentful is Vallejo of the state's neglect of education that he devotes an entire section in his memoirs to the deplorable training that he, Alvarado, José Castro, and other second-generation Californios received (MGV, 1:128, 255, 276–77). Vallejo recognized and wanted his readers to recognize that in the area of education, the situation had not been much better anywhere in the world at the beginning of the nineteenth century; in Spain and in the Spanish colonies, as well as in the United States, "education was the privilege of a select few, and ignorance, the patrimony of the majority of the inhabitants" (MGV, 1:179). Not until 1834 when Hartnell and Reverend Short established an institute in Monterey did a good school even exist, but the venture proved unprofitable and the school closed in 1836.

The at best rudimentary education available before 1834 would have severely handicapped Vallejo's and Alvarado's development but for the precedent first set by Vallejo's father,[32] a literate soldier who left copious notes on the early settlements, missions, and *presidios*, and the direction provided to the young Californios by their liberal mentors and their books.[33] The acquisition of reading material in Alta California was in general difficult, and there was a notable absence of texts of a liberal nature as a result of the missionaries' scrutiny of all written material that arrived from Mexico or elsewhere. In the early nineteenth century the Spanish Inquisition's *censura eclesiástica* was still very much alive:

> The missionary fathers were adamantly opposed to the circulation of books among us that might inspire liberal ideas and knowledge of the rights of free men in young people; they knew that books were the most fearsome emissaries of the goddess of liberty and consequently were relentless in trying to stop their circulation among us. (MGV, 3:109–10)

Books that the Californio José Antonio Carrillo, who had studied for a time in Mexico as did the sons of some of the wealthier families, had sent to California were on one occasion burned upon arrival—not even Echeandía tried to stop that *auto de fé* (MGV, 3:110). Carrillo, twelve years older than his cousin Vallejo, used to say that books were "the silent propagators of learning and illustration" (MGV, 3:110).

M. G. Vallejo, whose family had not had the means to send him to Mexico for an education, willingly risked excommunication in 1831 in order to become "the owner of the best library that until then existed in the Californias" (MGV, 3:111). Upon learning that Virmond's recently arrived frigate *Leonor* was to be boarded the next morning in Monterey by authorities in search of contraband, specifically to confiscate a small library said to be on board, Vallejo took a boat out to the ship at night to warn Fitch and Virmond and to offer to buy the books for one hundred hides and ten boots of tallow. Vallejo shared his books with Alvarado and Castro, but once it was known (through Castro's lover, who confessed it to the priest) that the library included works by Rousseau and Voltaire, and other liberal and anti-Catholic texts, in addition to books about Greek and Roman history and literature, the three young Californios were excommunicated for reading banned books (MGV, 3:111–12). Alvarado recalls with both glee and pride how he turned the tables on the missionaries at the time by arguing that he was precluded from turning over funds sent to Friar Durán as no Catholic could have dealings with one who was excommunicated. In the end, this maneuver directed at the mission's purse would bring about absolution for the three upstart Californios (Alvarado, 2:35–36). The three were allowed to continue reading as long as they made sure that Rousseau and Voltaire did not get into the wrong hands (MGV, 3:115–16). The entire episode had proved to be traumatic for the young men's families, but once the ban of excommunication was lifted, Vallejo would be able to write his fiancée Francisca Benicia in San Diego to let her know that he was no longer considered a heretic (MGV, 3:118). In 1834 a well-stocked library would come with the arrival of the Hijar-Padrés colony (Alvarado, 2:229) and thereafter, under liberal Mexican rule, the flow of reading matter into Alta California would no longer be problematic.

The third and last mentor of the second-generation Californios is José Figueroa, appointed governor and *comandante general* of California in 1833. His importance is not so much at the level of providing a philosophical/political framework, which Echeandía and Padrés had already made theirs, but rather in the manipulation of these liberal discourses to construct a counterargument to policies that the governor considered detrimental to Indian interests and to the Californios' own property aspirations. Figueroa would textualize these liberal discourses in his *Manifiesto,* published in Alta California, and in this way disseminate, even after his death, discourses that the Californios would make their own, as is amply evident in the testimonials. The new governor arrived after an uprising of Californio *sureños,* supported by Echeandía and Vallejo, succeeded in ousting Governor Victoria. Alvarado (2:190) recalls that the *yorkino* Echeandía was happy to hear of Figueroa's appointment, in view of the new appointee's *yorkino* affiliation, but the supporters of Zamorano, members of the *escocés* lodge, had an opposite reaction. For the young native sons who were without property and consequently interested in a shift in land tenancy in California, Figueroa meant the reintroduction of liberal policies in California. Called "el Aristides americano" and considered by both Alvarado and Vallejo to be the best governor that California ever had, Figueroa would be pivotal in the implementation of the secularization process initiated by Echeandía and halted by Victoria. The realignment of liberal discourses would be triggered by a major political conflict that erupted during Figueroa's governorship.

The acquisition of liberal-rationalist discourses constituted an important learning stage in the political development of second-generation Californios, as evidenced in their testimonials. Even Pío Pico acknowledges that when he heard the merchant Luis Bringas in Los Angeles refuse to be interrogated by a military officer during Echeandía's administration, arguing that "the civilians were the sacred core of the nation" and not required to declare before a military authority, he was so struck with this notion of civil rights that the next day he refused to go on an errand for the captain of the San Diego *presidio,* because he realized "that the citizens were the nation and that no military was superior to us" (1973: 34–35). The streak of independence and rebelliousness that characterizes the actions of Pico, José Antonio Carrillo, and Juan Bandini during the entire Mexican period can no doubt be tied to the introduction of liberal — and for others heretical — discourses.

Secularization

Secularization as a process of dismantling the mortmain property of the missionaries actually began as a movement within the church as early as 1554, with secular orders (priests) seeking to replace the regular orders (friars) within the parishes.[34] Throughout Latin America in the eighteenth century, little secularization took place, despite two royal decrees. In Alta California the process of secularization would be the trial balloon set off by Mexican liberals in their aim to restructure property relations (i.e., to appropriate and privatize church lands). Land tenancy has not always figured as the central consideration in studies of California's mission secularization, as is clear in the work of the historian Servín, who finds that it was particular Franciscan traits, like "zeal for Indian conversion" and "inflexibility," that "would bring them into conflict with civilian authorities, would arouse the jealousy of the non-aborigine, and would thereby ultimately contribute to the dispossession of their own missions" (1965: 135). As we shall argue, the personal traits of the Franciscans are largely irrelevant, for concrete economic and political interests as much in Mexico as in California will be behind the push for secularization. This political struggle for property rights would be carried out first within the ideological field.

The Franciscan friars established twenty-one missions in Alta California and controlled most of the coastal lands; one mission's lands were said to end where the next one's began. Beyond the land occupied by the mission itself, which included the church, housing for the priests and young neophytes, storerooms, and rooms for crafts and other industries, as well as the garden, vineyards, and orchards, were the mission *ranchos*, where mission livestock could graze. The friars, as Echeandía indicated, held the lands by occupation; no legal document granted title or designated the limits or boundaries of any mission. The missionaries coming to Alta California in 1769 had taken possession of the land in the name of the king (MGV, 1:53) and held it by use (MGV, 2:107). In fact, as originally set out, the missionaries were to be in charge of the missions, temporalities, and Indians for a period of ten years, after which the mission Indians were to be free (P. Vallejo, 23; Alvarado, 2:160). Previous Spanish governors had already foreseen, however, that the missionaries would not be overly interested in freeing the Indians, just as they were not concerned with doing away with coercive restraints and the corporal punishment of the mission Indians (Servín, 1965: 139).

Like the church in Mexico, the mission was a most powerful institution in Alta California and, since 1769, opposed both to the founding of *pueblos* and the concession of land to individuals. The golden dream of the missionaries, says Alvarado, was for a monastic colony (2:220). According to Servín, this opposition to *rancho* settlement was based on "a wish to pursue their spiritual labors untrammeled and unhindered" (1965: 137). But the Californios rightfully saw other than spiritual interests behind these mission colonies where the friars controlled the circulation of ideological discourses and all production. The missionaries themselves would make quite clear their economic interests by the wholesale slaughter of mission cattle upon learning that they would be dispossessed, as we shall see in chapter 4.

The impetus for the beginning of secularization can at least in part be traced to the liberal Spanish Cortes of 1812–13, to their prohibition of flogging of the Indians and their call for the secularization of the missions and the recognition of the Indians as full citizens (Junta de Fomento de Californias, 290; Alvarado, 1:189). The actual implementation of these measures would not begin until after Mexican independence. When Echeandía arrived in California in 1825, with specific orders to secularize the missions and emancipate the Indians, he found the missions still following the pre-Cortes Spanish system and restricting the neophytes to the *reducciones* of the mission. The purpose of the mission, said the liberal Echeandía, still was and had always been to tame but not to enlighten the Indian (MGV, 2:106). In view of the Indians' continued subjection in California missions, the Junta de Fomento, created for the development of the two Californias (Baja and Alta), had proposed that a new system be instituted that could "civilize them without coercion." In recognizing that the lands were the former Indian village sites (Junta de Fomento de Californias, 300), the Junta envisioned the process of secularization—at least in theory—as a return of the lands to the rightful owners, the Indians.

The recommendations of the Junta are the source of much of the liberal debate alluded to in these testimonials in relation to secularization and land distribution. Addressing the issue of property rights, the Junta acknowledged that the Indians did not have the same concept of ownership, but emphasized that they could not on that account "be denied the right they have to the soil on which they were born" (Junta de Fomento de Californias, 300). Interestingly, from the point of view of political practices, providing the Indians with the construct of private property was to be the first step. Vallejo mentions one incident in which this conceptual difference was made clear. He recounts that on one occasion an American immigrant wishing to express his appreciation for aid received from the Suysun Indians indicated that he would put in a good word for them so that they could receive land. The Suysuns' reply was that the governor of California had no lands in the north to give them, for all the lands belonged to their tribe and that, on the contrary, "it was they as owners of the land who could concede land to the government and not the other way around" (MGV, 4:103–4). In this particular case, the Indians' collective concept of possession of the entire northern frontier stood in sharp contrast to the Californios' and foreigners' legal notion of "private property." Of course, Vallejo did not recognize any "natural right" of the Indians to the land, but he did recognize the neophytes' contractual rights to mission lands as stipulated by the king, who entrusted mission lands to the missionaries on behalf of the Indians. Vallejo would later be authorized to grant northern Indian lands to incoming or relocating settlers (Alvarado, 2:199), and would do so.

In effect, the Junta would articulate the land rights of the Indians with the land needs of the Californios, but in the process leave out the emancipation of the Indians. In principle, after secularization land was to be distributed in accordance to a plan that favored the neophytes, the Christian Indians — old and new. The Junta left the formulation and implementation of the specific plan up to both Indians and interested settlers. Rather ambiguously it called for a distribution to be "arranged between them [the Indians] and the settlers, in proportions suited to their respective and peculiar circumstances," but the Junta also specified that the neophytes were to remain in "community life," i.e., at the mission (Junta de Fomento de Californias, 300). Their liberty, then, was to be conditional. Not every Californio or Mexican who requested land was to be given any, however — only those who were willing and could till the soil. Allotments were also to be made available for foreign colonists [Junta de Fomento de Californias, 300). The plan called for a *gradual* distribution of common mission lands lest the mission find itself unable to provide for a large number of neophytes and catechumens. The Junta also foresaw the need to proceed slowly in view of the "very backwardness of the neophytes of the mission" (306); for this reason the missionaries were to remain in the missions as "spiritual administrators," that is, as parish priests, not as administrators of the properties. The government was to assume the administration of the temporalities.

The Junta's recommendation was a typical liberal plan that indirectly sanctioned continued Indian servitude on the *ranchos* and *haciendas* that would be created as a result of secularization, as occurred throughout Latin America.[35] Its liberal policy, evident in its call for state appropriation and administration of ecclesiastical property and in its attempt to create private property owners through the distribution of mission lands, also implicitly recognized the Indians as citizens and as individuals with a right to property. At the same time, it was paternalistic and conservative in seeking to maintain the status quo of the Indians by keeping them in tutelage within a state-administered "community." Although never fully put into action, the Junta's general plan would serve as the basis for the Mexican government's secularization bill of 1833 and the Gómez Farías colonization bill presented before the Mexican Congress in 1833 (bill appended to Hutchinson, 408–18). More important, it would serve as Figueroa's blueprint for secularization. Differences between the three documents, as well as differences with reference to the 1824 colonization law that excluded mission lands from colonization and the 1828 colonization regulation that suspended colonization of mission lands for the time being (Hutchinson, 308), would be the grounds for the heated debate that was to ensue in Alta California.

In view of Indian insurrections in Alta California in 1824 (Lugo, 189) and the disaffection of the neophytes, Echeandía saw an urgent need to initiate secularization and to present the national government with a viable recommendation approved by the territorial Diputación. His call for emancipation of the Indians in 1826 would be amended in 1828 by a plan for the creation of Indian *pueblos* where the missions stood. A revised version of the latter would be the basis for the 1831 plan for secularization that was finally approved by the Diputación but never implemented, given the arrival of the new governor appointed by Bustamante, Manuel Victoria. A conservative supporter of the mission system, Victoria chose to ignore the secularization plan and instituted military rule, disregarding the Diputación as well as all municipal councils. One of Victoria's first acts upon arrival was to deport Padrés, who was considered a key player and principal agent in the writing of the secularization decree. By the end of 1831 Victoria was overthrown, and Pío Pico, Echeandía, and Zamorano were left in control of the territory.

Appointed in 1832, General José Figueroa arrived in 1833 as the new governor of California. Before his early death in September 1835, competing liberal plans for secularization would reveal serious inconsistencies and contradictions in the ideological field. Like Echeandía, Figueroa had been sent to Alta California with the precedent of the 1825 Junta recommendation and the 1824 and 1828 colonization regulations promoting settlement of vacant lands but exempting colonization of mission lands. The subsequent Gómez Farías secularization law, approved in late 1833 after his taking over from Santa Anna, and a colonization bill, not approved before Gómez Farías was ousted, would set in motion the liberal fragmentation that was to follow. The second measure dealing with colonization would have authorized land distribution, but the secularization bill simply created church parishes and converted the missions into secular institutions to be administered by the government. The colonization bill reflected the recommendations of the Junta and would have allowed for the distribution of land among Indian families, the military ("in arrears in their pay"), residents of California, new Mexican colonists, foreign families, directors of colonization projects, and convicts wishing to reside in California after completing their sentences. The measure as drafted placed limits on the amount of land that could be distributed to each individual; only those having fewer than the fifty-two acres specified in the act were to be entitled to land (bill translated and reprinted in Hutchinson, 408–18). In a territory where cattle raising was the primary form of production, this ceiling on the amount of land to be distributed ran counter to the views and aspirations of the land-hungry Californios and was consequently opposed by them. Article 25 of this bill called for the appointment by the governor of a director of colonization, who with subordinate commissioners would be in charge of the distribution of lands, cattle, and implements (Hutchinson, 416). Although the colonization bill was not passed, its content was known and would be the basis for debate in Alta California. In the meantime Figueroa began in 1833 a gradual program of secularization, distributing some land to the Indians at San Juan Bautista and San Antonio (Alvarado, 2:215–16), and fostered settlement, especially of the northern areas around San Rafael, by providing lands to foreigners as well as to Californios and Mexicans who wished to relocate in the north.

The various documents dealing with secularization and colonization, whether produced by the Spanish Cortes, the Mexican Junta, or Congress, would give rise to a number of competing liberal discourses, intersected as they were by other discourses within the ideological field. Aside from important differences within the liberal camp, the basic antagonism in the ideological arena had always been between the conservative mission supporters and the liberals who recognized the mission as an institution of coercive domination and advocated secularization. The conservatives, wishing to maintain the status quo, agreed with the head of the Fernandinos, Friar Durán, who was convinced that the experiment would fail, as the Indians were lazy and given to vices if unsupervised, and argued that their emancipation would only lead to servitude on the *ranchos*. The Indians, it was said, *needed* the protection of the missionaries (Alvarado, 2:92). Cleavages in the liberal camp hinged on the status of the Indian's right to private property (economic liberalism) and right to political equality (political liberalism) (see Mouffe, 1988a: 32). Two variants of these positions are reconstructed in the Californio testimonials by supporters of Governor Figueroa and by his adversaries in this case, fellow *yorkino* José María Padrés and José María Hijar. The latter was first appointed, then remanded, governor and with Padrés (slated to be the *comandante general* if Figueroa continued ill) headed the colonization project sent to California in 1834 by Vice President Gómez Farías. Both liberal positions are ultimately strategies for the appropriation of mission-held space.

California testimonial reconstructions of the disagreement over the issue of land ownership and land distribution are wrought with disjunctures and fissures that reveal critical differences over whether to transform or maintain existing property relations. More specifically, the overlapping of liberal and conservative positions characterizes the California ideological struggle, as it did in Mexico, where liberal positions on secularization also varied widely. The more economically progressive position claimed to be grounded in political rights, for now that the Indians were citizens, argued *letrados* like Mora, they had to be treated as equal citizens and integrated into society. Arguing that any kind of compensatory legislation implied that the Indian was inferior, Mora proposed that the government eliminate the distinction between Indian and non-Indian, replacing caste with a simplified category distinguishing rich and poor (Hutchinson, 171). Mora did not see any state responsibility for the social inequality produced by centuries of colonial oppression and marginalization. Once independence had brought legal equality, it was up to those able and qualified to profit from the new opportunities.[36] Sounding very much like present-day critics of affirmative action, Mora found the Indians to be themselves to blame for their lack of "progress" (Mora, 1984: 76); his only solution to the problem was his recommendation for the introduction of European, preferably Hispanic and Catholic, immigrants and the "whitening" of the population through miscegenation (Archivo, 35:151). In effect, the entire Mexican ruling class favored the fragmentation of Indian communities and feared their political potential and their capacity to organize, as occurred a few years later in the caste wars of Yucatán (Archivo, 35:72; Hale, 244). Clearly racist/caste discourses underpin all of Mora's proposals. The root objective of economic liberals like Mora and others was the appropriation of church and Indian communal lands to create small property owners and in that way develop a republic of small farmers (Ruiz, 190). These liberals, however, were too respectful of private property to consider expropriating the large landed estates owned by a minority (Hale, 228, 233), and they were also aware that "protection" of the Indians and their lands implied limiting the availability of land, a policy that would have hindered capitalist development of the country (Ruiz, 197; Hale, 180).

Some liberals in Mexico who were also hostile to communally held property saw the need to distribute the land to the Indians while others reaffirmed the right of the Indian communities to hold land (Hale, 227, 232). Some, like Juan Rodríguez Puebla, were early *indigenistas* who favored separate educational curricula for Indians to enable them to study their history and culture (Hale, 218). These took a more "affirmative action" stance, but were the exception; most liberals advocated close tutelage (Hale, 233). This paternalistic position matched that taken by the Junta de Fomento, which, considering that mission life had imposed a number of constraints on the Indians without providing them either with the proper compensation or understanding of a liberal social contract, proposed that the Indians be retained in communal life. These positions would be at the heart of the Hijar-Padrés conflict with Figueroa, with Hijar taking Mora's position and Figueroa that of liberals favoring tutelage. Neither side had a coherent program of integration for the neophytes or any plan for overcoming centuries of servitude and political disempowerment. Historically it has become clear that nineteenth-century Mexican liberals like Mora favoring the creation of a new propertied class through the dispossession of the Indians ultimately won the political battle, perhaps not then, but definitely a few years later under the Juárez administration. What is also clear is that although the more general "indigenista" discourses offered by Figueroa would continue to be echoed throughout the nineteenth and twentieth centuries they too would serve, as Mariátegui pointed out in reference to Peru, to maintain the Indian in a subaltern status. Both ideological positions framed by liberal-rationalist discourses intersected and collided with other ideological discourses and both would be proffered in Alta California to legitimate dispossession of the Indians. Only one position, however, would enable the state to create large privately owned landed estates in Alta California with a subservient labor force, and that position would be espoused by a good many of the ascendant Californios.

The Hijar-Padrés colony would be the liberals' experimental probe into "missionary-infested" terrain to assess the feasibility of appropriation of church lands in Mexico and the viability of a colony of small farms. To expedite matters before the end of Gómez Farías's ten-month term as interim president, an emergency bill introduced by Juan Bandini, the California representative to Congress, was approved that authorized the government to use every means necessary, including the estates of the Pious Fund, to ensure the colonization and secularization of the missions of Baja and Alta California (Alvarado, 2:226–29; Coronel, 5; Hutchinson, 190). This bill, which was in effect extracted from article 29 of the 1833 colonization bill that was never approved, was rapidly passed, enabling Gómez Farías to obtain a loan to pay travel expenses of the "colonos" who were to be part of the California experiment.

The role of Alta California until then had been as a penal colony and land of exile, but the territory was now to receive a group of colonists made up of teachers, artisans, craftsworkers, and farmers. This was exactly what the Californios had been asking for and continued to request years later, as evident in Vallejo's letter to the minister of war in 1841, asking for a large number of Mexican settlers, preferably artisans, to come to California to counterbalance an increasing number of U.S. immigrants (MGV, 4:233–34). Ironically, and for reasons tied to the administration and distribution of newly secularized lands, the Californios' reaction to the Hijar-Padrés colony would not be favorable in 1834 (MGV, 3:21).

The Hijar-Padrés colonization project would not be the only enterprise developed for California by liberal parties. While in Mexico, the San Diegan Bandini organized a commercial venture to establish a trade company in California. The plan was for this stock company to develop agriculture and manufacturing in California and promote its products on the world market. Among the shareholders were Padrés and other former California residents, such as Luis de Castillo Negrete and José María Herrera. A capitalist venture based on wage labor and increased productivity, the Cosmopolitan Company would at the same time improve transportation and foster colonization of the territory (MGV, 2:226, 243).[37]

The Hijar-Padrés settlers set out just at the moment that Gómez Farías was turning over the presidency to Santa Anna. Possibly for this reason Gómez Farías's written instructions authorizing Hijar and Padrés to secularize and take over the mission lands were rather brief and unclear. The assumption was that Hijar would be the new governor and Padrés the new *comandante general*, but by the time of their arrival Santa Anna, perhaps fearing, as Coronel (15) assumes, that the liberals ultimately wanted the territory to secede from Mexico, had revoked Hijar's appointment and asked Figueroa to continue as governor.[38] Padrés also found Figueroa in better health and not ready to relinquish his position as *comandante general*. What had started out as a promising venture quickly collapsed. Even the trade company, within a few months of its arrival, saw its ship the *Natalia* totally destroyed after crashing against the rocks, putting an end to the commercial venture. Shortly thereafter the leaders of the colonization project would be accused of conspiracy against the territorial government and deported. The colonists, however, would stay and serve as catalysts for a number of reforms in the territory.

These events take up considerable space in Vallejo's memoirs in volumes 2 and 3. Vallejo reproduces Figueroa's *Manifiesto* to provide the governor's position on the Hijar-Padrés affair and includes Hijar's responses to the governor's letters as well as his own comments explaining in part his role, as the commanding officer of the Sonoma *presidio*, in the arrest of the conspirators. That these three hundred colonists, men, women, and children who were going to settle in a relatively isolated area, were in fact plotting against Figueroa is unlikely, but their being armed played into the hands of Governor Figueroa, who was especially bent on being rid of the leaders of the colonization project.[39] The basic point of contention between colonists and Figueroa was the refusal of the latter and the territorial Diputación to turn over the mission lands to the colonization company on the grounds that the orders from the national government did not specifically indicate that the "administrators of the colony" should be in charge of secularization (MGV, 2:219). Even the never-approved Gómez Farías bill could be read as calling for a director who would allocate the land, livestock, and implements without also being appointed to secularize the missions, a necessary first step. Presumably, as Figueroa argued, only the governor had the power to secularize and appoint administrators; thus, once Hijar's appointment as governor had been revoked, he no longer had this power. Settlement, if it were to proceed, had to be done on vacant lands, especially in the north where it was important to establish settlements to ward off further incursions by the Russians and by American and British trappers.

Throughout this entire episode we have to distinguish between the legal and the ethical reasoning, documented in the *Manifiesto*, that Figueroa employed to justify his rejection of Hijar's proposal that the missions be turned over to him; such reasoning underscores the economic liberalism behind the Diputación's support for Figueroa's stance. Only Coronel, one of the colonists, questions the governor's motives, accuses the customs officer Angel Ramírez of being behind Figueroa's decision (Coronel, 15), and blames Vallejo for charging them with conspiracy in Sonoma. It is interesting that the main protagonists in this conflict were all liberals with Masonic ties; all were anticlerical, all were in favor of secularization, and all espoused the demographic and economic development of California. Their differences were in relation to property rights and political power, but all used an "enlightened" perspective on the plight of the Indians as a discursive strategy to defend their positions. Figueroa's argument was additionally positivistic and assumed an evolutionary development, with the Indians at a lower stage needing protection and assistance to develop to a higher stage. In a territory where the Indians represented the laboring class in Alta California, the real issue centered on wage labor on small *ranchos* or peonage on large *haciendas*. The crux of the matter was the mode of production, but the more immediate concern was the ongoing maintenance of the territorial administration, the soldiers, the missionaries, and other church officials, all dependent on the surplus labor of the neophyte Indians. Without the missions, whether as religious or secular institutions, there was no surplus production to call upon, no "captive" labor force to meet the needs of the entire California population (Figueroa, quoted in Hutchinson, 239). Figueroa's stance merely forestalled the inevitable by maintaining the status quo. Finally, yet another level to all this argumentation sheds light on why it is so extensively dealt with in the testimonials: when reconstructed in the 1870s, defense of the "possessors" of the land, the Indians, would serve as a trope for the situation of the now dispossessed Californios.

For the Californios, who argue strongly in support of Figueroa in most cases, the entire Hijar-Padrés plan was ill conceived, as the particular skills of the settlers were not those of pioneers who could survive in the isolated northern areas. They were not farmers (MGV, 2:310), and here again inability or unwillingness to till the land would serve, as much in the United States as in Mexico, as justification for not granting land to would-be settlers. What was left to the Hijar-Padrés colonists was to settle piecemeal in existing populated areas where they could find work (MGV, 2:347). Salvador Vallejo, José de Jesús Vallejo, M. G.

Vallejo, José Fernández, and Alvarado all agree with Figueroa and repeatedly point out that the colonists' urban skills were fit for cities and towns but not for undeveloped areas (MGV, 2:348). They had come with unrealistic expectations, the Californios argue, foolishly leaving their trades and property in Mexico City and Veracruz to seek their fortunes in California, expecting to be served and catered to upon their arrival by Indians and Californios alike (Fernández, 82). This sarcastic perspective is reiterated by several Californios apparently unwilling to recognize that these colonists were the very type of settlers that California needed to continue to develop—something M. G. Vallejo acknowledged years later. They were carpenters, farmworkers, silversmiths, tailors, shoemakers, hat makers, musicians, and medical attendants; two were printers. Especially critical for Alta California were the number of teachers who came with the colony, as Ord (1956: 30) recognized. The colonization project should have been supported by the Californios of "advanced ideas" as it is obvious that the settlers were liberal and reasonably educated individuals who had been hand-picked by the Californios' friend and mentor Padrés. Why then, forty years later, knowing full well that almost all of the settlers had stayed and done well—and in fact had in some cases become the most trusted friends (as seen in the relationship between Vallejo and his secretary Víctor Prudón)—did the narrators of these testimonials continue to criticize Padrés and Hijar so harshly? Why had the Californios stood with Figueroa against the leaders of the colonization project?

At one level, the Californios give exactly the same explanations provided by Figueroa: Hijar and Padrés had come to despoil and enslave the Indians, as Vallejo indicated (MGV, 2:349). But despite their calling on these discourses of political equality, clearly the reason for their support of Figueroa was tied to the concrete economic interests of the Californios vis-à-vis the colonists, whom they saw as potential usurpers of their own emergent status as the elite. Looking back on the episode in the 1870s, in view of the loss of Californio lands, economic liberalism needed to be wedded to "property" rights, for again it was critical to defend the position of "the rightful owners," the rights of "native sons" to the territory. The Indians' rights to their property, as Fernández (70, 78) indicates, could not be violated, no matter how uncivilized they were, lest everyone else's rights also be violated. Yes, the issue in 1875 was still land, more specifically, property rights, just as it had been in 1834, only the players then were different.

Thus in 1834 more was at stake than a debate of two positions on secularization; as in 1875, economic liberalism and emergent "national" interests were also at issue. These antagonisms led the Californios to break with their mentor Padrés, specifically, it is said, over the appointment of administrators to oversee the mission estates and the distribution of the mission lands and temporalities. Hijar and Padrés claimed to have been authorized to take over the mission lands and appoint their own administrators to supervise the mission properties. Upon hearing the rumor that among the newly arrived Mexican colonists were twenty-one administrators who had been handpicked by Padrés for the missions, Vallejo recalls, he and others resolved to back Figueroa against his rivals (MGV, 2:262).[40] As Alvarado notes, they were not foolish enough to let twenty-one "foreigners," that is, Mexicans, have a say-so in their affairs.[41] Nationalist discourses distinguishing between *mexicanos* and *californios* thus serve here to legitimate positions on property relations, for at issue were the mission lands, especially the large mission *ranchos*, which constituted the only capital in the territory (Coronel, 16) and to which, both Figueroa and Hijar agreed, the missionaries had no legal right (Alvarado, 2:197). Hijar's plan called for a distribution of lands to the new settlers and other interested parties. Given the emancipation of the Indians, they were to be treated as "equal citizens"; they were free, free to become wage earners or "colonos," and, like any settler, entitled to petition for mission lands. For Hijar, it was not a matter of dispossession, because the government rather than the Indians was the real proprietor and by "eminent domain" could dispose of all the property as it thought best (MGV, 2:326). But for Figueroa what was involved was confiscation without compensation for the second time: had not the missionaries done the same thing when they established their missions and *ranchos* on Indian land in the first place?

Figueroa took the stance that the Indians were the true owners of the mission lands and of the wealth therein. Only the vacant lands beyond the missions could be distributed to settlers by the government. For this reason, he accuses Hijar and Padrés not only of trying to rob the missions and reduce the Indians to peonage (MGV, 2:307), but of trying to deceive the Indians on the issue of their equality:

> [Hijar] alleged the ignorant, still beggarly and half wild Indian to be identically and absolutely equal, in terms of political rights, to any citizen, perhaps in order to deceive him or to take advantage of him more easily. According to these principles, we were to forgo all laws from our codes regulating *patria potestad*, those guaranteeing a man's authority as head of the family and all those stipulating the care and tutelage of minors, retarded, insane, and other individuals.
> (Figueroa, quoted in MGV, 3:48)

Figueroa here astutely recognizes that "political liberalism," that is, discourses on the equality of all citizens, can be manipulated to serve the interests of economic liberalism, for, given the subordination and quasi-enslavement of the Indians, merely turning them out of the missions did not mean that they were "equal" or should be "equal." For Figueroa, such notions of equality were nonsense, be they in relation to women, children, or Indians: "Equality before the law, taken to such extremes, would throw society into upheaval" (Figueroa, quoted in MGV, 3:48). Society required a patriarchal structure, social stratification, with women, children, and Indians under tutelage. Figueroa's *Manifiesto* combines caste, patriarchal, aristocratic, and semifeudal discourses with liberal discourses as framing strategies, ostensibly to defend the "property rights" of the Indians. In Mexico, the liberal Mora was then combining racist, anticorporatist, and procapitalist discourses to argue the opposite: the abolition of Indian communal property. Figueroa, fearing that the Indians were being overwhelmed with "rights" and deprived of property, combined feudal discourses with those of economic liberalism in defending the right to property of the Indians. Like peasants under feudalism, the Indians as producers were seen to be entitled to hold the land they worked (Brenner, 1990: 33), although the surplus produced was controlled by the missionaries. Figueroa's argument further recognized that in becoming neophytes at the mission, the Indians had entered into a social contract that the Mexicans now threatened to breach; the Indians had, moreover, produced all the wealth of the missions (MGV, 3:51) and for that reason were the legitimate owners of the land (Figueroa, quoted in MGV, 2:279). Figueroa asks, "Who then could deprive them of these rights without attacking all social guarantees?" (Figueroa, quoted in MGV, 2:268–69). The Indians, though not equal, were guaranteed certain rights, property rights; and now to avoid their being swindled, they, minors as they were in "the course of civilization," needed the firm paternalistic protection of the government (Figueroa, quoted in MGV, 2:281). Only the government could see to it that they did not sell or pass their lands to others. Figueroa thus made himself out to be the great defender of the Indians, a title under which the pillage of Indian lands was often carried out throughout Latin America.

Neither the Californios nor the advocates of the colonization project had the interests of the Indians at heart. What mattered to the Californios was that the newly arrived competition not gain control of the mission lands and other properties that they held to be their native land and over which they had prerogatives. One side saw the Indians as a potential wage labor force while the other preferred maintaining a patriarchal system resembling the existing semifeudal structure. Clearly the latter could be accomplished by retaining the Indians at the missions under lay administrators until the large landed estates had been created. Emancipation would thus be contingent and conditional. When it came to the allocation of lands only some of the Indians would be given land to work but they too, like those working the mission lands for their own subsistence, would continue living communally. What might have sounded utopian for Figueroa was nothing more than a reincarnation of the *reducciones* concept, nothing more and nothing less than a secular version of the mission system and a continuation of controls on movement and the disposition of space. One side, that of Hijar and Padrés, saw the possibility of new Mexican colonists with land for farming; the other side could only see non-Californios standing in the way of large land grants for cattle-raising. Whoever distributed the mission lands would have the upper hand in the balance of power between Mexicans and Californios but would also control the mode of production and thereby the size and nature of land allotments. Whoever implemented secularization would also determine who would control the productive forces, the Indian population.

The legal implications of secularization under Figueroa's plan were also alarming for Hijar. The governor, like Echeandía before him, claimed that upon being secularized, each mission was to be considered a *pueblo*, with its own *ayuntamiento*. Hijar, however, could only conceive of new *pueblos* in terms of Mexican *colonos* alongside old Indian converts, themselves *colonos* or laborers. The governor's plan was read as a swindle by Hijar, who accused Figueroa and the Diputación of trying to deceive the Indians about their rights of ownership (Hijar, quoted in MGV, 2:304). If the Indians were indeed the owners, Hijar asked, why were the governor and the Diputación planning to grant them only four hundred square *varas*? The Indians' continued retention at the mission, Hijar insisted, kept them subservient to mission administrators. How then could *ayuntamientos* be formed by people who had known only servitude? Suddenly Hijar found himself caught in a contradiction, tripped up by the premises of his own arguments. Could they or could they not be treated as equal citizens? The ideological field in California during the 1830s was full of contradictions and slippages from one position to another.

Figueroa's argument positing the Indians as the rightful owners of mission lands was supported by Californios like Vallejo, who insisted he was not against the colonization project in theory but rather against the intentions of the leadership, which had maliciously misled the settlers and sought only to serve its own interests, to the detriment of the neophytes (MGV, 2:348). Vallejo felt that despite their talk of equality, the directors of the colony did not wish to treat the Indians as rational beings; he reasoned that the discourses of equality were meant to mask their real intentions, "for undoubtedly they would have preferred to find them stupid, without any awareness of the rights of free men" in order to more easily keep them subservient and alienated from the rest of society (MGV, 2:297). All of a sudden in this line of Californio argumentation, the Indians, who all along had been described as not having received the proper education from the missionaries to make them aware of their rights, are seen to be very much aware of the rights of free men. Here again we have a projection of the notion of Californio rights: the Californios are the ones who seemingly are not stupid, who are very much aware of their political and property rights as well as their faculties to administer the missions themselves, and—with 1875 hindsight—who are keenly aware of having been dispossessed and defrauded by the legal system of the United States.

The issue clouds further still if we consider what Alvarado says about Figueroa's presentation to the Diputación upon his arrival. Figueroa's plan was first to secularize the mission lands and distribute them among the inhabitants of the territory (especially among the most needy); second, to free the Indians from the "tyrannical tutelage of missionary power," allowing them to be at the service of the townspeople or settlers as servants; and finally, to abolish the missionaries' monopoly of "retail trade" (Alvarado, 2:213). This view favoring land distribution to Californios and reducing Indians to servitude under *rancheros* and townspeople is totally contradicted by what Figueroa says in his *Manifiesto,* included in its entirety in Vallejo's testimonial. More than a representation of Figueroa's position, Alvarado's account serves best to summarize his own plan of secularization that he would put into practice five years later as governor.

The question of land property also led to debate on the "natives" as the real proprietors. The second generation of Californios felt that as native sons born within the territory they had as much right to the land as the Indians, as José de Jesús Vallejo recalls hearing the "principal leaders of the secularization movement" state (JJV, 41). This notion that California was for the natives, Indian and non-Indian, and not for the Mexican *foreigners* is dominant throughout the texts, running contradictorily alongside comments indicating the Californios' desire to welcome all foreign settlers. As Alvarado demonstrates several times in his testimonial, by "foreigners" the Californios also meant *mexicanos*. This becomes clear even in Vallejo's testimonial when he comments on the arrival of new Zacatecan Mexican friars to California, with their "ínfulas de marqués" ("airs of a marquis") and expecting to be served hand and foot by those considered inferior native "help":

> But the Californios had already had their eyes opened and knew how to put to their own good use what little still remained in the country, without having foreigners from faraway lands come live like great lords off the sweat of the native sons. (MGV, 4:78)

Whatever was in California was for the native Californios, *los hijos del país*. To underscore this claim, Alvarado resorts in his testimonial to having the missionaries assert as much. He recalls that when the Zacatecan friars asked the Fernandinos to sign a protest against Governor Figueroa's secularization plan, the latter abstained, arguing that the Indians were the sole owners of the land and that if they were to prove incapable of managing their property, it was only fitting that the "native sons," the descendants of the original heroic soldiers, receive the land (Alvarado, 2:220–26). Alvarado, who earlier (2:91–92) had quoted Friar Durán denying that the Indians were the owners of the land, now had the missionaries corroborating what he and all the other descendants of the original settlers and soldiers believed: it was only just that they inherit the land. Like the Spanish conquerors of the sixteenth century, these descendants of the early Californio conquerors were demanding their rightful compensation.

Property relations are thus masked by discourses of nativism and political liberalism. Figueroa, who is called the champion of Indian rights, should instead have been called the champion of the Californios, or, as Alvarado (3:60) called him, the "father of California." By refusing to let Híjar and Padrés take charge of secularization, Figueroa postponed matters and allowed the native Californios to determine who would administer the mission lands, who would become property owners, who would be granted the mission *ranchos*, who would be sold these lands, who would profit from the cattle and horses of the missions, and who would be able to lease out the neophyte Indians. If he did wish to protect the Indians, Figueroa only succeeded in guaranteeing their reduction to peonage. Had Híjar's plan been followed, it is as likely that the same servitude would have been imposed on the Indians, only it would have taken place on smaller ranches and farms. Obviously neither plan envisioned the Indians as large-scale property owners. Whether they would have entered into new relations of production, as wage laborers in an emergent capitalist system, is unclear. Figueroa did ensure the maintenance of a semifeudal system in Alta California, though not for long. In the end very few Indians received any land, and most of those that did lost it and the livestock they were given, even before 1846. Only in the ensuing dispossession would the Californios and the Indians find equality.

The fate of the Hijar-Padrés colony would be determined by Figueroa, who seven months after the colonists' arrival accused the leaders of the colony of plotting a conspiracy against the governor and forcibly returned them to Mexico. Contrary to a report submitted by Vallejo, Coronel is adamant in his insistence that there was no such conspiracy and in fact insinuates that the entire episode was the product of prevarication (Coronel, 13). Coronel fails to see that Vallejo, who took Hijar, Padrés, and a few others into custody in Sonoma, was only following Figueroa's orders (MGV, 3:33). It is unclear whether Figueroa was overly sensitive to any hint of conspiracy after long years of residence in war-torn Mexico as Hutchinson (367) alleges. In accusing the leaders of the colony of trying to divide the territory and secede (Figueroa, quoted in MGV, 2:231), Figueroa may simply have been conscious of events taking place in Texas where the liberal Lorenzo de Zavala was plotting with Texans to secede from the Mexican federation (Mejía Zúñiga, 208–9).

The fact that this colonization had been sponsored by the liberal Gómez Farías had led to rumors that the vice president was conspiring with the leaders of the colony to declare California independent from Mexico in order to establish a liberal stronghold outside of Mexico. This, Coronel insists, was the idea circulated by President Santa Anna. Rejecting such intrigues, Coronel adds that had the plans of the colonists actually been hostile, they would not have come with their entire families nor would the leaders have chosen artisans and educators over a fighting force (Coronel, 17). Hijar and Padrés also discounted the imputations of a conspiracy (MGV, 3:34), but Coronel (13) recognizes that events in Los Angeles could have led to these accusations.[42] In any event the alleged plot served as a perfect excuse for what the governor wanted to do: deport Hijar and Padrés. These same events allow Alvarado to vent his spleen against incoming Mexican settlers. The Hijar-Padrés colonists, he says, seeing their proposed project vetoed, conceived a plan to have a group of newly arrived Sonoran colonists push their agenda and start a revolt. Alvarado's comments about these Sonorans as poor devils, who had not in their wildest dreams thought it possible to have land and stock like the Californios (Alvarado,

3:4–5) and were consequently duped by the conspirators, reveal an aristocratic, condescending, and derisive attitude toward property-less Mexicans with pretensions to California land. Thus nation and class discourses interact in what is a strongly anti-Mexicanist testimonial.

Once the Hijar-Padrés colonization project was abandoned and the leaders deported, most of the colonists settled as best they could throughout California. The failure of this project, in view of the need for additional settlers in the territory, allowed economic interests to prevail over ideological ones, but clearly the victory had been political and possible only because the Californios' cause was championed by the governor. Within a period of two years after the governor's death the young Californios would ensure that they themselves controlled secularization and land distribution. The entire conflict offers an overview of the fuzzy ideological field in which liberal and conservative, procapitalist and residual feudal, democratic and aristocratic discourses intersect, creating a liminal space for the emergent Californio *rancheros*. It also allows one to see how advocacy for revindication of Indian rights serves as a strategy to affirm the rights of the "native sons" to the land. In the proffering of arguments and justifications, the Californios make it clear that they were fully aware that the mission lands and wealth represented the only capital in Alta California and that for that reason it was imperative that measures be taken to impede the appropriation of this wealth by any but themselves (JJV, 41–42). The Californios well knew that whoever administered the properties would have direct access to the wealth. Thus concern for the rights of the newly recognized citizens—the Indians—was a ploy. Coronel, however, simply perceived false pretenses:

> Their [the Californios'] alleged philanthropy toward the mission
> Indians in order to rehabilitate them, educate them, and see that their
> property rights were recognized was proven false by subsequent
> events known to all. (16)

Coronel, himself a Mexican colonist, saw the ethical argument put forth by the Californios as hypocrisy rather than as an ideological stratagem or a political ruse. He is the only one to comment on the self-interest underlying the Californios' Indianist discourses, however. The members of the Diputación who opposed Hijar and Padrés and set themselves up as the defenders of the Indians, recalls Coronel (16–17), were the very ones who would take possession of the mission lands and *ranchos* and render the neophytes destitute. Within two years of Figueroa's death, the notion of the Indian as rightful proprietor had faded away and the ex-neophytes were being rented out to *rancheros* and *hacendados*. Mission lands as well as livestock and implements would be distributed by the governors to friends, relatives, girlfriends, and supporters, as we shall explore in the next chapter. The next eleven years (1835–46) would in effect consolidate the position of a new landowning class, semifeudal rather than bourgeois. This is not surprising, for, as Brenner explains, precapitalist exploiters cannot be expected to seek change: "On the contrary, their rationally self-interested activity will, as a rule, have as one of its goals maintaining those precapitalist property relations, which structure non-development" (1986r: 26). All too soon, however, these Californios would see themselves at risk and threatened with displacement by yet another emergent class.

Ideological Positioning

The political positioning of these Californios during the process of constructing secularization is wrought with contradictions born of an ambiguous ideological field and shifts in property relations. The emergent dominant class, previously without land, still immersed within a precapitalist society, supported by a caste system and a religious framework, but enlightened by liberal-rationalist discourses dominant within a global capitalist system, was being interpellated by competing discourses and positioned within the fissures and disjunctures. The discourses are consequently at best fuzzy and characterized by slippages.

In the testimonials the Californios do as a whole look back and perceive secularization as their major accomplishment. What they gain in restructuring land tenancy is, in effect, their own "passive revolution" against the church, a struggle in which "political warriors" like Alvarado did battle against what he held as backward forces. If their soldier fathers had "liberated" California by conquering the heathen, they, the native sons of California, had participated in a different kind of contest, an ideological struggle against a more powerful—and worthy—enemy, the missionaries. The adversary to be conquered now lay within the very collectivity of Californios:

> It is satisfying to be able to recall that I participated in the struggle waged by the ideas of progress against fanaticism, and even more satisfying is it to report that the few defeated the many and that at the end of the battle, the stiff corpse of fanaticism lay prostrate, never to rise again, at least in my country. (Alvarado, 1:vi)

Like their heroic fathers they too had fought the good fight and broken the hold of religious fanaticism over the territory that had for so
long oppressed the inhabitants of this land and fettered its development (Alvarado, 1:iv–v).[43] This struggle would principally take place
within the political realm but have major economic consequences upon
the territory by opening up previously mission-controlled spaces to
private ownership. Significantly, Californio women had no role to play
in this "valiant epic" for they, Alvarado (2:30–31) laments, continued
totally submissive to the missionaries.

In casting his generation as warriors in a different kind of struggle,
Alvarado also reconstructs the image of Spanish soldiers, counters hegemonic representations of California history, and provides a corrective
to the prevailing version of history written by sympathizers or allies
of the missionaries. Such writers, including de Mofras, Gleason, Robinson, and others, fail to represent the contributions of the Californio
soldiers in the establishment and defense of the missions (Alvarado,
5:126). What is striking is that for Alvarado and other Californios, writing from the vantage point of postindependence/postinvasion California, the soldiers are never cast as agents of the Spanish Crown defending the frontier for the colonial power; they are instead pioneers
defending *la patria,* their homeland, from attacks by hostile forces, natives though the Indians might be. This is a telling inversion of rhetorical positioning; the colonists are bravely defending *their* territory against
the native "bárbaros infieles." Even when there is recognition of the
Spanish settlement of the territory, as the northwestern frontier of Nueva
España, Alta California is never seen to be conquered territory occupied by a foreign force in 1769. This is glossed over and stress is put
on the now "rightful possessors" of the land, who fear its being wrested
from them by Indians or encroached upon by the Russians. This logic
of course erases the representation of the soldiers as invaders involved
in the slaughter of the former occupants of the land and posits them
instead as the maligned and unsung heroes who valiantly faced "hordes
of savages" in order to guarantee the security of Alta California for its
rightful claimants. Once invasion and occupation are thus naturalized, defense of the land against its former occupants is seen as per-
fectly coherent. Those involved in expansionism are represented as "civ-
ilizers" whose brave deeds and accomplishments have too easily been
forgotten. Alvarado regrets not having a record of all the encounters
between soldiers and gentile Indians, for, to his mind, there has been
insufficient recognition and appreciation for the soldiers' efforts in defending their land and civilization itself. To compensate for this lack

of recognition, he proposes that those dictating their testimonials for Bancroft should in their reconstructions of the Californio past not omit the heroic contributions of the soldiers, lest those (i.e., the U.S. invaders) arriving after the Indians had been eliminated not realize the import of their continual military efforts and choose to denigrate them in their writings (Alvarado, 4:59). The implications here, that the Indians were successfully exterminated through warfare, are ghastly, but are in actuality more of an exaggeration than an accurate portrayal of the military might of the Californio soldiers. Though the Californios did indeed on several occasions carry out Indian massacres, the entire Indian population of California would be decimated and practically eliminated not by lances and firearms of the Californios and the missionaries but as a consequence of disease, enslavement, and exploitation.

In another revealing tirade aimed at self-vindication, Alvarado attacks these same pro-clergy writers for trying to defame him by distorting their accounts of events, simply because he, a republican, dealt the fatal blow to a worn-out system of education introduced by the decadent Franciscans to enslave the mission Indians.[44] Alvarado's overwrought denunciation is anticlerical, liberal, republican, positivist, and ethically self-righteous. His "liberating" intentions notwithstanding, Alvarado's discourses do not change the tragic outcome of his practices in the implementation of secularization, but as discursive artifacts they do carve a definite liberal niche for themselves in the history of Chicano literature.

Like Alvarado, the ideology of the emergent *ranchero* class in Alta California in 1831 is at best eclectic: liberal and federalist at a political level, semifeudal at an economic level, caste-conscious and racist at a sociocultural level, and both anticlerical and religious. It is not any more or less inconsistent than the dominant classes in Mexico during this period of transition, marked as well by ideological slippages and vacillations. In California this class will subsequently fragment along political and national lines, once again following patterns in Mexico. Regionalism will become a powerful discourse of dissension as Californios divide into two spatialized factions, *norteños* and *sureños*, as we shall see in chapter 5.

4

Spaces of (Re)Production

There is a plot whenever history brings together a set of
goals, material causes, and chance.

Paul Ricoeur

The spatialization of history evident in the Californio testimonials allows the narrators to position themselves as a collectivity, a caste or a
faction within or outside given geographical sites (territory, department,
region, nation, mission, *presidio, pueblo, rancho, hacienda, ranchería*, wilderness [*el monte*], the coast, the inland area, "the frontier," the capital,
and the "penal colony") and in relation to particular social and political positions. Two sociospatial realms predominate during the Spanish
period, one (the mission) viewed from the outside, and the other (the
presidio/pueblo) from within. From the vantage point of the latter sites,
identity is generated and alterity posited. This outside/inside antin-
omy will be sublated with secularization, a process allowing the state
to assume political ascendancy over ecclesioeconomic spaces, and the
rancho/hacienda to displace the mission as the central space of production. With this restructuring, that is, as the state penetrates the mission walls and privatizes the lands, private landholdings assume center stage as sites for the inscription of the California nation. The *rancho*
will now be the new site of domination, the target of all acts of rebellion, and a new site of representation, where the construct of the Indian shifts from being primarily one of "natives abused by missionaries" to one of Indians as hostile forces threatening the California family.
As we shall find as we detail specific testimonials, the *rancho* is also
the setting of narrative emplotment within these texts.

There is plot, Ricoeur explains, "whenever history brings together a set of goals, material causes, and chance."[1] In these dictated narratives plot construction is the primary strategy, for the testimonials, in reconstructing the past, provide explanation by emplotment, by the particular configuration of elements within the narrative. To say, then, that the Californio testimonials are representational spaces is not to deny that they are sites of emplotment, places of narrative activity (Ricoeur, 1:32). Against the notion that there is a gap "between narrative explanations and historical explanations" (Ricoeur, 1:179), we would have to argue that in these testimonials, narrative and ideological explanation are part and parcel of historical explanation.

The testimonials together constitute a macrotext, a collective effort to reconstruct the past from a variety of perspectives. Within these narratives, different versions of the same episode function as intercalated mininarratives or stories, and individual characters are configured as agents for particular "imagined communities" rather than as singular subjects. Events narrated are both contingent and determined, especially in the case of those subnarratives or mininarratives that serve allegorically to explain macrosocial relations. In one specific miniromance, dealing with events at the Rancho Jamul in 1837, the place and action take priority over the characters, to the point where there is often disagreement in the various reconstructions as to who was where although the sequence of what transpired is more or less the same. The story fits in with a fixture in the tradition of colonial literature: the kidnapping of a maiden by savage Indians. One can find this story of Indian hostility in Mera's *Cumandá*, the Ecuadorian novel of a girl kidnapped and brought up by the Indians in the jungles of the *oriente*, and in Echeverría's narrative poem *La cautiva*. In these two texts Indians are either idealized as noble savages (*Cumandá*), or represented as fierce savages (*La cautiva*). This common theme in Latin American literature is the basis for a Californio novel, *Who Would Have Thought It?*, written by Ruiz de Burton in 1872.[2]

At an ideological level the Jamul narrative has to be viewed as a romantic emplotment of historical antagonisms and as a reconstruction that attempts to legitimate other constructions in the testimonials dealing with social relations, social practices, and political policies in California history between 1825 and 1846. Central to this story is the construct of the *rancho* as frontier and nation. From the perspective of 1875, the tale, the site itself, structures a series of events and establishes hierarchies: *rancho* over *pueblo*, gender over caste, danger over safety, vulnerability over strength, and strategy over weapons—antinomies that

serve to provide historical and ideological explanations, through emplotment, for the state of affairs that led to particular policies in regard
to the Indians, the majority population of the territory, and in 1846 to
the Californios' conquest by the U.S. invaders.

Within a patriarchal caste system like that of Alta California, the construct of women as kidnapped property, especially fair-skinned women,
is the ultimate legitimation for political policies that kept settlements
along the coast (rather than fostering exploration and settlment further
inland) and for policies of mass killings of Indian raiders to protect
life and property. The story is meant to reconstruct the Californios'
worst fears and provide explanations for a continued caste-segregated
society: *gente de razón* versus Indians, with allowances for a few exceptions, and at the same time to posit the vulnerability of the Californio nation, exposed to a variety of hostilities from outside.

Several kidnapping episodes appear in these testimonials, but the
best known, recounted by Juana Machado, Apolinaria Lorenzana, J. B.
Alvarado, Pío Pico, Felipa Osuna de Marrón, Antonio Franco Coronel,
and José María Estudillo, is that of the Jamul *rancho*.[3] This most famous
episode took place in 1837; the year is important if we recall that in
December 1836 Alvarado, with the support of Vallejo, Castro, and other
northerners, had revolted against Gutiérrez, the acting commander general after Governor Chico's exit. The revolutionary governor was now
himself facing a rebellion by southerners favoring Carlos Carrillo, another native son, for governor. Like all other stories of Indian raids,
this narrative serves to argue for a united *gente de razón* against the
hostile barbarians who are a threat to the system of separate and unequal castes, to the mission and *rancho* systems, and to the health and
safety of the *gente de razón*.

In Juana Machado's account, the narrative is divided into five parts:
the warning (the interdiction), the villainy or attack, the kidnapping or
abduction and attendant pillaging, the escape/survival of the partici-
pant/witness (lack made known), and finally the subsequent search
(counteraction or quest) for the victims and kidnappers. In several of
these insurrection stories, warnings are provided by a Californio-loyal
Indian woman or by a young Indian boy. The warning, always taken to
heart by women, often leads to an averting of the insurrection.

Juana Machado's version of the events at Jamul begins with the warning. According to Machado, a lifelong resident of San Diego (11–17),
Pío Pico's mother, Doña Eustaquia, was at the ranch with her daughters Feliciana, Jacinta, and Isidora one afternoon when an Indian woman
named Cesárea approached her at the door, asking for salt. Doña

Eustaquia ordered that she be brought some salt but on seeing that the woman wanted her to go inside the house to get it herself, she entered and went into another room with Cesárea. The Indian woman told her in her Indian language (which Doña Eustaquia knew well) of a planned uprising to kill the men and kidnap the women. Doña Eustaquia immediately entered the next room where her daughters were sewing, told them to get their *rebozos* and go for a walk around the edge of the cornfield where she would catch up with them soon. She then informed the foreman, Juan Leyva, who was a relative, about what Cesárea had said and about her own suspicions, but the foreman assured her that there was no danger, that he and his men and their twelve rifles could defend the place. Doña Eustaquia wanted him to leave with his family but he refused. She then told him to send the wagon with the oxen down by the cornfield where she and her daughters would take it to the next ranch, Rancho Jamachá, which belonged to Doña Apolinaria Lorenzana. They arrived at Jamachá at midnight and after letting them know of the planned uprising, continued to the *presidio* at San Diego.

Savage, the interviewer for the Machado *testimonio,* includes a note indicating that Doña Isidora Pico de Forster, "one of the young women who escaped with their mother," had related the story "in almost the same terms." Pico, in his account (1973: 86–87), recalls that his family was fortunately not at Jamul but in San Diego when the incident occurred. Whether they were there the day before is not mentioned. Estudillo's version also recalls being told by Osuna, his mother-in-law, that Doña Eustaquia left the ranch with her three daughters upon being warned.

When asked about the event, Lorenzana at first cannot recall if the Pico family had been at Jamul but is inclined to believe that they were not. She had been at her *rancho* at Jamachá for two days to install a new foreman, Valentín Ríos, when the incident occurred. One of her servants, named Camacho, was at Jamul at the time, on his way back from Rancho de la nación, the *presidio* ranch where stray cattle were rounded up and could be picked out to return to their respective *rancho* owners. Camacho had gone to the rodeo with Juan Leyva to help him round up his cattle and that of Jamachá, and had planned to proceed to Jamachá with his steers the next morning.

According to the Lorenzana text, it was not Doña Eustaquia de Pico who was warned of the impending raid but rather Leyva's wife, Doña María de los Ángeles, who asked her husband to let her go to Jamachá because she was afraid. Upon hearing about the old Indian woman's warning, Leyva told her not to worry, that there were no such Indians around and that if they came she and the rest of the family could always hide in a room where the hides were stored. Leyva's failure to heed the warning, Lorenzana (33) recalls, was recounted to her by Leyva's wife.

The Indians indeed attacked the next day—in the morning, according to Lorenzana, and in the evening, according to Machado. In addition to Camacho and the Leyva family, two other Californios were at Jamul that day. One was Anastasio Molina, a servant at the Ortega house who was to marry one of Leyva's daughters, Tomasa, and had gone to the ranch to ask that she appear before the missionaries in preparation for the ceremony. Tomasa was then about eighteen or nineteen years old, and her sister Ramona was eleven or twelve. The other man at the ranch was a servant. Pico says there were four vaqueros at the ranch, and Machado says the fourth man was Leyva's young son José Antonio.

When the Indians attacked, Camacho and Leyva's servant were killed outside, one in the wheat field and the other in the corral. Leyva and Molina were on their way out when they heard the Indians hollering; they tried to run to the room where they kept their rifles, but an Indian woman ran in and locked the door before they could reach it. Machado indicates that the Indian woman (the hostile agent who betrays the family) had pocketed the key and flaunted it before Leyva, who then ran into the kitchen to fight off the Indians with live coals. Once the Indians had killed both Leyva and Molina, they rounded up the family. They disrobed the mother and sent her off with her two young sons, José Antonio (twelve years old) and Claro (six years old), after threatening to kill them if they did not leave. The two daughters, who screamed to stay with their mother, were taken by the Indians along with whatever they could find of value. Significantly, as relates to the construction of the threat posed to the Californio collectivity by hostile Indians, in Pico's version he makes the perhaps exaggerated claim that all his horses and nearly two thousand head of cattle were taken in the raid. Afterward the Indians burned the ranch house, with the two bodies inside.

Lorenzana recalls that the same day of the raid Doña María de los Ángeles arrived at her Jamachá *rancho* with her sons. Because she was naked she had one of the children go on ahead to ask for something with which to cover herself. She was handed a bedspread and once inside told her horrifying story and asked to be taken to San Diego.

After sending her on her way in one of her wagons, Lorenzana called her foreman Valentín Ríos and asked him to ride to the *ranchería* of the Secuá Indians, who were friendly gentiles, to ask for their assistance lest her ranch at Jamachá be attacked. (Three of Doña Apolinaria's servants were neophytes, she notes in the testimonial; the rest of the ranch workers were gentiles from Secuá and from other neighboring *rancherías*.) The Secuá Indians came in her defense armed with bows and arrows. Lorenzana, now the helper in the tale, also sent word to have the gunpowder she kept in San Diego sent to her ranch. Word of the attack was also sent to the foreman at the mission El Cajón ranch and to the San Diego mission, asking the missionaries there to send her paper for making cartridges. "La Beata," as Lorenzana was called, then sent her foreman with twenty-six Secuá Indians to Jamul. Once the San Diego *alcalde* (mayor) Don José Estudillo had arrived, the bodies were buried.

At that time no military force was stationed at the San Diego *presidio*; the few available soldiers were quite a distance away at the San Luis Rey mission. After the Indian attack, the local authorities had to send for Sergeant Macedonio González (the would-be hero), then a military commander at San Vicente, Baja California, and who was related to the Leyva family, to pursue the Indians in an effort to rescue the two kidnapped girls. González's expedition, said by Vicente Romero to have been made up of eighteen regular soldiers and thirty friendly Indians led by Chief Jatanil,[4] reportedly saw the two girls on a mountaintop; the Indians taunted González to go after them, but the soldiers were unable to reach them. Pico recalls that the Indians defeated the troops in pursuit at Jacumba. Three soldiers, including González, were wounded and fourteen of the horses were stolen as they attempted to scale the steep hills on foot (Pico, 1973: 86–87). Estudillo indicates that Bandini, his wife's uncle, hired a party of *chahuanosos*, Indian riflemen and traders from Chihuahua and New Mexico (Botello, 37), to pursue the Indians, but also to no avail. Lorenzana's testimonial indicates further that the girls were taken to the Colorado River where they were sold. One of her servants, named Muñoz, years later saw one of the girls in the desert of Sonora and she begged him to take her back, but he, fearing the Indians and having only one tired horse, dared not do so.

As to who the Indians were that attacked the Jamul ranch, "La Beata" says that the perpetrators were the same Jamul Indians who worked at the ranch and conspired with others to raid it. No other ranch in the San Diego area or in Baja California came under attack, nor did the Indians ever approach the Jamachá ranch, which was closest to Jamul. Estudillo (28–30) claims that the Indians were neophyte Dieguinos, Cahuillas, and other Indians from the Colorado River, led by the Indians Cartucho and Cabezón.

Coronel, however, asserts that the girls were killed once the soldiers began pursuing the Indians and entering the *rancherías* in search of the girls. The Indians wanted to be rid of them as they had become liabilities. According to Coronel, he had reason to know that the perpetrators were several Indian captains that, years later, joined Coronel on a trip to Sonora and admitted as much to him, but again personal safety led him to keep quiet about the matter once he reached Sonora (Coronel, 193).

Interestingly, Alvarado's northern version of events in the south is entirely different. In his account, the attack was planned by Claudio, the "Zampay of the South." Zampay was a famous northern California Indian who, along with Claudio, represents in these narratives the Indian who has learned to ride and use firearms; he is the equal of any Californio in the marksmanship and riding skills for which the Californios were well known. According to Alvarado, during the attack on the Jamul ranch Claudio and his raiders had to fight the neophytes working at the ranch who defended it. Some of the neophytes escaped, some were killed, and others were taken prisoner. Once in control of Jamul, Claudio is then said to have taken the girls, the livestock, and the horses and burned down the ranch—which, in Alvarado's version, belongs not to Pico but to Bandini. Alvarado, who disliked Bandini and considered him a liar for misinforming the Mexican government about fellow Californios from the north in his letters to Mexico City, then goes on to say that Bandini, upon hearing the news, reported having gone to the ranch where he was surprised by the Indians but was able to kill a large number of them. Not wanting to credit Bandini with any brave deed or even with the capacity to tell the truth, Alvarado questions that ending and says that what actually happened was that another Indian leader, Panto from San Pascual, not Bandini, followed Claudio and his men and was responsible for killing many of the raiding Indians.

Aside from the anecdotal and narrative value of the tales, this and other stories of Indian insurrections serve to deconstruct the heroic myth of valiant Californios able to lord over the "savage Indians." Far from heroic saviors of damsels in distress the Californios are represented as a valiant but defeated minority, unable to protect life, property, and nation from violent attacks by marauders, unable to save the maidens of the land from the grips of what are deemed depraved Indian monsters, and most important unable to protect the sanctity of the home. As in any typical folktale, the plot gives us a villainous force, two beloved daughters, a father, a messenger who forewarns, the departure of the family that heeds the warning, and the nefarious deed: the assault and kidnapping. What is missing is the rescue of the maidens and the punishment of the villains. The latter is projected to another spatial dimension, that of the macrotext, wherein punishment is effected in the subsequent killing of other Indians, on whom revenge for the acts is displaced.

As in the macrotext's reconstructing of the Californio past, the Jamul episode is constituted by a multiplicity of intersecting social spaces and discourses of family, gender, caste, nation, and religion. The agency of the Californio men is denied and women are forced to take action to protect what remains. The more powerful agency is that of the Indian raiders, against whom not even the soldiers with their weapons and their horses are a match (but note that these are not local Californio soldiers). The Indians are no longer on foot; they are armed with more than bows and arrows and they have become expert riders. Restructuring of the territory through secularization has created new agencies, new sites of production (the ranches), and renewed hostilities, but now by ex-neophyte Indians. The production of these new spaces has taken the Californio population into the no-man's-land of the interior where isolation puts them at risk. With the breakup of the missions and the dismantling of the *presidios* there are now frequent outbreaks of Indian raids and uprisings throughout the territory. The emancipated neophytes (*los manumisos*), left homeless with the secularization of the missions, have now joined forces with the gentiles and are threatening the survival of the Californio settlements.

The Jamul episode is also the Californios' story of the *rancho*-nation under attack by hostile forces. It will serve to legitimate continued armed aggression against the gentiles and insurrectionists from the ex-missions, for what is revealed is the vulnerability of the spaces of production and reproduction of the "white" *gente de razón*. Obviously the women (as possessions and vessels of "white" blood) represent the major loss in the story but equally vulnerable is the capital represented by the cattle, horses, saddles, and other articles of value. It is an inverse emplotment of romance, for here the few valiantly struggling against the many are ultimately powerless. The lesson is clear: the few will have to take coercive measures against Indian aggression. The emplotment can be configured through a semantic rectangle. The major opposition posited by the story is that of Indian raiders against *rancho* families:

Powerless ◄─────► Powerful
rancho   *ranchería*
California family   Indian raiders

The Indians are pursued by the Baja California soldiers, the only force to counter their power. In fact the soldiers, perceived as Mexican rather than Californio soldiers, underscore the powerlessness of the Californio nation. At a moment when Alvarado has tried to declare Alta California a free and independent nation (see chapter 6), Mexico is seen by some as the enemy and by others, especially residents of the south who are backing Carrillo for governor, as their only ally. In this picture there is no California force to counter the Indian marauders, at least not one separate from the Mexican forces. Only a united Alta California could have had such a force, but even the narrative, in its many versions, recognizes this lack in the political vacuum of 1837. What is

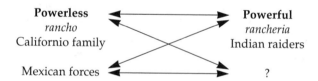

Powerless ◄─────► Powerful
rancho   *rancheria*
Californio family   Indian raiders

Mexican forces ◄─────► ?

missing from the story is an entity that will oppose the Mexican troops and negate the power of the Californios. That force, with which many of the Indians will ally, was only ten years away from the territory. In 1846 the United States would invade Alta California.

The Jamul episode is thus as much about the Californios' struggle with hostile Indian forces (and all the repression that this perceived threat justifies) as about the Californio nation that the northerners were trying to construct and the southerners were opposing on the basis of who would be in charge and where the capital/port would be located. In Alvarado's version, no Baja California troops are involved and the struggle becomes one of Indians against Indians. Indians are often employed as a trope for Californios in these testimonials, but the construct of the Indian is fuzzy; as a multivalent signifier it varies from one discursive site to another, from one articulation to another. This story also has to be read against other narratives made famous by the missionaries and their allies: stories of heartless Californio "wolves" devouring the defenseless Indians, slaughtering both men and women at some battles. Estudillo recalls a large uprising of the Cahuillas, Jacum Indians, Colorado River Indians, and neophytes from San Diego that led to a fierce battle with Californio soldiers near Tecate. Years later, in 1863–64, he recalls seeing piles of Indian skeletal remains at the scene of the battle, perhaps from insurrections of 1851 or from earlier encounters (Estudillo, 20).

Each region, north and south, had its horror stories to recount, vilifying both Californios and Indians. Vallejo, for example, is said not only to have participated as a twenty-one-year-old ensign in the massacre of Estanislao's people but to have ordered, in 1840, the execution of eleven of his Indian infantrymen, shot after rebelling and attacking his cavalrymen.[5] Each story posits an ethical argument that best serves particular interests. Given regional antagonisms, for divisions between north and south in Alta California went deep, the stories often serve to denounce bitterly the other side's incompetence. The unfavorable portrayal of Bandini, for example, who had little to do with the Jamul episode at all, provides Alvarado with the opportunity to criticize his political opponents in the south. The story also makes clear a number of inconsistencies in Alvarado's narrative; in his testimonial as a whole constructs of the Indians vary between their portrayal as pitiful beings and as heroic Cuauhtemocs striking out against their enemies. The latter representation in turn fully justifies portrayal of the soldiers that he as governor sent out on expeditions to kill Indian raiders and drive them away from settlements as heroic defenders of the homeland. After all, Alvarado will repeatedly argue, Californios were entitled to the credit they deserved for rescuing the territory from the domination of the "bárbaros infieles" (Alvarado, 4:204).

In several cases stories of rebellious Indians and rebellious women form one subgenre. In these episodes insubordinate subordinates meet a similar end: punishment or death. Coronel mentions the wife of Cosme Peña, who was abducted as she traveled with three men back to Mexico via Sonora; the men were killed and she was carried off. These anecdotes always include chance encounters years later with the hostages, by then acculturated to Indian ways but still hoping to be rescued back to civilization. Those spotting them always are at a numerical disadvantage and cannot rescue the Californio maidens. The Indian is thus viewed as desecrating what is most sacred, the family, and violating what is most prized by a Californio, his women (wife, mother, daughter, and so on). That Indian women were violated is acknowledged and, at times, regretted, but for the most part goes unremarked or accepted as natural. Kidnapping was not simply practiced by raiding Indians but by "civilized" Californios as well, who profited from kidnapping Indian girls and boys.[6]

Indian raids are most often presented as criminal acts rather than as acts of resistance, as would be the case after 1846 in newspaper accounts of Californio bandits. These raid stories are thus generally recorded alongside stories of vigilante actions by Californios. Juana Machado recalls that in 1838 or 1839, word of a planned insurrection of Indians in San Diego was leaked by a woman working for Captain Henry Fitch and his wife, Josefa Carrillo. According to the Indian servant, Candelaria, the plan was to enter Fitch's store, kill the clerk (Lawrence Hartwell), rob the store, burn the house, and kidnap the women. The conspiracy was said to be the plan of several Indians, three of whom worked for the Fitch and Estudillo households. The same story is told by Felipa Osuna de Marrón, who indicates that she, understanding the Indians' language, overheard a group of Dieguino Indians plotting to rob Fitch's store, kill the clerk, and kidnap Fitch's wife and Osuna herself. As in Machado's account, the Indians were local servants working at the homes of Marrón, Fitch, and Estudillo. Osuna de Marrón revealed the plot to her husband, Captain Marrón, who warned the Fitch family and that night waited at the Fitch home for the Indians to appear. When two of them appeared at Josefa's kitchen, Marrón and others are said to have fought them off.

The absence of *presidio* soldiers in town is in several accounts responsible for putting the *gente de razón* at risk. (As stated earlier, Juana Machado recalls that in 1839 no soldiers were at the *presidio*; the closest ones were at the San Luis Rey mission.) In Osuna's account, it again becomes necessary to seek the help of the famous Indian fighter González from Baja California, who comes to take the conspirators prisoner. She recalls that the San Diegans, fearing an attack by Cuyamaca Indians said to be in on the plot, also sought the help of foreigners, the hide and tallow traders, in the area. Once the would-be attackers were caught, there was no trial and the *alférez* from Baja California took it upon himself to judge and sentence them on the spot. After taking their declarations, González took them all to a gully and had them shot:

> Immediately thereafter they were taken to a canyon next to what is now the Protestant cemetery and there without even giving them Last Rites he had the five shot. The men were buried at the same place where they were executed. (Machado, 1878: 19)

Osuna recalls that the local judge disapproved of González's action: "The judge was Don José Antonio Estudillo and he disapproved of the violent action taken by Macedonio with the Indians" (23). The judge's son also recalls being a young boy at the time and upset when his family's Indian servant was killed without reason by González (Estudillo, 9). Osuna, who had turned the Indians in, felt guilty and was blamed for their deaths by other women, she says (22–23). For others, González was a hero who had stopped an insurrection, and the fact that the conspiracy was never proved was not an issue. The fear of the Californios justified González's actions. Machado's concern, what little is expressed, was for the souls of the Indians, not for their lives. After the execution, she says, nothing happened and tranquillity was restored: "Everything returned to normal after the Indian ringleaders were shot, and we considered ourselves out of danger" (1878: 18–19). The Osuna-Machado episode is like an epilogue rounding out the Jamul story. Revenge for the kidnapping and defeat at the hands of the Indians would be exacted by González and his men at the mere suggestion of impropriety—or even without it.

This type of vigilante justice against Indians is reconstructed in a number of testimonials that mention death sentences for relatively minor offenses or even suspicion thereof. Lorenzana recalls that one of her own Indian workers, whom she describes as "a hardworking man, peaceful and obedient," requested permission to leave her ranch to go to his *ranchería* in the sierra in order to bring his wife back to the ranch. Upon their return, the Indian fighter González showed up at Lorenzana's ranch and killed the Indian.

> He had already returned with his wife and was working when one day Sergeant Macedonio showed up at my ranch (I was at the mission) and, without giving reason or cause, killed the man. Perhaps he harbored suspicions about the poor devil, but I for one am convinced that the poor Indian was innocent. (Lorenzana, 42)

As a result of the apparently unprovoked killing, this Indian's brother incited others in town to join the conspiracy recalled in the Machado text. The various testimonial episodes now reveal themselves to be a longer story that the reader has to rearticulate. What seemed to be a linear narration is actually configured within separate testimonials. Once we become aware of the emplotment, the continuities and discontinuities of the macrotext become more obvious. Macedonio González is now the avenging hero who participates in several moves or sequences in an extended narrative.[7] In every case his action is described as force-ful and harsh: "Macedonio González acted with much forcefulness and severity" (Lorenzana, 43). González thus takes the law into his own hands in the south, where apparently no one questions his right to try and to sentence Indians on the spot. Afterward, in what takes on the appearance of a personal vendetta, those Indians leaving the area to work in Los Angeles and suspected of having participated in some uprising are tracked down by González, even though, according to Lorenzana, their good behavior is undeniable and worthy of praise:

> Often these same Indians would tire of their wild unruly ways and would move to Los Angeles to work as servants in homes there where their behavior was irreproachable. Apparently Macedonio González, believing one of these Indians who had been working at an orchard in Los Angeles and behaving well to be involved in something, went in and shot and killed him. (Lorenzana, 43)

Lorenzana, well served by both the neophyte and gentile Indians who worked her three ranches, notes the *dureza* of González but does not condemn him for this "harshness," even in the case of unwarranted ex-ecutions (the hero is allowed to kill all his assumed enemies). She goes on to relate that the theft of horses and cattle was often instigated by the very mission Indians who would organize the "gentiles" for at-tacks on Californios. Women introduce a note of uncertainty and hesi-tation in recalling Californio or *mexicano* actions against the Indians, but men, for the most part, who often participate in these reprisals, tend to exaggerate their own heroic action and even their slaughter of the Indian raiders (Lugo, 209).

There are a few counterstories in these testimonials, presumably told from the perspective of the Indian. These intercalated mininarratives reveal that the "emancipation" of the Indians in California did not lead to a recognition of Indian rights, to a genuine distribution of land to the Indians, to wage labor for the Indians, or to any improvement in their condition, despite the fact that liberal discourses countering their enslavement had served as justification for the secularization of the missions. The stories generally begin with the flight of the neophytes from the missions or ex-missions back to the "wilderness," a site from which they would initiate their raids. Comments by the Californios in their testimonials would suggest that the discourses of liberty served postindependence neophytes to construct their antagonism, to fight for an end to enslavement, but clearly other constructs, earlier discourses of resistance, had led to insurrections before 1822 and even to the killing of two missionaries, Fray Luis Jayme in San Diego in 1775 and Fray Quintana in Santa Cruz in 1812 (Alvarado, 1:97–99). The earliest Indian warriors celebrated by Alvarado are Marín and Quintín (Kintin); later, Pomponio, Zampay, Buenheme, and Daniel are all warriors plotted as worthy adversaries of the "glorious" Californio soldiers (Alvarado, 1:107; MGV, 1:147). Often the emplotment is romantic, as in the descriptions of the bandit and former neophyte Pomponio, said to be "the bravest and most fearsome of the Cainameros tribe" (Alvarado, 1982: 33) and of the handsome, haughty, and defiant Indian Chalpinich, who led an uprising of Indians from the Fresno, Tulare, Merced, Mariposa, and Kern areas in 1818 (MGV, 1:113). After secularization, the ex-mission Indians would continue to resist through mass protests, work stoppages, guerrilla action, and insurrection.

Two large-scale insurrections planned for the liberation of the entire territory from Californio domination stand out in the testimonials: those of Pacomio and Estanislao, both taking place long before secularization. Both leaders are described as educated ex-neophytes or *cimarrones* who wanted to free their people. Both insurrections failed, according to Alvarado (2:49–68), because the Indians (like the Californios) were divided. Pacomio, who would inspire a series of Indian revolts in 1824, is a typical romantic hero in these testimonials:

> There was in the mission of la Purísima an Indian named Pacomio, a handsome young man, well built, insightful, steadfast, extraordinarily intelligent, and provenly brave. (MGV, 1:351)

Pacomio's complex plans for insurrection called for building a fort, amassing weapons, and congregating thousands of Indians at the Purísima mission to rid the territory once and for all of Christians (MGV, 1:353). The weapons and fort were soon ready, but the messages to the Indians were intercepted and the plan foiled. Five years later, in 1829, Estanislao too organized gentile tribes friendly with the missionaries. They took positions near the Stanislaus River, hid in the forest, dug trap holes and trenches, and positioned snipers armed with bows and arrows. M. G. Vallejo, assigned to head the second squad sent to fight Estanislao, after the first squad failed, would gain the tactical advantage by smoking the Indians out of their hiding places, and the battle would end with a massacre of the Indians (Alvarado, 2:58–67). The failure of this mass action against the Californios would be the last organized effort of mass resistance. Smaller raids and other guerrilla tactics would continue until 1846. To demonstrate the settlers' fear, Alvarado notes that in the north no woman ever went out without carrying her own rifle (4:158).

Reconstructions of numerous neophyte and gentile uprisings signal a new and important element in the narratives related to conditions on the ex-missions, now in the hands of lay administrators who
were not providing for the neophytes' needs and who were often leasing them as if they were slaves, overworking them as much as or more
than they had been under Franciscan rule. It is understandable that
they should have not only fled but subsequently raided establishments
built entirely with their labor. The neophytes, of course, knew the disposition of the missions and what livestock and horses were available
at the various *ranchos* (MGV, 4:29). These raids would diminish in number, as much due to armed Californio reaction as perhaps to the smallpox epidemic that decimated the population of uninoculated Indians,
especially in the north (MGV, 4:29).

The image of Indian resistance functions in the testimonials to buttress the representation of the Californios as hardy pioneers who had
to undergo hardships, danger, and attack from hostile forces in this
Mexican frontier, far from military and economic assistance. But the
reconstruction of the raids also serves to construct Indian agency, an
important rewriting in view of the subjection the Indians continued to
face even after secularization. These narratives of resistance are countered by representations of Indian collaboration with the *rancheros*.
Several of the Indian caciques (including Marcelo of the Chologones
and Bolgones, Solano of the Suysuns, or Juan Antonio of Temécula
[MGV, 1:146; Lugo, 208]) would form alliances with the Californios in
order to defeat other tribes. Additional constructs are provided of Indians who, once defeated, like the great Marín, made their peace with
the Californios (MGV, 1:149), and either became their allies, like Sem
Yeto (Chief Solano), or acculturated, becoming respected *pueblo* residents, like Pacomio, who lived among *gente de razón* as a sought-after
cabinetmaker in Monterey (MGV, 1:8, 149, 358–69; Alvarado, 2:57).

Despoliation of the Mission and Neophyte Displacement

The battles and raids are only one dimension of this macronarrative.
In an examination of the constructs of the *ranchos* and ex-missions we
find an explanation of why secularization in California was both partial and conditional: if in theory the process called for the emancipation of the neophytes and the distribution of land and livestock to the
Indians, what in fact took place was the assignment of the missions
to secular administrators who further dispossessed and displaced the

neophytes. Previously, as Fernández recalls in what amounts to a flash-back, the missionaries had had the Indians do everything, both at the mission and at the *presidio*:

> The neophytes worked the fields, loaded the ships, constructed the houses, fabricated the adobes, looked after the stock, sheared the sheep, salted the meat, and did all the chores at the *presidio* and if it is true that the missionaries provided their upkeep and dressed them, one cannot however deny that the neophytes with their labor made the missionaries rich. (28–29)

Afterward the administrators despotically controlled the production of the neophytes for their own gain and that of the territorial adminis-tration and friends of the administrator and/or governor, until the missions had been totally ransacked and destroyed. All the neophytes who had not fled were leased by the administrators to other *rancheros*, much as the missionaries had leased them to the *presidios* and towns-people (Lugo, 206). Pío Pico recalls being appointed as administrator of the ex-mission of San Luis Rey in 1835 and attempting to "follow the same regime as the padres" (1973: 158). He claims finding the store-house empty and in total disorder when he arrived, but he soon had the neophytes planting, working at the various industries, and graz-ing cattle at the seven *ranchos* that were part of the mission, extending from San Diego into Riverside County. In an obvious attempt to vin-dicate himself, Pico goes on to state that when he was dismissed by Governor Alvarado in 1840 he left the storehouses full, along with thou-sands of sheep, cattle, and so on, a state of affairs corroborated by For-ster (206). One year later when Pico visited San Luis Rey he found that "there remained nothing but a small amount of liquor that was being manufactured" (Pico, 1973: 98), a comment demonstrating that "secu-larization" of the missions in reality translated into wholesale plunder by the Californios.

The despoliation of the missions meant the pillage of immense wealth in cattle, sheep, horses, mules, and the ruin of vineyards, or-chards, gardens, and fields of corn and wheat. Testimonial reconstruc-tion of this plunder serves to censure not only governors but also re-gional rivals who became the administrators of the ex-missions. To the crime of despoliation will be added critiques of land distribution to a favored few. The testimonials thus become not confessions but a means to condemn enemies and rivals. The southerner Botello, for ex-ample, will accuse the northerner Alvarado of having given a number of mission *ranchos* to his friends and cronies and of "lending" them livestock with no provisions ever made for their repayment (Botello, 94). Alvarado was also criticized for taking cattle and other goods from the mission to feed his soldiers and militiamen during the period of armed clashes with the south over the governorship claimed by both himself and Carlos Carrillo. Alvarado clearly is defending his actions by saying that his soldiers, by keeping Carrillo from coming to power, this man who would have made off with all the wealth of the missions, and by defending the neophytes from attacks by hostile gentiles, deserved to be rewarded with a few thousand steers. Thus "hostile Indians" are always marshaled as the perfect justification for whatever actions were taken and Alvarado is adamant about this fact in 1876, lest those no longer threatened by hostile Indians feel that he exaggerates (Alvarado, 4:57–58). Ensconced in this self-righteousness, Alvarado claims to be unconcerned by criticism:

> Public opinion matters little to me insofar as my conduct toward the emancipated Indians, for my conscience tells me that I did for them more than I should have; convinced as I am that if I have committed any error in my dealings with the Indians it has been on the side of humanity, it matters little what is said or written on this subject by those who, ignoring the state of affairs in my country during the period of my administration, are not able to fully appreciate the true merit of the measures that I then adopted. (4:55–56)

Alvarado was certain that history would vindicate his actions, especially his giving mission lands to (among many others) his friend José Castro and, as a payoff, to Guerra y Noriega for supporting him during the civil insurrection. Yet he was not so generous in his opinion of Pío Pico, whom he accused of giving land to all his relatives when he became governor in 1845 (Alvarado, 5:110). Vallejo expresses the same opinion about Pico, said to be especially eager to please beautiful women who caught his fancy, and uses the opportunity the testimonial provides to criticize President Grant by equating the nepotism and favoritism of the two (MGV, 5:42).

The testimonials thus become a vehicle for attacks on the *sureños* or the *norteños* in light of their dispossession of the neophytes and for charges of opportunism in the distribution of mission lands. But, at every turn, Vallejo, narrating in the 1870s, will indicate that the Yankees had no grounds whatsoever to censure the Californios, as their hands were equally tarnished by usurpation. Cast aside and forgotten in these regional struggles are all the liberal debates in defense of the neophytes in which these Californios had engaged upon the arrival of Hijar and Padrés. Only Coronel recalls the liberal discourses of the Californios and their self-righteous questioning of the motives of Hijar and Padrés, and comments with a great deal of sarcasm that secularization had in fact served to increase the property of a few administrators but done nothing to improve the lot of the Indians (16). What becomes clear is that all involved knew that the underlying objective of the *diputados* opposing Hijar and Padrés in 1835 had always been privatization of mission lands to free up the productive spaces in California. If in the process of dismantling the missions, the Indians had been cast adrift and left to fend for themselves in a highly unstable social and economic order, the rival faction was always to blame. Even in Coronel's critique, the ethical question is not his primary concern; he foregrounds instead the loss of labor power and production, and the despoliation:

> Mismanagement [of the secularized missions] and failure to take advantage of the labor power of more than twenty thousand Indians, which would have been useful for the nation's progress, resulted in the destruction of the lands that were at that time the only source of wealth ... the majority of the administrators that had come to their posts poor, in a very short time came to be the owners of the wealthiest mission *ranchos* stocked with great quantities of cattle and horses — the missions were soon left destitute. (16–17)

For Coronel it was utter folly to forfeit the potential gain, the surplus, that thousands of workers could have produced. Thus within the narratives there are those who even in hindsight mourn the economic loss more than the social injustice.

Coronel's assertions are also taken up by M. G. Vallejo, who felt that the administrators for the most part had taken advantage of their posts as mission managers to rob not only the Indians but what he in retrospect constructs as the Californio nation (MGV, 4:15). Vallejo, named military commander of the northern frontier in 1834 and sent by Governor Figueroa to secularize the San Francisco Solano mission, never served as a mission administrator but was nevertheless accused by missionaries and foreigners alike of making off with mission cattle and even the grapevines of San Rafael.[8] Aware of these accusations, Vallejo in his testimonial assumes a critical perspective, especially of Alvarado's judgment in naming administrators for the missions:

> In the majority of his appointments he did not manage to select
> individuals who had the requisite probity necessary in people placed
> in so responsible a position as to administer the estates of minors.
> (MGV, 4:17)

Despite mounting criticism of particular administrators from various
quarters, Alvarado found his hands tied, for he did not dare remove
members of influential families who were furthermore members of his
own inner circle and might be called on to make loans to a government
in need (MGV, 4:23–24). One of the administrators that he did remove
was his own uncle José de Jesús Vallejo. According to his brother, the
elder Vallejo was one of the few that kept receipts for everything that
he was ordered to turn over and was removed not for malfeasance but
for not cooperating with Castro, who wanted to make use of mission
properties and livestock (MGV, 4:16, 18). Also accused by "a mean-
spirited, shameless, and dishonest writer" of mistreating a missionary,
J. J. Vallejo, like other Californios, utilizes his testimonial to respond
to accusations levied against him (JJV, 58). Here J. J. Vallejo is obviously denying statements by de Mofras, who accuses him of putting
the missionary on rations and growing rich "from the spoils."[9] Evidently no love was lost between the missionaries and the Vallejos as
seen in the writings of several foreigners aligned with the church. Interestingly, among some sectors of the population who resent the collusion of the governor and the ex-mission administrators (called by
Coronel [216] "government satellites" or agents), the condemnation of
new administrators will now replace all critique of the missionaries.

Diminished production and lack of revenues, as well as failure to
distribute land to the Indians, become not problems of the territorial
government but consequences of corrupt practices of rival administrators. In other cases, however, the Indian paradoxically is blamed.
Previously, when Alvarado as governor had suspended the distribution of land and livestock to the neophytes, he had argued that the few
Indians receiving this property had rapidly abandoned it or sold it to
buy liquor (Alvarado, 4:60). This typical "blame the victim" strategy sets
up the Indians as deficient and incapable of dealing responsibly with
or benefiting from private property and justifies Alvarado's order that
all neophytes return to communal life in the ex-missions (MGV, 3:361).

The Indians previously cast as villains in the narratives are now
transformed and reconstructed as children by the Californio narrators,
falling back on the same constructs used by the missionaries to justify
their *reducciones*. In fact, during the first stages of secularization, the

majority of neophyte *manumisos* had remained restricted to communal life on the ex-mission, according to the conditional freedom advocated by Figueroa, a position backed by both Alvarado and Vallejo. Deteriorating conditions on the mission and the practice of leasing neophyte labor soon began to push the Indians out of the mission. Alvarado says that this "leasing of the Indians" accelerated by the mission administrators did not begin during his term, as suggested by some, but rather under that of governors Victoria and Chico. The practice was a return of sorts to the *repartimiento* in which the Indians were sent to *ranchos* needing workers, now allowing the governor (rather than the missionaries) to be paid for leasing secularized mission neophytes. That in California these "freed" Indians were "shamelessly" rented out to private individuals (Alvarado, 3:104) is a travesty that Alvarado condemns years later as a "retrograde policy" originating with Governor Chico:

> I have always thought that it was an injustice in 1839 to force the poor neophyte Indians to work for next to nothing at tasks that were not of their choosing. (4:59)

What this rather naive-sounding apology does not make clear is that the Californios had been all too willing to reinstitute the forced labor of the Indians after declaring them emancipated. Tracing the practice to a previous governor did not change matters; in fact, like other *rancheros* and *hacendados*, Alvarado himself acknowledges that he used leased Indians for the trapping of sea otters under Victoria's administration. For this reason he had allowed the leasing to continue, for how, he unconvincingly argues (4:59–60), could he stop a practice of which he too was guilty? Subsequently, as borne out by numerous testimonials, the abuse of Indian workers became so great that the leased Indians (sometimes entire families forced to put in long workdays and poorly fed) deserted the *ranchos* or tried to find another party to lease them (MGV, 4:17, 19). Flight now meant escaping from the *ranchos* rather than the missions, as the narrative assumes a spiral configuration with the restoration of forced labor.

The government would ultimately prohibit the practice of leasing, as even the remaining missionaries had begun to denounce the displacement of the neophytes from the mission to the *ranchos* (MGV, 4:20).[10] In 1839, when Alvarado left his secretary Jimeno Casarín in charge during an illness, the interim governor put an end to this practice. The precipitating event, Alvarado recalls, was the arrival of an old Indian from the San Juan Capistrano mission who complained before Casarín

of having been forced to work for the Cota ranch, where he was mistreated by the foreman:

> The old man ... left the Cota house and stealing a saddled horse rode
> up to Monterey where he presented his complaints to Mr. Casarín.
> Wishing to make known the extent of his resentment he said, "I am not
> an animal to be made to work for bosses who are not to my liking. You
> can do with me two things: have me executed, if you like, or set me
> free, if you are a just man; it is all the same to me. I am already old and
> know that I must die soon; it matters little to me to die today or
> tomorrow!" (4:126–127)

By this time we are dealing with acculturated Spanish-speaking ex-
neophytes who are being treated at best as indentured servants and at
worst as slaves, as they are not paid wages but simply provided with
subsistence (MGV, 4:27). Casarín named a commissioner to visit the
ranchos and *haciendas* with leased Indian workers, and he was informed
by Commissioner Estrada that, ostensibly unbeknownst to the owners
of the *ranchos,* leased neophytes were in fact treated harshly by the
foremen. As a result of this report, Casarín ordered all ex-mission administrators to stop the leasing of Indians (Alvarado, 4:127). True to his class
interests, Estrada (who was Alvarado's stepfather) found the foremen—
not the owners—responsible for the ill treatment of the Indians; the
property owners, of course, were exempted from blame. Ironically, in
view of his previous unwillingness to act on this practice, Alvarado,
upon resuming his office, states that he approved this "humane" and
"just" measure (4:127).

But Casarín's injunction on the leasing of Indians, contrary to what
Alvarado would have us believe, was not followed in practice. According to Vallejo, "that measure was merely written but things continued
going from bad to worse" (MGV, 4:19). Concerned with Indian deser-
tions as much as with the leasing, Hartnell, the supervisor of the missions, asked that the Indians be forcibly returned to communal life at
the missions and placed under the supervision of the mission administrators or ranch foremen. This additional measure, meant in reality to
favor the administrators who needed workers for harvest, reinforced
the abuse of the Indians, who by all rights, according to Echeandía's
decree in 1826, were, if of good conduct, entitled to freedom of movement (MGV, 4:21). Vallejo questions Hartnell's authority to use military force to remand the Indians "suffering hunger and a lack of clothing" to the missions (MGV, 4:22). According to Vallejo in his indictment
of Hartnell, "the foreigner" did not question or take into consideration

the implications of his order to use force to return the Indians to the ex-missions, subjecting them in the process to continued oppression (MGV, 4:22). Here Vallejo, an *hacendado* who had hundreds of ex-neophyte Indians at his service, advocates freedom of movement for the neophytes, yet, as the powerful feudal lord of the northern frontier, made use of a large labor pool of Indian labor and was able to keep his peons at his disposal by offering subsistence and little else.

Leased manumitted Indians, like mission neophytes, were more akin to slaves than to serfs, but an even more obvious form of servitude was practiced outside the mission. Apparently the kidnapping of Indian women and children for sale to Californio families was a profitable business. Among the northern California Indian tribes, Vallejo reports, slavery had been practiced before the colonization of Alta California, especially with the women of enemy tribes who were often kidnapped and enslaved (MGV, 1:11). During Alvarado's administration, a plot was revealed at New Helvetia where J. A. Sutter and his allies, both Indian and non-Indian, kidnapped "over twenty" Indian children to present as gifts to merchants and other foreigners who had extended credit to the Swiss entrepreneur. This traffic in Indian children was not limited to New Helvetia, for Vallejo also uncovered a scheme between several Californios and several Suysun Indians, including his ally, Chief Solano, to kidnap and sell Indian children. Both boys and girls were kidnapped, but girls were in special demand, for they were said to make "excellent servants," as Alvarado (4:216) recalls.

When Vallejo discovered that "over thirty" children, both boys and girls, had been kidnapped in the Californio/Suysun incident, he feared for his name (MGV, 3:331). The reputed friend of the Indians was concerned that he might be accused of hypocrisy and insincerity, for he well knew that he was constantly the subject of rumors, placing him in some cases under Indian siege or, given his alliance with Chief Solano, about to descend on Monterey with hundreds, if not thousands, of Indian soldiers at his disposal (Alvarado, 3:139). His aristocratic bearing, authoritarian ways, and wealth did not win him any friends, not among southern Californios and especially not among historians, whom he accuses of purposely falsifying the record (MGV, 3:341). For this reason, Vallejo's testimonial wishes to make clear that he went so far as to have his ally Solano arrested and jailed for his involvement in the kidnapping, even though in so doing he exposed all of Sonoma to attack by the chief's Indian allies. When Vallejo confronted Solano with his crime, the latter confessed and promised not only to reveal where the children had been sent but to help retrieve them, thereby averting the crisis. Vallejo attributes Solano's crime to the liquor that he had been given and further clarifies that he found that the Californios involved in the kidnappings were a group of men named Castro—not the Castro family "de sangre azul" with whom he and Alvarado were intimate, but other mestizo and mulatto Castros (MGV, 3:334). Thus caste and crime are conflated again in this instance by Californios to account for deeds deemed unworthy of white *gente de razón*.

In the emplotment seen thus far the heroes begin to look a good deal like villains and the narrators, in hindsight and faced with multiple contradictions, are forced to point to the "real villains": lower-class, mestizo-mulatto Californios and foreigners. Even villains could be subdivided into different categories, as the episode of Solano is meant to demonstrate. In inserting this incident, Alvarado seeks not only to lay out the Californios' abolitionist stance with respect to slavery (Alvarado, 4:218), but to contrast the behavior of Sutter to that of Solano. The Indian chief, considered ignorant and unaware of the consequences of his actions, recognized his crime and regretted having participated in a scheme that could have ruined the reputation of his friend Vallejo, whereas "the illustrious" Sutter, a foreigner who should have been above kidnapping children (Alvarado, 4:218), is revealed as less "civilized" than "even an Indian." Sutter did not desist from the kidnapping of young Indian girls, as Alvarado indicates by quoting from Sutter's letter to Larkin's wife: "Today I am sending Mrs. Larkin an Indian girl of a tender age, but as soon as I go out into the field I will send you an older one" (4:218). Here we find gender discourses wielded to underscore Sutter's crime and to compare him, unfavorably, to the Californios and even to Solano.

That the elite of California benefited directly from the breakup of the missions is made all the more clear when one considers what happened at the end of 1840 when the president of Mexico, through his secretary of the interior, asked that Alvarado return the missions to the missionaries. The California governor, says Vallejo, was unwilling to follow an order that would have alienated "the most powerful families of southern and northern Alta California" (MGV, 4:23). It was not in the governor's interest to return these establishments because they were the source of revenue for the government and the source of land and cattle for the new *rancheros* (MGV, 4:24). The fact that the Indians did not receive the land that the Californios had formerly argued belonged to the neophytes is explained in terms of the Indians' failure to apprehend the value of property. Vallejo's analysis here is again contradictory; there is a condemnation of the abusive practices of the ex-mission administrators and at the same time an insistence that the distribution plan had not and would not have worked. In the same breath he seeks to let the government off the hook, for although his account recognizes that neophytes had been dispossessed, it also blames the victims rather than the system that exploited them. In the end the Californios continue to make full strategic use of Figueroa's paternalistic discourses to justify the dispossession of the Indians, forgetting that they had previously made use of liberal discourses to condemn their dispossession. One discourse was meant to obviate the other; the only disjuncture, a liminal space of armed Indian struggle fleetingly seen in the testimonials, had by this time been obliterated. What remained was displacement and destitution or peonage on Californio *ranchos* and *haciendas*. These new spaces of production, constituting a new site of emplotment, would in effect be the new heterotopias.

Ranchos and haciendas

> For many years cattle-raising was the chief if not sole occupation of the Hispano-Californians. It was a mode of life well suited to their tempers and habits. There was little work about it, little of the drudgery of labor, such as attended agriculture and manufacture, and if in the pursuit there was little of the sweet power that displays itself in the domination of men, the *ranchero* might at least rule cattle.
>
> H. H. Bancroft

The often-repeated description of Spanish/Mexican California as a "pastoral" golden period found in several historical accounts is of course a romantic, idealized, and highly complex construction of the conquered Californios that all but begs for disarticulation. Behind Bancroft's "pastoral" configuration, for example, is an absolute disdain for the Californios, a typically racist portrayal drawn with disparaging remarks about lack of ambition, lack of industriousness, and lack of a desire for power and domination in men capable of standing tall only over cattle. The nineteenth-century historian here makes use of romantic emplotment to both deride the conquered and substantiate the flaws that led to their fall.

The term "pastoral" or "Arcadian" as regards the reality of Spanish/ Mexican California is also unfortunate in that it evokes an idyllic scene complete with green valley and stream in the background, a lonely shepherd playing a flute, his faithful dog by his side, and hundreds or thousands of sheep grazing nearby. If rose-colored glasses are removed and the historical reality is focused upon more closely, we see that instead of sheep, we have hundreds if not thousands of head of cattle before us and instead of a quiet contemplative boy or young man, there are six cowboys on horseback, riding hard in the dust after the cattle, with knives in hand to stab the livestock in the back of the head; right and left the cattle drop. These are Indian cowboys, *nuqueadores*, experts at their task, moving as the rest of the cattle scatter before them. To the right we have advancing toward the fallen livestock dozens of *peladores*, Indian skinners moving in like threshing machines to remove the hides from the dead animals. Right behind the skinners come the *tasajadores*, the butchers who cut and dress the meat, and finally behind these come dozens of Indian women to cut the fat and gather it in leather sacks while still other women prepare the fire where they cook the tallow in iron pots, allow it to cool, and then pour it into large leather pouches or boots. Instead of a placid meadow we see a gory sight of blood, meat, intestines — nothing less than an open-air slaughterhouse (MGV, 4:108–9). What was construed as "little work" for Bancroft meant hours of hard labor for the Indian ranch hands and servants on both missions and *ranchos*.

The scene enacted is an abridged version of Vallejo's reconstruction of an Indian laborer's day of *nuqueo* on a *rancho* or *hacienda*. This division of labor, of fast-paced activity involving both men and women, with each task requiring greater or lesser skills, produced meat not only for subsistence but for dried *tasajo* and *charqui* to trade with visiting ships. The tallow and hides would be traded for goods or currency, or exported to the Sandwich Islands, Peru, Canada, or Boston, subject to the transportation fees established by the carriers or the ships' masters (MGV, 4:110). Vallejo's description of the *nuqueo* is one of the few detailed accounts of production found in the testimonials, but any mention of wages or compensation for these workers is glaring in its absence. In a society in which hides and tallow were the commodities of exchange on a capitalist world market, the Indians who made that commerce possible remained locked in semifeudal relations and with nothing to show for their work but subsistence. The testimonials are thus full of these gaps, of unrecognized disjunctures, evident in the discursive fissures.

That the Californios' testimonials are in part romantic emplotments of the past is evident in the intercalation of miniromances. They are also contestatory texts narrated very much against the grain of the histories on Alta California written by others. Yet the romanticized "pastoral" myth has endured in museum and historical sites along California Highway 101 as well as in Hollywood's portrayals of Californio life. A reading of these testimonials requires a reading against the romantic grain, although elements of the "Arcadian" myth surface in some of the testimonials, especially sections that respond to interviewers' questions on customs and traditions, as in Coronel's *Cosas de California*, a testimonial that offers insightful critiques of Californio society from a Mexican and *sureño* perspective.[11] In his old age Coronel fell prey to staging simulacrums of Californio life, posing for pictures in period costume with guitar and boots, and dancing for the erstwhile ethnographers and photographers trying to "capture" a disappeared but picturesque "Olde California." Nostalgia would blur the testimonial critique and succumb through musical and photographic performance to hegemonic appropriation of residual discourses. Coronel was not to be the only co-opted Californio. In his romantic sketch "Ranch and Mission Days in Alta California," Guadalupe Vallejo (nephew of Mariano Guadalupe Vallejo) focuses on "the long pastoral age before 1840" in which lived a "peaceful happy people" made up of a Spanish, Mexican, and Indian population. All Californios, of course, were, in his reconstruction, well-to-do with plentiful servants: "No one need suppose that the Spanish pioneers of California suffered many hardships or privations" because in this utopia the Indians "reached the very perfection of silent, careful, unselfish service," the missionaries were well loved, the Californios enjoyed grizzly bear and bull fights, the Indian servants thrived on doing the family wash by the stream and then walked home singing hymns while the Californios rode their carts (G. Vallejo, 1971: 3–5, 22–24). "Ranch and Mission Days in Alta California," while approximating a California version of "happy slaves" in the South, does allow for the intersection of two dissonant discourses: both counterdiscourses are produced in the fissures and margins of the text. The first is introduced tangentially in reference to the dispossession of Californios by squatters who after invasion, by taking "advantage of laws they understood but which were new to the Spaniards," were able to take over their land. A second disjunctive form of reconstruction is evident in the testimonials' attempt to justify the missions' training of women in the care of children through a brief reference to the sadistic punishment of an Indian woman who lost her child, an episode presented in chapter 2. These two constructs, dispossession and gender repression, are mentioned only in passing but nonetheless are two threads that unravel the entire romantic tapestry woven by Guadalupe Vallejo.

The world of Alta California was not an idyllic "pastoral" society; on the contrary, it was a cattle-raising, labor-intensive, tallow-and-hide-producing economy with a largely "unfree" labor force made up of Indian men and women whose ancestors had lived on those lands for generations. Property relations had shifted, as was evident in the fact that the mission *ranchos* were now claimed as private domains, but for the Indians there had been little or no change. With the breakup of the missions and a scarcity of provisions at the ex-missions, the neophytes had few options. They could either become peons on *ranchos* and *haciendas*, domestic workers in the *pueblos* and *rancho* homes, or displaced neophytes on the road or on *pueblo* streets with no place to stay except the wilderness and nothing to do except try to rejoin gentile communities. But some of these *indios manumisos* were second-generation neophytes, acculturated, bilingual, and no longer interested in returning to Indian *rancherías*. The *pueblos* thus began to see homeless Indians, hungry, cold, and begging — no longer subservient to the missionaries, J. J. Vallejo recalls, but no longer clothed or sheltered (JJV, 62–63). Archives indicate that in 1830 there were 198 Indians living in the outskirts of the *pueblo* of Los Angeles, but by 1836, with secularization, there were 533, residing primarily in their own segregated *ranchería*.[12] As new settlers became interested in the land where the *"ranchería* of poblanos"* was located, the Indians were removed to new sites further away, until in 1847 the main settlement of Indians was razed and they were scattered throughout the area (W. Robinson, 157). Minutes from the town council indicate that employers of Indians were required to house those working as cooks or house servants, but those who were self-sustaining laborers were ordered to find lodging outside the town limits in a variety of segregated sites (W. Robinson, 171). These *pueblo* Indians would be subjected not only to segregation and enforced spatial fragmentation but to labor on public works, like fixing the baptistery and enlarging the town water canal, often as punishment for drunkenness or homelessness ("Minutes," in W. Robinson, 158, 161), in imitation of forced labor practices in Mexico and the Andean region in the nineteenth century.

Instead of bringing emancipation to the Indians, secularization simply displaced the neophytes and subjected them to further *pueblo* discrimination and exploitation. In private cattle-raising *haciendas* or subsistence farming *ranchos* there was no interest in accommodating thousands of neophytes nor was there a need for that many workers. Even an autarkic *hacienda* like Vallejo's Petaluma needed only a few hundred peons and servants, and few landed estates were of that magnitude. The displacement and homelessness of the Indians were exacerbated with a further blow, the outbreak of smallpox in the late 1830s, an epidemic that would decimate the northern gentile population especially. In southern California, destitute Indians would succumb readily to venereal disease and alcoholism (Coronel, 225). This devastation, however, is traced back and attributed exclusively to the missionaries. No Californio felt responsible for a situation that the missionaries had created by treating the Indians as minors and neglecting to train them to be independent (Coronel, 225). The testimonials let us see how, for the Californios, disarticulating the myth of benevolent missionaries and happy Indians had become by then a way of avoiding reflexive construction of their own collusion in Indian genocide and dispossession.

In the new emplotment promised by secularization the hero was to be the new landed class that promised prosperity through increased production. Neither the prosperity nor the productivity materialized, as José de Jesús Vallejo recounts, describing the years following the restructuring:

> When the missions were secularized, many believed that agriculture
> would take a great leap forward and that production in the various
> industries would increase, but what happened was just the opposite.
> (JJV, 63)

Before secularization, most of the Californios had been able to obtain their agricultural produce from the missions, though even then a few farmers were involved in subsistence farming (Coronel, 229). The end of mission industries that had produced blankets, shoes, boots, clothing, cloth, carriages, and leather goods (such as saddles) gave rise to a noticeable scarcity of these items (JJV, 63). Soon they were available only in a handful of autarkic *haciendas*, like Petaluma; thereafter all of these articles would have to be bought from foreign trading vessels (MGV, 4:233). Only the quest for land and the privatization of this capital had been attained through restructuring, for, with secularization, "the 260 leagues of the finest land in California" previously controlled by the missionaries had become available for concession by the governor (Fernández, 28–29). For most Californios, access to private land meant possession of vast cattle ranges, not the development of the necessary infrastructure for modernization.

Secularization increased the number of property owners to such an extent that Vallejo estimated that just in the northern frontier alone there were seventeen *haciendas* and twenty-five *ranchos*, all productive and able to expand, all with their own boat landing and potentially able to meet the needs of whaling ships that could be attracted to San Francisco if only the *aduana* were to be transferred there (MGV, 3:342–354). Testimonials like that of Vallejo remind readers that within California there were those who had analyzed the problematic and saw the need for the development of the territory's infrastructure. Vallejo's synoptic view of Alta California's demographics, trade, and production, though limited in focus and devoid of consideration of relations of production (that is, the serflike conditions of the producers that would have had to have been transformed for any substantive change to take place), does allow us to see that back in 1841 he had already imagined a new configuration of social spaces. Yet there would be neither time nor capital nor the necessary changes at the level of relations of production during the Mexican period to give rise to these spaces. History proved Vallejo right about San Francisco, as he is quick to point out, but the mode of production under which the port's transformation to the hub of the Pacific would take place would be entirely different and not far off in time.

The historical emplotment after secularization thus continues to oppose "unfree" producers and exploiters, although now the private *ranchos* are the single most important domain of production, with cattle as the principal source of capital. The configuration of *ranchero*-Indian peon relations is not the main plotted story in these testimonials, for at the same time the territory encompassed a number of small family farms. To understand these relations of production it will be useful to look at the distinction made by Vallejo between *haciendas* and *ranchos* on the basis of size and industries. An *hacienda* was an autarkic ranch, self-sufficient like the missions. Vallejo's ranch at Petaluma, a ten-square-league *hacienda* (now a historical site and still impressive), was known as "the palace": "it was then the best *hacienda* house that existed in Alta California, for there blankets, shoes, stockings for both men and women, ordinary rugs, tools to work the fields, saddles, bridles, and so on, were manufactured" (MGV, 3:294). The Californio *haciendas* of Buriburí, San Antonio, Pinole, San Pablo, Napa, and Santa Teresa, like Petaluma, were all characterized, Vallejo recalls, by their "sumptuous buildings," housing for Indian servants (often more than one hundred, in addition to the *gente de razón* foremen), multiple shops and rooms for tools, dairy products, storage of tallow and hides for trade with Peruvian or U.S. ships, quarters for guests, and of course by their large herds of livestock with thousands of head of cattle and large numbers of mares (MGV, 3:312–13).

Vallejo's friendship with the northern Indians was not strictly out of humanitarian feelings, Alvarado acknowledges in his testimonial, but rather out of a need for their labor. "More than three thousand" Indian "peons" produced the "colossal fortune" of M. G. Vallejo, but Alvaredo claims not to know what his arrangement with these workers was, although he reports having heard that "in addition to supporting them and feeding them, he [Vallejo] did give them some money, which the Indians invested in the purchase of liquor" (Alvarado, 4:162). Even if Alvarado exaggerates the number of Indians working on Vallejo's *hacienda*, the servile relations are made quite clear, as is the fact that they were not wage laborers except for the money received for the purchase of drink. Simpson is much more graphic in his description of the workers on Vallejo's *hacienda*; he says they are treated as "menial drudges or as predial serfs," "the sons and daughters of bondage." He is especially repulsed by their acculturation: "and it was truly pitiable to hear Vallejo's beasts of burden speaking the Spanish language, as an evidence that the system, whatever the fault lay, had not failed through want of time" (Simpson, 30). Of course the implication here is that the British would have accomplished a lot more in the same length of time and presumably in a more "humane" fashion for, if we recall Balibar, British racism/colonialism always posited itself as more "humane" than the Spanish or Mexican variety.[13] But there was a British intolerance for the particular type of colonialism practiced by the Californios in the territory, for it brought them into close contact with natives that the British found disgusting. The use of Indian labor for everything horrified the visiting Englishman, who could only see unkempt Indian women ("native drudges, unwashed and uncombed") in charge of preparing the meals, which he describes as unfit for British consumption. His disdain extended to the entire Californio population that could eat refried beans, hot sauce, beef and tongue, and potatoes in their jackets, all "poisoned with the everlasting compound of pepper and garlic," and drink "bad tea and worse wine" — comments that allow us to gauge the degree to which the Eurocentric eye viewed and condemned much of what it saw in California except the land and what it offered, including its women (Simpson, 25–26).[14]

The construct of exploitation of the Indians is not missing in the testimonials, only naturalized. Dominance over the Indians does not arouse self-censure; rather, the Californios seem almost proud of their control over hundreds of workers from whom they could "naturally" extract surplus production. Salvador Vallejo, looking back on the thousands

of Indians who had disappeared by 1875, best expresses the use of Indian labor on the *haciendas* as servants, cowboys, and peons, while still
making use of paternalistic rationale to justify the superiority of the
gente de razón vis-à-vis the "friendly" Indians:

> Our friendly Indians were missed very much, for they tilled our soil,
> pastured our cattle, sheared our sheep, cut our lumber, built our
> houses, paddled our boats, made tiles for our houses, ground our
> grain, killed our cattle and dressed their hides for market, and made
> our burnt bricks, while the Indian women made excellent servants,
> took good care of our children, made every one of our meals, and be it
> said in justice to them that, though not learned in the culinary arts as
> taught by Italian and French books, they made very palatable and
> savory dishes. These people we considered members of our families;
> we loved them and they loved us; our intercourse was always pleasant;
> the Indians knew that our superior education gave us a right to
> command and rule over them, and we, guided by the teachings of the
> good missionaries and counseled by our forlorn position that made it
> very plain that in case of a general uprising of the Indians we could not
> cope with them, always did our best to strengthen the bond of
> friendship that bound the two races together. (46)

For Salvador Vallejo, Alta California is the epitome of the perfect feudal family with a strict patriarchal structure and a large pool of indentured laborers. To keep them consenting to their exploitation it was
necessary to use a combination of strategies, both coercive and per-
suasive, for in the final analysis the Californio soldiers could not have
survived against thousands of Indian warriors. Alliances with the various gentile chiefs who were kept well supplied with meat and horses
also helped to maintain the peace and to allow for coalitions against
particular warring tribes, a strategy for domination well practiced by
M. G. Vallejo in the north.

The family romance thus emplotted takes on attributes of the southern plantation system when the Californios describe their domestic
Indian servants' tasks, especially on the estates where a large labor
force allowed for specialization. This division of labor also served to
distinguish the workers and to give them a sense of expertise, as one
visitor from Peru, Manuel Torres, discovered:

> While visiting the Vallejo mansion, I commented to Doña Francisca
> [Benicia] as to the extraordinary number of natives in the courtyard.
> These, she explained, were the domestics needed to run her large
> household. Each of her children (there were eight at that time) had his
> own body servant. Then there were seven women to do the cooking

and six to do the wash, while on festive occasions, seven or eight were kept to grind corn for the tortillas. Another dozen were employed to do the spinning and weaving. In addition there were those who looked after the cleaning and those who tended the gardens and looked after the horses. Each servant specialized in doing one task and would be insulted if asked to perform some other duty.[15]

Having had such extensive labor resources at her disposal, Doña Benicia had nothing but resentment for her son-in-law John Frisbie when, in her old age and near penniless on account of Frisbie's speculation and loss of Vallejo's money (he is estimated to have lost over $156,000), she found herself in the 1870s forced to do all the household chores. She was no longer able to afford a single servant and had hardly enough to eat. She addressed an amazing letter to Frisbie in 1873 that took her three months to write in her old wavering hand, but it was never mailed.

Though not wealthy in terms of urban luxury household goods or lifestyle, the Californio *hacendados* were rich in land, cattle, horses, and in their access to cheap labor.[16] No other Californio had access to as many Indians and no other Californio was as wealthy as M. G. Vallejo, who owned three major properties. These were lost after the U.S. invasion, a loss never described in any detail in his testimonial. Bancroft, however, provides the following information:

> He [M. G. Vallejo] held thirty-three leagues, equal to 146,000 acres, with 400–500 acres under cultivation, the rest being used for pasturing; of stock he had from 12,000 to 15,000 head of meat cattle, 7,000 to 8,000 head of horses, and 2,000 to 3,000 sheep. He had also 300 working men with their usual portion of females and children, all kept in a nearly naked state, poorly fed, and never paid.[17]

José de Jesús Vallejo indicates that his brother was able to make thousands of *pesos* just on pelts brought to him by the Indians, until 1841, when, as a consequence of overhunting by Californios, Russians, and British trappers, the sea otter no longer existed in the region. M. G. Vallejo had plans for increasing production and trade and was constantly urging people to migrate north, but he had little desire and no incentive to change property relations. His brother's dream after retiring from military service, José de Jesús Vallejo says, was to work on increasing production in his *hacienda* industries of blankets, shoes, soap, and other articles, all of which relied exclusively on Indian labor (JJV, 155–56). Simpson estimates that given M. G. Vallejo's enormous herd of cattle (more than eight thousand head), he probably made about ten thousand dollars a year, not a meager sum. But if each mission had

had two to five times as many head of cattle, then Vallejo's wealth, though noteworthy, was small in comparison (Simpson, 18). The missions, with over twenty thousand laboring neophytes, had produced immense wealth, which, once in private hands, did not in the short period of twelve years (1834–46) yield the returns that might have been expected.

Many foreigners who visited California, like Simpson, Dana, and Robinson, describe the Californio men as indolent: "The Californians are an idle, thriftless people, and can make nothing for themselves."[18] Similar descriptions had been proffered by the Spanish missionaries, who found the Californios "given over to idleness" and satisfied with working only for subsistence, although they much preferred to "hire pagan Indians to do this as well as whatever work [was] to be done around the house" (Zalvidea, 239). Zalvidea further states that "the one activity they engage in is to go about on horseback from one *rancho* to another" (239), a comment that would be repeated by hegemonic historians and contribute to the romantic construction of the Californio Don. Coronel, not a native Californio and given to airs of superiority over the *hijos del país,* also remarks on their inclination to part-time employment:

> The men dedicated themselves almost exclusively to the care of the cattle and horses, chores that occupied them only during roundups for branding and safeguarding their property and during the slaughter of cattle for the collection of tallow and hides to make their purchases and pay off debts, as these were the commodities used for exchange. (228)

The romantic emplotment of heroic soldiers and brave *rancheros* facing hostile Indians is thus constantly undermined and dismantled by nonnative Californios and foreigners. The latter all agree that the Californio women were hardworking, as we shall see in chapter 5. The strategy employed by these detractors is to feminize the men in order to put their virility into question. Few of the testimonial narrators actually focus on the labor involved in the upkeep of a *rancho,* preferring to distance themselves from "menial labor," except for Californios like Lugo, who offers a totally different construct of the *ranchero* as a hardworking farmer "who passed the day in labor in the fields ... preparing the ground for sowing seed, bringing in wood, sowing the seed, reaping, and so on" (216). Women, too, played a key role in production, especially on the smaller *ranchos,* either by working the land or managing the place.

The emplotment of the wealthy *ranchero*-merchant is also evident in other types of texts that, like the testimonials, reveal relations of production established between landowners, ranch hands, and servants. One of these interesting texts is the will left by Tomás Yorba, who inherited part of Middle Santa Ana and Lower Santa Ana from his father, José Antonio Yorba. Tomás and his brothers inherited over 150,000 acres, of which about a fourth was claimed by him.[19] In addition to these lands, the will indicates that Tomás Yorba left an adobe house of eighteen rooms, a soap factory, two vineyards, orchards, lands with cultivated crops, two thousand beef cattle, nine hundred ewes "with corresponding rams," three herds of mules, three burros, twenty-one broken horses, seven broken mules, and other horses and mules.[20] Robinson's description of Yorba as a well-dressed *ranchero* provides part of the myth of a Zorro-like *caballero* "dressed in all the extravagance of his country's costume," with a "blue damask vest, short cloth of crimson velvet," and a black silk handkerchief, all of which indicated not only wealth but a brisk contraband trade with visiting vessels.[21] Yorba was not only an *hacendado* with some seventy servants but also a merchant and storekeeper (Stephenson, 136), a collector of debts for Guerra y Noriega, a moneylender, and a small manufacturer of leather goods, soap, cigars, hats, wine, and brandy. His letters to Guerra y Noriega and other clients as well as his account book entered as evidence when his widowed and later remarried wife Vicenta Sepúlveda Yorba de Carrillo sought to have the court distinguish between her property and that of her four minor children (Stephenson, 13) are interesting "testimonials" of the 1830s and 1840s in Alta California.[22]

Most of the merchants in Alta California were foreigners, as we shall see in the next chapter, but several Californios too were storekeepers. Like the missionaries, they profited by dealing directly with the Yankee captains at various ports before Governor Argüello opened the territory to trade with foreign ships. Yorba's will includes an account book for his store at Rancho Santa Ana, and this ledger provides an impressive record of all the different classes in the area. This account book is a testimonial, for in studying the lists of debtors and their debts we become aware not only of the *rancheros* and others trading at this store—including the teacher Ygnacio Coronel, Pío Pico, and Juan Bandini—but also of the servants and workers whose wages are noted along with the credit extended to them for cloth, sugar, *aguardiente*, wine, beans, corn, paper, horses, and so forth. The workers' wages are given in *pesos*, as are the prices of the items, but the workers are actually paid in goods and the debts to the store are paid in hides, tallow, or labor (Stephenson, 146–47). Obviously the workers were always indebted; they and their families necessarily consumed more than they were paid. One Gabriel García, for example, is listed as earning eight pesos in wages per month, plus one peso worth of soap and a bullock every month. Yet each month his wages were deducted to pay on his store account. Between May 1841 and March 1845, he earned 368 pesos, but he owed the store 413 pesos during that same period. After working almost four years he still owed the store 45 pesos plus the purchase of a horse for 16 pesos (itemized in Stephenson, 138–41). Indebted labor thus ensured the maintenance both of Indian and of non-Indian labor; the ledger shows that Indian workers too paid off their accounts in work (Stephenson, 148). These documents of what amounts to a company store are in fact a narrative of indebted labor.

Haciendas generally had a store and many industries, but *ranchos* operated on a much smaller scale. The dwellings on these small *ranchos* were often "of rough timber roofed with tules" and "rarely had more than two rooms" (Lugo, 217). Land grants required that within the first year a house be built and the land stocked with cattle, so rough timber constructions often preceded the building of adobe houses, which might eventually be whitened with limestone, available in the Santa Cruz area (Alvarado, 4:161). Incoming settlers from Sonora and San Blas often established these small *ranchos* on vacant lands and practiced subsistence farming, concentrating primarily on corn and a variety of other vegetables while also raising some cattle for meat and hides, the only cash product (MGV, 3:312). Subsistence farming was also practiced by the townspeople in their *pueblo* gardens and orchards, especially after secularization when the missions no longer supplied these goods and the people were forced to grow produce for their own consumption (Coronel, 229). For those townspeople who were not self-sufficient, the loss of the missions' market services presented a crucial problem, for now it became more difficult to procure necessary items.

Vallejo, who advocated increasing agricultural production, preferred diversified agriculture to monocultivation, arguing that subsistence farming freed the Californios from being subjected to market prices. In the 1870s he was especially critical of what he termed a consumerist society that drives young men away from marriage and into sure ruin and debt (MGV, 4:335). A precapitalist market economy was for him more sensible and therefore desirable for Alta California, unlike the single-crop farming practiced in Virginia and Louisiana, where, by producing only tobacco or only sugar cane, farmers were forced to acquire all their staples at high market prices (MGV, 3:312). As Brenner indicates, the tendency of the precapitalist producers who have "direct (i.e. nonmarket) access to their full means of subsistence, that is, the

tools and land needed to maintain themselves" is to ensure the maintenance of their existing property relations and thus determine the pat-
tern of economic development.[23] Behind Vallejo's celebration in 1875
of subsistence farming and self-sufficient production with multiple industries at the *haciendas* was an argument for the mode of production
and property relations that existed in California before 1846. This argument is one of many veiled defenses of preinvasion California and
of the semifeudal *latifundista* system established late in Alta California. Paradoxically, in view of his early antimission stance, this defensive
position leads Vallejo only a few pages later to attack those in Mexico
calling for the appropriation of church lands on the basis of the lack of
development of these mortmain properties, considered an obstacle in
the introduction of new organizations of production and techniques.
Vallejo, who had previously advocated the secularization and distribution of mission lands, suddenly feels the need to support the ownership of large tracts of land and to criticize the notion of land distribution in order to encourage economic development, particularly in the
area of agriculture. Ironically, was this not precisely the rationale used
after invasion by the Anglo squatters to support their taking of the
Californio lands? An attack on Fondo Piadoso lands was similar to an
attack on Californio lands, and the taking of these funds and land was
an illegal measure in Vallejo's estimation (MGV, 3:325–26). His argument was framed by public concern, he said, for once the government
took over these lands and funds, they profited not the public but rather
private individuals and the military. The narrative thus offers an odd
twist as a Californio liberal in retrospect sides with Mexican conservatives. This entire discussion against the governmental appropriation
of church lands and properties is indeed strange, given Vallejo's past
political positions, but the anticlerical Vallejo, a *latifundista* himself, could
not in 1875 question the ownership of vast estates.

Social Stratification and Narrative Gaps

Californio society was highly stratified from the arrival of the missionaries, military officers, and soldiers with their families; restructuring after secularization would merely bring a new ruling class, an oligarchy made up of several wealthy landowning clans related by blood
and marriage. Secularization also meant the abandonment of the *presidios,* and with this reconfiguration of the territory, soldiers, once the
bulk and predominant component of Californio society, disappeared
from center stage. The return of most of the soldiers to private life was

also linked to their awareness that the territorial government never had enough money to pay their salaries. Only Vallejo could afford to keep and support a small detail in the northern frontier, soldiers he sometimes used as labor on his ranches; in Monterey, the governor and J. Castro also had a small contingent of soldiers. Thereafter whenever fighting broke out against the Indians or against a regional faction, a militia of civilians was called up by the district officers. The status of military preparedness, or rather lack thereof, would be mentioned in several testimonials and would play a crucial role as U.S. invasion approached.

Neophyte Indians also carried out military duties, serving not only as *arrieros* that transported cannon, ammunition, and provisions for the long treks across the territory, but sometimes, as in Vallejo's army, as regular troops, too. Indian warriors were used on a number of occasions by governors and officers in their factional conflicts, and by local landowners, like Lugo in San Bernardino, to fight Indian raiders. In the north, the Suysun Indians were a constant source of rumor, for it was assumed that Vallejo was capable of taking over the entire territory with thousands of Indian soldiers. The Indians thus played a variety of roles, real and imaginary. When Alvarado marched south to impose his authority over the *sureños* backing Carrillo for governor, he even took an Indian band with him to play as his troops entered the towns. Spectacle was important for political plotting.

Political and economic shifts during the decade of the 1830s would create new social actors and a more complex and stratified Californio society. In addition to the ruling elite of *hacendados*, there were the small farmers and *rancheros* as well as storekeepers and an emergent class of merchants, as we shall see in the next chapter. Not every Californio was a landowner, of course, and sometimes newly arrived foreigners willing to settle in the northern frontier had a better chance of obtaining a land grant than did mestizo Sonorans in the south, although coastal mission lands also seemed to go to those who could pay something into Alta California's empty government coffers (Alvarado, 3:4–5).[24] At the bottom of the social hierarchy were the ex-mission and homeless neophytes and the *ranchería* gentile Indians; just above them were Indian tenant farmers and Indian peons and servants. Mestizo ranch hands and other laborers in the towns and on the *ranchos* also belonged to these lower levels of the hierarchy. A middle sector of Californios occupied managerial positions as supervisors, foremen, and government clerks and administrators. In the *pueblos* and capital at Monterey there were also a few professionals (lawyers, teachers, doctors), craftsworkers, artisans, other workers, and a number of foreigners who were either merchants or trappers and hunters. What is often missing in these testimonials, except in occasional passing remarks, is the role of skilled acculturated Indian craftsmen in California who, after sixty-six years of mission life, had developed important skills as farmers, masons, tile workers, carpenters, soapmakers, and vaqueros. Many of these had petitioned Echeandía for permission to leave the mission back in 1826 and some, especially in the south, worked their own land.[25]

This heterogeneous society is not, however, the central focus of these Californio narrators. The social hierarchy constructed in the testimonials is primarily configured on the basis of discourses of caste, distinguishing *gente de razón* from *indios*, concealing in the process relations between exploiters and producers and blurring as well intra-Californio class differences. The latter become apparent in brief references to *pueblo* daily life and (almost by design) no attempt is made to include the landless *pueblo* inhabitants in the narrative figuration, except on occasion as humorous asides or in the mention of a robbery or murder. The testimonials do not homogenize the population, as if all intragroup differences had been dissolved or resolved; on the contrary, aristocratic remarks and derogatory comments are frequently made by members of the higher levels of the hierarchy in reference to plebians, ruffians, the uncouth, and the "poor but fertile" people among them, as if to underline further references to the elite, "the principal families, the select and the enlightened." Through this aristocratic/plebian dialectic, the problems of class divisions (that is, differences on the basis of relations of production) become blurred and reduced to problems of rich and poor, as is evident in the following example. During his governorship, Alvarado ordered all citizens of Monterey to work three days every winter repairing the roads and bridges. The "poor" had to do this work themselves but the "rich" could send their "peons or servants," a decree that, for Vallejo (who apparently missed the point), proved the "justice and impartiality behind a decree that dealt with both rich and poor alike" (MGV, 4:4). The other salient social difference cutting across this semifeudal patriarchal society is that of gender, the focus of the following chapter.

Although Indians as the social other of the Californios are a constant construct throughout these testimonials, there is little in these texts about Indian society itself, except in relation to Californio society. Their spaces, their social organization, is largely absent in these narratives. Their social site, the *ranchería*, is constantly mentioned as the abode of the Indians, both neophytes and gentiles, but never described from within. In reconstructing his visits to the Indian *rancherías*, Vallejo never goes beyond glowing descriptions of beautiful Indian women and tall, strong Indian men, all of whom, contrary to frequent characterizations of them as short and ugly, were, he says, graceful and marvelous dancers and runners (MGV, 4:342; MGV, 1:9). The Californios have curiously little to say about Indian history or living conditions, except for Vallejo, who in the first chapter of his first volume reviews the various tribes that inhabited Alta California before Spanish colonization, their animistic belief system, their customs and traditions, the role of the Indian astrologer, the place of the homosexual *joyas*, the Indian addiction to an herb called "pespivata," and other practices (MGV, 1:6–16). Vallejo's account of a different and complex culture stands in sharp contrast to that of Simpson, who upon being taken to an Indian village found the Indians to be

> the most miserable of the race that I ever saw, excepting always the slaves of the savages of the north-west coast, yet every face bears the impress of poverty and wretchedness; and they are moreover, a prey to several malignant diseases, among which an hereditary syphilis ranks as the predominant scourge alike of old and young. They are badly clothed, badly lodged and badly fed. As to clothing, they are pretty nearly in a state of nature; as to lodging, their hovels are made of boughs wattled with bulrushes in the form of bee-hives, with a hole in the top for a chimney, and with two holes at the bottom toward the northwest and the south-east, so as to enable the poor creatures, by closing them in turns, to exclude both the prevailing winds; as to food, they eat the worst bullock's worst joints, with bread of acorns and chestnuts, which are most laboriously and carefully prepared by pounding and rinsing and grinding. Though not so recognized by the law, yet they are thralls in all but the name; while borne to the earth by the toils of civilization superadded to the privations of savage life, they vegetate rather than live, without the wish to enjoy their former pastimes or the skill to resume their former avocations. (29)

In Simpson's description the afflictions of colonialism have been encoded on the Indian bodies. These gentile and ex-neophyte Indians who now work as peons on Vallejo's *hacienda* for subsistence are no longer willing or able to survive in the wild on their own, yet they are, despite acculturation, still living in the hovels of rush huts of yesterday. Against this graphic pitiable account stands the romantic view of Vallejo, who consistently claims that given the wild game, fish, crab and lobster, berries, nuts, acorns, and so on, available to these Indian hunters and gatherers, in addition to the daily rations of *atole* distributed to those working on the *hacienda* and as servants in Sonoma, the

Indians could seemingly not have gone hungry. With these idyllic descriptions of plenty, Vallejo thus attempts (but fails) to refute charges that the Indians were not provided for on the *haciendas*. By 1841, when Simpson visited California, there was additional evidence of calamity in the Indian villages, for after the smallpox epidemic at the end of the previous decade only a few hundred Indians remained alive in the north.[26] Whatever Californios might say about fierce, indolent, or happy Indians, there was no way to counter, whether by references to epidemics or to intertribal warfare, historiographic constructs of Californio exploitation of the Indians. The very same discourses that the Californios had used to condemn mission practices would in later years be used to condemn their own oppression, dispossession, and destitution of the Indians.

In view of their treatment at the hands of both Spain and Mexico, it is not difficult to understand why, when the U.S. invasion began, the Indians for the most part sided with the Americans (Coronel, 111), especially the more independent Indians of southern California. They would of course live to regret this alliance as well, as we shall see in chapter 7. Lorenzana recalls, for example, that the Indians of San Luis Rey who favored the invaders met at Pala to discuss their collective awareness and plan for action upon the arrival of U.S. forces (23). Here disidentification with the Californios signals a reconfiguration within the Californio narrative, for the romantic emplotment is about to overlap with what is potentially a tragic emplotment, despite attempts to forestall it. The Indians from the San Luis Rey mission were up in arms, recalls Lorenzana, and ready to attack "her countrymen" when Sérvulo Varela, who headed a group of Californios preparing to fight the U.S. invaders, was sent for in the middle of the night to defend the small group of Californios at the mission. Upon his arrival he asked to meet with the Indians, who came to the mission armed:

> When the Indians arrived, Varela lashed into them verbally, censuring them for being hostile to the native sons of the land, telling them that this was foolhardy, that they, the Indians and the Californios, were on the same side. The Indians promised to follow his advice; then they celebrated with food and drink after which time they left. (Lorenzana, 27)

Varela's appeal to the Indians for solidarity against the U.S. invaders worked on that occasion, but later these Indians, hoping to better their situation, would ask the American major Frémont to replace the mission administrator with an American. Although many southern Indians joined Kearny's and Frémont's forces against the Californios (Coronel,

111, 121), a few hesitated to do so and sided with the Californios in both the north and south (Coronel, 117).[27] These pro-Californio Indians were the exception, and, given the structural position they occupied, it is not entirely difficult to understand why they would have supported the invaders, assuming as they did that with political transformation their status could only improve. At this juncture so many Indians had died from disease, so many had died at the hands of military expeditions against them, so many had been left destitute after secularization, so many had been exploited for the gain of a few that their enemies' enemies must have looked like friends. In fact some Indians took advantage of the turmoil to attack the *ranchos*, as Lugo (208–9) recalls, although, as before, friendly Indians allied with the Californios joined Lugo and other *rancheros* in fighting the rebellious Indians from San Bernardino. This final act of Indian resistance against the Californios is minimized in the native Californios' testimonials as it will not be the determining force in their defeat. Only Coronel's testimonial explores what happened to the Indians afterward and makes clear that after invasion the Indians' situation did not improve at all; it only worsened, for now Anglos and Californios would join forces against them (Lugo, 212). As the aged Indian José María Flores, interviewed by Cerruti, indicates, the Indians now faced near total extermination (Cerruti, 80). The destruction of the *rancherías*—including the one at Temécula, as recalled in the novel *Ramona* by Helen Hunt Jackson—would follow in rapid order and reach even the gentile tribes that had survived by remaining distant from the Californios' settlements.

What is missing in Coronel's work is any comment on U.S. policies toward Native Americans throughout the rest of the nation. Apparently the California Indians did not know that the Indians of the Northeast, South, and Midwest had suffered a history of broken treaties, unjust wars, and dispossession.[28] The Indian Removal Bill of 1830 had in effect allowed U.S. expansionists to rid themselves of thousands of Indians from the South and the Midwest by forcing the surviving Indians to walk the Trail of Tears to the bleak lands of Oklahoma. The Californios like the remaining Indians, would soon learn that the dominant U.S. ideology was racist, ethnocentric, and intolerant of all who were not Anglo-Saxons. Even the earth was thought to be there exclusively for cultivation by white people only; the *United States Democratic Review* of 1858 would indicate that "no race but our own can either cultivate or rule the Western hemisphere" (Weinberg, 90). With these special "natural" and "divinely ordained" powers, the Americans would justify the taking of Californio lands and Indian lands, and even consider taking the silver mines in central Mexico (Weinberg, 90). Racism would overlap with expansionism and play a decisive role in the exclusion of all but the dominant race from partaking of equal rights.[29] Only some (i.e., white Anglo Protestants), it was said, are fit to reside "within the fold of civilization" (Weinberg, 162). One of the attractive things seen about California was that few Mexicans—few members of a "degraded" race—were there (Weinberg, 177).

Coronel's testimonial does add a narrative dimension to the Californio story by moving beyond 1846 to new postinvasion social spaces, such as the mining area that opened up after 1848. Overlapping with this space are sites of vigilantism and sites of massacres and lynchings. Coronel recalls working the mines in 1848 at the onset of the gold rush and finding that some Californios had joined American settlers in tracking down Indians said to be responsible for the death of one or two men. On one night, Coronel had camped outside Sacramento with his servants when the Californio Sisto Berreyesa and the Sonoran Molina arrived with a group of foreigners (i.e., Anglos) and about sixty Indian prisoners—men, women, and children. The Indians were tied together and made to lie stretched out and naked on the ground. Where they were being led was not clear, but early the next morning Molina stayed with the prisoners while the others rode off. Coronel followed them at a distance and saw them enter a *ranchería* near the site where two Americans had been killed. The foreigners and Berreyesa circled the *ranchería*, then waited until daylight. Coronel narrates what happened in one of the few instances in the testimonials that bear witness to scenes of Indian massacres, otherwise almost wholly absent:

> When the search party arrived at the place, it surrounded the Indian village and as soon as dawn broke they began to fire upon the village—a horrible scene then ensued as the aged, women, children, and everyone else started to pour forth and run, some armed with their bows, others empty-handed, running in every which way, some throwing themselves into the river. But all were stopped and cut down by bullets. I could not continue to witness that horrible massacre and I returned to my campsite. These events took place around the end of May 1849. (175)

The massacre of the entire Indian village was more than Coronel could stomach. He seemingly felt impotent to do anything, just as on another occasion he and other Californio friends, feeling outnumbered, had failed to take any action (other than offering to pay the allegedly "stolen" money) to stop the lynching of a Spaniard and a Frenchman who were falsely accused of stealing five pounds of gold. Continuing on his trip north, Coronel tells of seeing bands of armed men shooting at fleeing Indians as they ran toward the ranch of one Mr. Hicks, where they hoped to be safe—only to have the armed men enter Hicks's ranch, bring them out, and kill them.

> Such was the status of things at that time for those wretched beings [the Indians] that to kill one of them in cold blood was the same as to shoot a jackrabbit. These atrocities were such and so common that the military governor ultimately had to intervene, having to go himself to the area and put an end to these acts. (Coronel, 176)

Coronel condemns the lawlessness and violence but in the end his text ironically regards U.S. military intervention as the only guarantee of social order.

With westward expansion, Indian agency as evident previously in raids and insurrections would be quickly wiped out. Those Indians not exterminated before 1846 by disease, overwork, malnutrition, or military excursions against them would find survival very difficult after the U.S. invasion, except for those Indians who continued to live in isolated areas near the deserts and higher plains. With invasion the Indians would also cease to have a key role in the social order as the primary labor force, although they would continue to be used in work chain gangs and even "auctioned off to the highest bidder for private service" in Los Angeles when the city was unable to place them in sufficient public works assignments ("Minutes" from 1850, cited in W. Robinson, 172). Those few Indians who had received mission lands would ultimately lose them, like the Californios. Those in the *rancherías* would be driven out to make room for incoming farmers, ranchers, settlers, and miners. Some would continue to work as vaqueros and servants and become part of the marginalized Californio-Mexican population. Many would be homeless. Invasion would thus signal a true diaspora for the California Indians.

Conclusion

The accounts in these Californio testimonials are contradictory and some undoubtedly evidence bad conscience. The Californios interviewed in the 1870s knew full well that they were being accused of abusing, exploiting, and decimating (directly or indirectly) the Indian population, in a renewed version of the "Black Legend" of Spanish Conquest. They knew what was being said about secularization and about their role in that corruption-ridden enterprise. But they also knew American history and policies toward the Indians and used their conquerors' reasoning to defend their own subjugation and decimation of the Indian population.

The oppositions reconstructed by the Californios in these testimonials are contradictory. On the one hand, the Indians are posited as the Californios' antagonists:

Indians ◄────────► Californios
barbarism   civilization
non-Christian   Christian
enemy/villians   victims/heroes

Yet on the other hand the Indians were servants in their homes, cowboys and peons on their *ranchos,* and acculturated Indians living in the *pueblos* with them, like Pacomio, who even served on the town council (Alvarado, 2:53). Indian labor allowed the Californios to enjoy the life they led even while they feared the number and potential power of the Indians. Thus the Indians had a much different role from that of the marauding enemy attributed to them by the military and at times by the Californios:

Indians ◄────────► Californios
producers   exploiters
subordinated   dominant

In hindsight, of course, it was easier to blame the missionaries and the mission administrators for the abuse of the Indians; it was harder for the Californios to recognize and come to terms with the degree to which their society was dependent on Indian labor and the degree to which all Californios had exploited, abused, and benefited from the Indians. Like the Americans who would follow, the Californios preferred to justify their abuse by alluding to a higher intelligence and the rights inherent to members of a superior race. What is clear is that the Indians were an integral part of the colony, and even those gentile tribes not incorporated into production were tangentially integrated through trade.[30] The Indians were the very cornerstones of Californio existence; only when they resisted conquest and subordination did they metamorphose into barbarians—"bárbaros infieles," in Alvarado's often repeated phrase.

Whatever the position taken with regard to the exploitation of the Indians, clearly the Californio narrative is emplotted in relation to particular social sites and around the agency or subjected agency of the Indians, whose blood and sweat served to colonize California under both the mission system and the related—though relatively short-lived—feudal *rancho* system. We can now reconstruct the emplotment via Greimas's semantic rectangle,[31] but we must bear in mind that new oppositions begin to emerge in the early part of the decade of the 1840s with the arrival of growing numbers of "foreigners." These new oppositions will be dealt with in chapter 5, and those generated after invasion will be seen in chapter 7. Applying Greimas's semantic rectan-

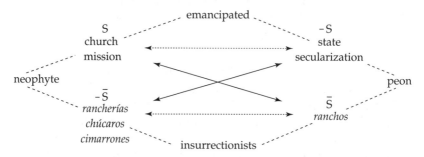

gle we can see an opposition between two social sites: church and state, as well as the corresponding negatives. Each side of the rectangle also generates a synthetic term.[32] Thus the contradictory or negative of the secularized or state-run mission (-S) is the *ranchería*. The missions and the *rancherías* generate a complex term (the neophyte): the Indians residing in *rancherías* within mission lands were transformed into neophytes. The mission was built on the premise of *rancherías* although in practice it negated their space, first by taking their youth (boys and girls) out of the *rancherías* and circumscribing their movement, and second by absorbing the *rancherías,* making them extensions of mission space. The mission's antagonist was the civil government, both before and especially after Mexican independence. Secularization meant the desacralization of mission space, the destruction (profanation) of mission order, the privatization of a corporate (missionary) despotic system, and the supposed emancipation of the neophytes. The complex term here is *manumisos,* the "free" neophytes, a contradictory term in that the neophytes were free legally but not in practice. Once the missions were state-administered, then dismantled and destitute, once the livestock and horses had been appropriated by the government or *rancheros,* the mission ranches (S) passed on to private hands (S̄) and at least some of the neophytes became a constrained labor pool of peons, vaqueros, and servants. Some stayed for a while at the secular missions; others (the *cimarrones*) fled to gentile communities; still others became vagrants and alcoholics. Secularization was thus a process that allowed Californios to petition for mission lands. The *ranchos* would face an antagonistic relation with the Indians of the gentile *rancherías* who, together with the *cimarrones,* in several instances raided the *ranchos* and made off with livestock and horses. In some cases Indian raiders would drive the Californios off the land, but the reverse scenario was clearly dominant throughout. The neutral and potentially liberating term here is that of the insurrectionist, the Indian who fled the mission and the *ranchos* and who, like Pacomio or Estanislao, organized Indian uprisings against the Californios.

This semantic rectangle does not consider the growing opposition represented by the arrival of foreigners, first merchants and later trappers, hunters, and settlers. In the next chapter we will examine several mininarratives given in the testimonials about women, emplotments that symbolically try to resolve this new contradiction and that attempt to explain, from the perspective of 1875, what went wrong with efforts to establish a Californio nation.

5

Politics of Gender

Las mujeres de los pobres probablemente trabajaban más
que las otras.

A. F. Coronel

In analyzing any ideological discourse, we are struck by its ambiguity
and fuzziness; both Chatterjee and Hobsbawm have pointed this out
in reference to the discourses of liberalism and nationalism, as we have
seen in chapter 3.[1] The same indeterminacy applies to discourses of
gender, for they also operate within an ideological field intersected by
a multiplicity of discourses. Consequently, there can be no essential gender discourse, only gender discourses in articulation with other discourses, like those of nation, race/caste, religion, family, class, and sexuality, all of which articulate with one another and generate a variety
of social identities. In a reading of a conflictive ideological field like
that found in the Californio testimonials, often what is perceived as a
multiplicity of individual subject positions points to nothing more (and
nothing less) than the instability of these dynamic intersections, these
different combinations, layerings, and "jagged edges." What must be
stressed is that the ambiguity or disruptions resulting from this interdiscursivity are historically and materially determined and not simply
a matter of instability in the processes of signification.

If the indeterminacy of gender discourses is a product of the ideological field, then what is implied is that gender can only be read chrono-
geographically, that is to say, across time and space, in its articulation
with other discourses, that is, across different spatial sites.[2] As Lefebvre indicates, the underpinning of social relations is spatial: "Social
relations, which are concrete abstractions, have no real existence save

in and through space."[3] In other words, when we posit that relations of class, caste, gender, sexuality, race, ethnicity, and so on, can only be grasped spatially or rather interspatially, we are suggesting that the *constructs* of these relations can only be analyzed spatially and historically. In what follows we propose to examine gender relations discursively and interdiscursively and across several spatial locations, for there is no one social space in Alta, California that is exclusively feminine, not even the domestic domain, often the site of labor for men and women, Indian and non-Indian. There are masculine-dominant spaces (for example, the Franciscan order, the military order, and, most notably, the political sphere), but these overlap and collide with other gendered spheres. Relating social spaces to structural positions and agential locations in these Californio testimonials implies, then, that one is always dealing with interspatial sites, for one site cannot be considered in isolation from all others that necessarily impinge on it. Interdiscursivity is a result of interspatial articulations and overlapping.

In view of these interspatial connections and shifts, the gendering of any particular space in terms of one or the other gender is at best a haphazard proposition. This has not impeded the gendering of the space of the subaltern as feminine, however, a logic underlying attempts by writers to gender what is perceived as colonized, inferior, and different as feminine. Yet once a strategy becomes obvious, it can always allow for its subversion. If gendering is a strategy for the subordination of others, can it also serve to frame antagonisms and resistance? Can constructs of gender serve as contestatory discourses, as sites of reelaboration of relations? In chapter 3 we examined discourses of liberalism and how they were manipulated to construct antagonisms between missionaries and the emergent *ranchero* class. Given this situation, and following Mouffe's analysis, it would be interesting to see whether discourses of individual rights and economic liberalism are articulated with discourses of gender to interpellate feminine subjects or whether the denial itself of subjectivity or of particular positionalities can become the basis for the construction of an antagonism.[4] The converse needs to be explored as well. How and when do gender discourses in their interconnection with other discourses lead to collusion with hegemonic and/or patriarchal strategies of domination?

Victims or Culprits?

In her work *Beyond Female Masochism*, the German Marxist and feminist critic Frigga Haug explores the collusion of women with their own oppression. She suggests that women, "by desiring marriage and motherhood, or at least by secretly longing for them or striving towards them, ... become willing accomplices in their own oppression."[5] The assumption that women consent to their oppression whenever no extreme coercive force is used backhandedly allows for the positing of more agential possibilities; admittedly the construct of women as victims could be said to be self-defeating (Haug, 7). The element of acquiescence that Haug explores considers women to be capable of changing themselves and their situation, as well as of collaborating with and enabling oppression. A similar line of inquiry, but now in relation not to women but to constructs of the feminine, is followed in the work of Hennessy and Mohan, who in an article on nineteenth-century British literature propose to examine how constructs of the feminine "enable and support global exploitation and domination"[6] and, rather paradoxically, how they simultaneously and conversely enable oppositional feminist readings. Discourses of gender in their articulation with other discursive formations may, according to the particulars, function ideologically to frame either modalities of oppression and exploitation or modalities of resistance.

The testimonials of both men and women provide ample evidence that women of Alta California not only often acquiesced to their own oppression and exploitation but to that of others as well; this is especially clear in the case of those who supervised Indian labor in the missions (such as Apolinaria Lorenzana and Eulalia Pérez) and those who were the wives or widows of wealthy *hacendados* (like Francisca Benicia Vallejo) with hundreds of Indian workers, including domestic workers. Within the testimonials, however, women are not explicitly constructed as exploiters and oppressors. On the contrary, Lorenzana and Pérez are said to be "nurturing women" caring for sick Indian women and newly arrived settlers, helpers of the missionaries, and talented purchasers, housekeepers, and supervisors, all functions crucial to the domestic economy of the mission. Yet their collusion is implicit in constructions of the feminine not at odds with constructs of the mission and *rancho* as spaces of production or with a caste system predicated on the patriarchal model. Gender discourses do not, however, simply support dominant patriarchal discourses and practices. Although the dominant discourses of religion and family construct women as subordinate subjects, in several cases recorded in these testimonials women put that (en)gendered subordination into question. In reality this questioning is transitory, for it leads in some instances to a new patriarchal subordination, but nevertheless it is crucial to see how gender discourses articulate with discourses of liberalism and class to permit the construction of certain antagonisms that will in turn be the catalysts for modification of the patriarchy (Mouffe, 1988: 95).

(En)gendering Subordination

Patriarchal discourses, which engender constructs both of the masculine and the feminine, are dominant in all the social spaces represented in these testimonials. Even the space of biological reproduction, generally marked as feminine, is seen to be dominated by patriarchal social relations in a territory where there were never more than six or seven thousand Californios, the pressure was on women to reproduce, and for this reason many of the *gente de razón* women had up to twenty-five children. Given the many deaths that came about from childbirth, men often married two or three times. Larios, for example, had twenty-two children from three successive wives (Pico, 1973: 115). Occupation of the land required not only the establishment of missions and *presidios* but the "upkeep" of frontier soldiers by recruiting families, men with women and children, for settlement in Alta California. Even a group of orphans, including both boys and girls, was recruited in 1800. The female orphans were discouraged from leaving, for they were expected to "contribute to the population of the peninsula" by remaining in California and marrying.[7] The importance of women for settlement was thus recognized at the highest levels; the establishment of families in the territory and reproduction itself were very much political, economic, and cultural acts.

The construct of women as a fertile field for reproduction is frequent in the testimonials. José de Jesús Vallejo recalls that Teresa de la Guerra de Hartnell had twenty-five children, of which sixteen survived (JJV, 145). In the large landed estates, where there were hundreds of Indian servants and workers, the wives of the *hacendados* had two tasks: to reproduce and to manage the servants. Francisca Benicia Vallejo, for example, would have sixteen children, of which six would die before the age of six years. As a rule female narrators do not speak out in their narratives against their use as breeders. Dorotea Valdez, who apparently neither married nor had children, condemns any type of birth control and points, on the one hand, to the imperative for reproduction and, on the other, to changed conditions by the 1870s:

> I must not forget to mention that during the early days of this country, in fact until the arrival of the Americans, our population increased very rapidly. It was then not an unusual thing to see a mother leading to

church twenty-four children all begotten by the same husband, and I am not far from the mark when I state that the average number of children raised by our mothers was rather above than below the number of eleven; but since the Americans have taken possession of this country, sterility has become very common because the American women are too fond of visiting doctors and swallowing medicines. *Éste es un delito que Dios no perdona.* [This is an unpardonable sin.] (Valdez, 5)

Who determines reproduction? In a society where impregnation is determined by men because women have little control over their fertility, reproduction cannot be said to be determined by women though they be the childbearers.[8] At most one could say that women were complicit. But given the low survival rate for children among some couples, women were probably not only expected to or forced to but also willing to be impregnated every year in hopes of having at least one or two children survive. Angustias de la Guerra de Ord had eleven children with Manuel Jimeno Casarín, her first husband, and only two survived. Cultural pressure (i.e., "a woman without children is a nonentity") generated as much by women as by men thus interpellated women to consent to their own conversion into reproductive factories. And yet, the dominant position notwithstanding, there is evidence that among even more subordinated women (Indian women), there was an effort to abort to save their children from servitude.

Patriarchal practices have to be specified in more detail if we are to understand the complex construction of the feminine in these testimonials. The term "patriarchy" needs to be delimited, as Delphy suggests, in order to specify "relations between patriarchy and the domestic mode of production" (Delphy, 260). There is no question about the subordination of women to men in Alta California, but even in this semifeudal society patriarchal conditions varied from site to site. We must also bear in mind that feudal models have not all evolved historically in the same way. Studies on the transition from feudalism to capitalism have tried to account for different models of development, often on the basis of differing demographic and/or commercial trade factors. Brenner demonstrates the importance of going beyond these types of analyses, to explain the transition in terms of property relations.[9] For Alta California we need to consider, then, relations of production, different economic phases, and different sites of production.

Changes in property relations within semifeudal society in Alta California, the result of secularization and land distribution, were effected within three different social spaces. This restructuring shifted production from the missions to *haciendas, ranchos,* and secularized ex-missions, as we have seen in chapter 4. Semifeudal property relations did not preclude women from owning or inheriting land, as in the case of Lorenzana and others. Women in Alta California could own land property separate from that of their husbands, who, as Weber indicates, "had no claim on property that their spouses acquired prior to marriage; wives [moreover] could not be held accountable for their husband's debts."[10]

Nor were women excluded from production. In the *pueblos* women were central to production, working both at home and in the *pueblo* gardens, where they sowed, harvested, and took care of livestock. In addition to their performing regular domestic chores, which were heavier and more strenuous than those of men, Californio women were also involved in domestic industries for the production of candles, soap, and clothing, as Coronel explains in his thorough account of the domestic mode of production. Articles of clothing, at least those worn by the Californios, were rather complicated to sew and prepare; Coronel (232–33) describes each item in detail, including the embroidery, ruffles, and fringes. Most Californio women did not have the luxury of hundreds of Indian servants, as did the wives of *hacendados,* but it was not uncommon for *pueblo* families to have at least one or two house servants, often Indian children.

What comes out in the testimonials is that the domestic economy is the one site of production and reproduction that more often than not is dominated by women, both Indian and non-Indian. Here too there are exceptions, for often Indian men were used as cooks. In the case of the small *ranchos,* women went beyond the domestic spheres: the farm, the *minifundio,* was a family enterprise with both men and women working the fields and taking care of the cattle. Interestingly, the representation of women on the small *ranchos* is provided, for the most part, by non-Californios, especially by Mexican men like Mauricio González and Coronel, who came to California when they were young men or adults. Their assumptions about non-Indian women and about nondomestic production as a masculine social space, given the expected construct of a male "head of household," have been so ingrained that any deviation astonishes newly arrived *mexicanos* like González, who is amazed to see Californio women working the land when he comes to Alta California in 1840. In what he assumes to be a traditional patriarchal authoritarian system, he finds, to his surprise, feminine agency, as he notes in the following example in his *Memorias:*

There was a woman in California named Fermina Espinosa, who was the owner of the Santa Rita *rancho*, where now the town of Sotoville is located. This woman was very masculine, she did all the ranch work like a man, riding horses, roping steers, and so on, because her husband was a man who spent the day eating, smoking, and sleeping, and increasing [i.e., reproducing] the family brood, which was quite large. Fermina was a very good and honest woman—at her death she left the *rancho* and other property, no longer owned by her descendants, except for the part owned by her eldest daughter who is married to the Peruvian Indian Manuel Soto. (50–51)

Note that González refers to Fermina as the owner of the *rancho*; she is the "*ranchero*" who leaves her property for her children to inherit. The space of production is still masculine here and for that reason her participation in a variety of ranch chores (roping steers, breaking colts, and so forth) is said to make her masculine: *varonil*. She is the matriarch. The man is emasculated; he is described like a woman (almost drone-like), the reproductive agent ("increasing the family") and indolent. This construct of the effeminate Californio appears in several of the testimonials and writings by foreigners, whether Mexican or British or American or French, as if the intent were to show the Californio men as weak and obviously ripe for conquest or domination.

González's relatively short testimonial offers us a glimpse of another side of women's roles not in keeping with the conventional model. But clearly the interviewer, especially interested in what a *mexicano* had to say about Californio women, perhaps to compare his assessment with that provided by British, French, and American writers, made it a point to elicit this information. On another ranch, Sal-Si-Puedes, González notes that Don Vicente Avila Linares and his four daughters work the land:

These four young women, who are pretty, very white with blue eyes, work like men and have the habit of going around in the hills dressed like men, looking after their livestock, cutting wood, loading country carts, and generally doing all kinds of work done by men. They have a loom where they weave blankets, and they produce other things like cheese and butter. (51–52)

Again he is struck by the fact that these daughters, though beautiful and criollo, are strong women who within their social domain (the small *rancho*) assume the role of men and are able to carry out all the tasks usually the prerogative of men, as well as those traditionally assigned to women, such as weaving, sewing, and cheese making. Particularly striking in these accounts is that no attempt is made by the women to hide their talents and abilities—everyone has seen them dressed like men driving their cattle in the hills. Even Coronel offers comments similar to those of González: women, he indicates, often learned to do work that was more fitting for men, like riding and using the lasso. He was surprised to see other things as well:

> The women too for the most part were good horse riders and I saw some of them rope, throw a steer, and even fight bulls with a cape, although such women were few in number. (245)

Women also could handle a rifle (Alvarado, 4:158), and Lorenzana knew how to make cartridges from paper and gunpowder (Lorenzana, 37). These pioneering experiences clearly lessened a number of social constraints, a semiliberation of sorts that would not otherwise have been possible within a strongly patriarchal society.

More typical constructs of feminine strength are also provided in these testimonials. For Coronel (237), Californio women are noted for their moral standards, attributed to their upbringing, industriousness, and cleanliness. José Fernández, a Spaniard who came in 1817 and spent most of his life in Alta California, also implies a matriarchal vein in the population, asserting that Californio women had a great deal of power over their countrymen (Fernández, 132). Representations like these make for overlapping constructs of both femininity and masculinity and point to an interspatial construction of gender discourses. Where Indian labor was not used exclusively, and that was particularly true on the small *ranchos*, gender discourses were more fluid and ambiguous and women were able to construct new identities for themselves and position themselves within the site of ranch production.[11] That they continued to be subordinate to men in society is evident, but equally clear is that within some family spaces, restructuring produced disjunctures and out of these fissures new constructions of feminine identity arose.

Lest one run the risk of exaggerating these instances where constructions of the feminine are at odds with convention, it is important to stress that for the most part the testimonials reveal stringent patriarchal domination in Alta California. Women, like Indians, are dominated by male heads of household and missionaries. This domination is especially clear with the marriage contract, for here women become commodities to be exchanged by their fathers. Coronel recalls that women could not choose their husbands freely:

The daughters had little liberty in choosing the men that they would marry. The marriages were arranged by the fathers of both the man and the woman and many times before the two who were to wed had even met. (229)

In fact, María Antonia Lugo became engaged to Ignacio Vallejo when she was one day old, as she was "the first girl of the race called *de razón* that had been born at Mission San José" (JJV, 2). Her father accepted for her and the two were married when she was fourteen years old. The scarcity of young women who were *gente de razón* in Alta California produced a number of child brides. In the case of Ana de la Guerra, the daughter of the prominent officer and *ranchero* of Santa Barbara, Guerra y Noriega, her hand in marriage was sought by Alfred Robinson when she was thirteen years old. Of course the marriage was acceded to by her father and took place when she was fifteen years old. As elsewhere, women obviously had little or no choice in the selection of husbands, and economic and social factors weighed heavily in the acceptance of a future son-in-law.

The semifeudal patriarchal structure not only subordinated women, but all offspring as well. As Coronel (230) explains, a man's sons, though adult, were expected to continue to live under the father's control, even after marriage, as if they were still minors. Tutelage thus binds not only the Indians and women but even the patriarch's sons, who were expected to work for their father. The patriarch in turn provided for everyone in the extended family and retained control of his children; even when they reached adulthood, he could still punish them (Coronel, 229). In view of this subordination of the entire family to the patriarch, the only means of liberation was either the patriarch's death or flight from the patriarch's home. In this sense the family home too served as a penal colony, a heterotopia of sorts. A son who left was disinherited, but a woman who left simply moved into a new patriarchal structure. Flight was not easy for those who were considered possessions. As Coronel (228) recalls, nubile women were protected and watched over by their mothers to the extent that a guest in the house might not even see them.

As a corollary to the familial patriarchal structure, the missionaries also exerted *patria potestad* over the women and Indians. The missionaries' domination of subservient women (Alvarado, 2:30–31) sometimes led to confessions that revealed the affairs of their male relatives or friends, as occurred when José Castro's mistress told the missionaries about Vallejo's acquisition of banned books (MGV, 3:113). Eulalia Pérez would seem not to be bothered by this stereotype, because she asserts that she saw the missionaries as both father and mother and for that reason, as a widow, married a man chosen for her by the missionaries. Lorenzana, however, clearly saw her role more as that of a companion than a daughter to the friars at the San Diego mission. Nevertheless, in a patriarchal semifeudal society it was socially unacceptable and economically difficult to survive without a man, be he husband, relative, or missionary—but not impossible, as Juana Briones de Miranda and others demonstrated. Given this type of patriarchal enclosure, women who wanted to flee from a situation of subordination had few options. They could stay single, but this still meant subordination to others, either in the mission or in the homes of other Californios. Whether married or not, "serving others" is the dominant discourse applied to women in these testimonials.

Constructs of the Feminine in Hegemonic Texts

Constructions of the feminine are prominent in the testimonials of non-native Californios and in the writings of foreigners, yet less so in Californio accounts: both men and women, tend to focus on public positioning rather than on domestic spaces (except for the domestic space of the mission, which is automatically othered as the space of neophytes and supervisors). In the writings of foreigners the strategy of gendering becomes obvious, as does the gender counterstrategy of some Californios, who by the 1870s were quite aware of what the de Mofras, Simpsons, and Robinsons of the world had written about Californios, both men and women.

In studies dealing with European literature and colonialism, the construction of the feminine is often tied to constructs of the colonized. The feminization of the colonized subject who is also racially, economically, and politically dominated is read as the construction of the European subject's alterity, a necessary process of identification vis-à-vis the colonized Other. In these studies the European attains subjectivity through a disidentification with alterity. This gendered rendition of the analysis of "power relations"—dominant/dominated—as well as the subject/Other narrative positing a colonial subject that oscillates "between identification with and alienation from the colonized other" (Hennessy and Mohan, 328) is an inversion of the difference/identity dilemma faced by the dominated vis-à-vis Europe. Given such a representation of the colonized, gender is a discourse that can be manipulated as much by the colonizer as by the colonized. Here of course it becomes important to recall that the Californio testimonials are narrated by colonized subjects who were in turn once the colonizers. It will be necessary to examine to what degree the construction of the feminine in these testimonials enables or constrains "modalities of oppression" or of "difference" in Alta California society as well as in postinvasion society, particularly in light of hegemonic representations of the Californios within dominant historiography by British, French, American, Spanish, and Mexican writers. Discourses of gender will be seen to be both complicit or contestatory in relation to (a) hegemonic constructs of the conquered; (b) racial oppression of the colonized; (c) openness to modernity; (d) resistance to colonization; and (e) disidentification with colonial culture.

The feminization of the colonized is a typical construct in the works of foreigners on Alta California, who perceive Californio men as different, as Others. Foreigners are attracted to California women and identify with them because they are seen to be industrious and pragmatic, "masculine" like themselves. Gender discourses thus serve for ethnocentric constructions of the enemy.

Inseminating California

The construction of Californio women that appears in the works of Robinson, Simpson, de Mofras, and Dana is underwritten by romantic tropes. Women are like the earth, healthy, wholesome, and desirable, a fertile site for reproduction and, like California itself, eagerly awaiting the arrival of equally strong foreigners. The Frenchman de Mofras, for example, describes Californio men as handsome but idle:

> Their days are spent mainly in idleness. A Californian never cultivates the soil. A stranger entering a ranch house will invariably find the men lying down smoking and drinking brandy. The women assume charge of the gardening and agriculture, which consists of hiring a few Indians and planting small areas. Most of the women are large and robust and have retained the type of beauty that characterizes the Spanish peasant. Their fecundity is extraordinary and women often have as many as twelve or fifteen children.[12]

Here de Mofras sees a healthy but not productive society, concerned with subsistence and no more. The Briton Simpson, who spends a short time in California as an agent for the Hudson Bay Company, shares this perspective:

> The Californian is too lazy to hunt for amusement.... As one might expect from the abundance of land, the fertility of the soil, and the indolence of the people, agriculture is conducted in the rudest possible way.[13]

What the foreigners see are the investment opportunities that the territory offers, and the women are like the land — fertile, big, and shackled to effeminate and indolent men. Moreover, women are seen as active in the art of pleasing, of serving the male ego and person:

> Of the women with their witchery of manner it is not easy, or rather it is not possible, for a stranger to speak with impartiality, inasmuch as our self-love is naturally enlisted in favor of those, who, in every look, tone, and gesture, have apparently no other end in view than the pleasure of pleasing us. (Simpson, 62–63)

Simpson also found that the women were not vain:

> Though doubtless fully conscious of their attractions, yet the women of California, to their credit be it spoken, do not "before their mirrors count the time," being on the contrary, by far the more industrious half of the population. (63)

Their beauty is said to be remarkable, considering that "they are subjected to the wearing effect of early wedlock, sometimes marrying at thirteen, and seldom remaining single after sixteen" (Simpson, 66). Simpson finds the men to be vain:

> The men are generally tall and handsome, while their dress is far more showy and elaborate than that of the women. (63)

In the eyes of these foreigners the Californios are too lazy — too lazy to hunt, to fish, to "clip and wash the raw" wool, to weave or spin, to farm, to make butter or cheese, to grow wheat and produce flour, and to cure meat (Simpson, 14–18). Yet they are also denigrated for being the butchers of Indian villages, shooting men, women, and children (Simpson, 52). In the end, after caustic remarks about the Californios, their ill treatment of the Indians and their lack of productivity, Simpson nevertheless finds that California is a veritable paradise, where "foreigners and natives cordially mingle together as members of one and the same harmonious family":

> In a word the Californians are a happy people, possessing the means of physical pleasure to the full and knowing no higher kind of enjoyment. (66)

It is a land of happy unsophisticated people, ripe, it seems, for the infusion of a better grade of genes. The women are beautiful and the men handsome but lacking in intelligence.[14] In the texts of foreigners, gender discourses are intimately interconnected with those of nation and class.

Robinson's comments in *Life in California, 1846* are equally full of praise for the women and disdainful of the men:

> The men are generally indolent, and addicted to many vices, caring little for the welfare of their children, who, like themselves, grow up unworthy members of society. Yet, with vice so prevalent amongst the men, the female portion of the community, it is worthy of remark, do not seem to have felt its influence, and perhaps there are few places in the world, where, in proportion to the number of inhabitants, can be found more chastity, industrious habits, and correct deportment, than among the women of this place.[15]

According to de Mofras, it is precisely because the women are so superior to the men that they prefer foreigners for husbands, as if the choice were that of the women:

> Among six thousand white inhabitants there are perhaps six hundred foreigners, whom the women prefer to their own countrymen, for they are usually more industrious, treat them more considerately, and take better care of their children. (11–12)

As one of the preferred foreigners, Robinson, who married one of Guerra y Noriega's daughters, disapproves of the "familiarity between the two classes," those of "virtuous" and those of "immoral habits" but he harbors hopes that the future will bring "a necessary distinction … among the various classes" (73). Robinson favored annexation of California to the United States and proposed an extension of the "area of freedom" in that fertile land, foreseeing bright prospects for the development of capitalism and a capitalist class society in California (226).

The construct of Californio women as strong and hardworking individuals is manipulated by foreigners to provide a negative construct of Californio men as essentially weak, ineffective, indolent, and fundamentally unworthy of either their women or their land. Those who are posited as worthy are, by this logic, entitled to take possession of both land and women.

Discourses of Gender and Liminal Spaces

McWilliams has indicated that foreigners were able to gain entrance into the dominant California classes by marrying the daughters of the Californio *gente de razón:*

> No matter what the nationality of the newcomer—French, Scottish, English, American, or German; and no matter what his social status— doctor, trader, sailor, or smuggler—he apparently had little difficulty in joining the *gente de razón,* provided he joined the Catholic Church and became a citizen of Mexico. Once affiliated with the *gente de razón* by marriage, he passed over completely into the orbit of their social life. The settlers ... who married Indian women, never achieved the status of *gente de razón.*[16]

Although clearly the agency noted in McWilliams's text is that of the foreigners who were able to penetrate the family (i.e., nation) closure, there are two further subtexts within the historian's comments. The first refers to the Californios' willingness to take in foreigners, no matter what their background or station in life, and the second, to the complicity of the women who married them. That the women, often mere children, might have had no choice in the matter given that fathers determined marriage within this semifeudal society is not addressed, nor is the fact that marriage to a foreigner might represent an "out," a means by which to escape from the family closure. For the fathers, these foreigners represented access to capital or cultural capital, for many of these young foreigners, though not wealthy, had had more schooling than most in the territory and had traveled much as well. For the incoming foreigners, commerce or ranching on their own land was a possibility after converting to Catholicism, becoming Mexican citizens, and marrying the daughters of influential families.[17] The role of women as collateral in these transactions or in the acquisition of land will be discussed later in this chapter.

As might be expected, women's relations to these newcomers are carried out in a fuzzy discursive field in which discourses of gender overlap and compete with discourses of class, nation, religion, and political orientation. The fact that these foreign merchants would be *compradores* and at the same time represent an emergent class of capitalists within the territory points to the mediating and complicitous role of women, particularly acute at the outbreak of the war upon invasion by U.S. forces. This constructed complicity functions both to challenge and reinforce patriarchal structures in the mininarratives of two women,

Concepción Argüello and Josefa Carrillo. The reconstructed relations between Californio women and foreigners, especially merchants, cannot be analyzed without an understanding of the social spaces of Alta California in relation to trade and commerce, both before and after secularization, spaces that are constructed in some detail in these testimonials.

The Princess and the Count

In the Spanish period before Mexican independence, the patriarchal political structure in Alta California enabled the representative of the king of Spain to determine a number of issues, advancements, and assignments on the basis of service and loyalty. Despite the Crown's regulations and guidelines, there was always a great deal of flexibility in a pioneering situation distant from the metropolis; moreover, there was colonial precedent in the New World for bending the rules dictated from Spain and for interpreting them in a way favorable to the local agents of power. The local *jefe político* and *comandante general* thus wielded some measure of power susceptible to local interests. It is clear in the testimonials that where local interests collide with royal interests disjunctures arise, within which discourses of gender become briefly decisive.

The narrative of the princess and the Russian count requires that we return to the Spanish period, when Alta California was even more isolated than after 1822. In a territory distant from the rest of the world, its relatively small settler population amid a hostile population, the missionaries and the dominant military powers determined one's station in life. Strategies for gaining any objective were not capitalist but feudal. Individuals were perceived as members of larger collectivities, be they those of family, caste, nation, region, religion, *compadrazgos, padrinos,* or friends. Identity and social worth were bound up with the attributes of these collectivities.

Before 1838, if one were an outsider (and here the dialectic of inside/outside is a spatial opposition based on caste, nation, religion, and family), one could, as McWilliams reminds us, gain admittance by becoming a Mexican citizen and a Catholic within a period of time, and/or through intermarriage. Women served as vehicles for gaining access to the collectivity; they were the additional cultural, economic, and political collateral necessary to become a part of the "Californio family," enabling "foreigners" to make trade contracts or become eligible for grants of land. As Friar Durán would remind Governor Alvarado as late as 1842, in view of his policies for the sale and concession of mission lands to foreigners, the Constitution prohibited the granting of lands to foreigners not married to Mexican women (MGV, 4:153). Of course the regulations being quoted were Spanish laws, although by 1821 Mexican concessions to foreigners not married to Mexican women but willing to become Mexican citizens had been made in Texas.[18] New regulations for California, including stipulations for land grants to foreigners, had been proposed by the California Junta de Fomento in 1825 and by Gómez Farías in 1833 (see chapter 3) but never had been duly approved by the Mexican Congress (Junta de Fomento de Californias, 309–12). The colonization laws of 1828, which continued to give Mexican citizens preference over foreigners in the distribution of land, further cemented Californio women's roles as links to inner Californio circles.[19] With Californio/Mexican wives these foreigners could have a stake in the game; without them there was little opportunity to participate in the contest.

During the early Spanish period, Californio women were a scarce commodity, especially during the eighteenth century, and thus highly valued within the patriarchal structure. Their value is fully appreciated in the testimonials reconstructing women as a fertile field for reproduction, production, and trade; here constructs of feminine gender are overdetermined and serve in the testimonials as allegorical representations of the nation or, more often the case, of the land itself. In the process feminine gender becomes spatialized as a site for bartering, for exchange, as the romantic legend of Concepción Argüello and Count Rezanov makes clear. The love story taken up in Bret Harte's poem "Concepción de Argüello" is a romance of two lovers separated by nationality, class, distance, and time.[20] In the poem the beautiful Californio maiden from the *presidio* of San Francisco waits for many years for the return of her betrothed, not knowing the Russian count's fate until Sir George Simpson visits California and, during informal conversation after a banquet, talk turns to the past and the Russian count:

> Quickly then cried Sir George Simpson: "Speak no ill of him, I pray!
> He is dead. He died, poor fellow, forty years ago this day,
> Died while speeding home to Russia, falling from a fractious horse!
> Left a sweetheart, too, they tell me. Married, I suppose, of course!"

When he asks if the sweetheart, surely married thereafter, still lives, "a deathlike silence" falls on the banquet guests and "a trembling figure," a "wasted figure" in a nun's white hood, rises:

> "Lives she yet?" Sir George repeated. All were hushed as Concha drew
> Closer yet her nun's attire. "Señor, pardon, she died, too!"

The poignancy of the ballad is not, however, what historians have noted in this episode. It is the construct of a maiden with no agency, manipulated by the Russians and the Californios alike, that appears in those accounts. In the testimonials, the episode is reconstructed as a tragic love story that overlies a successful trade transaction between Californios and foreigners.

M. G. Vallejo recalls that in 1806, during the governorship of José Joaquín Arrillaga (1806–14), Count Nicolai Petrovich Rezanov, chamberlain of the czar, came to Alta California and during his stay he proposed marriage to Concepción Argüello, then about sixteen or seventeen years old. She is described by José Fernández as a beautiful young maiden: "Doña Concepción María was a beautiful child, charming and of fine upbringing" (40). Vallejo's explanation is as follows:

> This man, be it that he wished to foster Russian trade, be it that he was taken by a fervent love or even for reasons that I do not know, proposed to Doña Concepción Argüello, daughter of Don José Darío Argüello and sister of Don Luis Argüello. His proposal of marriage was accepted and having made the necessary arrangements, he bid the family of his betrothed good-bye, promising to return within a year, or sooner if he was able to obtain the permission of the Emperor of Russia; but as fate would have it, four months later he fell from a horse and as a consequence of that fall, he died. That information did not arrive in due time and Doña Concepción, thinking that her lover had forgotten her, resolved to leave the world; she moved to the town of Santa Barbara where she lived for many years at the home of Don Pablo Noriega. (MGV, 1:102–3)

The fact that the news of the count's death did not reach California for many years led many to think that his proposal had been made with ulterior motives and that his promises were false. Only Concepción, according to Alvarado (2:31–32), continued to have faith in her lover until the day, years later, when his tragic end was known. Alvarado presents a tragic story of lovers separated by distance, time, and death and exaggerates the importance of the Argüello family at the time of the engagement to dramatize an affair that could have provided a potential link between Russia and Alta California. In his recollection of the oft-repeated tale, Vallejo is much more practical and willing to consider that the engagement may have been as much a pragmatic measure as an affair of the heart.

Historians have viewed this love story primarily from a pragmatic perspective, that is, as an attempt by the count to use the young lady as a means of procuring desperately needed provisions. When Rezanov's letter to his minister of commerce became available, it served to confirm this interpretation. In view of Rezanov's letter and the published travel observations of Dr. Georg von Langsdorff, a German surgeon and naturalist who accompanied Rezanov on his trip to California, Bancroft represents Doña Concepción as a naive young woman, without the proper training or noble birth that would have made her the desirable choice of a Russian nobleman. The courting of the Argüello maiden had only one explanation. She served to mediate between the Californios and the Russian settlers from Sitka who had come by boat to buy much-needed grain and foodstuff at a time when the Spanish governor of California, Arrillaga, was prohibited by the Crown from trading with foreign vessels. Given this impasse, an engagement with Doña Concepción served to bring Rezanov into an intimate Californio family circle and enabled him to induce the territorial administration to find a way around regulations prohibiting this direct trade:

> How Doña Concepción's black eyes won the heart of the imperial chamberlain has often been told in prose and verse; it is the famous romance of Spanish times in California. I have no wish to spoil so good a story, though history like murder will out, and it must be confessed that this celebrated courtship had a very solid substratum or superstructure of ambition and diplomacy.[21]

Bancroft assumes that Rezanov, in need of supplies to ward off starvation at Sitka, did not propose marriage until all other efforts to get Governor Arrillaga to trade grain for the cargo of goods on the Russian ship the *Juno* had been exhausted:

> It was not, however, until all other expedients had failed that Rezanov pressed his suit so far as to propose marriage, and herein lies the evidence that rather unpleasantly merges the lover into the diplomat. Doña Concepción consented; so did her parents; and so did the friars reluctantly, on condition that the betrothal should be kept secret and be subject to the Pope's approval. (2:73)

In this version Bancroft follows the narration published by Dr. G. H. von Langsdorff, who describes Rezanov's decision to propose marriage as a personal sacrifice for the welfare of the two countries (Bancroft, 2:65, 72).

The acceptance of Rezanov into the Argüello family led to an arrangement that made it appear as if both parties had bought each other's goods with money and there had been no trade deal. The missionaries were as interested in the trade as the Russians and most probably they too saw the engagement as a ruse, although to forestall the marriage they asked for papal permission. Rezanov left with the grain needed to stave off famine and promised to go to Saint Petersburg, then Madrid, to return with Spanish and papal permission to marry Doña Concepción. But he was never to return, for upon reaching Sitka, he left for Kamchatka and then started on an overland trip to Saint Petersburg. The Siberian snows, a high fever, and a fall from his horse led to his death en route about ten months later. Doña Concepción would not learn of his death for many years.

The publication of Rezanov's own letter to the Russian minister of commerce detailing his six-week sojourn in Alta California reveals that while at San Francisco (a) his situation began to get desperate as his men were beginning to desert; (b) the Argüello family treated him with graciousness; (c) he found Doña Concepción to be "the loveliest of the lovely sisters of Don Luis" and "the universally recognized beauty of Nueva California" (Rezanov, 18); and (d) he found her receptive and interested in a higher station:

> Associating daily with and paying my addresses to the beautiful
> Spanish señorita, I could not fail to perceive her active, venturesome
> disposition and character, her unlimited and overweening desire for
> rank and honors, which, with her age of fifteen years, made her, alone
> among her family, dissatisfied with the land of her birth. (36)

The alienation of the maiden from her immediate social space, as she grows tired of the "warm climate" and "abundance of grain and cattle" (36), and her ambition for something beyond Alta California, is not present in any of the Californio versions, in which she is afforded the role of the devoted woman who waits for her prince, rejecting all other suitors. Once betrothed, Rezanov becomes like a family member; he is therefore able to work out the deal for grain. We see then that agency is the prerogative of the dominant collectivity from which he is excluded until the woman provides the necessary and expedient entrée. Once inside, Rezanov, not oblivious to the implications for commerce, is confident that this transaction will be the beginning of trade and better relations with Spain and perhaps other countries on the Pacific. The juxtaposition of romantic and commercial discourses is revealing. Rezanov's letter acknowledges that the romance was strategic, but there is also the hint of something else:

> Should fate decree the completion of my romance—not begun in hot
> passion, which is not becoming at my age, but arising under the
> pressure of conditions, remoteness, duties, responsibilities, perhaps
> also under the influence of remnants of feelings that in the past were a

source of happiness in my life—then, and in such case, I shall be in a position to serve my country once again, as by a personal examination of the harbor of Vera Cruz, Mexico, and by a trip through the interior parts of America. (63–64)

Rezanov is thus a man with a mission, who identifies as part of a social whole, his country, and that organic connection is more important than the private sentiments that Doña Concepción may or may not have awakened. This marriage would afford all types of opportunities not to him, but to Russia and to the agent of the czar, political opportunities that otherwise would be forbidden because of the "suspicious Spanish temperament forbidding such investigations" (Rezanov, 64).

Historians thus would stress the count's proposal as "a purely business-like stroke of diplomacy whereby he gained the decisive official help of the Argüello family,"[22] but the fact that the count's love would never be tested, given his untimely death, does allow for two constructs of the affair: the romantic and the pragmatic-diplomatic. What is absent is the construct of individual agency, rare at this time, particularly in a woman, for clearly Doña Concepción in considering a Russian count is not only seeking to gain in social standing but attempting to find a way out of a tedious existence among settlers she considers beneath her station. As the daughter of the commander of the San Francisco *presidio* in an area fairly unpopulated by *gente de razón* (the northernmost frontier of the California territory at the time), she saw herself as a member of a literate criollo family headed by a liberal military officer, whose thirteen sons and daughters had been born in Alta California (MGV, 1:119) but who had few prospects of radically improving his situation. Although her father was a close friend of Governor Arrillaga, she faced the prospect of marrying a soldier or a low-ranking officer, for in 1806 almost no foreigners were in the area, other than fugitive sailors; most of the foreign merchants who would settle in Alta California would not come until the 1820s, after Mexican independence in 1821. Social mobility and escape from a dreary existence together with the illusion of a fairy-tale romance undoubtedly had a role in the fifteen-year-old's acceptance of the older Rezanov's proposal.

Given the patriarchal closure with all its restrictions and constraints when it came to women, especially young women, Doña Concepción's involvement must be seen as rebellious and in fact as rather assertive, for she deviates from the Californio norm of having her father choose her marriage partner, and she encourages Rezanov despite parental and missionary opposition to her engagement. His failure to return will lead to an inversion of roles: she, the individualist, will now live for the collectivity and spend a lifetime serving the poor and the Indians, and the count, in death, becomes the tragic lover, the individual. Yet even in this self-denial, in her abandonment of worldly pleasures and rejection of marriage, she counters established practices in Alta California, where women are expected to reproduce. For this reason Alvarado comments that he was pleased that she was the only Californio woman to become a nun, foregrounding Californio women's roles in reproduction:

> This is the only case until 1825 that a daughter of Alta California embraced religious life and I am very glad that it was this way, for our immense territory needed a large population and if women had gotten it into their heads to become nuns it would not have been possible to populate those sites that it was necessary to civilize to contain the heathen Indians. (2:32)

Cast in this light, reproduction was not only women's primary family obligation but also a civil duty, because "civilization" was seen as synonymous with occupation of the territory by *gente de razón*. Children were likewise an investment for a better future and guaranteed the retention of property within the family. Any woman, then, who turned from her assigned duty of having children was considered deviant and even unpatriotic, although women like Argüello or Lorenzana, in relinquishing the role of progenitrix, played other feminine roles in Californio society as teachers, nurses, and in service outside their own immediate family, but still fully within the patriarchal norm.

Yet Argüello enters the realm of textuality as a fairy-tale heroine. Even in the Californio testimonials of the 1870s she is the angel of romance, for these are narrated by a younger generation, for the most part, who were born after 1806 and heard the story from their parents. Alvarado will transform the role of Concepción Argüello from romantic angel to "guardian angel" of the embryonic Californio nation in his account of one particular experience in which she saved his life. His testimonial recounts how after he and his followers rebelled against the acting governor Nicolás Gutiérrez and pronounced the independence of Alta California in 1836, the northern rebels marched south, first to Santa Barbara and then to Los Angeles, to ensure by force the adherence of the *sureños*. To crush the continued opposition in the south and the support for Carlos Carrillo as governor, Alvarado months later had several of

the principal citizens of San Diego and Los Angeles imprisoned in
Sonoma; additionally, after a mysterious incident, Alvarado put Los Angeles, then the most populated *pueblo* in California, under a state of siege.
One night in 1838 while he was in Los Angeles, he recalls, a woman
who traveled incognito and dressed as a peasant approached his camp
to warn his guard of a conspiracy to kill the governor. Alvarado, upon
being notified, investigated, and is certain that the woman was Doña Concepción, as she was the only woman brave and daring enough to travel
from Santa Barbara to Los Angeles to warn him. Alvarado adds to the
intrigue by saying that she preferred to remain incognito to hide the
identity of her informant, another woman who had received the information from her lover (4:69–71).

For other Californios, this romantic angel who remained faithful to
Rezanov's memory and renounced marriage became little more than
a spinster dedicated to daily visits to the chapel, acts of charity, teaching children to read, and visiting Indian huts to care for the sick and
baptize them with water blessed by the missionaries. This role, contrary to the image of the exalted romantic maiden or the daring res-
cuer, exposed her to ridicule as well:

> During the many years that she lived in Mr. Noriega's house, young
> men from Santa Barbara and others from elsewhere tried by every
> means possible to convince her to change her mind and, if possible, to
> convince her to accept their marriage proposals, but it was all in vain—
> nothing helped, not the pleading, begging, or even attempts to mock
> her as she entered the Indians' huts to care for the sick or to teach
> Christian doctrine to poor children. (Fernández, 61)

If she was not to be a countess, then she preferred to be a nun. Her
saintly life of good deeds and her rejection of all suitors would make her
a laughingstock to her fellow Californios, for what else is left to a Cinderella that is not found by her prince? For those who mocked her vo-
cation of service, she became a pathetic figure. Caught in the double
bind of assigned feminine roles, she preferred to become an agent of
the church, baptizing the dying as the missionaries did. By participating in the patriarchal structure as a member of the Third Order Secular of Saint Francis in Santa Barbara, and later, in 1851, at the age of
sixty, joining a Dominican convent for women founded in Monterey, she
evidences penetration of male-dominated sites in a more formal way,
although "the feminine" subordinate element, represented by the neophytes, was always implicit in the mission domain. When the Academia

de Santa Catalina was moved to Benicia in 1854, Doña Concepción, now Sor María Dominga, accompanied the convent nuns, and she died there in 1857 (Fernández, 61; Rezanov, footnote, 99).

The construct of the manipulated/deceived/abandoned/gullible maiden thus competes with the construct of the fairy-tale Cinderella, favored by the count to be his wife. Her contemporaries emphasized the first version; sixty years later, the second-generation narrators of these testimonials still tend to inscribe the love story with more prosaic considerations, although for some the fact that she never married allows the romantic tale to endure. She becomes a symbol of faithfulness to her lover, as much in the testimonials as in Harte's ballad. The construct of the maiden in this story is a feudal construct, with the woman serving here for bartering, to link two "dynasties" and to suggest the opening of trade relations between two powers. Only Rezanov's version suggests some individual agency on her part in her desire to escape, but clearly she did not envision escape from the patriarchal structure, but only, perhaps, to trade the Californio patriarchy for a higher station.

Like Doña Concepción Argüello, Apolinaria Lorenzana was constantly in demand for her nursing and teaching services, but it bears noting that she was as dedicated to caring for the missionaries, the ill, and her pupils as she was to tending her three ranches. Both Argüello and Lorenzana were considered "beatas" ("pious ones," at best an ambiguous designation), but Argüello appears to have had a more religious disposition, and Lorenzana is the more enterprising of the two. Though she insists in her interview with Savage in 1878 that she lost all her property and "was loath to speak on this subject" (Lorenzana, introduction), Bowman finds, in his study of land grants and patents, that she sold her smaller *rancho* Cañada de los Coches to Anacleto Lestrade, who patented it in 1873, and her *rancho* Jamachá was patented to her for 8,881.16 acres in 1871 (Bowman, 1957: 158).

Reconstruction of the particular religious concerns of women afforded in Alvarado's testimonial give him an opportunity to comment on the total manipulation of women by the missionaries, noting that Californio men, unlike women, had been able to free themselves of the yoke of the missionaries (2:30–31). Constructs of the feminine are thus bound up in various ways with religious discourses and, for Alvarado, with fanaticism and domination. Males had escaped this phenomenon, Alvarado insists, because the missionaries had not established schools for young boys. Thus for Alvarado "enlightenment" is gendered, with the weaker sex said to be the one more prone to obscurantism (2:31). Not all women, however, felt the same way about the church, as we shall see in what follows.

The Maiden and the Merchant

If the myth of Concepción Argüello and the Russian count is a northern California emplotment of aristocratic pretensions during the Spanish period, the Mexican period and southern California offer a more prosaic counterpoint to the romantic fairy tale. The Fitch-Carrillo love story bears symbolic witness to changing times, to conquest and the reality of Californio-foreigner intermarriage. As Californio society begins to be transformed after the Mexican revolution and especially after secularization, male bonding and patriarchal practices (the cohesive elements that cement families, and thereby all of the Californio society together) start to unravel along political and regional lines.

The distance from the metropolis, Mexico City, allows for minor changes in relations of power, regarding caste as well as gender. Just as caste distinctions in the Spanish colonies gradually allowed for the removal of social barriers affecting mestizos and some acculturated Indians, so too in Alta California some tolerance and in fact a need for strong independent women emerged. Though insurmountable limitations along gender lines continued to be imposed, the frontier area, more conservative in some practices, proved to be more open in others. Here in the northern frontier towns, despite pressures by church missionaries and patriarchal family structures to abide by social rules, women found a degree of tolerance for changing social patterns, especially after Mexican independence. After secularization, certain women would take charge of a great deal of the production on the small ranches and become notable riders and farmers. As towns grew in size, women, especially widows such as Tía Gertrudis Boronda, for example, would begin to function a bit more independently, as she did with her small shop in Monterey (MGV, 1:267). This willingness to reduce social constraints on women after Mexican independence and secularization accompanies changes in property and other social relations, as well as increased contact with recent arrivals from Mexico (particularly with the Hijar-Padrés colonists arriving in 1834) and from other parts of the world. Linking the family with foreign economic interests now becomes desirable and in that linkage, of course, the primary nexus will be the Californio woman.

The love story of Josefa Carrillo and Henry Fitch takes place during this moment of transition, during the administration of the first Mexican appointed governor. Unlike the Spanish-period myth of Concepción and Rezanov, in this episode the hero is no longer noble: he is the captain of a merchant's boat involved in trade along the California coast. The heroine is one of nine children of a soldier and his wife living outside the San Diego *presidio* walls in the house and orchard of their uncle and former commander Francisco María Ruiz. San Diego at that time is small and desolate, site of the poorest mission but also of an attractive harbor and beach for four large hide houses, that is, barracks where hides were prepared and stored by the various trading vessels (Machado de Ridington, 18).

In 1829, twenty-three years after the Argüello-Rezanov episode, Henry Delano Fitch, a native of Massachusetts and then captain of a trading ship owned by the German merchant H. Virmond from Mexico, asked to marry Josefa Carrillo of San Diego—"an angelic maiden who captivated all who saw her" (Alvarado, 2:140). M. G. Vallejo notes that Fitch was not a Catholic (MGV, 2:118), but Pío Pico recalls that he joined the Catholic church, was baptized, and obtained the consent of her parents (Pico, 1973: 38). Vallejo, who would become Josefa's brother-in-law, recalls that Domingo Carrillo, the woman's uncle, opposed Josefa's marriage to a foreigner and asked Governor Echeandía to intervene and stop the wedding. He did, an act that Vallejo attributes to the governor's own personal interest in the girl (MGV, 2:118). Alvarado (2:141) alleges that the governor was interested in her for himself, although Echeandía, who had come to Alta California by himself, was a married man with a wife and children in Mexico (Hutchinson, 125). Pío Pico too makes Echeandía into the self-serving interloper in the Carrillo-Fitch love story:

> Josefa Carrillo was a very beautiful young woman who danced very well. Echeandía always favored her at the dances. (1973: 39)

Unlike the Argüello-Rezanov narrative, for this love story we have the version of the "heroine" herself. In her testimonial Josefa Carrillo Fitch recalls the climatic moment in her father's home: an altar had been set up, and the missionary Friar Antonio Meléndez had just come to the home dressed up in his appropriate vestments when Don Domingo Carrillo, under Echeandía's orders, appeared to stop the wedding. Fearing repercussions, the missionary fled and the bridegroom, Captain Fitch, left to seek the counsel of his friend Pío Pico (Carrillo de Fitch, 4), whose sole expertise, according to Vallejo, was the human heart (MGV, 2:119).

The Fitch-Carrillo story is in fact allegorical as reconstructed in the Californio testimonials, and anticipates what the Californios will narrate of the invasion of Alta California in 1846. Here the territory is feminized, courted by foreigners, and finally succumbs, despite Mexican intervention. The portrayals offered by the narrators encourage this particular reading. In true romantic fashion we find that the two lovers are presented by Alvarado as disconsolate, but Fitch, here the image of the would-be-conqueror facing unforeseen obstacles, is additionally described as acting first like an enraged lion who has lost his prey and then like a beggar pleading for help (Alvarado, 2:142). As in a fairy tale, there appears not a fairy godmother but the helper—Pío Pico—who intercedes to save the day. (And of course the conquerors of 1846 would have numerous "helpers," though Pico himself would favor the British rather than the United States.) Various versions of the ensuing elopement are textualized in the Californio testimonials. According to Alvarado the solution is suggested by Pico to Fitch, but Pico indicates that Josefa seeks his assistance. Josefa Fitch, however, cedes the initiative to Fitch, who works out the plan and in turn sends Pico to convince her of what she must do (Carrillo de Fitch, 5). Known as a lady's man, Pico, who is also Josefa's cousin, helps her to elope with Fitch by taking her to the beach that same night, where the bridegroom awaits with a boat. Josefa Fitch recalls that Pico gave them his blessing, asking only that Henry Fitch make her happy (6). (It would be this "blessing" to the conquerors that Pico would seek to avoid by fleeing in 1846.) That night the couple sailed for Valparaiso, Chile; after a trip of seventy-four days, they arrived and were married (Pico, 1973: 39).

The narrative reveals additional plot dimensions that capture social and political relations in a semifeudal society. It goes on to narrate how the "love couple," upon returning to California a year later with child in tow, was placed under house arrest by Echeandía in Monterey, and husband and wife were held separately (although Vallejo facilitated conjugal visits [MGV, 2:121–22]). After three months of this separation they were turned over to the ecclesiastical authorities in San Gabriel, where they spent yet another three months doing what was demanded as penance; thereafter the missionaries finally ruled that they were in fact legally married and could resume a normal life (Carrillo de Fitch, 9; Pico, 1973: 39; MGV, 2:122). Fitch tried to sue Echeandía for his meddling but nothing came of it. In the end the couple resolved to dismiss the suit and went into business in San Diego, doing quite well. The story thus reconstructs the power of the church, even during the administration of a liberal governor, and the power of a Mexican governor who was full of whims, antiforeigner, and able to interfere in the personal lives of a couple, a situation that would not be tolerated much longer. During the next decade, a number of foreigners would marry the daughters of Californio families with no problem. Though his testimonial is noted for its anticlericalism, in this case Alvarado finds the missionaries to be blameless and uses the opportunity to dismiss women as obstinate, as he recalls that Josefa Fitch always blamed the church, and not only Echeandía, for what had transpired:

> She was in the belief that the missionary fathers had led Governor Echeandía to initiate his persecution of her and her husband. I, however, have a different opinion on the matter and though I tried to make Mrs. Fitch see my point, I failed to convince her but that didn't surprise me, because experience has taught me that it would be less difficult for a man to carry Mt. Parnassus on his shoulders than to convince an old woman that she has lived for forty years prey to an erroneous idea. (2:145)

Alvarado was convinced that the persecution was initiated by a rejected lover and apparently did not know that Josefa Fitch had provided a version similar to his own in her testimonial. For her part, Josefa indicates that the governor had allowed his personal aspirations to cloud his "lofty liberal mind," but in time she forgave him, noting her identification as a Californio respectful of Echeandía's role against Victoria:

> A few years later, with all my heart I forgave him, for he had liberated my country from the yoke of the tyrant Victoria, and I figured that his persecution of me and my husband had been an act motivated by scorn that filled his soul when he became convinced that I had preferred a rival that he detested. (5)

Josefa Carrillo Fitch thus appears to have decided to reconstruct the dominant version of the episode, positing the governor's intervention as the despotic act of a tyrant and rejected suitor, as she presumably tells her father upon her return (Carrillo de Fitch, 8–9), but an act that she could ultimately forgive. Although she could make allowances for Echeandía's personal weakness, she would not forgive the church, which, upon their return home, had made incredible demands and kept the couple apart. Clearly the mission stay had embittered Fitch and explained her long-standing resentment against the church, evident in her refusal to give it a cent even in her old age, a fact that portrays the situation even better than do the personal accounts.[23]

In all of the reconstructions of this love story Josefa is presented as strong and passionate, willing to follow her heart, willing to risk losing her father's blessing, and determined to counter the governor's orders. Her decision to elope does not stray too far afield from boundaries established by the church (she marries within the church as soon as possible) yet upon returning the couple is surprised to be arrested and subjected to both civil and ecclesiastical jurisdictions. The couple, now duly chastised, is willing to abide, and Josefa even goes home to beg her father's forgiveness. The patriarchal structure is in no way rejected, though Josefa does make clear her prerogative to choose one patriarchy over another.

The multiple versions of this love story oppose personal interests to those of the state and church. In all, the individual subject's right to choose a partner is presented as preferable to the older generation's tradition of the parents' choosing for their daughters, with the daughters subject to both parental decision and church doctrine. The story also involves national and economic interests. The elopement is a challenge not only to the dominant semifeudal patriarchal structure, for Fitch represents a capitalist interloper, but also to any nationalist policy rejecting intermarriage with foreigners. This challenge did not signal a shift toward a more capitalist patriarchal family structure, but it did serve as a foreshadowing of what was to come. About eighteen years later, another Californio woman, this time from Baja California and a cousin of Josefa Carrillo, María Amparo Ruiz, would similarly provoke a spurned suitor to seek the church's ban of her marriage to a Protestant Yankee officer, Lieutenant Henry S. Burton.[24] Love stories in the Californio testimonials thus textualize both emergent and residual constructs in Californio history in a way that allows for a retrieval of the process of discursive shifts within the ideological field.

Many other Californio women of the ruling classes besides Josefa Carrillo would marry foreigners, merchants primarily, who replaced the missionaries as *compradores*, storekeepers, and bankers.[25] The wealth of Alta California, as Alvarado indicates, was soon primarily in the hands of foreigners linked through marriage to Californio women:

> The daughters of the most distinguished citizens of the territory had as husbands men who had been born beyond the Pacific. (3:72)

Intermarriage constituted an important nexus that not only incorporated foreigners into the California "family" but protected them from coercive action on the part of governors like Chico, who at one time thought of placing demands on foreigners to force them to loan the government money. Alvarado (3:74) recalls that once warned of the consequences, Chico desisted. Some of the leading Californio families were willing not only to defend these new family members, but also to assist them in competition with other foreigners. Spence, who originally worked for Hartnell and McCullock, was able to form his own business thanks to the support of the Estrada family network, with which he had become allied once he married one of its daughters. Against this northern oligarchy Hartnell could not compete.

In Santa Barbara the most influential Californio was the Spaniard Guerra y Noriega, who functioned as the missionaries' treasurer. In a territory where most of the early trade was with the missions, Guerra y Noriega was a key individual, as Robinson undoubtedly recognized when he married one of his daughters, Ana María. Robinson's marriage and links with the de la Guerra family were a stroke of good luck or astute planning, as José de Jesús Vallejo recalls:

> He was able to monopolize certain branches of commerce that proved very profitable for him. Mr. Robinson was, since his arrival in our country, very supportive of the clergy's interests and they in turn on more than one occasion showed him their gratitude. (JJV, 22)

Women function, then, as concessions made to men, as human capital. Once in the possession of males, women facilitate social interaction and material exchange. Adelaida Estrada is said to have enabled Spence to make the best deals, whether buying or selling.[26] In these intermarriages, however, women cannot simply be said to be manipulated by their families, or specifically by the patriarch of the family, and forced into marriage with the foreigners, although undoubtedly that was not an unheard-of practice. In several cases, the Californio women choose—not only in the early nineteenth century, like Concepción Argüello, but later, like Josefa Carrillo, and much later, like Rosalía Vallejo—to link with foreigners. Rosalía Vallejo's choice of partner becomes a significant issue: Timothy Murphy, an Irishman from Lima, had been admitted as a suitable husband for Rosalía by her brother and named to administer the San Rafael mission, but apparently Rosalía was not interested. Instead, she preferred in 1837 to marry the enterprising Jacob Leese, a man not to her brother's liking. The marriage would go through, but Leese, many years and several children later, would invest his capital and hers in a losing colonization project in Baja California and later abandon his family, leaving Rosalía Leese and her children penniless (Alvarado, 3:50–51).[27] Many of these foreigners, including Leese (originally from Ohio), would in 1846 ally with the incoming

U.S. invaders, despite being naturalized Mexican citizens; here too the women, at least those not forced into these marriages, could be said to be complicitous in helping to open doors for those who would eventually betray and dominate the Californios. In some cases, as we shall see in the next chapter, Californio women married to foreigners took an anti-U.S. stance, irrespective of their husbands' sympathies. Again, the discourses of gender, class, nation, and religion interconnect within the ideological field and cannot be seen as divorced from one another, or as layered in predetermined ways.

The Fallen Angels

Along with constructs of Californio women as romantic Cinderellas, daring maidens, and mediators, there is one additional construct of the feminine that appears in several of the testimonials that runs decidedly counter to the idealized representation of Californio women. Part and parcel of the Californio family's strategies of containment through patriarchal discourses of feminine virtue, propriety, and submissiveness are constructs of the fallen angel: the adulterous woman or the prostitute/mistress. Part of the figuration in the testimonials is that of women of "mala vida," prostitutes who since earlier times found their way into the men's quarters in the *presidio* (MGV, 1:69). Publicly recognized, living either in their parents' homes or independently as heads of household, these prostitutes are designated with the letters "M.V." in an early census of Los Angeles in 1836. Of 250 women living in the *pueblo*, fifteen are designated as prostitutes.[28] Representations of these women or of unfaithful wives are constructs of social deviation menacing the social fiber, just as hostile Indians threaten the social structure. Here too caste and class inform representations of gender. Like the hostile Indians, the female "monsters" represented within these testimonials,[29] while emplotted as not very powerful, are nonetheless acknowledged as disruptive. Also much like the neophyte Indians, they are contained within the early Californio patriarchy that saw itself threatened both from outside and from within.

The narratives of "fallen angels" in these testimonials, represented especially by Alvarado with a great deal of humor and condescension, have a dual function: first to counter the idealized version by foreigners of virtuous Californio womanhood alongside which male Californios are found lacking and, second, in a more conventional *machista* maneuver, to make fun of the husbands while berating the behavior of their wives, who in the end are treated rather patronizingly as naughty children. Interestingly enough, women like Juana Briones de Miranda, represented by hegemonic historians as "the most prominent woman of provincial California" who petitioned the bishop in 1844 to live apart from her husband (Bowman, 1957: 163), are not mentioned in the testimonials of northern Californios like the Vallejos or Alvarado, except perhaps to designate the North Beach area near her ranch where de Mofras suffered a rather ludicrous mishap (MGV, 4:254). Those episodes that are reconstructed do point to Californio women's willingness to defy the norms in their struggles against family constraints. Adultery, let us recall, was then a criminal offense.

The topic of Californio womanhood was often brought up as a point on which the narrators interviewed by Bancroft's agents were asked to comment. One of the more frequently mentioned cases is that of Ildefonsa (also called Alfonsa or Alfonsina) Herrera, wife of José María Herrera, a Mexican customs officer during the administration of Governor Echeandía and an enemy of the Californio "liberals." Herrera was deported in 1829 after it became clear that he had conspired with Solís and the missionaries to overthrow the governor (Alvarado, 2:111, 116), but he would return to Alta California in 1834 with a wife (a woman much younger than himself) to serve again as customs officer. The most extensive account of the affair is provided with undoubtable relish by Alvarado, who was one of the witnesses taken by the justice of the peace to the Herrera home when the husband made accusations of adultery upon discovering that Ildefonsa and José María Castañares, a customs office clerk, were having an affair. Castañares was married to Ana María González, and Herrera as customs officer was Castañares's superior (Alvarado, 3:88).

M. G. Vallejo, who considered Herrera not only an enemy but a generally disgusting fellow, offers a sarcastic perspective of the affair and appears to side with the woman when he explains that

> tired of living tied to a man whose disgusting presence and foolish words provoked nausea, she had opted for occasionally falling into the arms of Captain José María Castañares, whom she honored with the title of lover. (MGV, 3:128)

Despite sharing Vallejo's opinion of Herrera, Alvarado—who notes her infidelity rather than that of Castañares—goes on to impute effectively the reputation of a good many women of Monterey. He implies that both Ildefonsa and Cosme Peña's wife were led astray by the bad example established by Governor Chico's mistress, Doña Cruz (3:90). In 1836 Chico had scandalized Californio society by bringing his mistress, his *ramera,* as Vallejo indicates, a woman who had abandoned her husband in Mexico to follow her lover (MGV, 3:103, 120) and who during the short Chico governorship would be introduced in Alta California as his niece (Alvarado, 3:88–89).

In this episode gender, legal, and cultural discourses combine to reveal women's agency in a semifeudal society that was in the process of change. The episode begins not when the cuckolded Herrera had the justice of the peace come to his house to charge his wife and Castañares with the crime of adultery, but many months before, when Castañares's wife, Doña Ana, began gathering witnesses and evidence to prove her husband's infidelity. Ironically Herrera would subsequently sue Doña Ana for "defamation of his good name" with her rumors and insinuations. The slander suit was dismissed a few months later when Herrera made the accusation himself against his wife and her lover. Upon the arrival of the justice of the peace and witnesses at his home, Herrera reportedly took his wife by the hand and said:

> I hereby turn over to the legal authorities my wife, Alfonsa, as well as these documents that will prove her offense of infidelity. I ask that the judge file charges against her and her accomplice, the aggressor, according to our laws. (Alvarado, 3:88–89)

Vallejo offers a more risqué account indicating that the judge and witnesses were brought to view Doña Alfonsa in bed with her lover, whereupon the couple was made to get out of bed, get dressed, and led off to jail (MGV, 3:129). Because there were then no jails for women, the judge placed Alfonsa under house arrest in the home of the Pacheco family and jailed Castañares. What is especially interesting is that both the man and the woman were placed under arrest, not always the case in similar circumstances.[30]

Frequent references throughout the testimonials would indicate that adultery was not that uncommon in this patriarchal society. Adultery thus is in part a strategy for escaping from a patriarchal family closure. Another famous case often recalled is that of Cosme Peña and his wife, but in this instance escape from patriarchal closure would lead to a tragedy. Here too gender discourses are tied in with Californio politics. In 1834 Peña was a lawyer who came to California with the Hijar-Padrés colony, as did the lawyer Luis Castillo Negrete. During his stay Peña figured prominently in Alvarado's revolt and later in a conspiracy against Alvarado, although he was back in favor shortly thereafter. Like Herrera, Peña would have problems with his wife, troubles that were public knowledge and soon the subject of satirical verses by Castillo Negrete. The latter circulated a poem deriding three alleged leaders of the conspiracy against the interim head of the territory: the revolutionary ex-friar Angel Ramírez, the foreigner William Hinkley (captain of the *Don Quijote*), and the lawyer Cosme Peña. The text ridicules Peña for not being able to control his wife, and also for his ignorance and vices (Coronel, 187).[31]

Vallejo saw the poem as an attack from Castillo Negrete, a monarchist, on a liberal republican. Though not as well educated as Castillo Negrete, who had studied in the best universities of Spain, Peña had, Vallejo granted, developed his own style as a lawyer through his application, study of Mexican laws, and interaction with Mexican intellectuals (MGV, 3:188). This assessment of Peña is not shared by Coronel: "Cosme Peña was poorly educated, and not more than a two-bit lawyer; moreover he was fickle, given to pleasure and other vices, especially drink" (187). Peña is thus no threat to the Californios, not like the brilliant Castillo Negrete who had not backed Alvarado's revolution. If only for this reason, both Vallejo and Alvarado assume a defensive position in support of the wretched and cuckolded Peña. Whatever problems he might have had at home were not, according to these two narrators, politically relevant and had no business being discussed publicly (MGV, 3:189); moreover, it should have been beneath Castillo Negrete to do so (Alvarado, 3:167). The intimate life of a political ally is off-limits, and it is considered in bad taste to discuss it, but the intimate life of an enemy if not discussed is at least alluded to, as is evident in the case of Herrera. Pointedly all three unfaithful women are represented as *mexicanas*, unlike, of course, faithful Californio women. These examples capture the interconnection of discourses of nation, gender, and morality that pervades these various testimonials. In the end, for these narrators infidelity functions more as a sign of masculine weakness and, allegorically, of moral and political turpitude— for these are the wives of Mexican officials—than of women's condition within a semifeudal society. But the implications of these conditions are clear in the case of the nameless woman (Cosme Peña's wife), who preferred to take the risk of Indian attack in the desert in order to return to Mexico rather than remain in California subject to her husband and to rumors. Here too, however, Coronel's account of her abduction by Indians would indicate that she left one patriarchal closure only to be forced into another.[32]

Women are thus constructed as men's Achilles' heel, their weakness, but clearly the problem for these men is that women are not mere appendages and that they sometimes gain agency as women by going outside the social norms. But escape from a patriarchal structure is not to be found in a different caste, station, or order, as seen in neophyte women who married *gente de razón*; there are only shifts from one patriarchal structure to another. In a society without divorce, few options existed for married women; the bishop could grant requests for separation, as for Juana Briones (Bowman, 1957: 163), or women could simply live separately as did Teodora Soto (Bowman, 1957: 157). Adultery was also an option, though not an easy choice given that this act of transgression was punishable by both civil and church law and morally condemned by the Californios. One particular episode in Los Angeles would lead to the lynching of a woman. Alvarado, Botello, and Vallejo all recall the event, but the latter uses the story to adduce to Californio women the trait of being violently jealous:

> California women almost without exception were jealous to the
> highest degree of their husbands and although given their innate
> and proverbial prudence they overlooked their husbands' other faults,
> under no circumstances were they willing to forgive acts of infidelity.
> (MGV, 3:119)

According to Vallejo, a woman by the name of Villa, blind with jealousy, killed her husband and was later executed by the town without trial (MGV, 3:119). For Vallejo, the Suysun practice of punishing the man more than the woman in cases of adultery was more sensible (MGV, 1:10–11), yet recounting the Villa episode he prefers focusing on the initial cause and the final outcome, that is, the fact that this was the first lynching in California and presaged the many that were to follow after the U.S. invasion. In their telling of the story, Botello and Alvarado deal with intervening causes that led to the first act of vigilantism in California.

Alvarado's account of Domingo Felix and María del Rosario Villa, "hija de México" (an origin always meaningful for Alvarado), provides the construct of an unfaithful wife who intrigues with her lover in the murder of her husband. That her infidelity was an act of revenge for her husband's infidelity is remarked only in passing; it was to get back at her husband that she had become involved with Gervasio Alipaz (3:60). Alvarado indicates that the presumed infidelity of the husband was in fact a lie, saying that the whole town knew that Felix adored his wife (3:60). Seeing that she was unwilling to return to her home and preferred spending time with her lover, Gervasio, in San Gabriel, Felix, insists Alvarado, was forced to ask the *alcalde* of Los Angeles to order her to appear before him and remand her to his custody.

Botello's testimonial indicates that Villa was trying to separate from her husband and was having "illicit relations" with Gervasio Alipaz (20).

The discovery of Felix's corpse would lead the local *rancheros* to swear to avenge his death. Once the wayward wife and lover were arrested in the Los Angeles area and jailed, the authorities began taking down their depositions, but John Temple, Felix's brother, and other men resolved to save time and formed a vigilante committee headed by the Frenchman Víctor Prudón (who had come with the Híjar-Padrés colony) to try and sentence the accused. As Alvarado (3:67) indicates, this was the first vigilante committee to function in California. The townspeople armed themselves to forestall the intervention of the military authorities in the matter, but the latter did not intervene as several soldiers were in fact members of the committee. Only the *alcalde* showed up before the committee to remind it that the procedure was illegal, and that no town was authorized to take the law into its own hands. At the improvised hearing, each of the defendants blamed the other and both were found guilty. They were then sentenced to death and the committee sent for the missionary from San Fernando. When he did not appear within two days, they dispensed with religious formalities and carried out the sentence. Both Alipaz and Villa were executed and their corpses exhibited, as a deterrent to crime, until nightfall, when relatives took them away for burial (Alvarado, 3:60–67).

Alvarado was then head of the Diputación in Monterey and says he studied the case to determine if there was any doubt of the guilt of the sentenced couple but found none. Prudón, then a schoolteacher at San Gabriel, is said to have rather unwillingly acted out the role of judge at the townspeople's insistence. Popular power, argues Alvarado, in such instances is more powerful than written laws:

> Prudón had to accept popular fiat and preside over the first court in California outside of legal procedure but within popular dictates, which are much more powerful, much more strict, much clearer and more rapidly administered; the people are like a sleeping lion that while it sleeps does not care what is happening around it, but if any passerby should unwittingly step on its head, it rears up, looks about, shakes its mane, and falls upon the unhappy victim that soon falls prey to the agility and strength of the king of the jungle. (3:68–69)

Thus textualized, popular power in the hands of what is represented as a mob was of course what Alvarado feared most when he took over the administration of the territory near the end of 1836. Earlier that year, when the authorities were notified of what had occurred in Los

Angeles, they sent Captain Muñoz to investigate the case and to determine who had fired against the criminals, but no one would testify:

> In view of the fact that the exemplary sentence had been carried out by the entire town, not a single person was found who would appear to testify against those that the governor wanted to punish to set an example. (Alvarado, 3:70)

As in Lope de Vega's seventeenth-century play *Fuenteovejuna*, the town of Los Angeles in solidarity with the vigilante committee refused to turn over the men involved. Again in this story the leaders of the vigilante committee are said to be Prudón and Araujo, two Hijar-Padrés colonists who were new to the territory, and the Yankee Temple, all "foreigners." Botello recalls that the two leaders of what he considered a riot ("motín"), Prudón and Araujo, were expatriated as a result of the lynching but that Prudón later returned (20–21). The entire episode points out why Alvarado feared any political action that suggested political autonomy in Los Angeles and why he subjected it to a state of siege in 1838.

Again here in the Felix/Villa/Alipaz narrative the woman functions like the biblical serpent, enticing men to murder; no one seemingly entertains the notion that a woman should not be forced by authorities civil or ecclesiastic to stay with a man to whom she no longer wishes to be married, although Botello notes in passing that what the woman wanted was to separate from her husband (20). Moreover, the community seems especially enraged that Villa's infidelity should have led first to the fragmentation of the family and then to murder, so much so that at first they wanted her to die contemplating the corpse of her lover so that she would suffer more. After the execution of Alipaz, Alvarado (3:66–67) notes, the town changed its mind, "took pity on the criminal woman and spared her the sad scene even as they executed her." The fact that other murders in the territory had not provoked this type of *pueblo* response provides a good indication of the people's intolerance for what was perceived as the ultimate transgression on the part of a woman.

We have previously noted that in Mexico Alta California was seen as a penal colony. Ord (1956: 16) recalls the arrival of several "convict expeditions" to Alta California since she was a young girl. When Echeandía, the new governor, was met with Californio complaints about the number of convicts that were being sent to California, he argued that the Mexican government did not know that there were "decent and educated families" in Alta California (MGV, 2:71). This mind-set led many incoming settlers and governors to imagine that legal and moral restraints would be less stringent in the territory, but once they arrived they found that, with few exceptions, similar social and moral norms were imposed here as in Mexico. Thus, for example, when Governor Micheltorena arrived with his mistress, Doña Josefa Fuente, he was forced by the missionaries to marry her. Chico likewise arrived with his "niece," Doña Cruz, mentioned earlier in relation to the Herrera/Castañares affair. Vallejo remarks that what chagrined him and the other Californios was not so much that Doña Cruz had abandoned her husband to follow Chico, but that their affair was conducted publicly. Calling upon discourses of love, republicanism, and morality all in the same breath, he addresses his readers and states that he is not against love nor does he censure those blinded by love,

> but I do loathe intensely with all the strength of my republican soul those injudicious heads of state that are deaf to the cry for decency, and that indifferent to the call for reason and good morals boast publicly of their impetuousness and make known their disdain for the opinions of the virtuous. (MGV, 3:120)[33]

It was the effrontery of Chico, like that of Micheltorena and even Gutiérrez with his Indian harem, that scandalized the Californios, not the secret affairs of ruling-class men. As we shall see in chapter 7, moral superiority tied always to particular positions will in the end be the sole advantage that the Californios see themselves as possessing after all else has been taken from them. Even here women will be constructed as a constant threat, menacing to topple men from this remaining pedestal of moral and political righteousness.

Restructuring

With the restructuring of Alta California after secularization came a number of economic and political changes that affected the position of women. The infusion of foreigners to California, especially after 1840, similarly brought changes in social as well as property relations. Foreigners still had to indicate an intent to become naturalized Mexican citizens in order to be assigned vacant lands, but they no longer had to be married to Mexican women to petition for land. Unmarried men could also be considered for land grants (Junta de Fomento de Californias, 309–12). Although the colonization law spelling out conditions for land concessions to foreigners was never passed, it did serve as a precedent for determining a more open settlement policy. These new practices implemented by Alvarado and in part by Vallejo in effect no longer made marriage to Mexican or Californio women the sine qua non of land grants. In responding to criticism expressed by Friar Durán regarding Alvarado's land grants and sale to foreigners, Vallejo explains that in view of the importance of increasing the number of *gente de razón* in the territory to resist raids by hostile Indians, it was proper and necessary for Alvarado to make these land concessions even if they went beyond Mexican policy prohibiting "concessions of land to foreigners who were not married to native daughters," i.e., Californio women (MGV, 4:150–59). Vallejo's legitimation of their land concession policies might be seen as a liberal, even nonchauvinist discourse, but at bottom it is a racist one. Like Sarmiento in Argentina, the liberal Californios wanted to populate the territory with "white" immigrants, called *gente de razón*, to guard "civilized" portions of California from the "hordes" of Indian raiders. The dominant northern Californios were never as generous with Sonoran settlers, mestizos like Botello, who had been coming to Alta California since the 1830s. That Vallejo and Alvarado were prejudiced against darker mestizos, Blacks, and other non-European settlers is evident in the numerous comments made throughout their testimonials.[34] They did make land concessions to women, however, even Indian women, and Vallejo set aside land for Indian communities allied to him, perhaps keeping it in reserve for himself. In the south Pico had similarly been granted what were formerly the Indians' lands of Rancho Las Flores and provisionally of Temécula.

Beyond class and caste considerations there were of course pressing economic needs underlying these land grants. Although Vallejo indicates that the lands granted to Rowland, a recent exile from New Mexico, were a concession and not a sale as Durán insinuated, clearly the difference was difficult to determine in such cases. Had not the lands around Petaluma and Soscol been concessions to Vallejo by Governor Micheltorena in recognition of the two thousand pesos in gold and foodstuffs that Vallejo had made available to a bankrupt territorial administration (MGV, 4:387)? That too had not been an outright "sale," but nonetheless remuneration for goods or services received had played a part in the granting of lands, in this particular case a transaction that would not be patented by U.S. courts after invasion. Large land grants were thus clearly in exchange for some economic benefit, just as marriage to Californio women had formerly played a role in land transactions.

New policies, land concessions to women, and the allocation of lands to immigrant families (especially in the northern frontier) had definitely changed the role of Californio women as well as that of the foreigners who as settlers could be construed as a second wave of preinvaders, after the earlier arrival of the merchants, all preparing the way for the military forces and the U.S. occupation of Alta California. As it played out, almost all the foreigners in the territory married to Californio women or provided with land for settlement would betray their newly acquired Mexican citizenship and side with the invaders.

Gender and Social Change

When Vallejo looks back in 1875 he is forced to compare the women of the past with the Californio women now around him. He laments their transformation into what he calls spendthrifts and consumers of cosmetics, clothing, and all kinds of articles that he considers superfluous and extravagant, so much so that ostensibly many men were determining not to marry in order to escape debt and the economic burden a wife entailed. Sounding much like late-nineteenth-century Latin American naturalist novelists, Vallejo approaches misogyny as he goes on to state that women's love for luxury was the ruin of many a father and husband (MGV, 4:334). As to their role in reproduction and the stability of the patriarchal order, he says that all women used to marry, but now he finds old maids all around him—further proof, to his mind, that women were now considered to be the economic downfall of men and for that reason were being avoided, a turn of events that threatened the social fabric. Clearly Vallejo sees women as threats, as bound up with new social practices, and as the representatives of the new mode of production and the new ruling class, all made manifest in an excess of "liberty":

> The modern Californios wanting to give women all the freedom and privileges that they might desire have granted a dangerous liberty that in my view produces nothing more than the degeneration of the human species in the cities and causes an infinite number of moral and physical ills. No doubt my readers when they reflect on the previously written lines will classify me as retrograde, as a proponent of outdated ideas, and opposed to having young people enjoy the pleasures of life; for my part I have nothing to defend about what I have written, in view of the fact that my ideas and mode of bringing up young women are known by a good number of my fellow citizens who have on more than one occasion made known to me, orally and in writing, that they do not approve of the education bestowed on young women during the past twenty years. In this time those in charge of education have prepared them for nothing but how to behave in the theater, at dances, caring little that without instruction in home economics these "dolls" will be incapable of managing a household. (MGV, 4:337)

The importance of gender discourses becomes evident in this quote from Vallejo. On women's bodies and on the control exerted on them is transposed and displaced the frustration felt by the Californio male as he views from the 1870s what has been wrested from him. With restructuring after invasion, the Californio men felt that they had lost control over their women just as they had lost control over the territory, their property, and the political control of their native land.

In a culture where wives, daughters, and mothers are rarely mentioned in a male effort to protect *themselves* from rumor or misrepresentation, those constructs of women that do appear in these testimonials serve a variety of functions. When positioned as links to foreigners, the testimonials seek to counter hegemonic constructions of industrious Californio women in opposition to idle Californio men by, first, failing to recognize their labor and participation in production (inasmuch as it is principally the foreign narrators who stress the women's productivity) and second, by noting their participation in the fragmentation of the Californio "family." Within this familial space, women's infidelity is thus often a trope for division of the territory, which in its regional and political manifestations wreaked havoc on the Californio community. Finally, in constructs of their post-1848 acculturation as well as in their marriage to foreigners, women are symbols of betrayal, California Malinches who accommodate to the enemy and after 1846 threaten what is left of the Californio patriarchy. Whereas previously they were seen as conservative, manipulated by the missionaries, and linked to fanaticism, later they are deployed discursively as all-too-disposed toward change. These conflicting and negative constructs of women are not offset at all, of course, by the constructs of romantic maidens or angelic helpers included in several testimonials, or by the constructs of female managers and supervisors of semislave Indian labor, or by constructs of nurturing women found often in the women's testimonials. Rather they are countered in the testimonials by constructs of dissent that position women within the Californio collectivity but countering male expectations in spaces of production, family, and culture, by engendering productive spaces that are no more inherently masculine than feminine and that are suggestive of female agency.

6

Protonationalism in Alta California

Justicia y justicia seca es todo lo que exijo de la posteridad.
¡Cuidado con negár mela!

J. B. Alvarado

Nations, Hobsbawm insists, are the product of territorial states, nationalism, and particular stages of technological and economic development.[1] Before the formation of a state, the elite within a nationalist movement often produces constructs of "the nation-to-be" although in fact the "nation" produced afterward may be quite different. Nationalism as a mass movement, Hobsbawm indicates, is a final stage, coming after the formation of a state. To generate identification with this "imagined community,"[2] nationalist movements often call upon already existing constructs of community, what we can term "protonationalist" identities generated by discourses of religion, ethnicity, language, kinship, culture, and earlier "historical nations" that have long since disappeared. "Protonationalism," however, is neither essential for nationalism nor is it ever "enough to form nationalities or nations, let alone states" (Hobsbawm, 46, 73, 78). That territorial states are thus not automatically "nations" or national identification axiomatic with the end of colonialism becomes clear in the case of Mexico and its Alta California territory.

Mexican independence in 1821 would bring the formation of a territorial state but not the formation of a "nation." As the historian Ruiz has indicated, national identity during the first half of the nineteenth century was not particularly strong in Mexico.[3] This lack of nationalism became quite evident during the U.S.-Mexico war, when Mexico faced an invasion that took U.S. troops all the way to its capital. In the face of this national catastrophe, neither the church nor wealthy Mexicans felt called upon to contribute to the upkeep of the troops, many of whom — half-starved, poorly trained, and undisciplined — deserted the field.[4] Some Mexican states even threatened to secede, while others totally disregarded government decrees about taxation and customs duties; with the exception of the capital city, there appears to have been little interest on the part of the general population to defend the territory. Attesting to this is the fact that the local national guards throughout the republic never organized to come to the defense of the country nor did individual states arrest deserters returning to their areas, according to the minister of internal affairs, Luis de la Rosa, in his report to the interim government during the war (Archivo, 31:180). Given the situation of anarchy in Mexico prior to the breakout of and during the war, and the resulting national disaffection within the country, it is not wholly surprising that, in view of the distance and isolation of Alta California, Californios too identified with their immediate territory rather than with Mexico.

In Alta California the construct of *hijos del país*, native sons, embodied the notion of a native land, a homeland, an "imagined territorial community," and pointed to the Californios' nativist aspirations to establish a territorial state. This aspiration or "national consciousness" developed, as often happens, unevenly among the various regions of the territory and among the various social classes. It was constructed from above, by a faction of emergent landowning "native sons" of the territory, who faced a fragmented society, one divided not only by class and race but along lines of national origin, regional location, and political orientation. The dissensions within the collectivity would rapidly disarticulate the construct of "nation" as a territorial collectivity, restricting it to a small group of native Californios principally from the northern area. In Alta California Alvarado and his supporters would be the pioneers of "the national idea," a discursive construct that, although too soon truncated, would, in interpellating a collective subjectivity on the basis of bonds of territory, ethnicity, language, religion, culture, kinship, and blood, serve to generate a protonationalism to be sustained after invasion. These protonationalist constructs are linked to constructs of ethnicity today and emerge forcefully in the Californio testimonials under study.[5]

Nationalism in Alta California

To understand why these protonationalist discourses did not generate a cohesive nationalist movement for the formation of a separate state, even after a successful revolt to control the territorial government, we will have to consider a series of factors. First, Chatterjee suggests that nationalist struggles against colonialism involve a "struggle with an entire body of systematic knowledge, a struggle that is political at the same time as it is intellectual."[6] This framework of knowledge can lead to change only if the "social potentials exist for the change to occur" or if "determinate social forces, in the form of a class or an alliance of classes, which have the will and strength to act as agents of transformation," exist, perhaps even without an "elaborately formulated theoretical apparatus to think out the process of change" (Chatterjee, 27). These social forces and the ideological framework clearly existed in Alta California in 1836; as the Californios indicate in their testimonials, secularization had allowed for the rise of an emergent class of private landowners (the necessary "agents of transformation") following their acquisition of a liberal framework (explored in chapter 3) that, according to de la Torre, once acquired by "the principal men" had been disseminated throughout the territory (de la Torre, 62). The necessary "will and strength," however, appear to have been absent, as is apparent in the discussion of territorial dissensions based on regional rivalry and generational differences that pitted native sons against first-generation colonists, cleavages that never allowed them to form a cohesive alliance in the territory. There is also abundant evidence in these testimonials that their liberal discourses were compromised by residual colonial and feudal discourses, as well as by regional and individual interests.[7] Clearly ideological discourses can interpellate a colonized people to challenge their political domination by making them aware of their capacity to rule themselves and to modernize their country, but for the change itself to take place, the north (where these discourses were strongest) would also have had to have been economically and demographically more powerful than it was. In the absence of a national bourgeoisie, the dominant class of new *rancheros* and *hacendados* opted for what Chatterjee calls a "molecular transformation" (30) and continued under Mexican rule until change of a different order was thrust upon them in 1846.

The interconnection and competition between various ideological frameworks, some emergent, some residual, and various agencies in California after 1821 are thus important to consider. Critical in this regard is the diminishing role of another agency, the military, now primarily a volunteer militia paid by the governor, and its relation to the emergent enlightened class of *rancheros* and foreign merchants. This layered network of overlapping and often antagonistic discourses, especially those of family, caste, religion, region, and political orientation, will account for the numerous contradictions evident in the testimonials of these Californios.

After 1822 and more specifically after 1831, antagonisms develop in Alta California between "Californios" and "*mexicanos*" that go beyond local disputes over the consideration of Alta California as a penal colony for convicts or the periodic governor-initiated dispositions against meetings of the territorial Diputación.[8] Californios begin to refer to *mexicanos* as "foreigners" and to California as their *patria*, their homeland. A new differential is introduced to distinguish between *los hijos del país* and incoming settlers born in Mexico, Spain, or elsewhere. Thus the term *extranjero* formerly associated only with non-Mexican merchants and trappers becomes extensive to Mexicans. Alvarado's explanation for this phenomenon is that Californios were considered foreigners in Mexico:

> Given the great distance separating California from the capital of the Republic, the sons of that department were considered foreigners. (5:82)

This disidentification with the "stepmother," as Alvarado (5:106) calls Mexico, signals a fragmentation of the national "family" and the Californio population in terms of generation (Alvarado, 3:170). This generational difference is ideological rather than social, as all the more recent arrivals and the native sons coexist, intermarry, and interact as "friends" at other levels. Ideologically, the native sons develop an awareness of their colonial situation (Alvarado, 4:135). The assertion of national identity, as "Californios" rather than as "*mexicanos*," is thus here as in other colonial struggles, "a form of struggle against colonial exploitation" (Chatterjee, 18), and even in 1875–76 is an expression of continued resentment against Mexico. By the time of invasion, Alta California was "a populace ... divided by deep resentments against the Mexicans" (MGV, 3:56). And divided it would remain between those who like the Mexican José Abrego, an Hijar-Padrés colonist, refused after 1846 to serve in any position under the U.S. government "that had humiliated the flag under which he had been born" and those native sons of California, who, as Alvarado indicates, would see the invading U.S. forces as potential liberators:

> We, the Californios, that had for so many years been the victims of the Mexican heads of state, could not but recognize as liberators the American officials who, duly authorized, came aboard the warships to unfurl their government's banner in the Monterey and San Francisco forts. (4:135)

Alvarado's resentment against Mexico runs deep enough to call up discourses of liberation and seemingly legitimate the invasion of the territory by those he detested. His words here are a thousand times refuted in other chapters of his testimonial, and in this light need to be seen more as anti-Mexican than pro-United States. But it is precisely in the interplay of these double resentments that we see the creation of a disjuncture, a liminal "protonational" space neither Mexican nor American. In 1876 when the testimonial is being narrated Alvarado seeks to provide a new spatial construct, one outside the space of the new "American family" as well as beyond that of the Mexican family. This identity is neither hybrid nor compound; it is an identity as *Californios*. The formation of discourses of protonationalism in California and their eventual rearticulation as discourses of ethnicity interest us in this and the following chapter.

Geopolitical Relations

In the Californios' reconstruction of their past, geographical, demographic, and political concerns take precedence over relations of production. Californios seek to explain patterns of *pueblo/misión/rancho* relations with respect to regional dissensions, incompetence, and weakness of political authority, and their subordinate status vis-à-vis Mexico. Political decisions by Mexican authorities are seen to limit trade and the development of agricultural production. The impact of geography and demography on settlement and economic development, as well as on the mode of security and political structure, is the primary explanation offered for failure to advance productivity and their inability to resist the U.S. invasion of 1846.

Although these testimonials do not focus on the structure of class relations or class power after secularization, their discussion of a number of conflicts between *abajeños* (southerners) and *arribeños* (northerners) and between *rancheros* and governors allows us to piece together an idea of the emerging class power of the *rancheros* in Alta California, an agency generated after Mexican independence and made possible by the greater "distribution" of land grants. Interclass squabbles along regional lines would bring the north and south to the point of armed conflict at various times, with the northern faction of *hacendados* and *rancheros* taking power without ever gaining the consent of the southerners to be governed by what Botello (126) calls "el triumvirato" composed of Alvarado, M. G. Vallejo, and José Castro. Increased internal dissension is further exacerbated by rifts between the ruling partners, in what is an almost parodic replay of events taking place in Mexico. Given what Alvarado recalls as "the small number of inhabitants, the great distance between one *presidio* and another, and the notorious lack of harmony that existed between southern Californios and northern Californios" (5:30), the territory was in 1846 ripe for a relatively easy invasion and conquest.

This regional rivalry was based, Alvarado insists, on the differences of "politico-religious belief" and "place of birth" (2:198, 206). The *arribeños* and the *abajeños* were constantly at odds and challenged each other militarily on several occasions, though with few casualties. The more populated southern area was then the site of most newly arrived settlers (like Botello, who arrived in 1833), whose loyalty to their own place of origin, primarily Sonora, was more pronounced than any tie with the Californio territory. Moreover, in Los Angeles there were a number of Hijar-Padrés colonists from central Mexico, families like those of Coronel and Agustín Olvera, and southern Mexican families like that of Manuel Requena. For this reason, the *sureños* identified as much with the Mexican state as with their southern California region. Within the territory, regional rivalries were both economic and political and hinged upon the location of the capital, then at Monterey, which was also the site of the official port. In a territory where the only government revenue was produced by incoming ships paying customs fees, controlling the port was critical. As it was, all ships were expected to go to Monterey to declare their wares before they stopped in Santa Barbara, San Pedro, and San Diego.[9] All three areas of the territory consequently wanted the port: the more-populated south wanted it in San Diego or San Pedro; the north central area, referred to as "the north," wanted it to stay in Monterey, and the "autocrat of the northern frontier," as Vallejo was labeled (Alvarado 4:148), saw San Francisco as the best choice. Regional access to power thus often pitted one faction against another.

Regional economic interests are not the only factors dividing this heterogeneous population that included native Californios, Mexicans, Spaniards, and other foreigners, all *gente de razón*. Also comprising the population were a number of acculturated Indians, both native to the territory and from Baja and the Mexican northwest, as well as ex-neophytes working on *ranchos* and *haciendas* or still linked to former mission sites, and the thousands of native Indians who had avoided containment within the established *reducciones*. The population was also fragmented politically by ideological cleavages within the ruling families, the oligarchy of Alta California. Both the north and the south claimed to be federalist and liberal, but Santa Barbara, controlled by Guerra y Noriega, was known as a conservative, pro-missionary stronghold. Los Angeles and San Diego were considered rather independent and rebellious *pueblos,* unwilling to be dominated by the north. The Carrillos, Picos, Argüellos, Estudillos, and Bandinis were the dominant families in the south and they too were eager for power. The northern frontier was the realm of one man: Mariano Guadalupe Vallejo. In the words of his own brother José de Jesús Vallejo, he was considered "a sort of king in his Sonoma dominion" (JJV, 139). In fact he ruled the region much like a feudal lord: he was "the man who capriciously governed the northerners" (Alvarado, 5:121). In Monterey Alvarado and Castro had the support of the leading families. The fragmentation of the territory by local interests, political upheavals and *pronunciamientos,* economic difficulties, lack of a national market, subsistence agriculture, dependence on foreign ships for the sale of the two principal products (tallow and hides) and for consumption of the simplest articles, the lack of industries—all of these conditions and problems made Alta California almost a reduced simulacrum of the situation facing the larger Mexican state.

If local ties and frictions both bound and fragmented the population, national differences with Mexico were exacerbated by distance, both geographical and social. Geographically California existed in relative isolation, with limited contact with the rest of the world. Hostile Indian groups impeded frequent overland travel to Mexico, although trips across the desert to Sonora were not uncommon. The closest port by sea was La Paz in Baja California, then a sparsely populated and neglected area. Under these circumstances, consciousness of itself as a distinct cultural community was not entirely difficult to generate:

> Thus California, separated from the other states of the Mexican union, without ships at its ports that in case of emergency could take them to friendly shores, was for them [the Californios] their country, their everything. (MGV, 1:335)

The neglect of the territory by an impoverished Mexican government—"the Mexican heads of state were concerned about our future but they could not send resources that they did not have available" (MGV, 1:337)—and the population's blood and marriage relations also served to create local bonds and local self-reliance, especially in view of the economic and political conditions in Mexico during a period of instability and violence. Californio families who had previously received most of their supplies from San Blas felt further abandoned after independence.

As Machado, present during the change of flag in San Diego, recalls, this lack of provisions and nonarrival of salaries would promote divisions among the soldiers and lead to a failed revolt against the Mexican-appointed governor, Echeandía, in 1829 (Machado de Ridington, 6). While Alta California was a Spanish colony there appears to have been little interest in and awareness of movements for independence in Latin America, to the point that when Bouchard and his Buenos Aires insurrectionists approached the California coast in 1818, attacked the Spanish stronghold at Monterey, and raided and burned down the *presidio*, all attempts to get the missionary-influenced population to side with the rebels failed miserably (MGV, 1:186–98). Yet despite this territorial control by the *pro-realista* missionaries, there were already then "partisans of independence," as Ord (1956: 12) recalled.[10] José de Jesús Vallejo also knew from his experience resisting the Bouchard insurrectionists (JJV, 74–76; MGV, 1:199) that there were proindependence supporters in the territory, but these appear to have been primarily soldiers from Mexico rather than colonists or established soldiers.[11] In San Diego in 1812, several soldiers, including Pío Pico's older brother, were imprisoned after being accused of favoring independence and planning to overthrow the post. José Antonio Pico, then about eighteen years old, was soon released after the missionaries interceded in his favor, but two prisoners died in jail and another two were kept in irons until Mexican independence almost ten years later (Pico, 1973: 2). Back in Mexico the Spanish forces, with criollo support, had by 1815 crushed the first insurrection for independence led by Hidalgo and Morelos. The parish priest of Dolores had been executed in 1811 and Morelos was executed in 1815, but of course clandestinely the struggle for independence had continued.[12] In 1822, upon hearing that Iturbide, seen as the church's puppet, had successfully led a "bloodless revolution," the Californio youths were upset, for now they were to be the subjects of an emperor and the church. In the words of Salvador Vallejo, "during the king's reign, the missionaries enslaved the Indians only, but now they mean to enslave us as well" (cited in Alvarado, 1:207). These young rebels would shortly thereafter receive a new governor who shared their anticlerical views (Echeandía) and offered them the liberal discourses with which to analyze their situation, as we have seen in chapter 3.

If in Mexico the upper clergy favored countering the liberal Spanish Constitution proclaimed in 1820 (after having been annulled in 1814) by seeking the establishment of an independent Mexico in 1821 (Bazant, 24–25), so too in Alta California the first conspiracy tied to the notion of a "native-son" authority was said to be inspired by the missionaries. The anti-Echeandía revolt in 1829 instigated by Joaquín Solís, an ex-convict from Mexico, gained the support of several soldiers interested in protesting their destitution and the government's failure to pay their salaries. Surprisingly, the recently arrived Solís (1825) made further demands for a Californio-led government. This was the first pronouncement of sedition in California calculated to elicit the support of the general population and was, in Vallejo's opinion, the first threat to the unity of the Californio family, a rift provoked by the missionaries. This first act of rebellion would leave its "seed of political resentment" sown among them (MGV, 1:295).

Although the young liberal Californios all supported Echeandía and rallied in his defense, the rebels' call for a native-son governor, specifically the former interim governor Luis Argüello, did not fall on deaf ears. Argüello was an economic liberal who, as Vallejo recalls, had already proven that Californio native sons were "suited to govern" (MGV, 2:43). These nativist discourses were a ploy, it was charged, of the missionaries, and in particular of Padre Luis Antonio Martínez, who with the rebels had plotted to overthrow the liberal government of Echeandía and raise the Spanish flag anew in Alta California (MGV, 1:77–105). The friar would be banished from Alta California in 1830 for his complicity in the revolt.

The issue of non-Californio governors sent by the central government in Mexico without consultation with the population produced in 1831 a strong reaction on the part of the liberal native sons (a group of second-generation Californios then in their early twenties), especially when it became clear that there had indeed been consultation but only of the missionaries and their "party of order" (MGV, 2:137), who had sent for a governor who could undo all that the liberal Echeandía had initiated. That man was Lieutenant Colonel Manuel Victoria, considered a "despotic ruler" by Pico (1973: 40). Opposition to Victoria would serve to unite the Californios for more basic reasons than the fact that he failed to convene the Diputación and tried to restore military rule in the territory.[13] More important, as a conservative friend of the missionaries, Victoria would halt secularization, a policy favored by land-hungry Californios. The revolt against Victoria began in San Diego, under the leadership of Pío Pico, José Antonio Carrillo, and Juan Bandini (Pico, 1973: 42–47), and was supported by Echeandía, who continued to reside in San Diego, and in the north by M. G. Vallejo. The uprising was successful to the degree that it led to the wounding of the governor at Cahuenga Pass and ultimately to his decision to leave the territory. Thus after only nine months Victoria had been deposed and the native sons of California had come to see themselves as a potentially political force, with sufficient agency to take action and see their plans carried out. This regional alliance of *norteños* and *sureños* would be short-lived, as dissension soon irrupted over interim rulers.[14] It became evident that whenever political and economic interests divided the territory, other bonds, such as those of blood, marriage, and friendship, were not able to generate long-standing solidarity.

In the subsequent period, under Figueroa's governorship, as we have seen in chapter 3, native-son demands and politico-economic interests (the distribution of the secularized mission land) united Californios against Mexicans and buttressed the position of those who, like Alvarado, "professed advanced ideas" (3:114). All of the "enlightened" Californios had vested interests in the secularization of the missions and, in some cases, shared the liberal discourses, skills, and education to lead the territory in a different direction. After a brief interlude in 1836 with Colonel Mariano Chico, an ardent centralist and supporter of Santa Anna, the Californios, especially the young *monterreyanos* who had ridden out defiantly to receive Chico's party wearing red federalist insignias on their lapels, were ready for change (Alvarado, 3:52). Chico's administration, Alvarado recalled, had only increased "the gulf that existed between Mexicans and Californios" (3:9).

The "National" Movement

Nativism, then, is the form nationalism first took in Alta California until regionalism destroyed any notions of uniting the liberal factions for self-determination. These Californios prided themselves as being an enlightened younger generation, "a people without religious fanaticism," as Alvarado liked to say (quoted in MGV, 4:87), or, as Vallejo put it, a people free of the yoke of the friars, a people open to new ideas and civilization (MGV, 4:94). Both regional factions eagerly sought the naming of a native Californio as governor, but each wanted its own regional candidate installed. As reconstructed in hindsight in the testimonials, herein lay the downfall of Californio agency: the story told is that of a house divided.

Alvarado, the young Californio who would lead the movement for independence from Mexico, offers us a contradictory reconstruction of his revolutionary engagement conducted in the name of federalism. Given the way the plot unfolds, secession was the only possible outcome, an end that the agents themselves fail to acknowledge. From the beginning of his testimonial, Alvarado reveals his growing separatist inclinations and recalls how since an early age, when serving as secretary for the territorial Diputación, he had developed a sense of loyalty to what he considered his *patria*, California. Alvarado lays down this developing Californio identity by recalling how at the age of eighteen he had challenged Rodrigo del Pliego, a Mexican officer in Monterey, for his disparaging remarks against Californios (3:9); a few years later as secretary of the Diputación he would beat a Mexican who made a sarcastic remark about the Californio "donkeys in suits" (3:14). Things came to a head after Chico's departure when antagonisms broke out in Monterey between Mexican officials—"soldiers of the other band" (Alvarado, 3:12)—and Californios. As always, a handful of Mexican administrators sided with the Californios, but for the most part the *mexicanos* formed a group called "partido Mexicano puro" (solely Mexican party) set on countering the aspirations of the upstart Californios (Alvarado, 3:43, 60, 128). The construction of this national antagonism serves to introduce subsequent events in Alta California.[15]

The revolt in 1836 against the *comandante general* Nicolás Gutiérrez (a Spaniard in the Mexican army), left in charge after Chico's departure, was headed by Alvarado, then head of the Diputación, and José Castro, presumably with the support of M. G. Vallejo, his brothers, and a few other leading *monterreyanos*. In his testimonial Coronel (19) contradicts this and credits the revolt to Mexicans, suggesting that it was instigated by Angel Ramírez, the Mexican customs officer and ex-priest/ex-revolutionary.[16] In all of these episodes, as in the written speeches and proclamations offered by Alvarado or other Californios, Mexicans always assumed, and expressed so in their newspapers, that the writers or instigators were Mexican, in keeping with their low opinion of the intellectual and political potential of the Californios, as Vallejo recalls with indignation (MGV, 3:219). In this instance, the rebels, supported by a number of foreigners under Capt. Isaac Graham, a trapper from Kentucky, succeeded in capturing Monterey, declared the Diputación a "Constituent Congress," and named Alvarado as governor and Vallejo as *comandante general* of the new "estado libre." Their *Manifiesto*, declaring Alta California a free and independent state, made clear that the separation was conditional: "California is free and will cut all relations with Mexico until the motherland ceases to be oppressed by the present dominant centralist faction" (Alvarado, 3:171).[17] As the slogan of the rebels indicates—"¡Federación o muerte/es del Californio la suerte!" (Federation or death / is the Californio's fate!)—the Californios' rebellion against Mexico and declaration of independence had been provoked by Santa Anna's shift to a centralist government in 1835 and the establishment of a new constitution in 1836 that annulled the federalist constitution of 1824 supported by all the states and territories of the republic.

The northerners' call for unity as federalists and as defenders of the 1824 Constitution would be copied and distributed to all the *pueblos* so that it could be placed on the church doors and at the *alcaldías*. Beyond this declaration of loyalty to the federation, the rebellion would make known its insistence on a native Californio governor, its resentment against Mexico's neglect of the territory, its protest against being used as a penal colony for Mexican convicts, and its desire to split the position of governor into a civil *jefe político* and a military *comandante general* (Alvarado, 3:17–18). Several other states were threatening to secede as well, including Zacatecas and later Yucatán.[18] In 1836 Texas too had declared its independence but unlike Zacatecas, which was brought to its knees by Santa Anna (Bazant, 53), Texas would defeat the Mexican army. After Santa Anna's military misfortune at San Jacinto, Texas would declare itself an independent republic, although Mexico did not recognize its separation; by 1845 it was being annexed by the United States, thereby setting the stage for war between the two countries. Demographic and military conditions in Texas were quite different from those on the west coast. In 1825 only about 3,500 of 25,000 inhabitants in Texas were Mexican; the rest were settlers and troops from the United States, according to the Mexican statesman Manuel Crescencio Rejón (Archivo, 31:306). In Alta California, the total population in 1836 was close to 4,000 and only about 620 of these were foreigners.[19]

The contingency of the declaration in Alta California would become a fractious issue, especially when it became evident that upon Mexican Commissioner Castillero's visit to Santa Barbara and upon learning that Alta California was now a department rather than a mere territory, the rebel Alvarado agreed to take the oath of allegiance to the new 1836 Constitution. Thus, as head of the Diputación, Alvarado automatically became the interim head of the departmental government. In a territory where the revolt had been decided at the top and had not been fully supported, however, the return to Mexican control soon became more of an occasion for derision and scorn than for opposition. The entire episode is noteworthy if we consider that as a result of this rebellion, the power of the native Californios to form their own government was recognized. The taking of political power meant that native Californios would now be able to direct and control the formation of a new landowning class through the distribution of mission lands. Given the distance from Mexico, whether as a Mexican department or as an autonomous territory, the native Californios were now effectively in control. Equally important in a territory riven by regional schisms was that Alvarado's position as interim head meant control by the northern faction, a turn of events difficult for the southerners to accept.

To his critics Alvarado insisted that secession had always been contingent on Santa Anna's removal, and that once he was replaced by Bustamante, whose centralist policies converted California into a department, there was no longer a reason to secede (Alvarado, 4:22).[20] That Bustamante was as much a conservative centralist as Santa Anna does not appear to have had an impact on Alvarado's decision. What also entered into the Californio's consideration was the fact that Alta California did not have the military wherewithal to mount a resistance to the Mexican army like Texas did, nor did it have the political unity, despite bonds of kinship and political orientation. Clearly Alvarado's anti-Mexican feelings were not shared by all Californios (especially not by the more recent arrivals like Coronel or Botello), by Mexican administrators and officers, or by a number of *sureños* who favored remaining a part of Mexico and feared being invaded by a large military force, already rumored to be on its way from Mexico: "It was said that the expedition comprised 1,200 men well equipped to make the authority of the Republic respected and to punish those who had the audacity to ignore it" (Ord, 1956: 44). In reality, Mexico was in no condition to send troops. But more than fearing retaliation from Mexico, the *sureños* resented control of power by the *arribeños* and the fact that the new governor was not a southerner. When it was learned a few months later that José Antonio Carrillo, the California representative to the Mexican Congress, had convinced the government that the rebellion was against bad governors rather than against Mexican rule and that his brother, Carlos Carrillo, should be named governor (Alvarado, 4:24), the two regional factions prepared to do battle with each other, neither one willing to give up its regional claim on the governorship. The revolutionary governor from the north, Alvarado, twenty-eight years old in 1837, would be pitted against a southerner, his cousin and newly appointed governor, Carlos Carrillo, both native sons but the latter twenty-six years older.[21]

The family farce subsequently became more complicated when the appointment of Carrillo was countered by Mexico's recognition of Alvarado as head of the Diputación and interim governor. As Vallejo explains, California suddenly had two legally appointed governors, both named by the same president. Suddenly the strategy became one of stalling until new official orders came naming one or the other as fully recognized constitutional governor of California.[22] The entire episode of the armed confrontation between north and south during the decade of the 1830s, that is, between Californios who were related by blood and marriage, plays indeed like a sad farce, a pastiche of what was transpiring in Mexico. In California, north and south were continually at each other's throats but as soon as one or two individuals were killed, the confrontation ceased—or sometimes ended even without the spilling of blood. Cousins would then embrace and stay at each other's homes overnight before withdrawing their troops. In 1875 Alvarado, aware of what historians were saying about these Californio encounters, rebuts by alluding to kinship, *compadrazgo*, and territorial ties that bound them to each other but did not prevent their combating foreigners, even Mexicans (4:9).

Regionalism and nationalism are thus continually filtered through a cultural framework of kinship and friendship that ultimately seeks to reduce them to "family" discourses. Although political discourses are dominant ("I was the governor of the free and sovereign state of Alta California" [Alvarado, 3:217, 222]), their articulation with discourses of kinship relations will lead to a rather despotic yet paternalistic political framework that creates space for nonthreatening family considerations. What at a political level produced disagreements that led to imprisonment and armed confrontation could, at another moment, be set aside to satisfy a momentary cultural obligation, like a baptism (Pico, 1973: 85–86).[23]

Regional confrontation in California would entail for the most part a series of marches and countermarches with one side, Carrillo's, finally capitulating without a shot being fired (Coronel, 29–30; Botello, 66). Kinship here clearly was overdetermined by regionalism, political orientation, and economic interests, all powerful enough to divide or unite the closest family members. Even when Alvarado's interim governorship was recognized by the Mexican government, conspiracies were not totally eliminated. A subsequent move by Alvarado to imprison rebel leaders in the south, far from alleviating the regional conflict, only made it more acute.[24] Despite Vallejo's assurances in his testimonial that prisoners sent to Sonoma were treated as guests at his house rather than as prisoners, Botello (one of the prisoners) tells an entirely different story, one that reveals national distinctions made in the treatment of prisoners (81).[25] Men like Botello found Vallejo to be a heartless, despotic commander (Botello, 82–84), and in 1839 when Alvarado's and Vallejo's regular appointments arrived, Botello felt that Mexico was rewarding traitors rather than those who had always been loyal Mexican citizens (89). It is then not surprising to read that Vallejo, the wealthiest Californio and probably among the most intelligent and progressive for the times, despite or precisely because of his many contradictions, was also much hated and despised in the south.[26]

What had the makings of a "national" movement soon dissolved into nativism and subsequently this tendency dissipated somewhat as well. The "triumvirate," as Manuel Castro (151) and Botello (126) call the team of Alvarado, M. G. Vallejo, and José Castro, was finally in power and able to establish the direction of the department within their limited means. But far from leading the nation toward modernization, Alvarado's government merely reinforced semifeudal relations of production by availing a larger number of recently created *hacendados* and *rancheros* of unfree Indian labor to exploit. Economically the territory also declined, despite the continued production of hides and tallow for exportation, because secularization of the missions brought with it a marked drop in agricultural and craft production; at the same time, the government, with a growing bureaucracy, made ample use of mission properties to maintain its administration afloat. Soon political dissension began to eat at the bonds of the triumvirate to the point where uncle and nephew, Vallejo and Alvarado, could no longer work together. Vallejo, the military disciplinarian, saw only disorder in his nephew's administration and an unwillingness to follow his recommendations (although commander in chief, Vallejo was unwilling to leave his northern fiefdom, except on occasion, but was constantly sending out missives from Sonoma). Vallejo especially complained about Alvarado's failure to strengthen the *presidios,* about his various policies and priorities, and about his interference in northern frontier affairs.[27] Other difficulties ensued, including Alvarado's leaves of absence from the governor's office (perhaps to overcome health problems produced by his weakness for drink)[28] and his deportation in 1840 of a group of foreigners from California accused of conspiring with Graham against Alvarado's government (Escobar, 109).[29] The growing number of foreigners settling in the Sonoma-Sacramento area was causing concern and fear that what had happened in Texas in 1836 might occur in California unless measures were taken to deport foreigners heard making threats against Alvarado and Castro. What Alvarado did not realize was that a dependent and poor nation like Mexico was anxious to avoid confrontation with the powerful navies and armies of the world, especially after its experience with the French warship during the "Pastry War" of 1838 (Bazant, 54–55; Cosío Villegas et al., 100). When the California deportations provoked protests from the British and U.S. embassies, the Mexican government immediately determined that the deportees could return to California and moreover receive compensation for their troubles. With this turn of events, it became clear that Alta California could expect no support from Mexico.

By the 1840s foreigners, who had previously come more or less as single merchants and trappers and settled down with Californio wives, were now coming by the wagonload with their entire families. Given the small number of Californios in the territory, the arrival of foreigners who wished to settle in California was generally a happy occasion. The testimonials of Alvarado and the Vallejos often stress the kind treatment that Californios extended to the many foreign settlers that came to California, with or without passports, and express a resentment in reviewing the multiple cases of ingratitude manifested toward them after 1846. Vallejo is singled out by Alvarado as encouraging foreigners to settle in the north around Sonoma, an area that did not attract many Californios, who preferred the safer, more populated south. As governor Alvarado freely encouraged Californios to relocate; he also gave vast grants of land to men like Sutter, and even made choice mission lands available to foreigners (MGV, 4:152, 158).

The Texas example was constantly on everyone's mind but ethnocentric concerns also led Californios, like Castro, to be critical of the favoritism that Vallejo appeared to show toward the foreigners, especially in the years after the near extermination of the Indians in the north from the smallpox epidemic. Alvarado (5:144) recalls that these Californios resented Vallejo's courting the foreigners' favor so that they would settle in his domains: "they looked down on General Vallejo for being so friendly with a race whose education and customs were antagonistic to ours; for that reason, from among his own countrymen, he gained a large number of enemies." When Vallejo was imprisoned by the Bear Flag party, some among the Californios, instead of crossing the bay to come to his rescue, insinuated that it was a situation that he, who had been "flirting with the Americans," had brought on himself (Alvarado, 5:144). Of course this reasoning also served to mask Castro's cowardly unwillingness to cross the bay in order to attack the Bear Flag rebels, who at an early stage were fewer in number than Castro's troops. Once before, de la Torre (142–43) recalls, Castro had failed to confront Frémont's troops at Gavilán Hill and the commander's men had been on the verge of going forward on their own when Castro called off the attack.

Subsequent difficulties between Vallejo and Alvarado would lead the military commander in 1841 to ask the Mexican government to accept his resignation, citing the disorder in the territory and requesting that a new governor be appointed. In effect Vallejo's action strengthened the ties of the territory to Mexico and set back all nativist ambitions, at least for the moment. Interestingly enough, in his letter to the minister of war, Vallejo requested that the two offices (*gobernador* and *comandante general*) again be assigned to one individual — and to one who was not tied by blood or marriage to fellow Californios. He also informed the minister that the nation had no defense capability and was at risk of any military vessel that came to port (as would indeed be the case in 1842 when Commodore T. A. C. Jones of the U.S. navy took possession of Monterey for a short time). Vallejo requested an army of two thousand men to defend the nation against attack and invasion. Mail services, Vallejo explained, also needed to be overhauled as mail was constantly being read by others and delayed. He asked to be assigned to rebuild the port of San Francisco, which he had long insisted would stimulate production and industries that had disappeared with the secularization of the missions (MGV, 4:230–34). Vallejo insists (for there were those who claimed he wanted the new civil-military post for himself) he was ready to give up his military command to concentrate on his business affairs and join with other northern *hacendados* and *rancheros* in opening up a port for whaling ships in San Francisco. The northern region was rapidly changing with the arrival of an increasing number of immigrants from the United States, and Vallejo undoubtedly wanted to be a prominent part of whatever changes were implemented after invasion, which by this time everyone saw as imminent. What Vallejo most feared, he repeatedly tells us, was for invasion to occur "on his watch," as he explained in a letter to his friend Virmond in Mexico.[30] But as Alvarado (4:228) points out, it would ironically fall to Vallejo to be at the center of the invasion drama as he was the first prisoner taken by the invaders in 1846.

In 1842 the arrival of the new governor, Micheltorena, also brought on a renewal of Californio nationalist discourses against Mexico, this time for sending three hundred convicts as soldiers for the defense of the territory. A new rebellion against Micheltorena and his *cholos* would be generated by nationalist as much as by regionalist discourses, the latter provoked by the proposal of the northern *hacendados* to convert San Francisco into a port. The successful revolt against Micheltorena (led by Manuel Castro and supported by Alvarado) and his departure on the *Quijote* would lead to a quasi-reconciliation between north and south and to an orchestrated decision to share in the civil and military government of California, with the southerner Pío Pico (the head of the Diputación) as governor and the northerner José Castro as *comandante general*. Regionalism was for the moment put aside and the discourses of California nationalism became dominant once again, with native Californios left in charge of their *patria* for the last time, conscious too that Mexico was powerless and too impoverished to intervene (Alvarado, 5:98). During the few months that Pico and Castro headed the territorial government before the U.S. invasion, factionalism again reared its ugly head, for the two leaders were always at odds. The testimonials themselves serve to continue the political intrigue dividing north and south, with each informant doing his or her best to condemn particular regional antagonists (MGV, 5:42, 110; Botello, 94; Pico, 128). The south was still wary of the north, seen as power-hungry and unwilling to share power with the south, despite Alvarado's past policy of naming southerners to several administrative positions. Also feared was that the northern triumvirate would continue to dominate as long as the three lived, and it would have, says Botello (126), had not the invasion left them disempowered.

Even the invasion of 1846 would only temporarily unite the two factions, for, as occurred in Mexico, the forces of resistance were highly fragmented. Regionalism created schisms that were difficult to overcome and that undermined all nationalist efforts. Nevertheless, the testimonials do reveal that in the short period between 1836 and 1846 the Californio elite, though ill prepared to stop an invading army, struggled to establish itself as a social force capable of taking the political reins of the territory. The agency of enlightened native Californios and their strong distaste for *mexicanos,* considered colonial "satraps that treat the Californios like a conquered nation," stand out as the most prominent constructs in Alvarado's testimonial (4:29). This same agency, but now casting Californios as statesmen and *letrados* able to analyze their political options, would be constructed by Vallejo.

On the Eve of Invasion

One episode discussed at length by M. G. Vallejo in his testimonial, and also summarized by Alvarado and mentioned by Fernández, concerns a meeting that Bancroft (1885–86, 22:62) and Royce say never occurred; in fact, Royce calls it "legendary."[31] This famous nonevent, a genuine discursive conjuncture, can be viewed as a short apocryphal dialogue of Californio orators on the various positions assumed on the eve of invasion. Vallejo constructs the discursive encounter as a means of presenting the Californios' assessment of their political options. He textualizes that brief moment of indecision that allowed the Californios, in reconstruction at least, to assume agency as statesmen able to analyze their situation consciously and chart their future. This textualization offers a macroview of all the discourses intersecting the political field in Alta California: discourses of democracy, monarchy, federalism, liberalism, republicanism, centralism, religion, geography, and culture. But this conjunctural textuality neglects to consider other very ominous practices: U.S. policies with respect to Texas, U.S. slavery and racism, and Indian removal and extermination. It ignores as well the implications of U.S. expansionism and national chauvinism. Vallejo's construction does in certain sections consider the discourses of "Manifest Destiny" with a twist that in retrospect presages what is to come after 1846. The dialogical text reconstructs a number of positions that by 1875 were important to set down, especially given hegemonic historians' proclivity to erase the analyses of the subaltern by representing them as incapable of conceptualization and action. At the same time Vallejo felt a need to state that given relations with Mexico, some Californios had joined the union not unwillingly, clearly not expecting to be treated as a conquered population. These, then, are the positions presented in his construction of the Californio ideological field:

liberal federalist		promonarchist
independence	versus	British annexation
U.S. annexation	versus	French protectorate

The constructed meeting takes place during Pico's and Castro's short-lived administration, as Mexico undergoes one *pronunciamiento* after another with U.S. forces poised at the Rio Grande to attack and invade Mexico. Aware of the danger faced by Alta California, Governor Pico asked that the districts select delegates for a meeting to be held in Santa Barbara to plan for independence under the protection of a foreign power (M. Castro, 177). Regional dissension and plotting by the two leaders against each other led to a cancellation of the meeting.[32] Vallejo, however, indicates that Castro, the *comandante general*, decided to hold a similar meeting in Monterey in March 1846 to discuss the imminent threat of invasion by the United States and to plan for the defense of the territory. All of the individuals that presumably participated in this meeting were dead by the time that Vallejo narrated his testimonial, except for key figures like Alvarado and Pío Pico, then still living, who were said not to have been in attendance. Alvarado, though puzzled that this meeting should have been held at Consul Larkin's house (5:132), provides a synopsis of the positions based on his uncle's report.

Vallejo's construction of this meeting is the best assessment we have of the diversity of political views that divided the leaders of the Californios, for the most part coinciding with similar views held by criollos in Mexico. Vallejo offers a number of constructs on nation, language, culture, and religion, and allows us to consider the ideological frameworks, the masternarratives being opposed and defended. That he casts himself in a pro-U.S. position spouting the dominant hegemonic discourses of the period (the 1870s) may well be the result of an effort to appear as having been well disposed toward annexation at the time, in order to qualify and to a certain degree mitigate his critique of the U.S. treatment of Californios. Vallejo's construction of this meeting thus serves not only to delineate the contradictory ideological field of Alta California in 1846, but as a political strategy, as a way of grounding his protest, five chapters later, of the Californios' deterritorialization and marginalization in the postinvasion period. This last essay in Vallejo's testimonial should perhaps serve as his final assessment of the Californios' dispossession, disempowerment, and oppression. These two texts are contrasted in chapter 7 and read against the other voices that emanate from the testimonials.

Vallejo's telling of the Monterey meeting brings together a number of individuals, government officials, and businessmen, both Californio and foreign, representing a diversity of positions circulating for a good while in the territory. Possibly the one that had stirred more controversy in Alta California than any other was the pro-British proposal of Pico and his southern allies, called "los azules" because members of this "association" dressed in blue uniform and were said to have a sword at home (MGV, 4:243). "La plebe," the rabble, Vallejo notes, mocked them and scoffed at their "virgin swords" (4:243), as presumably these had never been unsheathed.[33] (Similar double entendres were often made by the south about the north, as Botello [89] demonstrates.) Alvarado, who also comments on activities in the south, particularly enjoyed rumors that Pico had been promised a title of nobility—"Duke of Jamul"—if California became part of the British kingdom. The sarcasm and constant put-downs traded by *abajeños* and *arribeños* are part of the common humorous discourses running through these testimonials.

Pico, in his own testimonial, records his interest in procuring British support in view of Mexico's lack of attention to what was a critical situation in California. After his official appointment as governor of the department in 1845, he recalls sending his secretary José María Covarrubias to Mexico to inform the government of California's "absolute lack of resources to defend itself in case of foreign invasion." If not heard, Covarrubias was to seek the help of the British.

> I requested of Señor Covarrubias, moreover, that in case his efforts were not heeded by the government, he was to approach the head of the English naval forces in the Pacific ... and propose to him in my name that in case the general government of Mexico should be disinterested in our protection, obliging us to rebel against it, California would place itself under the protection of His Britannic Majesty. (Pico, 1973: 123)

This preference for the British appears to have been favored at one time by Alvarado as well, who, disillusioned with the likelihood of Mexican intervention in case of invasion (5:117), considered already in 1836 seeking protection from the British.[34] Yet he too had misgivings. British annexation subsequently becomes a good excuse to justify a number of actions. Frémont, for example, is said to have participated in the Bear Flag revolt to stop the British from claiming California (Bancroft, 1964: 151; see Royce). José Antonio Castro is said to have plotted against Pico on account of his pro-British stance as well as because of his sale and granting of mission lands to relatives and friends (MGV, 5:49).[35]

Vallejo points out that the British annexation project had originated in Mexico. According to Vallejo, Sloat lifted anchor and sailed for Monterey when he found out that the British frigate *Collingwood* was leaving for the same port (MGV, 5:88–89). The British interest in California was more than imaginary. Published London correspondence between the Mexican ambassador and British minister during the years 1844–50 reveals the extent to which England was interested in California and in having Mexico, like France and England, recognize Texan independence. Lord Aberdeen, the British minister of foreign relations, suggested that an independent Texas would open the doors to British and French intervention to guarantee the independence of Texas and in that way impede U.S. annexation of the territory.[36] This was not news to Alvarado, who was well aware that both England and France "secretly did all they could to prevent Texas and California from becoming part of the United States of North America," and he was not surprised when the visiting French admiral Cyrille Laplace, on a "research expedition" aboard the *Artemisa*, stopped briefly in Monterey in 1839, warning him that the United States planned to take Alta California (Alvarado, 4:173). By 1845 the Mexican ambassador was appealing to Lord Aberdeen for support to defend the Californias against U.S. expansionism. To justify intervention, the London minister now suggested, British interests in California would have to be created either through the concession of lands to a British colonization company or by using California lands in payment of the Mexican foreign debt (Archivo, 15:51–52). In one meeting, Lord Aberdeen recalls having already received offers from Californios seeking British protection and warns the Mexican ambassador that the attack by Commodore Jones on Monterey is a sign of what is to come if Mexico gets bogged down in a war with the United States. For this reason, he reminds the Mexican ambassador that similar British recommendations with regard to Texas had gone unheeded, and intimates that California should perhaps be allowed to be independent (53). These various strategies were apparently never seriously considered, because in 1847 the new Mexican ambassador to London, Mora, was again bringing up the issue with the Mexican government. It was better to sell part of the territory to England, he advised, to ensure the sovereignty of what was left than to lose it all.[37]

But not all Californios favored British protection. Neither did they favor annexation to France, as was rumored to be Sutter's objective in New Helvetia. When de Mofras, French attaché of the Mexican legation, arrived in California with letters from Virmond (MGV, 4:244), the Californios were put on guard. Proponents of the British and the French positions were opposed by others, like Larkin, who was known to look favorably on U.S. annexation. Larkin, U.S. consul at Monterey, was actually an agent for the United States, working toward this end. Vallejo claims to have been aware of all the maneuvering by the various "proponents of foreign domination" and states that, had it been necessary, he would not have hesitated to take action to stop them (MGV, 4:242).

At the apocryphal meeting in March 1846, Castro is said to have opened with a statement lamenting Mexico's neglect and inability to provide the necessary manpower, firearms, and military materiel for defense of the department at a time of imminent danger of foreign invasion. He also expressed concern over the increased immigration from Oregon and Utah, and suggested that California's defense called for protection under the French flag. Castro's proposal favoring France over England, for reasons of religion and culture, is said to have surprised his audience:

> There are in Europe two great powers and both claim the supremacy of the sea. The two rich nations yearn to extend their dominion to the American continent. Both are nations of warriors, both possess squadrons and armies, both desire to possess the Californias and between them there is no difference except that one zealously advocates the spread of Catholicism and the other, the spread of Protestantism; the first one is the one that is more convenient for us. Gentlemen, I propose that this assembly declare itself in favor of annexing California to France! (Castro, quoted in MGV, 5:72–76)

That religion and culture should have been the determining factors for Castro is somewhat difficult to believe given that he and Alvarado, who favored independence, were "uña y carne," i.e., intimate friends (Botello, 125). Yet Alvarado himself refers to Castro's ethnocentrism with respect to his comments about Vallejo's being a "friend of the foreigners" who had nothing in common with Californios. Vallejo may have been more insightful into Castro's conservatism than Alvarado was, or perhaps resented his inaction, and therefore chose him as an exponent of the position least favored by Californio liberals.

This promonarchist, pro-French perspective was then being espoused in Mexico by the upper clergy and their landowning supporters. Since 1821 the church had wanted to bring in a European prince from a reigning dynasty to rule Mexico (Bazant, 28) and by 1840 the Francophile Gutiérrez Estrada was calling for a constitutional monarch.[38] By 1847, according to Ambassador Mora, the French already had tentatively selected the duke and duchess of Montpensier for the Mexican throne and gained the approval of conservatives in Mexico (Archivo, 35, 41). In effect, the crowning of the Hapsburg Maximilian by the Mexican oligarchy in 1864 had been in the works for a good length of time.

Pico's position (he was not present) in favor of British protection was supported by the merchant Spence. Rafael González favored independence, as did Pablo de la Guerra and Alvarado, neither of whom was present. De la Guerra was known as a champion of independence; he was

> the most assertive champion of absolute independence for Alta California, and he equally detested the French, English, and North Americans. (MGV, 5:63)

Alvarado and de la Guerra represented the voices of California nationalism. In his testimonial Alvarado assures us that had he been present he would have spoken for absolute sovereignty and independence (5:134, 138; MGV, 5:71). Alvarado's position had always been clear to everyone who knew him. He was a nationalist, content with nothing short of Californio sovereignty. Independence was of course also seen as a necessary first step in any plan for annexation and therefore supported by the British, for they saw greater possibilities in a newly independent and politically weak California.

The final position, favoring annexation to the United States, was introduced by Prudón, Vallejo's trusted secretary. Prudón did not see independence as a possibility: "I, gentlemen, recognize that a free, independent, and sovereign state is at present impossible" (MGV, 5:79). He saw advantages in annexing California to the United States, and his proposal was seconded by Vallejo, a strong republican who rejected annexation to European countries so distant that they could have nothing in common with California and moreover were monarchical. California, Vallejo said, would never kneel before a crown:

> Would it be glorious and worthy of us to turn to Europe, so distant from us, in search of a master? What could we have in common with two nations separated from us by two oceans? But even if these problems were to disappear, isn't there one major insurmountable obstacle that it is impossible to liquidate? I refer, gentlemen, to the fact that we are republicans and that it is natural that we should prefer to suffer, to withstand poverty, and if necessary face death itself before agreeing to be ruled as subjects by a monarch. (MGV, 5:81)

Vallejo favored a preliminary declaration of independence to be followed by annexation to the United States:

> Gentlemen, I am of the opinion that Mexico can no longer harm us, that our future requires that we declare our independence, that is, if we have not done that already by expatriating the governor that Mexico had sent to govern us; only one thing remains to be done and that is to declare the annexation of our country to the United States of the North. I now make this motion, gentlemen, because I maintain that only in this way will we be able to overcome the ills that hold us back from developing our resources. (MGV, 5:82; see also Alvarado, 5:141)

As Vallejo indicates, California was for all intents and purposes functioning as an independent nation and could consequently determine its own future. Development of its natural resources would only come about by joining the American union, which panegyrically he calls the most free, most industrious, most enlightened country in the world (MGV, 5:83).

At this point Vallejo succumbs to nineteenth-century U.S. hegemonic discourses by deterministically inferring that he sees a guiding principle operating in the destinies of nations:

> For it is written in the great book of the Director of the Universe that they [the Americans] are destined to run our same fate and there is nothing that we can do to delay for much time the realization of the great plan that consists in making the Californias the temple in whose halls the virginal daughters of the Pacific join hands with the indomitable adventurers who, overcoming all obstacles placed in their way by nature, have come to share with us the fruits of their experience acquired at the cost of great sacrifices. (MGV, 5:84)

Through this pompous speech Vallejo appears to have accommodated entirely to the dominant imperialist ideologies that provide "Manifest Destiny" as the justification for invasion and occupation of Mexican territory. Yet his speech also reveals a sense of impotence ("there is nothing that we can do"), an incapacity to halt the process. There is as well a veiled revulsion against the union of these "adventurers" (which he came to detest after the "trappers" imprisoned him during the Bear Flag revolt of 1846) with "the virginal daughters of the Pacific." The feminization of California taken by the indomitable male adventurers presages not a happy marriage but the rape that was about to take place. Thus despite voicing the platitudes of American hegemonic discourses, the speech reveals a wariness of violation, disempowerment, and dispossession.

This meeting, which allegedly broke up without a vote being taken, is an after-the-fact construction rather than a reconstruction, providing us with the array of the political spectrum in California in 1846 and a synthesis of the ideological positions in relation to nation and invasion. By the time of the supposed meeting, Mexico was the object of a deep resentment for its policies regarding California; its failure to provide military aid and its neglect of an area of not more than six thousand inhabitants were seen by Californios as an open invitation to interlopers and to any foreign nation for invasion. Vallejo reflects this attitude in a comment full of resentment for Mexico:

> Whoever wants to appropriate its fertile valleys, its green forests, beautiful bays, and flowing rivers can do so knowing for certain that the government of Mexico will not come to its defense. (MGV, 5:40)

These accusations against Mexico for its neglect and indifference toward the northernmost territories were not unfounded, for some Mexican leaders in Mexico City were ready to downplay the importance of the loss of what they considered "desert lands of savages":

> The territories that we are being asked to concede have never been in our full possession; for the most part these are deserts, the mansion of wild Indians, who not only have not recognized the sovereignty of the government of the Republic but rather have led hostile and barbaric raids against our towns. (Archivo, 31:196)

So spoke a group of Mexican congressmen on the foreign relations committee in 1848 after reviewing the treaty that would cede half the Mexican territory to the United States. In light of this mentality, the secessionist proposals of the ruling Californios are coherent, for clearly there were few ties between the Californios and the conservative Mexican elite.

Notably missing from the discussion of the apocryphal Monterey meeting is the view of first-generation Californios whose ties with Mexico ran deep and who felt that their only option was to resist. Alvarado (5:137), for example, is amazed that González, "a man who was considered an advocate of the Mexican cause," should have been the one to propose independence. In this case, the constructed González-subject represents the "coming to terms" even of the "Mexicans" in California, faced as they all were (native sons and first-generation Californios alike), with insurmountable odds and no possibility of stopping the invaders at the door. Even Vallejo, despite all attempts to present himself as the strong supporter of annexation to the United States, reveals on several occasions that the position at which he arrived was not his first reaction. He had first urged Mexico to send troops for the defense of Alta California, without any success. By 1846, despite his generosity in distributing land to foreigners, Vallejo was having second thoughts about the demographic changes taking place in Alta California. It was becoming clear to him that the growing number of settlers arriving from the east who had received land and assistance were already looking down deprecatingly at their Californio benefactors: "they considered us beings inferior to them in bravery and intelligence" (MGV, 4:168). The Californios felt that the foreigners would betray them in the event of an invasion or even create disorder to dispossess them, as eventually happened: "with the arrival of the Americans came disorder and in its shadow some adventurers took over all that was good in our land" (MGV, 5:373).

It is interesting to see Vallejo's vacillation as he alternates between affirming his loyalty as a Mexican citizen/soldier and identifying as a friend of the North Americans, even while seeing himself first and foremost as a Californio. His entire military career had evidenced only one clear participation in a rebellion, the early one against Victoria; thereafter he not once rebelled against Mexican officials. He never openly supported rebellion against Micheltorena, or even against Gutiérrez, although his name was used to gain further support; he almost backed Carrillo for the governorship once he became aware that it was a legitimate appointment, though he subsequently denied this. Alvarado (5:225) recalls that Vallejo refused to allow the Hudson Bay Company to build a Protestant church in San Francisco, despite his anticlericalism, arguing that the Mexican Constitution forbade the construction of non-Catholic temples throughout the republic. In his testimonial he always finds a pretext to justify his loyalty as an officer in the Mexican army; he had refused, he says, to participate in the revolt against Micheltorena because the governor had been sent to California upon his request. Vallejo had learned well from Echeandía to make distinctions between what one did and said as a Mexican military officer, as a public representative, and as an individual (MGV, 2:172), although at times these roles were in conflict. If as a Mexican officer he was loyal to Mexico and exasperated by the territory's defenselessness, as a Californio *hacendado* he was interested in the prosperity of the territory and in his own economic advancement. His economic interest in the settlement of the northern frontier had led him to counter Mexican settlement policies and offer lands to all the families of American settlers that arrived, whether they had passports or not, instead of sending them back in the dead of winter. By 1875 all of his economic plans had been reversed and he saw himself ruined by the very foreigners that he had helped with land, livestock, and tools; he bitterly recalls this ingratitude throughout his testimonial (MGV, 4:387). The contradictions are many. As a political individual, he was an admirer of liberal federalist republics like the United States, but he also wanted to retain authoritarian control of his fiefdom in Sonoma. Thus in Vallejo's narration, all Californio perspectives intersect and allow for ambiguous and highly contradictory positions, evident in the fuzzy discourses of his testimonial. The inconsistencies of his representation construct the dilemma of these Californios, who saw and argued various political possibilities but whose real choices by 1846 were extremely limited.

The Rape of California

The crisis of 1846 and the urgent need for unity to defend Alta California should have rallied all the Californios to join together to fend off a well-equipped army supported by warships, for only when they organized guerrilla-type hit-and-run action through the countryside, as they did on two or three occasions, were the Californios, fine horsemen that they were, able to mount a viable defense. All knew, however, that the cavalry was not just over the hill, that no one was coming to their rescue, not Mexico, not England, not France; all knew they did not have the manpower or the weapons to resist. But at the hour of peril, the small Californio population, split for so many years over regional interests, divided once again: some aligned with the invaders, some struck back in haphazard fashion, and some assumed a passive attitude of resignation, especially those, as Alvarado (5:219) recalls, who were indifferent and did not care whether they were a part of Mexico or some other government. Others, like Escobar or Marrón, conveniently chose to stay out of the conflict (Escobar, 125; Osuna de Marrón, 13), which meant, in effect, to support the invasion passively. The testimonials are full of contradictory discourses with respect to the war, none more so than that of Vallejo, who had discharged his soldiers at the time of the revolt against Micheltorena (in which he did not take part) and who was the first to be imprisoned during the initial confrontations. Three decades after the invasion Vallejo still resented Castro's incompetence and his lack of adequate resistance during the Bear Flag incidents. Even though he recognized that it was a losing battle, that the Californios did not have the troops or the arms to defend themselves, there is still a particular shame hidden behind all his ostentatious applause of the North Americans, the shame of knowing that the Californios resisted neither fully nor successfully. He does note with pride the skirmishes in which Californios fought back, and the action of those whose passive resistance against the invaders in Monterey took the form of going on strike and neither providing foodstuff for the invading forces nor cooperating with them.

The actual invasion begins with the Bear Flag revolt of 1846, a covert operation engineered by U.S. intelligence in the person of J. C. Frémont and carried out by trappers and other adventurers recruited by the explorer (attempts have of course been made by historians to make this look like a nongovernmentally sponsored act). This first act of aggression against the Californios by the U.S. operatives would lead to the incarceration of Vallejo and several other Sonoma residents in Sutter's prison. Although condemning Frémont's involvement with the "filibusterers," Vallejo is careful never to implicate the U.S. government directly in the Bear Flag assault, but his awareness is implicit in his questioning of the government's willingness to condone and dismiss Frémont's seeming betrayal of his nation upon pledging to another flag. The arrival of regular U.S. forces to counter the chaos of lawless trappers is nevertheless welcomed by Vallejo as restoring some degree of law and order (MGV, 5:148–90). The U.S. naval forces arrange for the prisoners' release about three months after the Bear Flag attack, once they give their word not to take up arms against the invaders, a compromise that Vallejo defends as honorable.

Alvarado, who had always railed against Mexico and who considered California his *patria* and wanted its independence, goes to great pains to explain his resistance at the moment of invasion on the basis of "one's duty as a Mexican citizen":

> Despite my having strong and powerful reasons to complain against Mexico, which had for so many years been our oppressor and robbed us without pity, we, always generous, didn't want to take advantage of this moment when the Mexican Republic was involved in a foreign war to avenge family grievances; neither I nor the other citizens who had read the newspapers and knew the Constitution of the United States ignored that Alta California would have a lot to gain with a change of flag ... but ... we preferred to undertake a life of shortages, uncertainty, and ambushes ... until the motherland triumphed or was defeated in this lopsided contest carelessly provoked by its powerful neighbor. (5:221)

Here Alvarado totally rejects the notion of being liberated by the incoming invaders, as he had previously claimed (4:135). Despite recriminations, complaints, and expressions of disidentification with Mexico that have pervaded his entire testimonial, in the end, at the moment of crisis and political excision, Alvarado reidentifies as a member of the Mexican "family." He insinuates that annexation to the United States seemed preferable in terms of economic advantages, but he recognizes that discourses of nationalism in California had been generated out of similar discourses in Mexico; an attack on the one was an attack on the other, and those historic bonds of national kinship could not be so easily cut. Californios had not ceased to think of themselves as members of an "imagined community" although there had always been talk of starting a "family" of their own. Or, as Alvarado explains, now, when Mexico was suffering the aggression of foreigners, was not the time "to avenge family grievances."

A description of specific acts of resistance taken by the Californios is offered in the testimonials of Alvarado, Lugo, Manuel Castro, and Coronel, who note that a brief reconciliation between north and south enabled some measures of defense against the invaders. The alliance quickly disintegrated given the lack of cooperation, the struggle for power of particular factions, and the co-optation of others in the last instance. The Californios were poorly armed and few in number, and many, like Escobar, simply stayed at home, perhaps, as Alvarado and Vallejo indicate, because they welcomed a change in government or simply because they considered it futile to resist (Alvarado, 5:209). But in the south, where resistance could have triumphed, according to Vallejo, the Californios were led by "a pusillanimous governor and a commander general who had lost faith in the star that had in the past led him to safety in one hundred battles" (MGV, 5:203). Here Vallejo clearly mocks Castro, who was no military man and had in the past "triumphed" by avoiding battle. As Botello (138) indicates, Castro had no intention of fighting the U.S. soldiers, but then the Mexican Botello says the same thing about Andrés Pico (Botello, 155), who defeated the invaders at San Pascual. As Lugo (207) indicates, the *mexicanos* considered the Californios to be incapable of standing up to the U.S. forces, but he personally would prove the contrary with other Californios and friendly Indians at the battle of Chino. This same assessment of the Californio leadership is made even by Californios like de la Torre (142) and Ord, the latter especially critical of the ineffectual men who headed the Californio government in 1846 (1878: 137).[39]

The testimonials reveal a sense of impotence and frustration in the midst of events that the entire territory was not equipped or ready to control. From the start, faced with preinvasion reconnoitering forces, it was said that Castro had wavered instead of advancing resolutely to take care of the brazen Frémont, who had unfurled a U.S. flag on Gavilán Hill (de la Torre, 142). His leadership was further put into question when a U.S. warship, the *Cyane*, arrived in Monterey purportedly with a sick man aboard who hoped to restore his health in California. The invalid, Archibald H. Gillespie, was in fact a naval lieutenant of the Marine Corps sent with secret instructions for Frémont and the U.S. consul Larkin (MGV, 5:106–8; Alvarado, 5:178). Talk of Gillespie's trip "to improve his health" did not fool Angustias de la Guerra de Ord:

> I must confess that neither I nor Señora Spence was deceived by the recommendation because we found it difficult to believe that the government of the United States would send a ship of war solely to bring a young invalid to California. (1956: 58)

Ord clearly suggests that the women were less naive than the men, who were duped by the U.S. officers. At a ball given in honor of the captain of the *Cyane* (Alvarado, 5:173), Ord and Mrs. Spence called Castro's attention to the suspicious nature of Gillespie's arrival on a military ship, but Castro dismissed their suspicions, alleging women's propensity to be ever more distrustful than men.

> But Castro told us that we were thinking ill of a sick man, accusing all women in general of thinking ill of others, much more so than men, to which we replied that we were almost always right. (Ord, 1878: 141)

In a series of testimonials in which the narrators always assume keener insight than those around them, Ord's is different only in that it presents a woman's viewpoint. Yet despite her comments on Castro's nasty dismissal of her allegations, Alvarado and Vallejo provide information indicating that Castro was not unaware of what was transpiring, including the fact that merchant Spence, who favored an English protectorate in California, had received a secret communiqué about Gillespie in a false-bottom box containing quinine sulfate (MGV, 5:107–8). Despite their suspicions and wariness, however, the Californios feared taking any action against a U.S. soldier with a warship in port; or as Alvarado (5:176–77) puts it, they could not act against Gillespie without subjecting Monterey to the cannon of the *Cyane*. Thus Castro's comment to Ord appears to have been the typical chauvinistic and paternalistic remark dismissing women's fears in order "to protect them" rather than one arising out of ignorance. The low esteem in which Ord held Castro was extended to other Californio men who administered the department. (At this time Ord was married to the Mexican Manuel Jimeno Casarín.) Although Ord was opposed to the U.S. invasion, she is willing to suggest that the situation in the department was indeed in need of administrative change:

> The occupation of the country did not please the Californios at all, especially not the women. But I must confess that California was on the road to complete ruin. On the one hand, the Indians were dispersed, committing robbery and other crimes on the *ranchos*, and little or nothing was done to put a stop to these raids. On the other hand, there was dissension between the people from the north and those from the south and both were estranged from the *mexicanos* from the other side. But the worst cancer was the plunder that was widespread. There was such a waste of government funds that the treasury coffers were totally empty.(1878: 144)[40]

In her assessment of internecine conflict within the department of Alta California and of the administration's misuse of public funds and incapacity to deal with Indian raids, Ord reveals her frustration with the territorial disorder and with the military corps of officers around Castro, who drew their salaries but did not perform as expected or as was necessary to defend the nation:

> When the time came to defend the homeland against the foreign invasion, the majority did nothing more than what the figure on the prow of a ship does. (1878: 144)

The poor performance of Californio officers at the moment of invasion is a central issue in many of the testimonials, even though there is a general recognition of the territory's inability to mount a war of maneuver. There were a few cases of armed resistance in the north after the Bear Flag party uprising and the taking of Monterey by Commodore John D. Sloat and his warship *Savannah*. Sloat, according to Alvarado (5:220), considered it foolish for Californios to leave town to try to organize against his forces; given their suffering under Mexican rule and his "good intentions," resistance, in Sloat's eyes, was said to be akin to "the behavior of the demented." Passive resistance increased with the arrival of Commodore Robert F. Stockton on the warship *Congress*, who took command of the Pacific squadron, declared a curfew, and sought to exonerate Frémont, who had instigated the declaration of California's independence at Sonoma on July 4, 1846.[41] To register their opposition, civil servants in Monterey refused to work and the *rancheros* stopped bringing their produce to town for the soldiers (MGV, 5:186).

Once the South saw itself subject to invasion by Stockton's soldiers, as Coronel recalls, the assembly placed all responsibility for eliminating the forces of occupation on Mexico and proposed that Governor Pico leave the country so that he could not officially surrender. The flight of Pico and José Castro would be viewed as a cowardly act by Vallejo, de la Torre, and even Botello, who saw Castro as a lover of intrigue but fundamentally a coward (Botello, 139).[42] Vallejo's censuring of the two leaders for having fled ("they refused to combat the invaders and cowardly fled toward areas where they were in no danger of being attacked" [MGV, 5:190]) and his conviction that had they confronted Stockton after his landing at San Pedro, the south would have been covered with U.S. corpses, is a good indication that Vallejo's apparent acquiescence was in part a convenient if not convincing facade, even in 1875. Had not these two cowards been in command, he says, the road between San Pedro and the city of Los Angeles would probably have been covered with the stiff corpses of the daring commodore and his obedient subordinates, as anyone knowing something about military arts would agree that a thousand armed men in control of all the winding roads that lead from San Pedro to Los Angeles would have been able without difficulty to annihilate three or four hundred foreigners who had resolved to conquer this town, the inhabitants of which had not the least liking for the invaders. (MGV, 5:203)

Are these the words of a man ready to acquiesce? Or the wishful musings of the vanquished thirty years hence? Of course the Californio men in the south willing and able to do battle, both civilians and soldiers, were poorly armed and never numbered more than five hundred (Coronel, 123), including the northerners who had joined their forces, among them Manuel Castro and Alvarado. For this reason, upon the arrival of Commodore Stockton by sea and Frémont by land, Los Angeles surrendered and was declared under state of siege. Some of the principal families, Coronel recalls, became intimate friends of Frémont and accommodated to the invaders:

Frémont's behavior, in my opinion, pointed to his plan to gain the approval of the Californios and in this he succeeded to the point that many of the more prominent men declared themselves supporters of the Americans and even their allies. (78)

But not all Californios were so ready to submit to U.S. forces:

He [Frémont] established relations with the then considered principal families, but many of these continued to be strongly patriotic and refrained from any friendly association with the Americans. (78)

Accommodation and resistance thus continue to divide the Californio community at a crucial moment.

With the flight of Pico and Castro and the surrender of Los Angeles, the Californio resistance fragmented and Alvarado and Manuel Castro, with their contingent of soldiers, headed back north (Alvarado, 5:249). But constructs of acquiescence would be rapidly replaced with those of resistance. In Los Angeles, where conquest was seemingly effected with a minimum of opposition, Gillespie, who had been left in charge with only about fifty men, began imposing strict regulations on the townspeople. Coronel recalls that Gillespie became "a small odious tyrant" (80). Sérvulo Varela, who for some minor infraction was under order of arrest, determined to make light of his orders of detainment by shouting "Viva México" and playing a drum in the middle of town. Upset, Gillespie began to take even more drastic measures, attempting to arrest prominent citizens like José María Flores, who escaped thanks to a ruse of his wife and went to join Varela's small group, which had grown to about three hundred men.[43] In September 1846 this Californio contingent would force Gillespie to retreat to San Pedro, where with his troops he boarded a boat to San Diego.

This successful act of resistance was followed a few days later by the battle of Chino. José del Carmen Lugo was at his ranch in San Bernardino when word came that Benito (Benjamin) Wilson had organized a group of foreigners and was coming to take him prisoner. What is clear is that Wilson, David Alexander, John Rowland, and others gathered at the ranch of Lugo's brother-in-law, Julian (Isaac) Williams, in Chino to stock up on ammunition on their way to Los Angeles to help the besieged Gillespie (Lugo, 200). At this point Lugo organized a group of men and sought the assistance of Californios from Flores's forces, who were organizing at Paredón Blanco against Gillespie. Like the Mexicans, the foreigners tended to underrate the Californios' fighting capacity and so, despite finding that the ammunition had been taken by the Californios, they resolved to stay and scare off the Californios with a few shots.[44] Some thirty men, including Ramón Carrillo, Sérvulo Varela, and Diego Sepúlveda, were sent to join Lugo's men and together all went to Chino, to the home of Williams, where Wilson and his men were waiting (Coronel, 87). After setting fire to the house and some shooting (which killed a Californio and wounded two others), Lugo and his men took some forty (twenty-four, according to Beattie) foreigners prisoner and confiscated their firearms and ammunition (Lugo, 204–5; Beattie, 160). Interestingly enough, the accounts by Wilson and White make out Williams, who had been married to Lugo's sister but was by then a widower, to be a traitor to their cause by backing the Californios (Beattie, 150), where by all rights *they* were the traitors given that most of then not only were married to Californio women but had recently pledged allegiance to the Mexican flag. The successful action at Chino undoubtedly contributed to the planning of additional engagements and strategic acts in the following days, such as stampeding Gillespie's horses and enacting mock attacks (Coronel, 92–93).

After retaking Los Angeles, the Californios organized under the command of Flores into three squadrons to fight against the invaders. These were headed by Andrés Pico, José Antonio Carrillo, and Manuel Garfias, but even then the internecine conflict persisted. Lugo (207) indicates that the Californios did not trust Commander Flores, a Mexican who thought little of the Californios and who was said to be "an intriguer and a thief." That factionalism and personal ambition should have led the Californio José Antonio Carrillo to organize the northerners and some Angelenos to try to remove the Mexican Flores as commander at such a critical moment amazes Coronel, himself a Mexican (115), but obviously the Californios did not trust him. Nativism and factionalism had again served to exacerbate the lack of unity but differences would be quickly patched up between the parties, if only temporarily (Coronel, 116). In Mexico, of course, dissensions between factions were common. In fact, General Paredes would similarly initiate a coup against the Mexican president in the middle of the U.S. invasion (Cosío Villegas et al., 100).

Coronel's discourses of armed confrontation, including J. A. Carrillo's stand at the Domínguez's ranch and the final battle at the San Gabriel River (Coronel, 100–102; 123–28), offer but a glimmer of resistance in what is otherwise primarily a body of testimonials marked by discourses of defeat, resignation, and acquiescence. For this reason his discussion of the scarcity of firearms, the inferior quality of the gunpowder, the production of lances from barred staves, and their lopsided struggle despite limited resources provides a token sense of agency in what is an attempt at resistance doomed from the start. When Coronel is sent to Sonora by land to procure arms and gunpowder, he is stopped at the Colorado River by Indian horse thieves and the approaching U.S. forces led by Kearny. Making a heroic effort to escape in order to get word to Andrés Pico, who was then camped with his troops north of San Diego (already under U.S. military control), Coronel hides in the chaparral and walks a distance without shoes until a group of friendly Indians provides him with a horse. When he finally reaches Californio settlements, he sends word to Pico at San Pascual that the U.S. forces have taken his horses and mules and are on their way — but to no avail, for the Californio apparently put no credence in his warnings (Coronel, 116). Botello (138) recalls having heard Andrés Pico, the hero of the resistance, say that he had no interest in fighting the Americans; here again, comments coming from Mexicans about Californios are generally negative. Still, despite the lack of preparedness on the part of Andrés Pico, who did not believe the reports of his own countryman and who, according to Coronel, was not alert and had allowed the men to unsaddle their horses, the Californios, armed primarily with lances and a few muskets (Coronel, 117, 123–24), were able to inflict serious damage on Kearny's troops northeast of San Diego and later surround the fleeing soldiers, some of them wounded, cutting off their access to food and water until Stockton sent reinforcements. The battle of San Pascual was to be the Californios' only major victory. The San Gabriel battle shortly thereafter against Kearny's forces would be inconsequential and with the occupation of Los Angeles by U.S. troops a few days later, the military phase of the war in California was effectively over. At that point, Californio forces scattered; some went to join the war effort in Mexico while others retired to their homes.

Before the final retreat of Flores, Manuel Castro, and others to Mexico, there were a few skirmishes in the north, as well as acts of bravery in which women played a part. Manuel Castro, following orders given by Flores, had organized three companies of about thirty men each (the third formed with a group of *mexicanos* and settlers from New Mexico) to create a diversion that would draw Stockton's attention from the southern front. One of the encounters of Castro's group with enemy soldiers is reconstructed by Alvarado (5:264–67), Ord, and Vallejo, who recall the confrontation at Natividad between U.S. troops and a small party of Californios who had just taken Consul Larkin prisoner at the *rancho* of Los Vergeles. As a result of that battle, which left two Californios dead and several wounded as well as four U.S. casualties, Lt. José Antonio Chávez would be wounded (MGV, 5:168–70; Ord, 60). He would be taken to Monterey and hid first by some Indians and later by the Californio wife of Francisco Day, who was a partisan of the invaders. Upon her husband's return, Chávez managed to flee (Ord, 1878: 148). Ord's description of her willingness to hide Chávez after his escape from Day is another of the heroic acts of resistance to be narrated in these testimonials. Before agreeing to this clandestine act, Ord, whose husband was away, consulted her imprisoned brother Pablo, who was not sure that she could pull it off:

> I was very angry at the Americans because they were dealing harshly
> with my brothers [Pablo and Miguel] by holding them prisoners
> without cause or reason and [consequently] I angrily asked him if he
> truly thought that the Yankees would be able to find a person I chose to
> hide. (1878: 150)[45]

Patriotism and gender, that is, personal pride both as a woman and as a native of Alta California, intersect in this retort to her imprisoned brother and lead Ord to succeed in devising an elaborate plan to hide Chávez in her home.[46] When he is finally able to leave, she shifts from patriotism to an ethical positioning:

> Then Chávez came out of his hiding place and Mrs. Silva applied her remedies to his foot. He told me: "Señora, I am alive because of you." To this I answered: "What I have done for you today, I will do tomorrow for an American if you unjustly try to hurt him." (1878: 156)

Thus despite her participation in 1846 in an act of resistance, she is willing to accommodate to the interviewer, Savage, and to the dominant society of 1878; here her words seek to bracket the discourses of nation by replacing them with discourses of humanitarianism, universal justice, and morality. Now "suffering humanity," and not the "conquered nation," moves her to hide a wounded soldier. Notwithstanding this final accommodation, in Ord's testimonial discourses of nation and gender, for the most part, overlap to reveal resentment both toward the conquerors and notably toward the Californio men who allowed the nation to be conquered; yet clearly by the decade of the 1870s it was the readers' sympathy for the underdog and recognition of her righteousness and ethics that she hoped to elicit.

The testimonials further record several instances in which women astutely hid or saved Californios pursued by U.S. troops. In addition to the participation of Mrs. Day, Mrs. Ord, and Flores's wife in the struggle, the testimonials record that Doña Bernarda Duarte de Valencia saved Agatón Ruiz, wounded at the Olompali fight (MGV, 5:96, 132) and Doña Felipa Osuna de Marrón hid Pico's secretary Matías Moreno at San Luis Rey (Osuna de Marrón, 12). In Los Angeles, it is the women who move rapidly to bury the cannon in the garden of Antonio Reyes right before Stockton's entrance into the city with his troops (Botello, 147). Women's perspectives on conquest, like those of the men, are not homogeneous. Osuna de Marrón, for example, saves Moreno but then she and her husband, upset at being mistreated and robbed by those resisting invasion, leave their ranch, taking their cattle with them, and move to San Diego, putting themselves under Stockton's rule — an act, she proudly recalls, sure to chagrin her countrymen, who were interested in procuring the rest of their cattle and sheep (17–19). Here protection of private property stands above any sense of national solidarity. Lorenzana, who like other *rancheros* would lose her lands after 1851, resents events in San Diego and San Luis Rey, especially Frémont's action at the latter mission:

I was very sad because of the occupation of the country by the
Americans and for that reason I did not want to return to San Diego....
I was deeply disturbed with the American invasion—I don't know what
I thought, perhaps that if I left, the Americans too would leave. (19)

Invasion spelled the end of her role as a confidante and housekeeper
to the missionaries, although she continued to reside for a time at San
Juan Capistrano, even after the death of Friar Oliva. With the capitula-
tion of San Diego to the enemy and the loss of prestige of the church as
an institution, she found herself defenseless and unable to retain possession of her three ranches, one of which, Jamachá, would be permanently
"loaned" by her friend Juan Forster to one Magruder to use for pas-
turing horses of U.S. troops (Lorenzana, 29). The invasion thus created
resentments based on national, cultural, and economic interests rather
than strictly on gender, which did not play a determining role in reac-
tions to invasion. Women as a group were not more resistant or more
acquiescent, not even in the case of those married to foreigners, as is
demonstrated by Mrs. Day. Nor were entire Californio regional, political, or generational factions noted for their resistance or accommodation, although clearly most of the foreigners in California sided with
the invaders. Oddly enough, among those in the south who had vocif-
erously attacked Alvarado for declaring the territory's independence
would be several supporters of the invaders, including Bandini, Santiago Argüello, Miguel Pedrorena, Pedro Carrillo, and others, mainly
foreigners such as Abel Stearns (Alvarado, 5:188). In the final contest,
allegiance to the Mexican flag undoubtedly lost out to opportunism.

Of all the episodes narrated about the invasion and sporadic acts of
resistance, in the north two stand out and set the stage for what will
be ensuing years.of oppression, intolerance, racism, and lynching: the
killing of José Berreyesa and the Haro brothers, and the killing of Cowie
and Fowler. Vallejo, Alvarado, Coronel, and Antonio Berreyesa all recount in their testimonials the murder in cold blood of the old man
José Berreyesa, who was traveling from San José to Sonoma to see his
son, the mayor of the town, who he feared had been imprisoned by
the Bear Flag party. With him were two young men named Ramón
and Francisco Haro, all of whom were unarmed. Shortly after they
crossed the bay from San Pablo on a small boat that landed at the San
Rafael wharf the three were killed by Frémont's men as they walked
inland. This crime came apparently in retaliation for the killing of two
members of the Bear Flag party. It seems that after the taking of Sonoma,
the imprisonment of M. G. Vallejo, Salvador Vallejo, Prudón, and Leese,

and the raising of the bear flag, two of the Bear Flag party were sent to Fitch's ranch to acquire some gunpowder from the foreman, Moses Carson, brother of Kit Carson. On the way Thomas Cowie and William Fowler were stopped by a group of *rancheros* that had organized under Juan Padilla and Ramón Carrillo (brother of Benicia Vallejo), who took them prisoners and tied them to a tree. Vallejo indicates that one of Padilla's party was Bernardo García, a man known as "Three-Fingered Jack" who was made famous by Ridge's novel on Joaquín Murieta. García stabbed and killed Fowler and Cowie and mutilated their bodies, one of them sexually, before the group could come to a decision as to what to do with the foreigners (MGV, 5:122–23; Berreyesa, 3). It was this act that was being avenged in the killing of the three unarmed Californio travelers.

There would be other deaths, but these two cases have become fixed in the history of each national group as proof of the other's savagery. Even Vallejo has to recognize that conquest created national as well as racial antagonisms that pitted Californios and *mexicanos* against Anglos, with the latter designation inclusive of U.S. forces as much as of Frémont's Bear Flag party. In reconstructing the ethnic clashes and conflicts, Vallejo, always contradictory, apologizes for rehashing old wounds, insisting he would prefer to make peace between Californios and Anglos:

> As long as I am alive I propose to use whatever means are available to me to enable the two races to erase the disagreeable actions that took place in the frontier of Sonoma in 1846 and if, before I am called to account by the Supreme Creator, I succeed in witnessing this reconciliation between the victors and the defeated, between conquerors and the conquered, I will die sure of not having worked in vain. (MGV, 5:133)

This ethnic and national antagonism of course would not disappear, especially not after the land loss and disempowerment that followed, not even nearly 150 years later. In effect these testimonials provide an introduction to postinvasion antagonisms that presage the ethnicism that was to predominate in the twentieth century.

In this chapter we have focused primarily on protonationalist discourses, interdiscursive constructs of various "imagined communities," differentiated on the basis of region, nation, generation, culture, class, and political orientation. Out of these discourses came several positions questioning the relationship of the territory with Mexico and positing various alternatives to invasion. In most of the Californio testimonials, as opposed to those of Mexican settlers, there is, despite differences of opinion, a clear construction of Alta California as a homeland, a construct that would be subsequently shattered, but at the hour of territorial occupation it would both unite and divide the population. Given the various political rifts, the ideological field represented in these testimonials is understandably ambiguous and full of fissures and disjunctures, which become even more pronounced once these Californio discourses are intersected by U.S. hegemonic discourses and once all Californio space is deterritorialized. In the fissures, however, liminal spaces are created; here these same protonationalist discourses again intersect and overlap, now with discourses of resentment and defeat, to generate new discourses of ethnicity, as we shall see in chapter 7.

7

Constructs of Ethnicity

El mal está hecho y no tiene remedio.

M. G. Vallejo

Well over a hundred years after the narration of the Californio testimonials, their descendants, the Chicanos, continue to face a number of social problems and contradictions that first came to the fore in the nineteenth century with invasion and modernization, that is, with conquest, the collapse of feudalism and the definitive inclusion of the territory within capitalism. The contingencies of social reality and politics, specifically an emergent dislocation and shift in social positioning, gave rise to an initial "space of indeterminacy" that ostensibly allowed the Californios to infiltrate and advance within the new system. By 1870, however, it had become quite clear, even to those Californios who had initially accommodated to the invaders, that as a collectivity they were now subject to new structural capacities and racist practices that had rapidly pushed them toward the periphery and threatened to obliterate prior historical identities. To counter this marginalization and increasing violence against them throughout the state required, in part, a new cognitive mapping, that is, consciousness of a new identity, ethnic in nature. This ethnic construction, as much a construct of the oppressor as a counterconstruct on the part of the oppressed, would give rise to new discourses that are still very much part of Chicano struggles today.[1] Thus, the Californios' legal, economic, political, and cultural demands came to be articulated around ethnism, a strategic discourse that was meant to transcend class, generational, origin, gender, and linguistic differences, especially during periods of xenophobic violence against Latinos, and enable the creation of a "historical bloc." Unfortunately, class, political orientation, and even generational and regional differences proved again to be major stumbling blocks in establishing long-term alliances across Latino sectors in nineteenth-century California. Since then, too, the politics of ethnic identity, while a significant strategy and catalyst for consciousness-raising, have proven inadequate for a committed identification with a Latino "imagined community" whenever ethnicity has been the only shared discourse.

Seen in this light, these testimonials provide a crucible for deconstructing the myth of essential identity, once the constructed differences among Californios are accounted for. At the same time they serve to show that ethnicity is a readily available discourse, a type of umbrella construct that often subsumes a number of economic, political, and social antagonisms that also call for disarticulation. As an identity of subalternity,[2] ethnicity can seemingly allow for a collective identity across classes, at least momentarily, especially when the community as a whole suffers the brunt of racist attacks, but the fact that ethnicism does not obliterate class distinctions and ideological differences leads invariably to group fragmentation. In the case of the Californios, it meant that socially mobile members of the same ethnic community could be found riding alongside vigilantes out to lynch Mexicans.

The violence against the Californios in the latter half of the nineteenth century is in part cultural racism, an intolerance not only for the landowners (MGV, 5:227–28), but for all Latinos, including Californios, considered foreigners by what was then an Anglo-Saxon majority. Racist practices here, as elsewhere, generate segregation, exclusion, and new spaces of marginalization, social sites (barrios) produced by concrete social relations and in turn central to the construction of identity as an ethnic collectivity. As economic and ethnic/racial segregation further exacerbates displacement, the need to rewrite and thereby reterritorialize Alta California becomes crucial. The Californios' claim to the land, to the territory as a national space, is what is historicized and reconstructed in these testimonials. The more decentered the Californios are, the more space assumes center stage and the more collective is the perspective in these narrations.

Conditions at the end of the twentieth century are far different from those facing the Californios in the 1870s — globally and nationally, technologically, economically, demographically, and politically — and yet, perhaps because of the way in which the past sits in judgment of us and makes us aware of "what we are not yet,"[3] these nineteenth-century texts continue to allow for an analysis from within. Looking back, then, implies first, a gauging of the textual strategies used for maneuvering and reworking hegemonic discourses and representations, and second, an examination of the constructed contradictory and clashing social, economic, and political relations operating within the ideological field. It is not surprising that the gaps and interstices generated in the rewritings of history and identity invariably contain strategies of accommodation, resentment, resignation, and resistance, all mechanisms adopted by the Californios in these testimonials for a reconstruction not only of their past but of their present relations to their own conditions under U.S. rule and monopoly capitalism.

Modernization and Marginalization

At least six major interrelated social processes characterize the political and economic development in California between 1846 and 1876: (a) the transition from a feudal Mexican model to a capitalist mode of production and a U.S. political system with the incorporation of California as a state in the union in 1850; (b) a major demographic shift initiated with the gold rush, migration and immigration that would bring in thousands so that by 1879 California had an ethnically and racially heterogeneous population of about one million; (c) the diversification of the economy (mining, agriculture, ranching, and manufacturing); (d) the spread of antagonisms and racism directed primarily against Mexicans and Asians; (e) the emergence of corporate monopoly capitalism; and (f) the rising levels of labor/political struggle.[4] These new economic and social conditions will consolidate the displacement of the Californios.

For the Californios, changes came quickly, destabilizing and then replacing existing structures. Only briefly did feudal relations of production on existing *haciendas* continue as the basis for local production and consumption and only until the first Constitutional Convention in 1849 did local *alcaldes* and judges continue in charge of local government. The rapid increase in population attracted first by the discovery of gold and then by the promise of "public land" available for agricultural production and manufacturing would bring not only the eclipse of the Californio *hacienda*, especially after the droughts of 1863 and 1864, but the subordination of the Californios themselves.[5] Migration west and state policies promoting farming over ranching facilitated the dispossession of the Californios, sanctioning racist/nativist movements calling for driving out all "foreigners," including second- and third-generation native Californios, actions that in turn provoked the revolt of some of the younger generations of Californios and Mexicanos. Not only the collapse of their economic and political system but their parallel displacement, dispossession, disempowerment, and proletarianization lead to a keen consciousness on the part of the Californios of their status as second-class citizens and as a marginalized ethnic minority.

This consciousness of subalternity, this awareness of having been conquered and displaced, informs (implicitly or explicitly) every narrative. Faced with their decline and impoverishment, the surviving population of dominant Californios is forced to contemplate its potential disappearance, as feared by Soledad Ortega Argüello (cited in Cerruti, 83). But several among the Californios who are acutely aware of the lack of self-representation see the need to reconstruct the past from their own vantage point if the collectivity and its history are to survive textually and if they are to envision a future. The effect of this reconstruction of the past and the construction of an ethnic identity, the "imagined community" of la raza, is thus twofold: historical and political.

The development of these discourses of ethnicity can be traced through several stages, some of which we have already examined at length in previous chapters. First there is the separation from the country of origin that begins with first-generation Californios, a distancing that leads in time to identity with their local space. For the second generation, the shared experience of local space and time is always already enabling a separate identification. This new territorial identity subsequently produces an ambivalent position on secession, initially repressed but later reactivated upon recognizing Mexico's incapacity to intervene on their behalf upon invasion by U.S. forces. Mexico's failure to negotiate an adequate treaty that safeguards their properties will in part give rise to a sense of betrayal ("our stepmother, cowardly Mexico, that sold the Department of Alta California to the North Americans" [Alvarado, 1:43]) along with a sense of solidarity with the vanquished (especially after Mexico suffered the invasion of French troops in 1863 [Alvarado, 5:180]). The stage beginning after 1848 with dispossession and rising social inequality, despite guarantees made by the United States to respect all the Californios' rights as new citizens, brings disillusionment with the new regime, a full awareness of marginalization and disempowerment, and a concomitant reassertion of national roots. This last stage is of particular interest to us here in this chapter, in view of the fact that these conditions continue to be the basis for identification as Chicanos today.

The sociospatial practices leading up to the forging of this new ethnic identity all implicitly or explicitly figure in M. G. Vallejo's last essay, the last chapter of his five-volume testimonial, and in Coronel's recollections of the period after invasion, especially his comments on the gold rush and banditry. Both of these texts will serve to frame the dialogue in the narratives of several Californios textualizing their plight in the 1870s when the testimonials were taken down.

Dispossession and Denunciation of the State

After five long volumes reconstructing the past in his narrative, M. G. Vallejo provides a single last essay in which he addresses the Californios' displacement and finally reveals his outrage, his underlying reason for narrating and reconstructing the past. Now the various arguments that he, Alvarado, Fernández, his friends, his brothers, and even the southerners have been making come together for a synoptic view of the period twenty-five years after invasion. Here he provides ethical and political arguments to denounce the judicial system of the United States, the unfulfilled promises of the U.S. government, the dispossession of the conquered Californios, and the economic and political displacement of a cultural minority sold out by Mexico and deprived of its rights by a duplicitous U.S. government. The essay is strongly worded, full of resentment, pained with resignation. The strategy throughout is one of contrasts and oppositions (before and after invasion), whether directly given or implied. The arguments are sometimes ethnocentric and aristocratic but reveal a clear conception of the problems faced by this ethnic minority after 1846 and project a collective identity. Central to all these arguments is the Treaty of Guadalupe-Hidalgo, a text that was to serve as the grounds for both struggle and resignation after 1848.

The treaty, ratified by the U.S. Congress in March 1848, not only ended the war between the United States and Mexico, and defined boundaries, land concessions, and war costs, but also included articles that concerned Mexican residents remaining in the conquered territory. As far as the Californios and other Mexicans in the Southwest were concerned, these articles, as well as an appended protocol explaining eliminated articles and reiterating the rights of Mexicans remaining in the occupied territories, were state guarantees, that is, legally binding agreements. What the Californios soon discovered, however, was the degree to which within a capitalist system the state functions as a coercive system of authority that serves the interest of capital even if this implies breaching its own agreements.[6] Its economic and coercive functions had already been clear in its expansion into Mexican territory in 1846 and would later establish the groundwork for the acceleration of capital investment, including subsequent government subsidies for the railroad monopoly (Olin, 31). With the gold rush and massive immigration, the issue of seeding the newly acquired soil with a U.S.-loyal population was rapidly solved, just as incorporation into the union guaranteed California's not taking an independent direction of its own, as Congress feared (Olin, 7). Subsequent depletion of gold and silver deposits, as much as a need to find new areas for capital investment, spurred on designs on the hundreds of thousands of acres of fertile land in the hands of a small Californio population, a usurpation achieved through "legal means," as Josiah Royce noted in his history of California:

> But as for us, who thus sought to despoil by legal means those whom we were too orderly to rob on any grand scale by violence, we could not altogether escape from the demoralization that we tried to inflict.[7]

Legal maneuvering as well as the manipulations of moneylenders constituted a form of violence as effectual as if the congressmen and legislators had sent out troops with drawn bayonets to force the Californios off the land.

A key strategy in the denunciation of the state by the Californios involves a reworking of discourses in the Treaty of Guadalupe-Hidalgo and warrants further comment. As Vallejo came to recognize, the treaty had in fact been imposed on the defeated nation. With it the United States wrested half of the Mexican territory (81,730 square leagues out of a total of 161,586 square leagues [Archivo, 31:344]) while allegedly preserving "Mexican sovereignty" over the rest of the land, as proponents of the treaty in Mexico had argued.[8] In view of Mexico's lack of military preparedness after thirty-six years of revolts and chaos, the Mexican commissioners seeking Mexican congressional approval of the agreement evidently considered themselves lucky not to have to forgo the entire national territory. The northern half, they argued, had been lost in the war and not as a result of the treaty, which merely ratified their losses (Archivo, 31:141).[9] Considering that more territory was then under control of U.S. forces than was conceded under the treaty, the commissioners preferred to think of it as being "more properly ... an agreement for reappropriation rather than of concession" (Archivo, 31:141–42). In view of this, some Mexicans felt relieved, while others, like Manuel C. Rejón, were outraged:

Gentlemen, it is our death sentence that is being proposed in these
wretched treaties and I am surprised that there should have been
Mexicans willing to negotiate them, underwrite them, and consider
them good for our unfortunate country. This circumstance alone
saddens me and makes me despair for the life of the Republic.
(Archivo, 31:325)

The aggressors not only had extended the legitimate Texas border from
the Nueces River to the Rio Grande but had taken the New Mexico
territory and Alta California as well, as if entitled to it, Rejón protested.
To add insult to injury, the United States had offered eighteen million
dollars for losses, subtracted three million for Mexico's debt, and dictated
terms of payment of the remaining fifteen million dollars. It was not
lost on Rejón that the appropriated territory, if sold at the cheap rate
of $1.25 per acre offered to homesteaders interested in settling on "va-
cant" lands in the newly expanded United States, would have been
worth at least 480 million dollars in gold. The sum to be paid by the
United States to Mexico was thus not for the sale of land but rather a
token amount given to assuage U.S. critics of the war; it was simply
an attempt to legitimate invasion under the guise of compensation.
The antiwar sentiment in the United States encouraged Rejón to suggest that Mexico should not ratify the treaty, lest, as he argued, within
fifteen years the United States resolve to invade the entire Mexican
territory and displace the mestizo and Indian population, the whole
of which it hated and considered unworthy of forming part of the same
nation (Archivo, 31:327). The Indian removal policies in the United
States, Rejón warned, were a good indication of what was to befall the
Californios and the other Mexicans remaining in the occupied territory.

The racism alluded to by Rejón would not of course be the sole
problem faced by the conquered population; it would in effect always
appear in conjunction with class. This becomes clear in the Californios'
major battle, the legal struggle to retain their land. Their loss of property was in part traceable to the failure of the vanquished nation to
ensure the rights of its citizens after defeat. The treaty as originally
negotiated had included specific articles that safeguarded the rights
of Californios and other Mexican citizens, but once before the U.S. Congress several of these had been unilaterally deleted. Californios were
not unaware that articles 8 and 9 of the treaty, for example, specified
that all those Mexicans wishing to remain in the occupied territories
could stay and that their property and individual rights would be respected. Article 10 further stipulated that all land concessions made
by the Mexican government or a qualified government authority would

be respected as valid, that is, all land grants made by authorized personnel until May 13, 1846, were to be recognized as official.[10] In the final version of the treaty approved by the U.S. Congress, article 10 was eliminated and replaced by a new streamlined version that stipulated that all Mexicans remaining in the territory would in due time, as determined by the U.S. Congress, become full citizens of the United States and in the meantime would enjoy all property and civil rights as well as freedom of religion. The suppression of article 10 by the United States led to further negotiations but despite assurances in appended explanations that the United States had no intention of annulling land titles that were legitimate under Mexican law, the statement by the commissioners that the grantees had no more than to present their titles before U.S. tribunals to have them acknowledged in effect already guaranteed the loss of all these lands (Archivo, 31:404).[11] It is precisely this process of validation that was instituted by the Land Act of 1851, which ruled that all land claims were invalid until ratified by the land commission or the courts. Far from furthering the recognition of property, it would lead to protracted and costly litigation and the ruin of most of the Californios, whose debts and mortgages to meet court costs, pay taxes, and continue fighting squatter appeals proved disastrous. Military occupation of the Mexican territory had meant loss of autonomy for Alta California, but, for many, the treaty discourses themselves enabled territorial amputation and guaranteed the dispossession of Mexican property owners throughout the Southwest. Had the Californios themselves negotiated the treaty, Salvador Vallejo argues in hindsight, they would never have been dispossessed, for they would have drawn up the documents of annexation in such a way that their property claims would have been safeguarded: "Instead of that, the Mexican government turned us over to the United States, in the same manner that a flock-herder turns over [his] sheep to a purchaser" (1874: 74). The assertion by Mexican writers "that every inherent right of the native Californians had been assured them by the treaty," he retorts, "is blasphemous, is adding insult to injury" (74). That Mexico had been forced to accept the U.S. version of the agreement was difficult for some Californios to accept even in the 1870s.

The treaty did allow for some leeway, however. Then, as today, legal constructs regarding entitlements served as the basis for struggle through institutional channels. Californios necessarily focused on those articles that had not been deleted and dealt in general terms with civil and property rights, using them as the basis for protest and denunciation, as is clear in the petition seeking redress of their grievances submitted to the U.S. Congress in 1859 by Antonio María Pico and forty-nine other Californios who had lost their land as a consequence of the Land Act of 1851 (Pico et al., 199). But the judicial system itself proved to be a minefield for Californios subjected to constant litigation and forced to pay court costs and lawyers to validate their land titles, only to find after endless appeals that *"the Californian claimant almost to a certainty was awarded a decision against his claim"* (MGV, 5:230). Vallejo's underlining and shift to English in a text written in Spanish not only express his exasperation with a system that made many promises to the Californios but kept few if any, but also pinpoint the ethnocentricity of a judicial system that as a rule found in favor of the Anglo squatters who settled on land under litigation and against the conquered.

Vallejo's strongest outrage is reserved for the hack lawyers from Missouri and other states who conspired to deprive the Californios of their land and means under protection of the law (MGV, 5:233–34). These pseudolawyers who colluded with the local sheriffs and were favored by juries and judges, some of whom were squatters, did not hesitate in filing suits against the Californios. Unfamiliar with the judicial system and with the language, Californios were at a disadvantage in organizing their defense, but then the U.S. courts also proved to be conveniently ignorant of Spanish and Mexican laws when they invalidated a number of legitimate land grants (MGV, 5:237). Local court findings, of course, could be appealed to the Supreme Court if one had the money to pursue the matter, but Vallejo recalls that most lacked these means and for that reason "lowered their heads before the California tribunals and allowed the squatters to take possession of their properties" (MGV, 5:237).

Ironically, even those Californios who would win their appeals and finally legally prove the validity of their titles—and a good many of the 813 claims (346 of these made by non-Mexicans) were validated— would nevertheless lose their lands to loan sharks, banks, and mortgage companies, as a consequence of the high costs involved.[12] Interestingly enough, some of the early foreign merchants, like Abel Stearns, who came in 1829 and married Arcadia Bandini, would profit immensely from these very same mortgages, taking possession of thousands of acres of foreclosed land (Alvarado, 3:227).[13] Other Californios would lose their land when the U.S. attorney general argued fraud and alleged that some of the land titles had been fabricated. But despite what the attorney general may have argued in support of the U.S. entrepreneurs coveting these lands, relatively few of the claims were fraudulent.[14] Clearly some of these claims were by common agreement the property of particular Californios, despite the fact that delineations of boundaries were ambiguous or inexact or that some grants had been made by the governors, others by *presidio* commanders, and still others by the missionaries but never brought before the territorial assembly for confirmation, as it was considered unnecessary at the time.[15] Pío Pico's particular trials and tribulations—the eventual loss of Santa Margarita (now Marine Corps Camp Pendleton) to his brother-in-law John Forster in 1883 and the loss of the balance of his property to moneylender Bernard Cohn a few years later—are typical of what would befall the formerly dominant Californio families.[16] In 1894 Pico would be buried in a pauper's grave.[17]

Broken Promises

Vallejo's revealing last chapter begins with a bitter recognition of what he now sees as the irreversible U.S. appropriation of Alta California and is framed by an ironic comparison of two social spaces and two legal systems. Before 1846, he recalls, no one ever went hungry or was hanged for cattle rustling in California as occurred after the U.S. invasion when the conquerors imposed new political structures. The new judicial system placed property above human life and allowed the death penalty for cattle theft, but, interestingly enough, hypocritically tolerated squatting on a Californio's land and shooting of a Californio's cattle for straying into squatted farmland. The property rights of some were obviously more sacred than those of others.

Vallejo's words voice both a denunciation and the lament of a conquered population, colonized and subjected to alien laws by a conquering government that made promises it did not intend to keep. What kind of a government denies minorities the right to protection in accordance with the principles of U.S. law? Vallejo appears to have no hope at this point; resignation and defeat are evident in the last line: "Of what use is it to complain? The evil deed is done and there's nothing to be done" (MGV, 5:229). Yet even here, in the very construction of disillusionment and resignation, the narrator assumes a confrontational stance to denounce those who have been hostile to the native population of California.

In this essay Vallejo summarizes the various complaints addressed by other Californios in their testimonials, although each in turn offers an added dimension. In all, the discourses of democracy and justice are articulated with those of ethnicity and class. The testimonials are in this sense appeals for justice, appeals to the very system that sanctions their dispossession and the denial of their civil rights. There is no other framework to which they can appeal, for Mexico has been proven to be weak and is then just coming out from both a civil war and a war against the French, who were allied to the Mexican conservative oligarchy. The Californios' only recourse is seen to lie within the very same system of government that has reduced them to their subaltern status.

The importance of unmasking false promises of equity and protection will be reiterated throughout this chapter, as will the need to reveal the institutional prejudice against Californios underpinning many of these illegal maneuvers. Vallejo recalls that when Commander Sloat and later Commander Stockton first imposed their control over Alta California, they invited the Californios to accept their annexation, promising to close the jails, abolish the scaffold and the bloody laws established by the Mexican government, and free the Californios from their ties to Mexico in order to "lift them" to the level of the invading nation. By 1876 Vallejo has no patience with these ethnocentric racist statements. He regrets that many defenseless and gullible Californios fell all too willingly for these promises and consequently into the maws of the beast:

> These stupidities and others along these same lines deceived many unsuspecting individuals who ... defenseless, fell into the maws of the astute adventurers that had crossed the sea to come to this virgin soil, not to work in a decent and honest way but to exploit the situation. (MGV, 5:231)

Here Vallejo referred as much to himself as to all the other Californios that had favored annexation and considered the offer of the United States ideal, little realizing that in the very promises there were implications of Anglo superiority and Californio inferiority. There was to be no "improvement" of their condition; instead, the immigrants that they had received with open arms, to whom in many cases they had ceded their daughters, had come to despoil them. These had been only the front lines of a voluminous wave of immigrants from all over the world, but already this vanguard had made resistance during the invasion quite difficult (MGV, 4:231).

The role of the state in the dispossession of the landed Californios particularly provokes the resentment of someone like Vallejo, who had originally thought it possible to articulate the interests of the landowning Californio aristocracy with those of the emerging California bourgeoisie. But the state was primarily concerned with laying the groundwork for capitalist expansion in the new territory and was indifferent to the imposition of an alien political structure in a language not "our own" over the conquered population:

> The language that is now spoken in our country, the laws that rule over us, and the faces with which we daily interact are new for us, the owners of the land, and of course antagonistic to our interests and rights, but, what does this matter to the conqueror? He looks after his own interests and not ours, a trait that I consider natural in individuals but that I condemn in a government that had promised to respect and to have others respect our rights and to treat us like sons and daughters, but, of what use is it to complain? The evil deed is done and there's nothing to be done. (MGV, 5:229)

In effect, the government espoused the interests of banks, moneylenders, lawyers, land entrepreneurs, settlers, and squatters and denied the Californios full protection under the law when with the Land Act of 1851 it deemed their land titles invalid, thereby facilitating their eventual land loss and reduction to second-class citizenship.

Like other Californios, Vallejo too would be despoiled of his lands by the people he had trusted to protect his property. Aware of the arguments in favor of this dispossession, he counters hegemonic objections to the Mexican grants for taking up too much of "the finest agricultural lands of the State" (Royce, 485) by reiterating as often as he can the legal basis for their just claims to these lands (MGV, 4:388). Let us recall that at the time of narration in 1875 Vallejo is close to sixty-seven years of age. The wealthiest individual in California before 1846, Vallejo, who had kept his word not to take up arms against the invaders after being released from the New Helvetia prison and who subsequently cast his lot with the new regime, was by then feeling his ruin most acutely. By 1862 he had lost his Soscol *rancho* to squatters after years of costly litigation, land that he had held since 1843 when Governor Micheltorena had granted him this *rancho* in payment for a loan to the government in grain, supplies, and other provisions (MGV, 4:387). His title to Petaluma had been recognized, but, as Alvarado mentions, not until he was already ruined.[18] If in the 1860s Vallejo had been able to assume a stance of resignation whenever he considered the injustices, after the 1876 crash of bonanza stocks, which left him further impoverished, he was totally depressed. Vallejo's wife Benicia, in her letters to her son Platón, provides an intimate view of a moody, downcast, irritable Vallejo, left destitute by his son-in-law Frisbie's speculation (Carrillo de Vallejo, carta a Platón Vallejo, abril de 1877).

This sense of deception, betrayal, loss, and total destitution pervades and underlies these testimonials. These narrations, as much as the Californios' personal letters, become their only means of reconstructing their oppression and of venting their resentment and frustration. For the Californios it is only too clear that the loss of property, this "usurpation of the Americans,"[19] underpins all their other losses, for it deprives them as a conquered population of economic and, consequently, political power. What is evident here is that it is not their minority status but their lack of economic and political power that reduces them to their subaltern status.

Dislocation and Relocation of the Californios

The process of dispossession that would bring down the Californios by the 1870s did not make itself immediately evident, at least not during the first decade after 1846. García has documented that in San Diego in 1850, for example, the wealthiest landowners, according to the taxpayers' roll, were the Californios; ten years later, decline was evident and the Anglos owned most of the property:

> Their decline resulted from the intense competition for land from Anglo miners, Anglo settlers, and Anglo speculators. It did not originate, as Pitt claims, from a clash of divergent cultures.[20]

With the change of flag had come modernization, that is, a capitalist system and numerous technological and social changes and innovations that had greatly improved transportation, education, and mail services. Even Alvarado, who resented the invaders, was willing to recognize that annexation to the United States had brought a new "era of progress," which, despite the suffering of the Californio minority, had undoubtedly improved things for the majority.[21] The *rancho*, though a profitable cattle-raising industry during the gold rush when fresh meat brought a good price in the mining camps, had, with new competition from the northern and central parts of the state, begun to decline in the south and, with it, so had the lot of Californio landowners. The final blow and the ruin of many a *ranchero* would be the famine years of 1863 and 1864, with the starvation of millions of head of cattle (Guinn, 46) providing additional impetus for increased urbanization facilitated by new means of transportation.[22]

The restructuring of California after 1846 would lead to the creation of new social spaces, new geographical centers of accumulation, and the diversification of production, brought about by a subdivision of the land into farms, the development of the fruit industry, urbanization, and the growth of manufacturing industries. For the displaced Californios, including mestizos, criollos, and Indians, relocation signaled a double shift from *ranchos* to cities and towns and from property owners to wage labor. This occupational shift or proletarianization meant manual labor in cities and towns and sometimes on farms, where Mexican laborers competed with Chinese workers. The construction of the Californios as farmworkers, service workers, and laborers is absent in these testimonials (although the loss of land is a dominant issue), but it does appear in the 1885 novel by Ruiz de Burton, *The Squatter and the Don*, a historical romance tracing the dispossession of the Californios. Here the sons of the elite are forced to become unskilled workers—as in the specific example of Gabriel Alamar, the son of a formerly wealthy Californio *ranchero*, who becomes a hod carrier—in order to support their families.[23] These intersecting occupational, geographical, and demographic shifts will produce a new spatial configuration of urban areas. Los Angeles, for example, by 1860 had become "a two-tiered city," with *mexicanos*, no longer a majority, residing in the center of town, and Anglos in the growing suburbs.[24] These barrios, social spaces segregating the working-class population of Mexican/Latino origin, would allow for the construction of a strong sense of community and develop an awareness of shared exploitation. The barrio would thus enable the strengthening of the construct of "imagined community" across the state and throughout the entire Southwest.

This economic restructuring not only relocated the Californios within new social spaces but peripheralized them politically as well. Before their economic decline, a few among the elite, especially those espousing the U.S. cause at the moment of invasion, like Miguel Pedrorena, Pedro Carrillo, Bandini, and Argüello (Alvarado, 5:136), and those accommodating to the invaders afterward, like Vallejo, Coronel, Andrés Pico, Pablo de la Guerra, Botello, Pacheco, and del Valle—several of these tied by blood and marriage to the new dominant majority—would participate in the new political system as customs officers, justices of the peace, delegates to the 1849 Constitutional Convention, mayors, sheriffs, judges, and even state senators and assemblymen. Some, like Alvarado or the Hijar-Padrés colonist Abrego, who had served as department treasurer under Governor Alvarado, were unwilling to participate in the conqueror's system (Cerruti, 89). By 1880, the political participation had declined with the aging and demise of the former ruling class, some of whom, like Vallejo, had already had problems being elected (Weber, 149). Even by the 1870s only a handful continued to serve in the state assembly (like Reginaldo del Valle) or in the state senate (like Pablo de la Guerra). Only one Californio, Romualdo Pacheco, considered atypical by the historian Weber (149), would become acting governor.[25] After that, representation of the population of Mexican origin in local, state, and national governing bodies and politics is almost nil.[26] This lack of what they considered their rightful political representation will further exacerbate the resentment of the Californios in the 1870s and lead to their acerbic critiques of the political and especially the judicial system.

The loss of status, land, political power, and comfortable lifestyle was especially difficult for the formerly wealthy ruling classes, especially for conservative aristocrats who saw modernization as a destructive force that melted all that was solid into air.[27] Thus when Cerruti (with Vallejo) visits the old widow of the first native-son interim governor of Alta California, Luis Argüello, to interview her, he finds her bitter and resentful with the situation in which "instead of being the rulers of the strangers that have taken up their residences in our town they rule us in the same manner that the owner of a large farm rules his slaves" (Cerruti, 83). Soledad Ortega de Argëllo resents the displacement of the Spanish language, finds the judicial system lacking, and notes that alien intruders now not only occupy their properties but rule the land. The foreigners have spread their technology and material innovations (such as steam engines and larger houses) but the Californios, "our race," are no longer a happy family. They have been dispersed to the winds, and undoubtedly, she says, "the change has not improved our condition." The equally aristocratic Vallejo, ever aware that the conversation is being transcribed, attempts to refute her arguments by pointing to the improvements in housing and the availability of furniture even in the homes of the poor; her response, however, is presumptuous and classist and reeks of the resentment of the déclassé. Adobe houses, she says, are much better than the new wooden ones:

> As to furniture, she claimed that the poor people did not feel the want of it because they did not know its use, and added that the Argüellos, Amesti, Alvarados, la Guerra, and several other families of note possessed since 1824 handsome bureaus, large looking glasses, and tables inlaid with shells that sailing vessels brought from China or from Peru. (Cerruti, 84)

The collectivity alluded to is that of the elite, but as used by other Californios, even Vallejo, the phrase "nuestra raza" is generally inclusive of all Californios and Mexicanos here before 1846. The discourses of class will not long remain aristocratic, however, for in time the wealthiest of Californios will be reduced to the position of beggars. The servant's announcement of dinner stops short the conversation with widow Argüello but not before we are made aware of the definite class position of the Argüellos, who, despite the family decline in status, still manage to have servants. Argüello moreover sees the situation of the fallen elite as the only significant one, signaling the poor as incapable of judging on social change. Cerruti, for his part, intervenes in the testimonial to point out the pettiness and limited resources of the family in describing the "scanty repast" that is offered to them for dinner and the family's disdain for history expressed in their own destruction of the family's archives. The latter is a dying aristocratic family's pathetic ultimate revenge, a discursive "scorched earth policy" in an ultimately futile attempt at safeguarding their past from hegemonic appropriation and interpretation.

The Californios' standing as a conquered population is thus often articulated with class resentment as a dispossessed landowning aristocracy, as is obvious not only in Argüello's testimonial but in that of another woman as well, María Antonia Rodríguez Soberanes, widow of Feliciano Soberanes. When Cerruti interviews her, Soberanes, who previously owned the Alisal ranch, San Lorenzo, and the mission Soledad, is highly cynical, but just as aristocratic, in her response:

> I asked her, if she was pleased with the change of rulers, and she replied, that though the Americans had taken away from her nearly the whole of her lands, she had no grudge against them; for, she said, "it is the law of nature that the poor should steal from the rich; we Californians in 1846 owned every inch of soil in this country and our conquerors took away from us the greater part; the same thing, I suppose has happened over and over again in every conquered nation." (Cerruti, 108)

Soberanes best captures a sense of history as cyclical violent transformation, revealing in her comments both determinism and resignation. Of course she neglects to note that the Californios had dispossessed the Indians in a similar fashion, but perhaps she had that in mind when she chose to naturalize conquest, dispossession, and oppression, as if it were a "law of nature" rather than an economic, political, and military enterprise. In any event, the tenor of her remarks, whether cynical or philosophical, reveals a very thin veneer of civility that at every turn belies her disdain and hate for "our conquerors" and all they represent.

Class and citizenship are always articulated within these representational spaces with ethnicity and with culture in view of the fact that modernization produced its own cultural dominant, within which the entire population, including the marginalized and conquered population of Californios, found itself. As seen in chapter 6, modernization brought a reification of social relations, the fetishization of commodities, and the commodification of culture.[28] The impact of this new social order, capitalism, becomes more obvious in the lifestyle of the younger generation. Salvador Vallejo, like his brother, is especially adamant about the loss of "cleanliness, good living, and economy" after 1846, all traits attributed to the California past. Before conquest young men had been trained to be "good farmers and artisans" and young women "to be good housewives," but now disdaining the healthy constitutions of yesterday, "California's fair daughters" were all made up with cosmetics and forced into ridiculous fashions. Although he admits that modernization brought improvement to the lower classes, "the females of the upper classes have lost what the less fortunate members of our race have gained: the women so as to keep pace with civilization are now compelled to wear straight laces and corsets, veritable instruments of torture that imprison the body and prevent it from growing to its full size" (S. Vallejo, 1874: 99–100); Vallejo argues that this leads to consumption, an illness formerly unknown in California. The use of "whale bone, peacock feathers, high heels, cotton breasts, and long tails of rustling silk" he holds in contempt when he laments the disappearance of

> the good ole times in which men, women, and children untrammeled by etiquette were free to roam at will through hills and plains, through meadows and ravines with no critics' eyes to fear, no scandalmongers to dread, no loquacious servants to bribe, and no money required when journeying from Sonoma to San Diego or vice versa. Those days were indeed happy, but alas gone, never again to return. (S. Vallejo, 1874: 100)

The spaces of fashion and consumerism are here representative not only of the cultural changes that Salvador Vallejo perceives but also of the closures established by the market and the limitations that commodification of transportation have imposed. It is especially the new "restrictions" placed on women's bodies, the impositions of distortions as far as size, apparel, and makeup, that become synecdochic (dress constraints for political/economic constraints) for the Californio men's powerlessness (feminization, so to speak) and sense of being contained within imposed norms and relations, all again grafted onto the body of woman in a discussion of their loss of power to dictate what their women should do or wear.

Cultural Racism

Cultural racism, currently a widely recognized phenomenon, is in fact a long-standing tradition in the United States, where cultural differences as much as race have been the basis for discriminatory practices. "Cultural racism" is a form of racism whereby "differences in culture, in way of life, in systems of belief, in ethnic identity and traditions, now matter more than anything that can be traced to specifically genetic or biological forms of racism."[29] Whether this form is more evident or matters more today than in the past, as Hall indicates, is debatable, although there is definitely more interest today in studying differentialist racist practices, perhaps because these practices also affect members of otherwise dominant groups, like white middle-class gays or women, for example. Social recognition of this form of racism has generated concern on the part of the political right, ever conscious and fearful of the strategic importance of politically organizing around issues of racism. It is not surprising, then, that at the same moment when ethnic and racial minorities, women, gays and lesbians, and other discriminated groups are forming alliances to counter racism and making demands for affirmative action and nondiscriminatory practices in the public sphere, works like that of Peter Skerry should be published and awarded prizes when they argue precisely against the identification of Mexican Americans as an oppressed racial minority.[30] That Chicanos have suffered "cultural racism" since 1846 as an oppressed ethnic and linguistic minority, despite the heterogeneous nature of the Mexican origin population, is a historical fact. It was more than abundantly clear to the Californios who recognized that a reconstruction from their own vantage point was called for in order to mitigate against dominant discourses in the midnineteenth century in the U.S. Congress, where they were being described as a "degraded" race,[31] and in California, where they were interpellated as "greasers" (Cerruti, 93). In the case of the population of Mexican origin, the racism suffered has always been intersected by ethnocentrism, classism, linguistic oppression, and judicial prejudice.

The constructs of cultural racism offered by the Californios in their testimonials to denounce their own oppression do not of course obliterate the discourses of racism we have presented throughout this work, proffered by the Californios themselves as evidence of their superiority with respect to Indians and Blacks. The Californios were, if anything, quite contradictory. But when the invaders were white, the discourses of caste were displaced and replaced by those of class and ethnicity. Yet destitute aristocrats like Vallejo, in discussing their situation in the 1870s, will continue to use discourses of cultural superiority as a defense mechanism, now primarily residual class discourses, vestiges of a feudal mode, positing differences between plebeians and aristocrats. What especially irks Vallejo is that those who uprooted the Californios, that is, the incoming squatters, settlers, and gold-struck adventurers, were nothing but "first-class" rabble (MGV, 5:234), as he ironically puts it. Vallejo's class biases and rancor as a displaced aristocrat are obvious.

Racist discourses and practices are especially virulent in California during the period of the gold rush, when xenophobia swept the mining country. During the two decades following invasion (1846–66), racist vigilantism would lead to mob violence and the lynching of numerous Californios, Latinos, and Chinese immigrants, more often than not denied a fair trial and swiftly executed by vigilance committees. The combination of dispossession and racism has been linked by Vallejo with a period of Californio banditry, but in the testimonial of Coronel we find the best reconstruction of the hostility toward Latinos during the gold rush and during the period of restructuring of the state.

Coronel's testimonial recounts how in 1848, when gold is discovered in Sutter's Coloma mill, he, Ramón Carrillo, Narciso Botello, and several other prospectors set out from Los Angeles to Placer Seco but end up in the *campo de Estanislao* where New Mexicans, Californios (called "personas españolas" by Coronel), and a few Americans are mining (Coronel, 145). After several months of working on the Stanislaus, Coronel and his servants leave to explore an area further north on the invitation of Ramón Carrillo, who reports better findings there. By the time they begin the journey, word reaches them that Carrillo has sold his horses, left his Indian workers with someone else, and returned to Sonoma. Frustrated with this change in plans, Coronel tells of deciding to make a trip into Sonoma with Padilla. What is narrated next is a scene out of the Wild West. The Anglo townsmen, still fighting the war with Mexico and out to gain revenge for the deaths of Cowie and Fowler (two of Frémont's Bear Flaggers), lay an ambush for Padilla at a cantina and attack him violently, claiming that he was part of the Carrillo band responsible for the killing of Cowie and Fowler. Padilla is left half-dead with no one interested in tending to the Californio's life-threatening injuries. Coronel stays on with him in Sonoma until he is able to fend for himself. The description of the events indicates that the war between Mexico and the United States continued to be played out at a moment (late 1848) when the full consequences of U.S. occupation of California are yet unclear to the Californios, who, like Vallejo, still enjoy possession of their properties. In hindsight, the fate of the ambushed Padilla anticipates what is in store for the Californio collectivity.

The testimonial goes on to tell of how Coronel returns to the mining area with supplies several months later, after a trip to the coast, to find ever increasing ethnic diversity and racism. By then the number of miners has multiplied: Californios, Mexicans, Chileans, Peruvians, U.S. migrants, Germans, and so forth (Coronel, 165). The mines are thus constructed as a trope for the California of the 1870s, for already in 1849 the diverse population had established certain spatial patterns of work and housing. Not unlike our barrios and residential communities today, the camp sites would be segregated according to nationality. When rumor circulated that "foreigners" had no right to work the placers and would be pushed out of the mining area (Coronel, 165), the Californios began to recognize that invasion had brought an inversion of both discursive and power relations. No longer dominant, the Californios had now become the dominated population and also the "foreigners," foreigners in their own native land, as Seguín and, later, Vallejo put it (Seguín, iv; MGV, 5:74). Coronel (169–70) notes, not without bitter resentment, that this antiforeigner sentiment would increase once the incoming Anglo miners had learned from the more experienced Latin Americans how to work the placer mines.

In his account, Hittell dismisses the notion of skilled miners from Latin America and makes out placer mining to be a simple task not requiring any particular skill or assistance:

> In 1848 the gold hunters of the Sierra Nevada did not need a scientific education. The method of washing gold was then so simple, and they were so skillful in many kinds of industrial labor, that they learned it quickly. Capital, like scientific education and technical experience, was unnecessary to the early placer miner. With the savings of a week's work he could buy the pick, shovel, pan, and rocker which were his only necessary tools.[32]

Contrary to Coronel's reconstruction of mining camps marked by lawlessness, drunkenness, and lynchings (169–70) and by miners of many nationalities, Hittell literally whitewashes the entire period by asserting that all the miners were "intelligent, enterprising, young and strong men" (34). Deftly erasing the presence of the Other, historian Hittell asserts that there were no foreigners present; it was an entirely "American" enterprise:

> The discovery of the mines was an American achievement. It was the result of the American conquest, and of preparation for American immigrants. It was made by an American, one of a little group of laborers in which all the white men were Americans, as were the first men who devoted themselves to mining. They also were Americans who subsequently invented the sluice and the hydraulic process of placer-washing, and who planned and constructed the great ditches, flumes, and dams that gave a distinctive character to the placer-mining of California. (36)

One of the great advantages of power is that the dominant society is allowed to write and publish its own interpretative schema. Hittell's piece is a prime example of hegemonic historiography. In his account the lynching and assaults on Latinos never took place; mining moreover rapidly developed into a highly technical job requiring a keen mind, technology, and industriousness, suited naturally to the new "white" arrivals. Hittell makes the mining camps sound like hygienic laboratories, as if whatever promoted occupation of invaded lands and stimulated capitalism was good and could not be the work of invaders, despoilers, and lawless, racist, and chauvinist "Americans," but of intelligent and enterprising young and strong men. Hegemonic racist discourses thus work to counter critical/liberal hegemonic perspectives like that of Royce, who would dismiss Hittell with the following: "The common talk about our national divine right to all the gold in California was detestable mock-pious cant, and we knew it" (359). Royce, of course, tries to be fair by finding degenerate individuals among all the miners, both "American" and foreign, at the mining camps. The problem he sees is the lack of reaction by honest men:

> But if the foreign criminals were not the great source of mischief, the honest men certainly did all that they could to make these foreigners such a source. The fearful blindness of the early behavior of the Americans in California towards foreigners is something almost unintelligible. The avaricious thirst for gold among the Americans themselves can alone explain the corruption of heart that induced this blindness. (357)

Royce had good reason to know what could and had happened in the mines, for his parents were part of a gold mining camp when they first came out to California, as his mother's published diary, *A Frontier Lady*, testifies.[33]

Throughout this period, threatening discourses against foreigners proliferated and a veritable "ethnic cleansing" program was put into effect. Coronel thus presents a genealogy of racist practices against Californios and Latinos from the perspective of one situated within what he sets out to recount. In 1848 Coronel witnesses at a mining camp the lynching of a Frenchman and "un español" (it is not clear whether the individual was from Spain or California); both had been accused of stealing. To save them, the Californios try to restore the gold ostensibly stolen, but to no avail. The two are summarily hanged without any kind of armed resistance on the part of the Californios, who feared meeting the same fate. The state of course participated in this discriminatory action as well—were they not all foreigners, all "invaders"?—by approving the Foreign Miners' Tax Law in 1850, which required each foreigner engaged in mining to pay a tax of thirty dollars a month (Royce, 358; the tax was twenty dollars according to Olin, 18). This tax, another evidence of the intersection of race and politics, only promoted more attacks on the foreign miners, who were generally more skilled. When mob violence against Sonoran miners and world reaction to it began to affect commerce, the tax was finally repealed in 1851. Although another law, more moderate, was approved later (Royce, 364), the racism and outrages against foreigners continued, forcing out between five thousand and fifteen thousand foreign miners in a few months (Olin, 19). Juan Antonio Sánchez, a Yaqui Indian from Sonora, was one of the "foreign" miners driven from the mines by the "Missourians" and interviewed by Cerruti (Cerruti, 23–24). By the 1870s Sánchez was making a living in California as a woodchopper.

Coronel makes the point that he initially hoped to avoid the bigotry by leaving the camp where the two Latino men had been lynched, for clearly Californios were just as Latino-looking as South Americans and Sonorans and subject to the same treatment. He moved north where instead of beginning his diggings again, he bought a small store that traded articles and foodstuff for gold. On a trip to Stanislaus to buy goods for his mining post, he tells of witnessing a different type of brutality in which Californios as well as Americans were involved: the slaughter of an entire Indian village, the ultimate in "relocation" practices (see chapter 4).

Royce corroborates Coronel's recollections of the Indian genocide in recognizing that there were even more brutal assaults than mob violence against foreigners. More despicable, he says, were massacres of Indian men, women, and children:

> So ill we indeed did not treat them [the foreigners] as some nations would have done; we did not massacre them wholesale, as Turks might have massacred them: that treatment we reserved for the defenseless Digger Indians, whose villages certain among our miners used on occasion to regard as targets for rifle-practice, or to destroy wholesale with fire, outrage, and murder, as if they had been so many wasps' nests in our gardens at home. (363)

Coronel, after witnessing so much carnage, decides to sell what he has and return to Los Angeles, but friends persuade him to try again, arguing that after all he is a Californio and in theory at least as entitled to prospect for gold as the "americanos."[34] In what follows in the testimonial we see the construct of assimilation rapidly deconstructed. When Coronel's party returns to the placers and finds a rich vein along the American River, they are first visited by "Americans" and by the end of the week are invaded by a group of armed men. The invaders allege that the claim is theirs, whereupon the Californio party, seeing itself surrounded, relinquishes the diggings (Coronel, 184). Coronel recalls that although he could not understand all the English of the invaders, he realized that it was better to leave than to die over a claim. That would be the end of Coronel's mining days. Thus the text bears witness to yet another concession of space, here productive and labor space, to the invaders.

Banditry

The racism and lynching evident in the mines would be paralleled by what Olin calls a "period of lynch law" and vigilantism in the towns and cities (16). Vigilante raids on the barrios and *ranchos* by Anglo settlers were frequent, especially after the young, uprooted *rancheros* and dispossessed miners sought retaliation and revenge in banditry. Vallejo recalls the moment in a double-voiced commentary, at the same time condemnatory and understanding:

> The majority of the young men that had so unjustly been dispossessed, thirsty for vengeance, took off to join the band of Joaquín Murieta and under the command of this fearsome bandit they were able to avenge some of the wrongs inflicted upon them by the North American race. (MGV, 5:237–38)

Here Vallejo adopts the version of the bandit "Joaquín" provided by "Yellow Bird" (John Rollin) Ridge in his romance of Joaquín Murieta in order to reconstruct the pervasive Californio rage against the invaders. In a context in which grievances could only be redressed outside a law that clearly favored one "race," that is, the Anglo-Saxons, any hostile raid against the invaders evoked support from others likewise dispossessed. Whether in fact these were social bandits or common criminals is not in essence the issue; what is decisive is that they were constructed as social bandits by the native population. This construct is taken up not only by the Cherokee Ridge to protest indirectly his own tribe's forced relocation from Georgia to Oklahoma but serves the Californio narrators to denounce their displacement as well. Thus, Vallejo, in part, reconstructs these bandit raids as acts of resistance, as attempts to gain some measure of satisfaction outside a legal system that discriminated against Californios. Given the dominant tendency to represent them simply as criminals, Vallejo here assumes a counter position.[35]

This construct of the bandit as our first rebel with a cause is not, however, what we find in Coronel's testimonial, at least not overtly. Coronel, a small businessman (grape grower and real estate agent) who would serve as local mayor, councilman, and state treasurer (1867–71), was not one to identify or ally himself with outlaws and escaped criminals threatening law and order in Los Angeles:

> One of the most famous outlaws was Murrieta whose band, or at least several of them and perhaps he himself, visited the city, where various crimes were reported. (Coronel, 197)

In his narratives recounting the deaths of General Bean, Sheriff Barton, two members of his posse, and the lynching of several bandits, Coronel goes to great pains to dismiss Ridge's insinuation and the generally held belief that Californios as a group were supportive of the bandits. Given the invasion of Los Angeles by outlaws of all nationalities fleeing south, he argues, the citizens of the city were forced to create their own "voluntary police force," that is, their own vigilante committee (197). As Pitt (164) points out, Coronel, Andrés Pico, Tomás Sánchez, and Juan Padilla served on a committee with nine "Americans" to bring "order" to the city by arresting all suspicious characters and determining on their own whether these men should be expelled from the community or allowed to stay. Coronel, for his part, insists that when he and Manuel Requena were appointed to one such commission after the murder of General Bean, he was at first unwilling to participate, not wishing to proceed outside the law, until it was explained that all he would have to do was to take down the declarations of the arrested and submit them to the public to avoid accusations of partiality (Coronel, 198–99). Although the three held men were found to have committed other crimes but not the murder of Bean, the vigilante committee and the town itself decreed that the important thing was that someone pay for Bean's death, and so the three Californio bandits, along with a fourth accused murderer, were lynched (Coronel, 199–200). Similar lynchings took place, with several accused being taken out of jail and hanged on the spot (Coronel, 202). As told by Coronel, the bandits, who formed part of Murieta's band, were a murderous lot who turned on each other and killed innocent people. The fact that they were Californios led the Anglos to suspect that they were being aided and abetted by other Californios, suspicions that led to ethnic divisiveness until the Californios "righted" matters by agreeing to participate in the formation of a posse that brought the criminals to justice, albeit vigilante justice (Coronel, 207). In one case dealing with the death of a merchant in San Juan Capistrano, the vigilantes, headed this time by Tomás Sánchez and Andrés Pico, apprehended the outlaws, hanged three of the bandits, and brought the rest in to be tried and hanged in town (Coronel, 207). Far from condemning this vigilante action, it is important to note that Coronel credits Californio cooperation and especially the participation of Sánchez for putting an end to the ethnic conflict and bringing about a reconciliation between the two sides.

As elsewhere in the Californio testimonials, the issue of the addressee of the dictated narrative becomes painfully clear as Coronel acquiesces to dominant society, represented here by Savage and Bancroft, by revealing himself more concerned with countering rumors of Californio collaboration with banditry rather than with using these reconstructed accounts for denouncing unequal treatment of "la gente del país," as he refers to fellow Californios. Nor is he ready to condemn rampant vigilante violence and the lynching of many Californios throughout the state, as the editor of the Los Angeles El Clamor Público, Francisco P. Ramírez, so frequently did (Weber, 174; Ríos-Bustamante and Castillo, 99). In one letter published in El Clamor, we learn that vigilante committees made up solely of Anglos (and in one case including the justice of the peace from San Gabriel) were indiscriminately lynching and butchering Mexicanos. The "strange fruit" upon a hanging tree, viewed by a visiting Frenchman, were all Mexicans (El Clamor, 1857, in Weber, 176).

And yet, the apparent accommodation of a leader of the Mexican community in Los Angeles is interestingly dealt with and deconstructed as Coronel ends his account of the bandits with a coda recounting the less than glorious end met by the Anglos who pursued the bandits: one dying violently, killed by his own father-in-law; one paralyzed; one dying in poverty due to alcoholism; two others gunned down as they fired indiscriminately into Abel Stearns's home on the day of a party (Coronel, 209–10). The focus on this final outcome, a sort of ironic twist, and the construction of these vigilante leaders as villains ultimately reveal Coronel's condemnation of vigilante action against Californios and the law's complicity in its failure to prosecute those who robbed and killed *mexicanos*. Coronel was neverthless reticent to tie the banditry to the dispossession and disempowerment of the Californios as Tiburcio Vásquez (Vásquez interview in Weber, 227) or Vallejo would do.

During the decades of the 1850s and 1860s, Tiburcio Vásquez was known first as a cattle rustler and stagecoach robber, for which reason he was sentenced to San Quentin in 1857 and released in 1863; later, he was known as a robber and murderer. In 1874 he was again arrested, tried, and ultimately hanged in 1877. Before his death Vásquez gave an interview in which he represents himself as a social bandit and expresses his resentment against the invaders displacing Californios in all spheres of social life:

> A spirit of hatred and revenge took possession of me. I had numerous fights in defense of what I believed to be my rights and those of my countrymen. The officers were continually in pursuit of me. I believed we were unjustly and wrongfully deprived of the social rights which belonged to us. (227)

To avoid violence, he resolved to live distant from populated areas, but even there, he says in his testimonial, he felt persecuted. Finally, he goes to his mother and tells her that he planned to begin a life of crime as he was constantly being falsely accused: "I asked for and obtained her blessing, and at once commenced the career of a robber" (228). After his first imprisonment, finding himself repeatedly accused of one crime or another, he goes back to a life of crime, although he insists he "always tried to avoid bloodshed" (228). Similar accounts are provided by other Californios, as, for example, Francisco Peralta, who reports that Vásquez was whipped viciously during his first time in prison for horse stealing, and for this reason "young Tiburcio took to the life of a banditti" (Cerruti, 72). Displacement, persecution, false accusations, and unequal and brutal treatment are said to drive Vásquez to a life of crime; his mother's blessing, in turn, provides the necessary closure, the older Californios' recognition that for the dispossessed generation there was no recourse within the system.

Vásquez, the grandson of José Tiburcio Vásquez, one of the founding fathers of San José, is not mentioned by Vallejo, who prefers to refer to the "constructed" Murieta, composed by Ridge on the basis of a state reward posted on the capture of the bandit "Joaquín."[36] Only after a bandit was captured and beheaded was he assigned the last name "Murrieta" (later "Murieta") (Jackson, xxiv). Like Vásquez, the fictional Joaquín Murieta from the novel by John Rollin Ridge began a life of crime after he was provoked by injustice. Unlike Vásquez, the fictional Murieta was not a native Californio but an immigrant who came from Sonora to California during the gold rush. As emplotted in the Rollin Ridge text, this young handsome man of noble sentiments, full of hope and accompanied by his girlfriend Rosita, begins working a mine in the Stanislaus placers at the age of eighteen. Within a short period he is displaced from the mine, he is beaten, and he sees his girlfriend raped; subsequently displaced from a farm where he tries to work and again is falsely accused and flogged, he learns that his half-brother has been lynched. The injustice, displacement, and dispossession suffered by Murieta lead him to a life of crime, bloody killings, and robberies. What is interesting about this 1854 "dime novel" is that what starts out as a quest for individual revenge becomes by the second year of murders and assaults a collective movement, said quite mechanically to be headquartered and masterminded in Sonora, Mexico. The goal of the bandits is to steal thousands of horses and enough money to support an army of fifteen hundred to two thousand men able to invade southern California to inflict collective revenge for the dispossession, lynching, and mistreatment of all *mexicanos* and Californios. Upon the bandit's death, the "movement" is said to become undone. Hegemonic forces win out at novel's end when the ranger Harry Love cuts the head of the bandit and reestablishes law and order in the state of California.

Vallejo, who saw the young disenfranchised Californios as social bandits willing to seek revenge for the injustices suffered at the hands of the invaders, incorporates some of these Ridgian constructs into his own analysis, but he does remind the reader that these bandits failed to "avenge ... the grievances inflicted upon them by the North American race" (MGV, 5:237). Vacillating between condemnation and sympathy, Vallejo's comments are contradictory, for while the bandits' objective is constructed as just, like that of the fictional Murieta, they are also called "incautos," naive and reckless, for proceeding outside the law; as a consequence they end up lynched or in prison (MGV, 5:237–38). Some of the bandits end up in insane asylums, in some cases undoubtedly due to alcoholism—a rare ailment before invasion, Vallejo goes on to insist, rejecting in this way the stereotypical portrayal of Californios as indolent drunkards. National origin or ethnicity is thus closely linked in Vallejo's analysis with economic and political positioning and with retaliation. This clustering of identities, this awareness of the overlapping and intersection of discourses, would become a constant in subsequent Chicano literature, as would the notion of resistance, whether through the courts or by other means.

Resistance is throughout paralleled by resentment, frustration, and psychological trauma. Along these same lines, other Californio testimonials point to insanity as an increasingly prevalent consequence of dispossession and disempowerment. In his comments on the murder of his uncle José de los Reyes Berreyesa and the two Haro boys by Frémont's men, Antonio Berreyesa, son of Nicolás Berreyesa, recalls that the assassination of his brother, the loss of thirty-five or forty horses robbed by Carlos Weber for the pro-U.S. California Battalion, and the raid of his home and that of other *rancheros* drove Don Nicolás to a state of depression. By 1849 the elder Berreyesa had suffered the invasion of squatters who staked claims on his land at Milpitas and killed his cattle and horses. The harassment of the Berreyesa family by squatters and ruthless land speculators interesting in taking over his lands while he tried to prove his title was valid in the end drove the old man insane. To add to his troubles he learned in 1854 that another Berreyesa (Demesio), accused of the murder of an American, had been arrested and lynched:

> My father, upon hearing the news, abandoned all his business affairs, became sad, and ended up losing his mind completely, without being able to have Jakes or the butcher-lawyer removed from his lands. (Berreyesa, 14–15)

In his moments of lunacy, Berreyesa writes Alvarado expecting help from the former *gobernador*, but in his few moments of lucidity he advises his sons to leave the country, where mob and legal violence against Californios have become prevalent.

> Of all the Californio families, perhaps ours is the one that has more cause to complain against the bad faith of the adventurers and squatters and against the disloyalty of the American lawyers. (Berreyesa, 21)

The impact of land loss and disempowerment on the Californio families is likewise narrated in the Californio novel *The Squatter and the Don*, written in 1885 by Ruiz de Burton. The specific plight of the Berreyesa family would be the focus one hundred years later of the Chicano novel *Reto en el paraíso* (1983) by Alejandro Morales. In Morales's novel lunacy becomes a trope for displacement and dispossession. Ethnic identity is here displaced by family identity and the latter, in turn, by lunacy, a liminal space in the disjuncture created by disempowerment and a lack of political direction. In *Reto en el paraíso,* a century after the death of Nicolás Berreyesa his great-great-grandson Dennis Berreyesa Coronel, a technocrat serving the capitalist interests of the Liffords (modeled after the Irvine family), who dispossessed his ancestors, is displaced anew, but now psychologically rather than in terms of land and power. In need of an anchor to ground himself within consumer society, he reaches out to an imaginary space, nineteenth-century California, constructed in the memoirs left by his great-grand-uncle Antonio Francisco Coronel. This manuscript allows for a temporal and spatial shift not to utopia, but rather to the time-space after banishment from paradise, when the Californios were beginning to be geographically, economically, and politically displaced and dispossessed to the point of their proletarianization and marginalization. Paradise is not attainable; it is an inaccessible aristocratic utopia that the main character Dennis can only reconstruct parodically, by creating a simulacrum, a living-room forest made up of numerous potted plants among which he can crawl naked. The collision of these various time-spaces will produce in this case not a liminal ethnic space, which he rejects from the onset and with it all ties to the Chicano Movement, but a solipsistic state of lunacy and self-absorption, a dysfunctional individualist space that offers escape from social contradictions and conflict, repeating a route taken years before by his ancestor Nicolás Berreyesa.

Ethnicism

Unlike Morales's novel, the Californio testimonials produce spaces of collective identity. Here for the first time in California we find widespread use of the construct of "la raza," "la raza latina," or, as Coronel (198) prefers, "la raza española," a construct that allows for an alliance of Latinos of different nationalities in similar situations, concretely those during the gold rush and during what Pitt calls the "race war" in Los Angeles (148), when in-group differences are blurred and they are all perceived as one and subject to the same racist violence. This construct does not arise during the Spanish-Mexican periods, for then the distinctions are *gente de razón* versus *indios* ("bárbaros infieles"); later, generational differences and economic/political interests pit *los hijos del país*, that is, *los californios* against *los mexicanos* and later, *los extranjeros*. After invasion, when Californios, *mexicanos*, and, by extension, any Latin American become undifferentiated "greasers," as both Salvador Vallejo and Alvarado explain (Alvarado, 5:164; S. Vallejo, 124), and reside in the same barrios under similar economic conditions, there develops an "imagined community" of Spanish speakers, dispossessed, disenfranchised, and subordinated by a majority Anglo population.

Like Argüello, Vallejo will also speak of "la raza latina," "el futuro de mi raza," and of a necessary reconciliation of the two antagonistic ethnicities — "las dos razas" (MGV, 3:332; 4:371; 5:133). The testimonials thus open up a new liminal space of ethnicity that is comprehensive and defined only in its antagonism to the conqueror (MGV, 5:133). This ethnicism, this new social space, enables the construction not only of an aggregate identity that goes beyond national origin and unites all the Spanish-speaking population of Latino/Mexicano/Spanish origin in California, but also of a site from which the subaltern can launch its ideological/political "war of position."[37]

The articulation of ethnicity with language in the construction of an "imagined community" of "la raza" is further enabled by the publishing of several Spanish-language newspapers from the 1850s to the 1870s in Los Angeles, San Francisco, and Santa Barbara. Especially crucial in Los Angeles were *El Clamor Público*, *La Crónica*, *Las Dos Repúblicas*, and *El Joven*, all dedicated to a defense of the community. As Ríos-Bustamante and Castillo indicate, "the press took the lead in condemning lynch mobs, job discrimination, illegal land seizure and racial violence." Most important, these publications developed "ethnic consciousness among Spanish-speaking Angelinos" and protested segregation and racism (101–2).

Ethnicity and language are frequently conjoined in several of the Californio testimonials and additionally are intersected by a strong sense of citizens' rights. In these narratives there is already a modern notion of civil rights, including the rights of linguistic minorities to an appropriate education, a precept validated with the Lau decision only in 1974 and the Equal Educational Opportunities Act, also of 1974.[38] Although the institution of public education after 1846 is praised by several of the Californios, including Vallejo and Alvarado, who often recall the poor instruction offered Californio children in the past by *presidio* soldiers, there is at the same time a critique of government deception for not keeping its pledges to the Californios and providing them with the promised schooling. The French had their school, the Germans had theirs, but, asks Vallejo, where was the school for Spanish speakers?

> In the schools of San Francisco they teach French and German. Why is there not a class to teach Spanish? Is the Californian population less deserving perhaps than that of the French and German? Is it perhaps less intelligent? Perhaps it is and in that case its only chance for redemption is through an education. Why is it being denied? The reason is clear: the German population controls thirty thousand votes, while the number of Hispano-American voters is barely four thousand; the former are praised while these are detested. (MGV, 5:240)

Vallejo comes out as one of our first advocates for bilingual education and instruction in the Spanish language for Spanish-speaking children. In effect he was here a spokesman for positions that were daily assumed in the Spanish-language press in the state, for language then as often today was linked to ethnicity, and language maintenance to resistance to cultural erasure.[39] Perhaps not so amazingly, the problems that Vallejo pinpoints in these lines are still the major issues today: a minority and fragmented Latino society lacking in significant political power. The power of the vote is his underlying theme, and in this Vallejo validates the very system he criticizes.

The question of minority rights is also clearly spelled out in Vallejo's essay. The lack of equity is a political issue that Vallejo recognizes to be "harmful and prejudicial for the Californios" (MGV, 5:240). We have been treated like a conquered nation, he protests, and not like citizens who remained in the United States of their own free will, entitled to rights and representation:

> The time has not yet arrived for commenting on or judging the actions of the authorities that have governed the country during the past twenty years, but the coming generation will fulfill this task. I do not doubt that it will agree with me when I declare that despite the Treaty of Guadalupe-Hidalgo, the North Americans treated the Californios like a conquered people and not like citizens that voluntarily agreed to become part of the great family that, protected by the glorious pendant that flew proudly over Bunker Hill, challenges the European monarchs who, seated on their tottering thrones, look enviously toward California and other cities that are included within the great federation of the sons of liberty. (MGV, 5:240–41)

In this, his final jeremiad, he traces the oppression of this population and stresses a number of problems still with us today. More important, he opens up the problem as one to be dealt with in the years to come: future generations will provide the ultimate verdict on the injustices suffered by the Californios during the nineteenth century and will seek to have their grievances redressed. Yet even at this low point in his life, Vallejo wants very much to see himself represented as antimonarchist, federalist, and the liberal defender of the republic, his inner bitterness and resentment notwithstanding.

The dominant antagonisms presented in these testimonials are thus ethnic (racial) and political: "our race" versus the foreigners/invaders. This antagonism is intersected by discourses of territoriality (homeland versus conquest) and language, tied not only to education but to countering strategies, as made clear by Rosalía Vallejo de Leese, who, like Argüello and Vallejo, resented linguistic oppression as much as the Yankee invasion. When asked by Cerruti to recall the events of the Bear Flag party, she provides a brief account and ends with these words:

> I could relate many a misdeed of the Bear Flag crowd, but not wishing to detain you any longer I will close with the remark that those hated men inspired me with such a large "dose of hate" against their race that though twenty-eight years have elapsed since that time, I have not yet forgotten the insults they heaped upon me, and not being desirous of coming in contact with them I have abstained from learning their language. (Vallejo de Leese, 6)

Implicit in these ethnic/linguistic distinctions are discourses of religion, for throughout this period there is a strong bias against Catholics, as is evident in portrayals of villains in contemporary nineteenth-century American historiography as dark and Catholic.[40] Each ethnic construct, then, embodies several subconstructs and exemplifies a basic economic and political antagonism:

Californios ("our race")	versus	Yankees ("foreigners")
Spanish language		English language
Catholic		Protestant
conquered		conqueror

This complex construct of ethnic identity blurs to a certain extent upon closer examination in view of particular contradictions. First, among the leading families, men like Alvarado and Vallejo were at best nominally Catholic, given their liberal ideas and anticlericalism. Their ideas were more akin to those of Freemasonry, but they never broke with the church and became Protestants, as did the Freemason Romualdo Pacheco in the 1860s.[41] The conqueror/conquered dialectic running throughout the testimonials also conceals the degree to which some members of the ruling families accommodated to the new political system, at least for a time, until the restructuring of the economy led to the dissolution of particular social spaces, like the *ranchos*, and to the ruin of these *hijos del país*. Many of the younger Californios, and even older ones like Coronel and the widowed Angustias de la Guerra, would marry Anglos, learn English, and adjust to the changing times. But among the older Californios, even those who participated in the new political structure and to a certain extent controlled the Latino vote, there remained a strong sense of obligation and allegiance to fellow Californios, especially among men like Pablo de la Guerra, Coronel, and Reginaldo del Valle.

In the Californios' various accommodations to hegemonic discourses and practices we become intensely aware of the mediated nature of these testimonials, for clearly Coronel, Vallejo, and others are careful about what they say given that the ultimate addressee is envisioned principally to be the ruling class of the United States. The very conditions that make these mediated narratives possible are what make the concealing of resentment and bitterness difficult but unavoidable. Yet Vallejo, who tried to convince his friends that he accepted his dispossession because it was a situation that he had brought upon himself (i.e., by advocating annexation to the United States), is unable to continue suppressing his bitterness and resentment in his last chapter.

In other instances, and despite an awareness of being stripped of political and economic agency and being the targets of race hatred themselves, the Californios reassume nativist positions that in the past often led them to distinctions between themselves and *mexicanos* and now lead them to derogatory remarks about newly arrived "gambusinos" (miners) and other immigrants, including Mexicans, Peruvians, and Chileans, alongside Australians, Mormons, Frenchmen, Italians, and Germans, all seen as part of an invading population. Thus Vallejo in his final essay assumes an aristocratic distance from all the Latin Americans that have come since 1846 by including them in his broad list of foreigners with undesirable characteristics such as alcoholism, prostitution, gambling, indolence, lasciviousness, and delinquency. Rather than using the concept of "la raza" to encompass all Latinos, Vallejo, like other Californios, was seemingly bent on a course of divisiveness, the same counterproductive practice they had maintained in the past and that had led to regional and political divisions within Alta California. The diversity within the barrios would in time blur national differences between working-class Latinos, Mexicanos, and Californios, especially when they were a small minority. Among the elite Californio families, as between the Carrillo and de la Guerra families, political feuds and dissension would continue into the 1870s (Genini and Hitchman, 56).[42]

Faced with racism, unequal treatment before the law, dispossession, and disempowerment, the Californios will ironically not only assume an aristocratic position in relation to newly arrived immigrants, the very people that at one time Vallejo had been eager to welcome to the northern frontier, but construct a parallel imaginary space as well: the space of moral superiority, deployable equally against Anglos and Latinos. Thus Vallejo, while noting the commercial and agricultural benefits accrued since annexation, ends his memoirs regretting the moral deficit in the state and, notably, the deterioration of the patriarchy with the influx of immigrants of immoral character:

> In conclusion, I will say that in my humble judgment, the change of government that took place in California on the seventh of July, 1846, has redounded in the benefit of agriculture and commerce of the young state but in detriment of the morality of the inhabitants, whose patriarchal customs have little by little been demoralized with daily contact with so many immoral persons who from all the corners of the known world emigrated to this my homeland, and a large part of the blame and responsibility can be rightfully laid at the feet of the government of the Union and the state. (MGV, 5:239)

After venting his spleen and offering his political and economic critique, Vallejo returns to an ethical ethnocentric posture, reducing the problem to a moral question. Why? After being displaced economically, politically, and culturally, the high moral ground was the only terrain to which the Californios could lay claim. All they could summon up was a sense of moral superiority and indignation, a sense of being victimized by inferior immoral beings immigrating to California in unprecedented numbers.

Nativism and haughty self-righteousness are part of the discourses of resentment that the Californios wield to express their bitterness and acute awareness of disempowerment. In their attempt to demonstrate their superiority to foreigners, they are often prone to voice hegemonic prejudices against Chinese immigrants. Vallejo's most ethnocentric/racist comments are reserved for the Chinese, accused of damaging the moral fiber of the populace through prostitution and the introduction of syphilis. Of course the syphilis and other venereal diseases as well as smallpox and measles that the Californios themselves had spread among the Indians go unremarked. Vallejo's disparaging comments against the Chinese are not the only racist comments against Asians in these testimonials. Sinforiana Cárdenas, who had come to California from Mexico in 1850, refers in a similar fashion to the Chinese who "like the locusts of Egypt invaded our state" (Cerruti, 47). Unfortunately this racism would be more than discursive. After 1849 both Californios and Anglos would participate in mob violence against the Chinese in the cities and towns of California, as occurred in the massacre in Los Angeles in 1871 that left at least eighteen Chinese dead.[43] The Chinese population was also often the target of bandits (Pitt, 77) and as late as 1881 Representative Pacheco was speaking in favor of a Chinese Exclusion Bill in Congress (Genini and Hitchman, 158). Thus in their statements against Asians and Blacks throughout their testimonials, the Californios, despite being the object of prejudice and mob violence themselves, express a bias and an animosity against the Chinese and African Americans similar to that voiced by the new majority Anglo population. Forged in a race- and caste-based society, the Californios unfortunately fell back on these operative categories, incapable of constructing an interethnic identity and alliance on the basis of class and ethnic oppression, an "imagined interethnic community" still in the making and necessary today.

Looking back into the Future

> Para que los que lean mis escritos se formen una idea de la manera en que los norteamericanos trataron a los californios cuando se posesionaron de este país.
>
> M. G. Vallejo

The Californio testimonials are above all sites of counterdiscursive engagement, full of resentment and bitterness, written to protest and deauthorize hegemonic reconstructions of the past as well as to protest practices of oppression and displacement. Vallejo makes known the objective of these testimonials when he explains that he feels compelled to write so that future generations will know what happened to the Californios in the process of becoming a minority population in California. The new majority treated them not with the same goodwill that the Californios had extended to them when as newly arrived immigrants they were provided with land, tools, and food; no, they treated them as a conquered population, Vallejo declares angrily. The Californios' resentment at having been betrayed and abused runs deep:

> The Americans as soon as they saw that they were a majority treated us not like brothers but like a conquered people. (MGV, 4:388)

In addition to a deep resentment against the invaders, there is a thinly veiled sense of frustration with themselves as leaders for not having rallied and struck back, and an accommodating facade of resignation at being powerless and devoid of agency before a conquering majority.

Their strategy in the testimonials is to marshal ideological correctives against dominant historiography; assume a collective stance against racism, linguistic oppression, dispossession, vigilantism, judicial inequality, and historical erasure; and reconstruct their own history, however contradictory it may be. Textually, then, the testimonial narrators reconstruct pre-1846 social practices, defined by exploration, civilization (i.e., exploitation) of the Indians, violence against the Indians, regional Californio conflicts, primitive accumulation, land distribution, and struggles first against the church and then against the invaders, all of which they invariably articulate with postinvasion practices. These subsequent clashes and conflicts opened up new social spaces but their limited options in the new game plan cast the Californios as pawns with a circumscribed field of action, where survival took precedence over dominance and where inscribing themselves textually was the vehicle sought to mitigate against discursive annihilation.

If in the 1870s the Californios see themselves devoid of agency after dispossession and disempowerment, in the reconstructed narratives they reacquire a measure of imaginary control as a collectivity (what we have termed a reclamation or recovery project). They also participate discursively in the production of a new social space, the space of ethnicity, generated by intersecting territorial, genealogical, liberal, cultural, and nationalist discourses as much as by discourses of oppression and marginalization. This ethnic space, erased within hegemonic historiography, was in part already being produced in Spanish-language newspapers published within communities of Mexican origin (Neri, 198–99). In view of Neri's comments that in the late nineteenth century the focus of the Spanish-language press is still on Mexico, what distinguishes these testimonials is that the focus is not Mexico at all, but California and the United States, for the collective subjectivity that these narrators seek to construct and reconstruct is that of Californios, not Mexicans. Through the construct of collective ethnic identity these

Californios seek to reposition themselves and secure for themselves agency and a self-authorized place in the history of California and in the social formation within California.

But the testimonials present us with more than a textualized struggle through the reappropriation of the past and a construction of ethnic and class identities. They are a reconstruction of the Californio ideological field and as such allow for a charting and disarticulation of Californio discourses of racism, caste, patriarchy, class, nation, gender, region, and finally ethnicity, and of the shifting ideological parameters since 1769. This ambiguity within the ideological field is, as we have sought to show, conditioned and characterized by socioeconomic restructuring, social displacement, and relocation as well as by interdiscursive relations. It has been our purpose here to disarticulate these interconnecting and intersecting discourses and to reveal the contradictions embedded in these nineteenth-century narratives in hopes of revealing insights into ensembles of relations and networks of ideological discourses still with us today.

As pointed out by Jameson, the past speaks to us about our present and about our future, especially about present and future struggles, about present and future social spaces, and we are compelled to respond to that past in the degree that it is a measure of the future. In a way it is ironic that only in this century has Mexico for reasons not of her own making begun to populate actively what was her northern frontier. By reactivating these Californio discourses, Chicanos are also no doubt similarly engaged in a process of reterritorialization of representational spaces and in setting down the terms of engagement for present and future political and ideological struggles.

Notes

Parenthetical citations in the text refer to works from the testimonial references list (which follows this notes section) or to works already cited in that particular chapter. All English translations of original Spanish material, unless otherwise documented, are my own.

1. Testimonials as Dependent Production

1. Fredric Jameson, *Postmodernism; or, The Cultural Logic of Late Capitalism* (Durham: Duke University Press, 1991), 54.

2. The denial of property rights to Californios led assemblyman Pablo de la Guerra, on his 1855 trip to Havana, to warn that what took place in California may well occur in Cuba or Sonora should either come under U.S. control (de la Guerra, 4).

3. Spencer C. Olin Jr., *California Politics 1846–1920: The Emerging Corporate State* (San Francisco: Boyd and Fraser, 1981), 15, 35, 37.

4. Treaty of Guadalupe-Hidalgo, cited in David J. Weber, ed., *Foreigners in Their Native Land: Historical Roots of the Mexican Americans* (Albuquerque: University of New Mexico Press, 1973), 164.

5. Annotations for Seguín and M. G. Vallejo, as well as for all nineteenth-century testimonials, speeches, letters, diaries, and so on, both published and unpublished, can be found in the testimonial reference section at the end of the book. Hereafter all references to Mariano Guadalupe Vallejo's testimonial are cited as MGV, and those of his brother José de Jesús Vallejo as JJV.

6. Partha Chatterjee, *Nationalist Thought and the Colonial World: A Derivative Discourse* (London: Zed Books, 1986), 11.

7. Terry Eagleton, "Nationalism: Irony and Commitment," in Terry Eagleton, Fredric Jameson, and Edward Said, *Nationalism, Colonialism, and Literature* (Minneapolis: University of Minnesota Press, 1990), 31.

8. Antonio Gramsci, *Selections from the Prison Notebooks* (New York: International Publishers, 1978), 88.

9. Paul John Eakin, ed., *American Autobiography: Retrospect and Prospect* (Madison: University of Wisconsin Press, 1991), 15.

10. Anthony Smith, *The Ethnic Origins of Nations* (Oxford: Basil Blackwell, 1986), 149.

11. E. J. Hobsbawm, *Nations and Nationalism since 1780* (New York: Cambridge University Press, 1992), 73.

12. See, for example, Thomas Jefferson Farnham, *Travels in the Californias and Scenes in the Pacific Ocean* (New York: Saxton & Miles, 1844).

13. See John Beverley, "Anatomía del testimonio," *Revista de crítica literaria* (Lima, Peru) 13 (1987): 10. See also Genaro M. Padilla, "The Recovery of Chicano Nineteenth Century Autobiography," *American Quarterly* 40, no. 3 (September 1988): 287.

14. See Elena Poniatowska, *La noche de Tlatelolco. Testimonios de historia oral* (Mexico City: Biblioteca Era, 1971). See also Oscar Lewis, *Cinco familias* (Mexico City: Fondo de Cultura Económica, 1961).

15. See Rigoberta Menchú, *Me llamo Rigoberta Menchú y así me nació la conciencia,* ed. Elizabeth Burgos (Mexico City: Siglo XXI Editores, 1988).

16. Hugo Achugar, "Historias paralelas/historias ejemplares: La historia y la voz del otro," *Revista de crítica literaria latinoamericana* 18, no. 36 (September 1992): 57.

17. George Yúdice, "El conflicto de posmodernidades," *Nuevo Texto crítico* 4, no. 7 (1991): 20.

18. Jorge Ruffinelli, "Los 80: ¿ingreso a la posmodernidad?" *Nuevo Texto crítico* 3, no. 6 (1990): 39.

19. David Harvey, *The Condition of Postmodernity* (London: Basil Blackwell Ltd., 1992), 159, 271. See also Jameson (1991: 36).

20. Although Padilla in his analysis classifies these testimonials as autobiographies, there are clear and significant points of difference that warrant their classification as testimonials rather than as autobiographies. See Padilla (286).

21. Georges Gusdorf, "Conditions and Limits of Autobiography," *Autobiography: Essays Theoretical and Critical,* ed. James Olney (Princeton: Princeton University Press, 1980), 29.

22. Arnold Krupat, "Native American Autobiography and the Synecdochic Self," *American Autobiography,* ed. Paul John Eakin, 179.

23. George Tays, "Mariano Guadalupe Vallejo and Sonoma," *California Historical Society Quarterly* 16, no. 3 (September 1937): 229.

24. See Ruiz de Burton's biography of her grandfather, José Manuel Ruiz, completed on Bancroft form.

25. Hubert Howe Bancroft, *Literary Industries* (San Francisco: The History Company Publishers, 1890), 399.

26. English translation from Bancroft (1890: 440). Vallejo's actual words, from *La Voz del Nuevo Mundo* (November 30, 1875), are as follows: "aunque durante muchos años he ocupado en California una posición prominente, sólo he aludido a mi persona, cuando me ha sido forzoso hacerlo en cumplimiento de las exigencias que son el norte del historiador imparcial." As is clear, Bancroft took liberties with the Californios' discourses even when translating their letters: the last clause should read, "only when the impartiality demanded of the historian required it."

27. John Beverley, "Through All Things Modern: Second Thoughts on Testimonio," *Boundary 2* (Summer 1991): 21.

28. Doris Sommer, " 'Not Just a Personal Story': Women's Testimonios and the Plural Self," *Life/Lines: Theorizing Women's Autobiography,* ed. Bella Brodzki and Celeste Schenck (Ithaca: Cornell University Press, 1988), 119.

29. Gayatri Chakravorty Spivak, "Imperialism and Sexual Difference," *The Current in Criticism,* ed. Clayton Koelb and Virgil Lokke (West Lafayette, Ind.: Purdue University Press, 1987), 324.

30. Gayatri Chakravorty Spivak, "Can the Subaltern Speak?" *Marxism and the Interpretation of Culture,* ed. Cary Nelson and Lawrence Grossberg (Urbana, Ill.: University of Illinois Press, 1988), 287.

31. Benedict Anderson, *Imagined Communities* (London: Verso, 1983), 40.

32. Hubert Howe Bancroft, *History of California* (San Francisco: The History Company Publishers, 1885–86), 4:649. The various history tones will hereafter be cited by volume and page.

33. In 1825 Augustín Vicente Zamorano, a Mexican army officer accompanying the new governor of the territory, José María Echeandía, as his executive secretary, brought over a small seal press for the purpose of stamping and imprinting government seals on official papers and documents. There would be no printer in Alta California until 1833, so official transactions requiring the use of "sealed" paper (*papel sellado*) were dependent on a supply from Mexico before 1825. See Herbert Fahey, *Early Printing in California: From Its Beginning in the Mexican Territory to Statehood (September 9, 1850)* (San Francisco: The Book Club of California, 1956), 6.

34. Fahey's research indicates that the press was contracted for in 1829 or 1830 and shipped from Boston to Henry Augustus Peirce in Honolulu on the *Lagoda* by James Hunnewell, his partner. Because Peirce, a trader, apparently had a change of plans and rejected the equipment, the ship had it on board when it set anchor in 1833 in California, where the press was acquired by Zamorano. The Ramage printer was in operation by 1834 when Zamorano printed a circular, *Aviso Público*, informing the public that his printing services were available. The press would henceforth serve for the printing in Spanish of announcements, laws, proclamations, procedures to be followed in the secularization of the missions, orders of deportation (as in the case of the Padrés and Hijar colonists), and for the publication, for example, of Governor Figueroa's *Manifiesto* (Fahey, 26–29).

35. A chaplain-journalist on the frigate *Congress*, which had dropped anchor in Monterey, and a dentist-printer who had participated in the Bear Flag revolt took over the press and published the first California newspaper, the *Californian*. Most of this newspaper's text was in English, although a small portion was in Spanish, as was an extra edition published to list the rules and regulations under the new U.S. government. In his study of early California newspapers, Kemble notes the many daily and weekly newspapers published in English and lists as well several French-language newspapers published in California during the decade of the 1850s, but cites only a handful of Spanish-language newspapers with the views of "los hijos del país"; see Edward C. Kemble, *A History of California Newspapers 1846–1858* (Los Gatos, Calif.: The Talisman Press, 1962), 235. Neri, however, notes the publication of several Spanish-language newspapers in Los Angeles and San Francisco during the nineteenth century; see Michael C. Neri, "A Journalistic Portrait of the Spanish-Speaking People of California, 1868–1925," *Quarterly of the Historical Society of Southern California* 55, no. 2 (Summer 1973): 194.

36. John Watson Caughey, *Hubert Howe Bancroft: Historian of the West* (Berkeley: University of California Press, 1946), 57–66.

37. Hubert Howe Bancroft, *Retrospection, Political and Personal* (New York: The Bancroft Company Publishers, 1912), 329.

38. Leland Stanford was among the individuals who agreed to pay thousands of dollars for the inclusion of their biographies. When Stanford complained about the agreement and refused to pay, the article on his life was "killed" (Caughey, 323). See H. H. Bancroft, *Chronicles of the Builders of the Commonwealth: Historical Character Study*. 7 vols. and index (San Francisco: The History Company, 1891–92).

39. Actually, Vallejo was then only a lieutenant colonel, but after being named commander general in 1836 he was often called "General" by his friends.

40. Fredric Jameson, *The Ideologies of Theory: Essays 1971–1986. Volume 2: The Syntax of History* (Minneapolis: University of Minnesota Press, 1988), 153.

41. David Levin, *History as Romantic Art* (New York: Harcourt, Brace & World, 1959), 25–26.

42. Rosaura Sánchez and Beatrice Pita, "Introduction," to *The Squatter and the Don,* by María Amparo Ruiz de Burton (Houston: Arte Público Press, 1993).

43. English translation from Bancroft (1890: 440). Clearly Bancroft took liberties in the translation of Vallejo's letter, as is evident when compared with the original text of the letter published in *La Voz del Nuevo Mundo* (San Francisco, November 30, 1875): "Su trabajo tendrá mejor aceptación que el mío, pues mientras no faltaría quien me tachase de parcial, Ud. amparado por su fama tan laboriosamente adquirida, no tendrá que vencer los obstáculos que en mi daño levantaría la envidia y el rencor." Once in his power, the letter, like all the testimonials, was subject to reconstruction by Bancroft's staff.

44. Vallejo's words are as follows: "Hasta ha poco, tuve intención de hacer imprimir mi manuscrito y presentarlo al mundo tal cual está" (*La Voz del Nuevo Mundo,* San Francisco, February 30, 1875).

45. After his historical account was destroyed in a fire, Vallejo had almost lost all hope: "Desde entonces perdí la esperanza de ver escrita una historia completa de nuestra querida patria. Por fortuna el señor Bancroft ha asumido la ardua tarea; él es dotado de inteligencia, posee una fortuna colosal y guiado por nosotros puede ser el Mesías de los californios" (MGV documents, 597).

46. Andrew Levine, Elliot Sober, and Erik Olin Wright, "Marxism and Methodological Individualism," *New Left Review* 162 (March–April 1987): 67–84.

47. Albert K. Weinberg, *Manifest Destiny: A Study of Nationalist Expansionism in American History* (Baltimore: Johns Hopkins University Press, 1935), 211.

48. Thus the annexation of Mexico called for by the *United States Review* was said to be in the order of " 'the regular growth' of the Republic" (Weinberg, 213).

49. Hubert Howe Bancroft, *California Pioneer Register 1542–1848* (Baltimore: Regional Publishing Co., 1964), 137.

50. Josiah Royce, *California from the Conquest in 1846 to the Second Vigilance Committee in San Francisco: A Study in American Character* (New York: Houghton, Mifflin and Co., 1886).

51. Carey McWilliams, *Southern California: An Island on the Land* (Salt Lake City: Peregrine Smith, 1983), 40.

52. In Cerruti's transcription of the testimonial of Isidora, the widow of Chief Solano, he edits her Spanish syntax during the first part and later indicates that, given her stature as the wife of an Indian chief who was Vallejo's ally, it is inappropriate to change her sentences; he then provides a transcription of what he says are her actual words. The length of sentences in all testimonials along with parenthetical constructions that allow for subsequent continuation of previously dropped sentences would indicate that much editing occurred in the copying of notes taken during the interviews.

53. Several of the testimonials are translated into English before they are submitted to Bancroft. In the case of Rosalía Vallejo, who hated the Americans so much that she never learned English, it is almost criminal to have done so.

54. Angustias de la Guerra Ord is allowed to add footnotes to her testimonial but not to change the original text. More examples are provided in Rosaura Sánchez, "Nineteenth Century Californio Narratives," in *Recovering the U.S. Hispanic Literary Heritage,* ed. Ramón Gutiérrez and Genaro M. Padilla (Houston: Arte Público Press, 1993), 279–92.

55. Roy Bhaskar, *Reclaiming Reality* (London: Verso, 1989), 186.

56. Fredric Jameson, *The Political Unconscious: Narrative as a Socially Symbolic Act* (Ithaca: Cornell University Press, 1981), 144.

57. Ilya Prigogine, "Beyond Being and Becoming," *New Perspectives Quarterly* 9, no. 2 (Spring 1992): 26.

58. Ilya Prigogine and Isabelle Stengers, *Order out of Chaos* (New York: Bantam Books, 1984), 293.

59. Perry Anderson, *In the Tracks of Historical Materialism* (London: Verso, 1988), 55.

60. M. M. Bakhtin, *Speech Genres and Other Late Essays*, ed. C. Emerson and M. Holquist, trans. V. W. McGee (Austin: University of Texas Press, 1986), 103.

61. Karl Marx, *Capital: A Critique of Political Economy* (New York: International Publishers, 1967), 1:174.

62. Barry Hindess and Paul Q. Hirst, *Mode of Production and Social Formation* (London: Macmillan Press, 1977), 19–20. In rejecting this relationship between external reality and the objects of discourse, Hindess and Hirst propose that epistemological discourses or metanarratives be conceived merely as discursive practices in relation to "other social practices" that condition their formation (22). Any consideration of "social practices" must, however, account for their social conditions of formation and interaction with other social practices, both discursive and nondiscursive. In fact, these "other social practices" — economic, political, and cultural, necessarily considered at a discursive level but not reducible to discourse — constitute "reality."

63. Pecheux distinguishes between different discursive formations on the basis of genres and subgenres (rural sermon versus sermon to aristocrats, for example) and notes their function within ideological formations. See Michel Pecheux, "Formación social, lengua, discurso," in *Lingüística y Semiología*, reprinted from *Languages* 37 (March 1975): 27.

64. Stuart Hall, "Signification, Representation, Ideology: Althusser and the Post-Structuralist Debates," *Critical Studies in Mass Communication* 2, no. 2 (June 1985): 91–114.

65. Erving Goffman, *Forms of Talk* (Philadelphia: University of Pennsylvania Press, 1981), 124.

66. Göran Therborn, *The Ideology of Power and the Power of Ideology* (London: Verso, 1980), 32–40.

67. Alex Callinicos, *Making History: Agency, Structure and Change in Social Theory* (London: Polity Press, 1987), 155.

68. Nicos P. Mouzelis, *Post Marxist Alternatives: The Construction of Social Orders* (London: Macmillan Press, 1990), 55.

69. Karl Marx, *Grundrisse* (New York: Vintage Books, 1973), 84.

70. Clearly, for the marginalized, exploited, and oppressed, discourses of resistance and struggle have always been necessary and even today, far from "metaphysical," still pose a threat to the status quo.

71. Perry Anderson, "The Antinomies of Antonio Gramsci," *New Left Review* 100 (November 1976–January 1977): 5–75.

72. Stuart Hall, "Gramsci's Relevance for the Study of Race and Ethnicity," *Journal of Communication Inquiry* 10, no. 2 (Summer 1980): 26.

73. Stuart Hall, "Culture, the Media and the 'Ideological Effect,'" ed. J. Curran et al., *Mass Communication and Society* (London: Arnold, 1977), 339.

74. Henri Lefebvre, *The Production of Space*, trans. D. Nicholson-Smith (Oxford: Basil Blackwell Ltd., 1991), 53.

75. See Lefebvre (83) and Edward W. Soja, *Post Modern Geographies* (London: Verso, 1989), 78.

76. Fredric Jameson, "Modernism and Imperialism," in Terry Eagleton, Fredric Jameson, and Edward Said, *Nationalism, Colonialism, and Literature* (Minneapolis: University of Minnesota Press, 1990), 60.

77. See Lefebvre (163) and Michel Foucault, "Of Other Spaces," *Diacritics* 16 (Spring 1986): 23.

78. Even an orphaned individual like Apolinaria Lorenzana, "la beata," had been the owner of three ranches while living and working for the friars at the San Diego mission. She had held a supervisory position there, conducting purchases for the mission from visiting ships (assisted always by Indian servants) and watching over the Indian workers. She was an administrative aide and companion to the missionaries as well as a mission employee. Her privileged position was much like that of Eulalia Pérez, said to be the oldest person in California in 1878, who had been the official housekeeper of the richest California mission, San Gabriel Mission, and was in charge of procurements as well as overseer of the Indian servants who cooked, cleaned, and sewed at the mission. She too became a landowner.

79. The longer, more extensive texts are those of Mariano Guadalupe Vallejo (five volumes; 1,875 handwritten pages) and Juan Bautista Alvarado (five volumes; 1,253 handwritten pages). Other long (one-volume) testimonials that we will consider are those of Antonio Franco Coronel, José de Jesús Vallejo, Salvador Vallejo, José Fernández, Narciso Botello, Estevan de la Torre, José del Carmen Lugo, and Manuel Castro.

80. The English translations are our own unless otherwise indicated.

2. The Mission as Heterotopia

1. Robert Glass Cleland, *From Wilderness to Empire: A History of California 1542–1900* (New York: Alfred A. Knopf Inc., 1947), 5.

2. Cited in Mario Góngora, *Studies in the Colonial History of Spanish America*, trans. Richard Southern (Cambridge: Cambridge University Press, 1975), 235.

3. Michel Foucault, "Of Other Spaces," *Diacritics* 16 (Spring 1986): 23.

4. Francisco Palou, *Historical Memoirs of New California*, ed. Herbert Eugene Bolton (New York: Russell & Russell, 1966), 90.

5. See Madie Brown Emparán, *The Vallejos of California* (San Francisco: The Gleeson Library Associates, University of San Francisco, 1968), 156. Also see Cerruti (51) for information on the construction of a chapel in Sonoma in 1874 where the former mission church, now in ruins, had stood.

6. Enrique Semo, *Historia del capitalismo en México. Los orígenes. 1521–1763* (Mexico City: Ediciones Era, 1983), 67–68.

7. E. J. Hobsbawm, *Nations and Nationalism since 1780* (New York: Cambridge University Press, 1992), 46.

8. Etienne Balibar, "Is There a 'Neo-Racism'?" in Etienne Balibar and Immanuel Wallerstein, *Race, Nation and Class: Ambiguous Identities* (London: Verso, 1991), 22.

9. Angel Rosenblat, *La población indígena y el mestizaje en América*, 2 vols. (Buenos Aires: Ediciones Nova, 1954), 2:180.

10. The 1781 census of Los Angeles, for example, lists twelve families among the founders, among them a good number of mulattoes, Indians, and mestizos, and only two Spaniards; see "First Census of Los Angeles," *Historical Society of Southern California Annual Publication* 15 (1931): 148–49.

11. Bancroft's *California Pioneer Register 1542–1848* (1964) offers a compilation of the names of the original settlers who came to California between 1769 and 1848. See also Leon Rowland, *Los Fundadores* (Fresno, Calif.: Academy of California Church History, 1951), which lists the first families that came to California with the Portolá party (1769), the Anza party (1776), or during the first fifteen years of settlement.

12. Salomé Hernández, "No Settlement without Women: Three Spanish California Settlement Schemes, 1790–1800," *Quarterly of the Historical Society of Southern California* 72, no. 3 (Fall 1990): 222.

13. Etienne Balibar, "Racism and Nationalism," in Etienne Balibar and Immanuel Wallerstein, *Race, Nation, Class: Ambiguous Identities* (London: Verso, 1991), 39.

14. Gilberto Cárdenas, "United States Immigration Policy toward Mexico: An Historical Perspective," *Chicano Law Review* 2 (Summer 1975): 40.

15. Governor Manuel Victoria (1830–31) was said to have ordered the execution of several men for petty or unproven crimes (Alvarado, 2:171).

16. The first land grant in California was given to a Catalonian soldier, Manuel Butrón, who married a neophyte Indian woman, Margarita, of the Eslen tribe (MGV, 1:88; Rowland, 18).

17. See Manuel P. Servín, "California's Hispanic Heritage: A View into the Spanish Myth," *Journal of San Diego History* 19, no. 1 (Winter 1973): 1–9. See also Ralph H. Vigil, "The Hispanic Heritage and the Borderlands," *Journal of San Diego History* 19, no. 3 (Summer 1973): 32–39, as well as Mario García, "A Chicano Perspective on San Diego History," *Journal of San Diego History* 18, no. 4 (Fall 1972): 14–21.

18. C. Alan Hutchinson, *Frontier Settlement in Mexican California: The Híjar-Padrés Colony and Its Origins* (New Haven: Yale University Press, 1969), 15.

19. Upon Echeandía's arrival to California, for example, the forty soldiers in charge of sixty convicts are described by Vallejo as "un piquete de soldados de infantería, todos de color negro, caras feas, bocas jetonas, ojos de guajolote y genio retobado" (MGV, 1:63).

20. Robert Brenner, "The Social Basis of Economic Development," *Analytical Marxism*, ed. John Roemer (New York: Cambridge University Press, 1986), 27.

21. The Pious Fund, set up by the Jesuits in 1697 with donations from wealthy patrons for the purpose of establishing missions in the Californias, was subsequently also subsidized by the Crown and secularized by the king after 1767. See María del Carmen Velázquez, *El fondo piadoso de las misiones de Californias* (Mexico City: Secretaría de Relaciones Exteriores, 1985), 15–17, 35.

22. Góngora (56) notes that seventeenth-century nationalism and royal prerogative were an attempt to distance Spain from former official views of full sovereignty in the Indies on the basis of papal donation.

23. Carey McWilliams, *Southern California: An Island on the Land* (Salt Lake City: Peregrine Smith, 1983), 29.

24. J. N. Bowman, "The Resident Neophytes (*existentes*) of the California Missions, 1769–1834," *Southern California Quarterly* 40, no. 2 (June 1958): 147–48.

25. Following the analyses of Marx, Cohen, Brenner, and Semo, we would have to call the mission an imposed despotic system.

26. See G. A. Cohen, *Karl Marx's Theory of History: A Defence* (Princeton: Princeton University Press, 1978), 13.

27. Henri Lefebvre, *The Production of Space*, trans. D. Nicholson-Smith (Oxford: Basil Blackwell Ltd., 1991), 366.

28. Richard James Blackburn, *The Vampire of Reason: An Essay in the Philosophy of History* (London: Verso, 1990), 185.

29. Albert K. Weinberg, *Manifest Destiny: A Study of Nationalist Expansionism in American History* (Baltimore: Johns Hopkins University Press, 1935), 86–87.

30. In Alvarado's words, "miles de indios bárbaros, sedientos de sangre cristiana" (2:19).

31. Theodore H. Hittell, *History of California* (San Francisco: Pacific Press Publishing House and Occidental Publishing Co., 1885), 1:728–29.

32. As Vallejo constructs the Indian he strives to underscore that even the Indians were immigrants, ostensibly to argue from that position that they had no more claim to the land than subsequent natives, i.e., the Californios. See MGV, vol. 1.

33. Cited in Hubert Howe Bancroft, *History of California* (San Francisco: The History Company Publishers, 1885–86), 1:437.

34. This speech was written in 1831 primarily to defend the estates composing the Pious Fund, which originally paid the missionary synods in California.

35. Richard Edwards, *Contested Terrains: The Transformation of the Workplace in the Twentieth Century* (New York: Basic Books, 1979), 19.

36. According to Friar Zalvidea, "the time of the day is so arranged that they labor with ease for five hours a day in the winter and from six to seven hours during the summer" (243).

37. Vallejo, the leading military native son in California, goes into great detail outlining the duties, weapons, gear, and regulations and ranks established by the Spanish Crown for *presidio* soldiers (MGV, 1:25–28).

38. Here we see another example of how often the testimonials serve to counter pro-missionary reconstructions of California history. Alvarado (2:66) suggests that Corporal Joaquín Piña's diary on the assault (the basis of this accusation) was the work of the missionaries and was produced after the fact. M. G. Vallejo was then twenty-one years old and the ensign in charge of the attack.

39. Estudillo's diary indicates that "por este tiempo mandaba tropa a recoger y llevar amarrados a todos los cristianos huidos y gentiles, y a matarlos si no querían que se fuesen a apresarlos" (Estudillo, 2).

40. Marín replied: "Mira, hombre: yo veo tú tienes caballo que lleva montura y tienes caballo que pegas al calesín; si tú pones caballo que lleva montura al calesín él patea y no camina y si tú pones montura al caballo del calesín, el tampoco quiere caminar, nosotros indios somos mismo caballos, somos acostumbrados a vivir en montes y no queremos vivir misión, en montes somos libres como ciervos y venados, en misión somos presos lo mismo caballos llevan montura y calesín" (Alvarado, 1:95–96).

41. Pico recalls that after secularization of the San Luis Rey mission the commander general, visiting the mission with his officers, asked the *alcaldes* "not to permit any of the Indian boys or girls to walk in the corridors of the mission after sunset" as he "knew the weaknesses of these gentlemen" (99).

42. See McWilliams (32).

43. Sir George Simpson, "California, Its History, Population, Climate, Soil, Productions, and Harbors," from *Overland Journey Round the World* (Cincinnati: J. A. and U. P. James, 1848), 29.

44. A square *vara* equals 1,122.25 inches or 7.8 square feet. See Keld J. Reynolds, "Introduction" to "Principal Actions of the California Junta de Fomento, 1825–1827," *California Historical Society Quarterly* 24, no. 4 (1945): 289–94, note 69.

45. By 1830 about fifty *ranchos* had been granted (Bancroft, 1885–86, 2:663).

46. According to Coronel, "el grado de parentesco no se podía calcular hasta qué punto lo llevaban: estaban todas las familias tan ligadas que eran parientes casi todos los habitantes de California, si no era de derecho, a lo menos por costumbre" (230).

47. Certain alliances and rivalries, despite kinship, would last even beyond 1848. Thus we find Alvarado and Pablo de la Guerra supporting Coronel against Romualdo Pacheco, backed by the Carrillos, in the election for state treasurer in 1867. All except Coronel were related by blood or marriage. See Ronald Genini and Richard Hitchman, *Romualdo Pacheco: A Californio in Two Eras* (San Francisco: The Book Club of California, 1985), 42.

3. Theoretical Disjunctures and Discourses of Liberalism

1. C. B. Macpherson, *The Real World of Democracy* (New York: Oxford University Press, 1981), 7, 47.

2. Chantal Mouffe, "Hegemony and New Political Subjects: Toward a New Concept of Democracy," *Marxism and the Interpretation of Culture,* ed. Cary Nelson and Lawrence Grossberg (Urbana: University of Illinois Press, 1988), 102.

3. Charles Adams Hale, *Mexican Liberalism in the Age of Mora, 1821–1853* (New Haven: Yale University Press, 1968), 83–115.

4. E. J. Hobsbawm, *Nations and Nationalism since 1780* (New York: Cambridge University Press, 1992), 38.

5. Mouffe (1988: 32) cites Macpherson as the writer who has shown that the articulation of democracy with liberalism is a product of the nineteenth century.

6. Archivo histórico diplomático mexicano 35. *La gestión diplomática del doctor Mora.* Con una adventencia de Luis Chávez Orozco (Mexico City: Editorial Porrúa, 1970), 74–76.

7. Partha Chatterjee, *Nationalist Thought and the Colonial World: A Derivative Discourse* (London: Zed Books, 1986), 11.

8. Roy Bhaskar, *Reclaiming Reality* (London: Verso, 1989), 140.

9. Robert Brenner, "The Social Basis of Economic Development," *Analytical Marxism,* ed. John Roemer (New York: Cambridge University Press, 1986), 26.

10. Robert Brenner, "Agrarian Class Structure and Economic Development in Pre-Industrial Europe," *The Brenner Debate,* ed. T. H. Aston and C. H. E. Philpin (New York: Cambridge University Press, 1990).

11. Beatriz González Stephan, *La historiografía literaria del liberalismo hispanoamericano del siglo XIX* (Havana: Casa de las Américas, 1987), 27.

12. Joyce Appleby, *Liberalism and Republicanism in the Historical Imagination* (Cambridge: Harvard University Press, 1992).

13. Stanley J. Stein and Barbara H. Stein, *The Colonial Heritage of Latin America: Essays on Economic Dependence in Perspective* (New York: Oxford University Press, 1970), 131.

14. Antonio Gramsci, *Selections from the Prison Notebooks* (New York: International Publishers, 1978), 106.

15. Raúl Mejía Zúñiga, *Valentín Gómez Farías: Hombre de México, 1781–1858* (Mexico City: Fondo de Cultura Económica, 1979), 119.

16. Sacvan Bercovitch, *The American Jeremiad* (Madison: University of Wisconsin Press, 1978), 17.

17. Luis J. Zalce y Rodríguez, *Apuntes para la historia de la masonería en México.* 2 vols. (Mexico City: n.p., 1950), 2.

18. Pierre Vilar, *Historia de España,* trans. M. Tuñón de Lara (Paris: Librairie Espagnole, 1975), 51.

19. Mario Góngora, *Studies in the Colonial History of Spanish America,* trans. Richard Southern (Cambridge: Cambridge University Press, 1975), 170, 180.

20. Ramón Martínez Zaldúa, *La masonería en Hispanoamérica, su influencia decisiva en la revolución mexicana* (Mexico City: B. Costa-Anic. Editores, 1965), 41.

21. Jan Bazant, *A Concise History of Mexico from Hidalgo to Cárdenas, 1805–1940* (New York: Cambridge University Press, 1988), 38, 42.

22. Andrés Lira, "Selección, introducción y notas," *Espejo de discordias* (Mexico City: Secretaría de Educación Pública, 1984), 22.

23. Gustavo Alberto Escobar Valenzuela, *El liberalismo ilustrado del Dr. José María Luis Mora* (Mexico City: Universidad Nacional Autónoma de México, 1974), 58.

24. Ramón Ruiz, *Triumphs and Tragedy: A History of the Mexican People* (New York: W. W. Norton & Co., 1992), 197.

25. In 1835 Texas would declare its independence and in 1836 Santa Anna, defeated at the Battle of San Jacinto, would sign an armistice recognizing this independence; the agreement, however, would not be acknowledged by the Mexican government.

26. These are the three individuals credited by the Californios in their testimonials. Tays credits the foreign merchants for hiring the Californios in their stores and teaching them to read French, Spanish, and Latin; see George Tays, "Mariano Guadalupe Vallejo and Sonoma," *California Historical Society Quarterly* 16, no. 2 (June 1937): 106.

27. The direct connection between the Junta and the liberal Spanish Cortes is specified in Keld J. Reynolds, "Introduction" to "Principal Actions of the California Junta de Fomento, 1825–1827," *California Historical Society Quarterly* 24, no. 4 (1945): 291.

28. C. Alan Hutchinson, *Frontier Settlement in Mexican California: The Híjar-Padrés Colony and Its Origins* (New Haven: Yale University Press, 1969), 164–65. This neglect in matters related to Alta California is also one of the sore points with the Californios, who felt abandoned and betrayed (especially by the Padrés and Híjar project) and therefore justified in their own attempts at forging a Californio nation.

29. Alta California, as Vallejo saw it, was "un pueblo que había sacudido el yugo de los frayles, un pueblo en que la civilización y nuevas ideas habían hecho progreso" (MGV, 3:94).

30. Alfred Robinson, *Life in California, 1846* (New York: Da Capo Press, 1969), 121.

31. Richard Henry Dana, *Two Years before the Mast: A Personal Narrative (1840)* (Boston: Fields, Osgood & Co., 1869), 85.

32. Sir George Simpson, "California, Its History, Population, Climate, Soil, Productions, and Harbors," from *Overland Journey Round the World* (Cincinnati: J. A. and U. P. James, 1848), 24.

33. Ignacio Vallejo, who was also Alvarado's grandfather, came to California in 1773 (1774, according to Bancroft, 1964: 364) after fleeing in 1769 from a Guadalajaran seminary where he was a novitiate (MGV, 1:225–30). He was one of the more educated soldier-settlers in Alta California.

34. Manuel P. Servín, "The Secularization of the California Missions: A Reappraisal," *Quarterly of the Historical Society of Southern California* 47, no. 2 (March 1965): 134.

35. José Carlos Mariátegui, *Siete ensayos de interpretación de la realidad peruana* (Mexico City: Ediciones Era, S. A., 1979), 37, 323.

36. José María Luis Mora, "Una visión de la sociedad mexicana," in *Espejo de discordias*, selections by Andrés Lira (Mexico: Secretaría de Educación Pública [SEP], 1984), 77.

37. The estates of the Pious Funds were used by Gómez Farías to secure a loan to purchase a ship, the *Natalia*, for this commercial enterprise (MGV, 2:285). On this ship about three hundred colonists, all artisans, craftsworkers, teachers, and several political prisoners, with wives and children, arrived after trekking across Mexico in a wagon train with sheep, goats, and luggage (Coronel, 5). Their departure produced a great deal of commotion, for neighbors and others feared that these families were going off to a wild country (Coronel, 6–7). Coronel made the trip and recalls that it took three months, from April to July, to reach Tepic and then San Blas, from where they would go to California.

38. Hutchinson indicates that in a letter to the Ministro de Relaciones dated July 20, 1833, Figueroa warned that there were Californios interested in fighting for the independence of California and that "they looked upon Mexicans much as Mexicans looked upon the hated Spaniards" (226).

39. One plot involving a group of Sonorans and two of the colonists had been uncovered in Los Angeles (Coronel, 13). There is indication that the colonists were upset at finding that none of the promises of land, tools, livestock, and stipends were to be met (Alvarado, 2:231). The California treasury was then practically empty and the missions were able and willing to provide only a small part of what the settlers needed.

40. Vallejo explains his break with Padrés as follows: "Cuando regresó de su destierro acompañado de tres cientos colonos nos preparábamos a apoyarle de cuales-

quiera manera, pero como que no tardamos en descubrir que entre los colonos venían veinte y un administradores de misiones traídos y escogidos por Padrés entre sus amigos mexicanos para que viniesen a California a disponer a su antojo de todo lo creado; nosotros que teníamos miras particulares que servir (pues si bien la filantropía entraba por algo, el interés personal tampoco podía descuidarse) nos rebelamos contra la idea de ver la riqueza del país pasar a manos extrañas y en vez de apoyar, combatimos el plan y miras de ese astuto engañador" (MGV, 2:262).

41. Alvarado's actual words are as follows: "Esa medida fue la que hizo fracasar su proyecto favorito, pues los californios no eran tan sencillos hasta el extremo de permitir que veinte y un extranjeros (nosotros llamábamos a los mejicanos extranjeros y los apreciábamos mucho menos de los norte americanos y europeos) viniesen a su tierra a sentarse sobre silletas mientras que a ellos no quedaba otro asiento más que el suelo" (2:228).

42. As previously noted, two disappointed colonists in Los Angeles tried to instigate a group of Sonoran settlers to revolt against Figueroa. Pico recalls the short-lived movement, which led leaders to approach the *alcalde* and *ayuntamiento* for support in overthrowing Figueroa. Once the rebel leaders became aware of the lack of support in the town and of the instigators' lack of money for such a campaign, they turned the colonists in (Pico, 61–64).

43. The young generation of Californios, according to Alvarado, "con brazo fuerte rompieron los vínculos con que los esbirros del fanatismo habían riveteado el cuerpo y el alma de los primitivos moradores de este hoy próspero Estado" (1:iv–v).

44. Alvarado's anticlerical speech is as follows: "Quince años después pusieron en berlina a los monjeríos y frailerías, y libertaron a la Alta California de la dominación que durante sesenta y nueve años habían en ella ejercido los jesuitas, disfrazados con el nombre de frayles franciscanos que nadaron en la abundancia a costillas de treinta mil neófitos … bien me consta que Mofrás, Gleason y otros escritores asalariados por el clero han tratado de manchar mi memoria y tergiversar mis hechos gubernativos porque en despecho de sus protestas di el golpe de muerte al carcomido sistema de educación de los indios introducido por los frayles franciscanos, pero sépanlo ellos, sépanlo sus mermellones, sépalo el mundo entero que si yo me resolví a dar libertad a los indios, lo hice impulsado de sentimientos de humanidad, lo hice porque mi educación republicana no me podía permitir que continuase a ser el pimpollo de los hombres de sotana, que gris tenían el hábito, gris el capucho, pero negra el alma que insensible al grito de angustia que salía del pecho de treinta mil indios que privados de su libertad no eran más que muñecos en manos de los adustos sacerdotes que predicaban pureza de alma y cuerpo, al mismo tiempo que ellos casi públicamente se engolfaban en todos los vicios que la humanidad y decencia vituperan" (1: 208–9).

4. Spaces of (Re)Production

1. Paul Ricoeur, *Time and Narrative* (Chicago: University of Chicago Press, 1985), 1:170.

2. María Amparo Ruiz de Burton, *Who Would Have Thought It?* (Philadelphia: Lippincott and Co., 1872).

3. The ranch, which would in time have a central role in the life of the novelist María Amparo Ruiz de Burton, was then the property of Pío Pico. Pico had received title to it in 1829 and had it confirmed in 1831. Jamul is situated in southern California, in San Diego County.

4. Cited in footnote 32 of the English translation of Juana Machado de Ridington's "Recollections, 1878" prepared by Raymond Brandes.

5. Hubert Howe Bancroft, *History of California* (San Francisco: The History Company Publishers, 1885–86), 3:723. The Englishman Simpson of course reports it not as an act

of mutiny but rather one of many acts of despotism on the part of Vallejo: "On one occasion, a regiment of native infantry, being an awkward squad of fifteen Indians, having conspired against the general, were [sic] shot for their pains; and more recently the Californian soldiers, disdaining to drive bullock, were cashiered on the spot, and replaced by new levies" (Sir George Simpson, "California, Its History, Population, Climate, Soil, Production, and Harbors," from *Overland Journey Round the World* [Cincinnati: J. A. and U. P. James, 1848], 32).

6. The kidnapping of Indian girls was not a practice limited to the Californios. Alvarado recalls being told by Mrs. Larkin that Augustus Sutter used to supply his friends with kidnapped Indian girls (4:213, 218, 220). The testimonials, recalling that young Indian girls were raped by the missionaries, offer several stories about the friar Jesús María Vásquez del Mercado and his several children by the young neophytes under his "protection" (Alvardo, 5:87) and mention the need to remove Friar Gerónimo Boscana from San Juan Capistrano for similar activities (Alvarado, 3:113).

7. Vladimir Propp, *Morphology of the Folktale* (Austin: University of Texas Press, 1977), 92.

8. Duflot de Mofras, *Travels on the Pacific Coast,* trans. and ed. Marguerite Eyer Wilbur (Santa Ana, Calif.: Fine Arts Press, 1937), 237; also Simpson, 41. Platón Vallejo indicates in his testimonial that after secularization the mission cattle was distributed to the neophytes, who upon finding themselves under attack by other Indians, "entrusted" Vallejo with their cattle, sheep, and horses, and he in turn saw after their needs: "The proceeds from their stock was placed to the credit of the proper owners, on which they were entitled to draw at will. It was expended mostly in the purchases of various articles of use or luxury — the prized colored blanket, cooking utensils, useful implements, and tools" (P. Vallejo, 26). Bancroft (1885–86, 3:720) provides similar information.

9. de Mofras, 223–24. De Mofras would be denounced by Hartnell's wife, Doña Teresa de la Guerra, in a short narrative published in *El Heraldo de Monterey* in 1875 and reproduced in MGV's testimonial. She exposes his bizarre behavior and lies at their Rancho del Alizal (MGV, 4:246–49). The situation would come to a head in 1878, when church officials delayed granting permission for M. G. Vallejo's daughter Jovita Vallejo de Haraszthy to receive last rites from the San Francisco Cathedral. This denial of funeral honors would be a severe blow to her seventy-year-old father; see Madie Brown Emparán, *The Vallejos of California* (San Francisco: The Gleeson Library Associates, University of San Francisco, 1968), 360–61.

10. At one point in 1839, Hartnell was informed by the administrators that the majority of the Indians from San Diego, San Juan Capistrano, and San Luis Rey missions had fled to Santa Barbara; some were servants, others were vagrants without jobs.

11. Antonio Franco Coronel's *Cosas de California* (1877) is a 265-page manuscript that reconstructs a variety of political events and situations in Alta California after his family's arrival in 1834. The last forty pages deal with everyday life in the territory, including customs, family traditions, dress, dances, and other recreational activities. These pages generate constructs of fine horsemen (245) and a patriarchal society of protected women and authoritarian men, all generous to a fault, perfect hosts to travelers, and so on (228).

12. W. W. Robinson, "The Indians of Los Angeles," *Quarterly of the Historical Society of Southern California* 20, no. 4 (December 1938): 156.

13. Simpson conveniently forgets that English settlers in Virginia, for example, had massacred the Powhatan Indians in 1610, and in 1636 in Massachusetts had massacred an entire village of six hundred Pequot Indians. See Howard Zinn, *A People's History of the United States* (New York: Harper and Row, 1980), 12–15. The British policies had been to remove the Indians, dispossess them, and take their lands, one way or another. Simpson also manages to avoid the issue of the role of England in the slave trade in the

late eighteenth century. See also E. J. Hobsbawm, *Industry and Empire* (Baltimore: Penguin Books, 1972), 54.

14. Simpson also laughs derisively at the Hawaiian furniture ("the gaudy chairs from Woahoo") imported by these wealthy Californios who were "obliged to borrow the means of sitting from savages" (Simpson, 24).

15. Cited in James B. Alexander, *Sonoma Valley Legacy* (Sonoma, Calif.: Sonoma Valley Historical Society, 1986), 22.

16. Not until 1844, for example, did M. G. Vallejo and two other Californios acquire pianos; see George Tays, "Mariano Guadalupe Vallejo and Sonoma," *California Historical Society Quarterly* 17, no. 2 (June 1938): 154. M. G. Vallejo's new house, Lachryma Montis, was not built until 1850, and was completed in 1852.

17. Hubert Howe Bancroft, *California Pastoral, 1796–1848* (San Francisco: A. L. Bancroft, 1888), 335.

18. Richard Henry Dana, *Two Years before the Mast: A Personal Narrative (1840)* (Boston: Fields, Osgood & Co., 1869), 84.

19. Bruce Conde, "Santa Ana of the Yorbas," *Historical Society of Southern California Publication* 22, no. 2 (June 1940): 71.

20. See Terry E. Stephenson, "Tomás Yorba, His Wife Vicenta, and His Account Book," *Historical Society of Southern California Publication* 23, nos. 3–4 (September–December 1941): 135. See also Robert Glass Cleland, *From Wilderness to Empire: A History of California 1542–1900* (New York: Alfred A. Knopf, Inc., 1947), 17.

21. Alfred Robinson, *Life in California, 1846* (New York: Da Capo Press, 1969), 29–30.

22. See Tomás Yorba, "Letters to José de la Guerra, et al.," in Wayne Dell Gibson, *Tomás Yorba's Santa Ana Viejo* (Santa Ana, Calif.: Santa Ana College, 1975), 184–293.

23. Robert Brenner, "The Social Basis of Economic Development," *Analytical Marxism*, ed. John Roemer (New York: Cambridge University Press, 1986), 26–27.

24. M. G. Vallejo claims, for example, that there was no exchange of money for the concession by Alvarado to one Juan Rowland for the *hacienda* La Puente from San Gabriel, but this hardly seems likely. Vallejo states that his nephew's sole aim was to increase the number of *gente de razón* (MGV, 4:156).

25. C. Alan Hutchinson, *Frontier Settlement in Mexican California: The Híjar-Padrés Colony and Its Origins* (New Haven: Yale University Press, 1969), 129.

26. Platón Vallejo (30) recalls that gentile tribes from as far as the Yuma and Sonoran deserts established a trade of wool blankets for horses and even a slave trade of sorts with the Californios of young Indian children who were for the most part bought for domestic service in Californio homes.

27. The year of the invasion eleven Californios from San Diego resolved to avoid the conflict by leaving town and staying at the Pauma ranch until they could ensure safe passage to Baja California. While there they were taken from the ranch by several Indians and killed, according to Juana Machado de Ridington, at the instigation of Juan Garras and Bill Marshall. The two allegedly misled the Indians into thinking that General Kearny had authorized the killing of any Californios in the area. For this act Garras and Marshall were eventually tried and several years later found guilty and hanged in San Diego (Machado, 39–40).

28. Albert K. Weinberg, *Manifest Destiny: A Study of Nationalist Expansionism in American History* (Baltimore: Johns Hopkins University Press, 1935), 73.

29. Etienne Balibar, "Racism and Nationalism," in Etienne Balibar and Immanuel Wallerstein, *Race, Nation and Class: Ambiguous Identities* (London: Verso, 1991), 48.

30. Coronel (50) recalls that gentile tribes from as far as the Yuma and Sonoran deserts established a trade of wool blankets for horses and even a slave trade of sorts with the Californios of young Indian children who were for the most part bought for domestic service in Californio homes.

31. Fredric Jameson, *The Political Unconscious: Narrative as a Socially Symbolic Act* (Ithaca: Cornell University Press, 1981), 83.

32. Fredric Jameson, *The Ideologies of Theory: Essays 1971–1986. Volume 2: The Syntax of History* (Minneapolis: University of Minnesota Press, 1988), 13.

5. Politics of Gender

1. Partha Chatterjee, *Nationalist Thought and the Colonial World: A Derivative Discourse* (London: Zed Books, 1986), vii; E. J. Hobsbawm, *Nations and Nationalism since 1780* (Cambridge: Cambridge University Press, 1992), 6.

2. Ilya Prigogine and Isabelle Stengers, *Order out of Chaos* (New York: Bantam Books, 1984), 272.

3. Henri Lefebvre, *The Production of Space,* trans. D. Nicholson-Smith (Oxford: Basil Blackwell Ltd., 1991), 404.

4. Chantal Mouffe, "Hegemony and New Political Subjects: Toward a New Concept of Democracy," *Marxism and the Interpretation of Culture,* ed. Cary Nelson and Lawrence Grossberg (Urbana: University of Illinois Press, 1988), 94–95.

5. Frigga Haug, *Beyond Female Masochism: Memory-Work and Politics,* trans. Rodney Livingstone (London: Verso, 1992), 7.

6. Rosemary Hennessy and Rajeswari Mohan, "The Construction of Woman in Three Popular Texts of Empire: Towards a Critique of Materialist Feminism," *Textual Practice* 3, no. 3 (Winter 1989): 325.

7. Salomé Hernández, "No Settlement without Women: Three Spanish California Settlement Schemes, 1790–1800," *Quarterly of the Historical Society of Southern California* 72, no. 3 (Fall 1990): 219.

8. Christine Delphy, "Patriarchy, Domestic Mode of Production, Gender, and Class," in *Marxism and the Interpretation of Culture,* ed. Cary Nelson and Lawrence Grossberg (Urbana: University of Illinois Press, 1988), 263.

9. Brenner discusses three different outcomes from feudalism: one in Eastern Europe, one in Western Europe, and one in England. Without going into the "historically significant patterns" of development of the agrarian classes in these three posited models, we need to consider that the specific form of transition that took place is related to relations between the peasant, landlord, and state, and that historically these varied, with different outcomes in different areas of the world. Thus particular property relations and serf struggles account for the more rapid transition to capitalism in England, for example. See Robert Brenner, "Agrarian Class Structure and Economic Development in Pre-Industrial Europe," *The Brenner Debate,* ed. T. H. Aston and C. H. E. Philpin (New York: Cambridge University Press, 1990), 46.

10. David J. Weber, *Foreigners in Their Native Land: Historical Roots of the Mexican Americans* (Albuquerque: University of New Mexico Press, 1973), 215. In a study of land-grant papers of the "Spanish Archives" (part of the National Archives in Washington) and the "Spanish Records" (part of the State Archives), Bowman finds the listing of sixty-six women who petitioned for a land grant in Alta California. Of these, thirty-seven received full or part of the concession, among them at least two Indian women. After invasion and following the Land Act of 1851, only twenty-two women petitioned before U.S. tribunals to have their titles confirmed, with patents being issued to either these women or their heirs. See J. N. Bowman, "Prominent Women of Provincial California," *Quarterly of the Historical Society of Southern California* 39, no. 2 (June 1957): 151, 161, 165.

11. There are several representations of strong women in the *pueblos,* too. Doña Paz Espinola, for example, was a washerwoman and *fondera* in Monterey; she sold fried fish

and corn tortillas from her front door to passersby, primarily Californio and Indian workers, and on festive occasions she sold meat pies and apple cider in the evenings from a bench placed near the church doors. Alvarado (5:33) recalls that she approached Governor Micheltorena several times to demand restitution of items stolen by his ex-convict soldiers.

12. Duflot de Mofras, *Travels on the Pacific Coast*, trans. and ed. Marguerite Eyer Wilbur (Santa Ana, Calif.: Fine Arts Press, 1937), 11.

13. Sir George Simpson, "California, Its History, Population, Climate, Soil, Production, and Harbors," from *Overland Journey Round the World* (Cincinnati: J. A. and U. P. James, 1848), 27.

14. The only exception made by Simpson is M. G. Vallejo, "who has risen in the world by his own talent and energy" (Simpson, 24).

15. Alfred Robinson, *Life in California, 1846* (New York: Da Capo Press, 1969), 73.

16. Carey McWilliams, *Southern California: An Island on the Land* (Salt Lake City: Peregrine Smith, 1983), 53.

17. The four daughters of Guerra y Noriega, the wealthiest man in Santa Barbara, all married foreigners. Teresa de Jesús married the merchant Hartnell. María de las Augustias married a Mexican, Manuel Jimeno Casarín, whose two brothers were missionaries and who was an educated man and later became Governor Alvarado's secretary and served as a vice governor. After his death Augustias married a doctor, J. L. Ord. Ana María Guerra married Alfred Robinson. María Antonia married Cesario Lataillade, a Spaniard of French descent and a businessman; after his death she married Gaspar Oreña, another Spanish trader.

18. Archivo histórico diplomático mexicano 31. *Alqunos documentos sobre el Tratado de Guadalupe y la situación de México durante la invasión americana* (Mexico City: Editorial Porrúa, 1970), 76, 80.

19. C. Alan Hutchinson, *Frontier Settlement in Mexican California: The Híjar-Padrés Colony and Its Origins* (New Haven: Yale University Press, 1969), 113.

20. Bret Harte, "Concepción de Argüello," in Bret Harte, *Complete Poetical Works* (New York: P. F. Collier and Son, 1899), 76–82.

21. Hubert Howe Bancroft, *History of California* (San Francisco: The History Company Publishers, 1885–86), 2:73.

22. Josiah Royce, *California from the Conquest in 1846 to the Second Vigilance Committee in San Francisco: A Study in American Character* (New York: Houghton, Mifflin, and Co., 1886), 18.

23. We need to remember that at this time there was no separation of church and state in Mexico, although in Alta California the missionaries and the governor were not one entity or of one mind. In fact since 1769 they were often at odds. It is possible that Echeandía, who was known to be a liberal federalist republican and whom the missionaries tried to overthrow with the Solís revolt that same year, 1829, was interested in demonstrating that his motives for planning for the emancipation of the Indians and secularization of the mission were the freedom of the neophytes and not antireligious feelings. In Mexico the *yorkinos* were liberals and anticlerical but good Catholics. This does not deny that Echeandía used the political situation and religious practices to do what he may have wanted to do for personal reasons.

24. Rosaura Sánchez and Beatrice Pita, "Introduction," to *The Squatter and the Don*, by María Amparo Ruiz de Burton (Houston: Arte Público Press, 1993), 8–11.

25. The enterprising foreigners who would figure prominently in Alta California's history came to the territory right after Mexican independence and during Argüello's interim governorship or Echeandía's governorship: William Hartnell (1822), William Antonio Richardson (1822), John Bautista R. Cooper (1823), David Spence (1824), Henry

Fitch (1826), John Wilson (1826), Abel Stearns (1829), Alfred Robinson (1829), Thomas Oliver Larkin (1832), Jacob Leese (1833), and John Forster (1833). Many others would arrive during the 1840's. Spaniards like José de la Guerra y Noriega (1801), Estevan Munrás (1820), the Basque José Amesti (1822), and the Peruvian criollo Juan Bandini (1824) are generally not considered foreigners, except during the period of Mexican independence when anti-Hispanism was rampant in Mexico and the rest of Latin America.

26. Spence, from Scotland, though a naturalized Mexican citizen, becomes a close friend of the more prominent Californios. Like other Californio merchants, he is said to participate in contraband trade: "Don David Spence, a la par de todos los otros comerciantes de su época se dedicó al contrabando y por ese medio, ilegítimo hoy, pero sancionado entonces, logró reunir una gran fortuna que a su muerte, por carencia de hijos pasó a ser propiedad de sus nietos" (JJV, 17). José de Jesús Vallejo's comment is not shared by his brother Mariano Guadalupe, who considers Spence to be a model citizen — a Californio, in fact: "David Spence aunque nacido en Escocia era considerado como californio pues tenía papeles de ciudadano mexicano" (MGV, 2:26), a man often elected as *diputado, alcalde,* or prefect on account of his honesty and respect for the law (MGV, 2:27).

27. M. G. Vallejo was said to love Rosalía best of all his sisters because of her spirit of independence; she had married Leese during her brother's absence from Sonoma.

28. Gregg J. Layne, "The First Census of the Los Angeles District," *Quarterly of the Historical Society of Southern California* 18, no. 3 (September–December 1936): 82.

29. Sandra Gilbert and Susan Gubar, *The Madwoman in the Attic* (New Haven: Yale University Press, 1984), 17, 28.

30. The entire Herrera/Castañares/Chico episode became increasingly ridiculous and in effect led to the governor's removal. Events initiated by the governor's mistress, Doña Cruz, precipitated Mayor Estrada's subsequent resignation in Monterey, and the visible discontent of the town in turn led to the governor's exit from the territory with his mistress, who was presumably bored to death in the California hinterlands (Alvarado, 3:100). Herrera would later dismiss libel charges against Doña Ana and she would countersue him, until finally the last suit was also dismissed. In 1836 Herrera would again be exiled by Alvarado.

31. Vallejo's version is slightly different (MGV, 3:186).

32. There is an interesting sidelight to the Peña episode. When Peña's wife, who is never mentioned by first name in the testimonials, determined to leave her husband in 1837, she tried to return to Mexico overland with a servant. In San Diego the two joined two men traveling to Mexico by way of Sonora. After crossing the Cuyamaca mountains and the Colorado River they reached the desert, where they were attacked by Indians. The three men were killed and she was kidnapped. Coronel thinks that he might have seen her during one of his overland trips through the desert to trade in Sonora. His party of nine men (four of them his servants, plus an Indian friend from San Felipe, Capitán José, who served as interpreter) came across a group of about three hundred Indians from various tribes (Amayanes, Cochanes, and Yumas) with whom he had trading relations; they used to take their wool blankets and hides to town to trade for horses, mares, and used clothing (Coronel, 189). The Indians were awaiting them in full dress and party paint, for the captains of the *rancherías* had had word of their trip and were expecting a big treat of barbecued horse meat (Coronel, 130). Coronel's party had camped nearby, and he was told by Captain José that a *mujer de razón* was among the Indians, the wife of one of the Indian captains. Although Coronel was unable to talk to her, he did see her from a distance, totally transformed in terms of hairstyle, clothing, blanket, and face paint. From information he had two years later from an Indian child, he assumed this was the wife of Cosme Peña. He subsequently informed the

authorities of San Diego but nothing ever came of it (Coronel, 192). Alvarado and Vallejo do not mention what happened to Peña's wife, but perhaps Vallejo is recalling this outcome when he makes a comment about the wounds of Peña and his two children that have healed and should not be disturbed: "recuerdos desagradables, que quizás ya están relegados al olvido y cuyas llagas hace años que han sido cicatrizades" (MGV, 3:189).

33. Vallejo indicates that when he first saw Doña Cruz he was struck by her beauty and that had not his wife always been on his mind, he too might have succumbed (MGV, 3:90). Clearly the church plays an important role in determining what the Californios will tolerate and what they will not, but the administrators of the territory often thought they were above this popular mission-given consensus. There appears to have been no public outcry about Indian mistresses, except for the instances when missionaries or an interim governor were involved; Lieutenant Colonel Gutiérrez, who twice was interim governor, was known to have several Indian concubines. After Chico returned to Mexico, he had his mistresses travel to Monterey to reside in the "palacio de gobierno" as his housekeeper, washerwoman, cook, maid, and so forth (Alvarado, 3:117). He would be overthrown by Alvarado shortly thereafter and severely criticized in the testimonials for his conduct. The private life of liberal men that these Californios supported is off-limits in these testimonials—the only private lives commented on are those of their antagonists. The revolutionary ex-monk Ramírez, who participated in the wars for independence, is said to have fled from Mexico to California with an ex-nun, Doña Pachita Arancibia (MGV, 3:80). He would be both an ally and a rival to the Californios at different moments but he managed to evade deportation, an action that would have meant his imprisonment in Mexico.

34. Alvarado's comment on the Mexican ambassador to the United States, Matías Romero, is typical: "un triste cholo de Oaxaca" (1:220), and reveals the racist and aristocratic disdain he feels toward Indian-looking individuals who do not "know their place." But of course this was not his attitude toward Figueroa or Padrés. The discourses of caste or racism are wielded only when it is expedient to do so.

6. Protonationalism in Alta California

1. E. J. Hobsbawm, *Nations and Nationalism since 1780* (New York: Cambridge University Press, 1992), 10.

2. Benedict Anderson, *Imagined Communities* (London: Verso, 1983), 15.

3. Ramón Ruiz, *Triumphs and Tragedy: A History of the Mexican People* (New York: W. W. Norton & Co., 1992), 195.

4. Archivo histórico diplomático mexicano 31. *Algunos documentos sobre el Tratado de Guadalupe y la situación de México durante la invasión americana* (Mexico City: Editorial Porrúa, 1970), 172–75, 180.

5. These discourses of territoriality have been orally transmitted, for the most part, given the nonavailability of these discourses in print.

6. Partha Chatterjee, *Nationalist Thought and the Colonial World: A Derivative Discourse* (London: Zed Books, 1986), 42.

7. As Chatterjee indicates, "liberal, secular and rational attitudes" are "invariably compromised by concessions to scriptural or canonical authority or, even more ignominiously, by succumbing to pressures for conformity or to enticements of individual material advancement" (28).

8. "En 1834 y aún en 1842 se creía en todos los Estados de la Unión Mexicana que la Alta California no era otra cosa sino una colonia de presidiarios" (Alvarado, 2:226–27).

9. In reality there was a great deal of contraband, with ships often stopping off in Santa Barbara or one of the other ports before sailing into Monterey to declare their wares.

10. Vallejo, a child in 1814, indicates that the supporters of Mexican independence in California also favored the interim and liberal governor José Darío Argüello and did not take well to the news that a new Spanish governor, Pablo Vicente Solá, was being appointed (MGV, 1:119).

11. Manuel Gómez is said to have been a partisan of the insurrectionists and uncle of one of Bouchard's officers (MGV, 1:203).

12. Jan Bazant, *A Concise History of Mexico from Hidalgo to Cárdenas, 1805–1940* (New York: Cambridge University Press, 1988), 19–23.

13. Victoria's quick death sentences in the case of individuals whose crimes had not been proven beyond a doubt or were minor alarmed the population as did his willingness to exile his nonsupporters, men like José Antonio Carrillo and Abel Stearns (Alvarado, 3:171). As Alvarado recalls, Victoria "contaba con el apoyo de los soldados, de los frayles y de los mexicanos" (3:171).

14. Although initiated in the south, the rebellion against Victoria united most of the native sons around Echeandía, but once Victoria was removed, dissension between the north and the south again broke out, with the north supporting Zamorano, the military officer in charge at Monterey, and the south, Echeandía (as military head) and Pío Pico (as head of the Diputación) (MGV, 2:163). But here friendship intervened, and Echeandía (a *yorkino*) and Zamorano (an *escocés* who had come to Alta California with Echeandía) were able to resolve the conflict peacefully by each retaining military control of his own area until the new governor was appointed.

15. The perspective of the Mexican bloc or *banda* is also present in the testimonials. Botello (22) goes so far as to say that the Californios tended to emphasize their suffering and to forget that the *mexicanos* also were mistreated by Governor Chico.

16. Coronel (19) suggests that Ramírez provoked this revolt because he could not control Gutiérrez but thought he could control Alvarado.

17. Alvarado's actual words are as follows: "California es libre y cortará todas sus relaciones con México hasta que la madre patria deje de ser oprimida por la actual facción dominante titulada gobierno central."

18. Daniel Cosío Villegas et al., *Historia mínima de México* (Mexico City: El Colegio de México, 1977), 100.

19. Hubert Howe Bancroft, *History of California* (San Francisco: The History Company Publishers, 1885–86), 5:524.

20. Ord insists that "the plan of the revolution was to make California independent" (43).

21. Carlos Carrillo's mother, Tomasa Ignacia Lugo de Carrillo, was the sister of Alvarado's grandmother, María Antonia Lugo de Vallejo, who raised Alvarado.

22. In effect Carrillo's appointment had been that official order. Unwilling to accept it, Alvarado, who claimed Carrillo's appointment was not valid because it lacked the president's signature, determined to impose his authority by force. For this reason Alvarado and José Castro marched south with a contingent of soldiers and civilians to confront the armed Californios and *mexicanos* that had gathered around Carlos Carrillo and José Antonio Carrillo.

23. Political enemies are often said to be friends: "no digo enemigos pues aunque opuestos en política Pío Pico, Carrillo, Ibarra y yo siempre fuimos buenos amigos personales" (Alvarado, 4:195).

24. In 1838 after several revolts against Alvarado, many of the leading men in the south, including José Antonio Carrillo, Pío Pico, Andrés Pico, Ignacio del Valle, Gil Ibarra,

Roberto Pardo, Narciso Botello, José María Ramírez, and Ignacio Palomares, were arrested; all but Pío Pico, who was ill, were sent to Sonoma as prisoners.

25. Botello bitterly indicates that Vallejo divided the group in two, with Carrillo, Andrés Pico, del Valle, and Carrillo's servant Juan Padilla receiving better treatment. The rest were locked up in the mission without beds, blankets, or sheets (81). The food was bad too, but things were to get worse. After eight days, Vallejo divided the mission prisoners into two groups, one of native Californios and one of *mexicanos*. The four *mexicanos* (del Valle, Ramírez, Pardo, and Botello) were placed in a narrow, dirty, flea-infested back room of the mission. After a few days, Vallejo allowed the Mexican men to rejoin the other prisoners in the main room of the mission.

26. Charles H. Shinn, "Pioneer Spanish Families in California, with Special Reference to the Vallejos," *The Century Magazine* 41, no. 50 (January 1891): 385.

27. Alvarado recalls that "muchos californios denominaban al general Vallejo el aristócrata de Sonoma debido a que él en esa frontera no dejaba imperar más leyes que su voluntad" (4:149).

28. Hubert Howe Bancroft, *California Pioneer Register 1542–1848* (Baltimore: Regional Publishing Co., 1964), 34.

29. Although Graham's riflemen had played an important role in support of Alvarado's revolution and would again play a role years later in support of Micheltorena, Alvarado placed forty-seven English, Irish, and American foreigners on a boat and shipped them to San Blas.

30. Vallejo's actual words are as follows: "que de ninguna manera permitiese que 'el monigote se me muriera en las manos'" (MGV, 4:236).

31. Josiah Royce, *California from the Conquest in 1846 to the Second Vigilance Committee in San Francisco: A Study in American Character* (New York: Houghton, Mifflin and Co., 1886), 173–74.

32. Some testimonials, for example that of Fernández (120–21), indicate that the Santa Barbara meeting was in fact held.

33. The pro-British group "los azules" was said to have conspired against Vallejo's life. One of the Mexicans who had been held in Sonoma for supporting Carrillo wrote to Vallejo, presumably to warn him (MGV, 4:243).

34. "Yo pensé en procurar para mi patria el protectorado de la Inglaterra con el fin de impedir que ella fuese a caer en manos de los demagogos, mientras que el gobernador Pío Pico hizo revivir ese proyecto cuando ya los demagogos estaban en vísperas de entronarse cuales dueños en nuestra misma casa" (Alvarado, 5:149).

35. "Don José A. Carrillo detestaba a los ingleses y deseoso de impedir que se consumase el sacrificio de las libertades de su patria resolvió con un golpe bien dirigido libertarla del tirano [i.e., Pico] que después de haberse robado los terrenos pertenecientes a las ex-misiones, estaba moviendo cielo y tierra para entregarla maniatada a un déspota europeo" (MGV, 5:49).

36. Archivo histórico diplomático mexicano 15. *Lord Aberdeen, Texas y California*. Con una introducción de Antonio de la Peña y Reyes (Mexico City: Editorial Porrúa, 1970), 51–52.

37. Archivo histórico diplomático mexicano 35. *La gestión diplomática del Doctor Mora*. Con una advertencia de Luis Chávez Orozco (Mexico City: Editorial Porrúa, 1970), 38–40.

38. Charles Adams Hale, *Mexican Liberalism in the Age of Mora, 1821–1853* (New Haven: Yale University Press, 1968), 27.

39. Castro, who always found a way to resolve confrontations between Californios through mediation and the firing of a few shots, had also been unwilling to chase Frémont out of Gavilán Hill in 1845, "where the stars and stripes waved" (Ord, 1956: 58) even after he had ordered him out of the department. Castro had rescinded his previous permis-

sion to the engineer and his men to rest in the San Joaquín Valley after a "tiring trip of exploration" as soon as word from Mexico identified him not as an explorer of routes but as a U.S. military operative (MGV, 5:97–98). As Ord recalls: "The opposing forces never met, because Frémont did not wait for the attack. As was said with considerable truth, Castro wasn't anxious to make the assault, though he was urged by Alvarado and others who accompanied him. But Castro was not addicted to exposing his interesting person to bullets. He preferred to settle things [amicably], or [through intrigue] or in any manner that would not risk his hide" (1956: 58; note changes in brackets based on original, 1878: 137).

40. The first sentence of this quotation has been mistranslated in the English edition as "The conquest of California did not bother the Californians, least of all the women" (1956: 59). But the gist of the sentence is not too far from the mistranslation, as Ord seems to suggest that given the ruinous conditions she stipulates anything would be better.

41. Frémont had had himself named "gobernador del Estado Independiente de California" (MGV, 5:147)—an act that clearly compromised his pledged allegiance to the United States.

42. In Vallejo's words, "pues esos dos jefes con su comportamiento cobarde probaron hasta la evidencia más completa que carecían del valor cívico y marcial que conviene al ciudadano en un héroe" (MGV, 5:190).

43. When the soldiers arrived to search the home, Flores's wife made him get on all fours, draped a sarape around him, and sat on him until the soldiers left. Afterward he left the house and escaped (Coronel, 83).

44. Wilson is quoted in George William Beattie, "The Battle of Chino," *Quarterly of the Historical Society of Southern California* 24, no. 4 (December 1942): 148. Beattie thinks Lugo's reasoning "fanciful" and even indicates that in his testimonial "his narrative shows an impairment of mental faculties." Beattie of course prefers the versions of the Chino battle offered by Benjamin Wilson, Michael White, and Stephen C. Foster (Beattie, 144–46).

45. The last sentence of this quotation is mistranslated in the English edition of Ord's testimonial (1956).

46. Ord's plan called for Chávez to be brought into the house on the shoulders of another short man; two days later when the U.S. soldiers came to search her home at night, she hid him inside a couch. When Chávez was finally able to leave his hiding place, he thanked her for saving his life.

7. Constructs of Ethnicity

1. Terry Eagleton, "Nationalism: Irony and Commitment," in Terry Eagleton, Fredric Jameson, and Edward Said, *Nationalism, Colonialism, and Literature* (Minneapolis: University of Minnesota Press, 1990), 30.

2. Fredric Jameson, "De la sustitución de importaciones literarias y culturales en el Tercer Mundo: el caso del testimonio," in *Revista de crítica literaria latinoamericana* 28, no. 36 (September 1992): 131.

3. Fredric Jameson, *The Ideologies of Theory: Essays 1971–1986. Volume 2: The Syntax of History* (Minneapolis: University of Minnesota Press, 1988), 175.

4. Spencer C. Olin Jr., *California Politics 1846–1920: The Emerging Corporate State* (San Francisco: Boyd and Fraser, 1981), 1–40.

5. Terry E. Stephenson, "Forster vs. Pico," *Quarterly Historical Society of Southern California* 18, no. 2 (June 1936): 61.

6. James Petras and Morley Morris, *U.S. Hegemony under Siege* (London: Verso, 1990), 66–67.

7. Josiah Royce, *California from the Conquest in 1846 to the Second Vigilance Committee in San Francisco: A Study in American Character* (New York: Houghton, Mifflin, and Co., 1886), 487.

8. "Nosotros sufriremos un menoscabo de territorios, pero en el que conservamos, nuestra independencia es plena y absoluta" (Archivo histórico diplomático mexicano 31. *Algunos documentos sobre el Tratado de Guadalupe y la Situación de México durante la invasión americana* [Mexico City: Editorial Porrúa, 1970], 344, 141).

9. "Esas posesiones eran perdidas el día que se disparara el primer tiro."

10. "Serán respetadas como válidas, con la misma extensión con que lo serían si los indicados territorios permanecieran dentro de los límites de México" (Archivo, 31:122–23).

11. Article 10 was totally eliminated by the U.S. Congress; the U.S. commissioners later clarified in a separate note that articles 9 and 10 as originally formulated were implicit in understandings expressed in article 3 of the Louisiana Treaty and valid here as well.

12. The figure of 813 claims is from N. Ray Gilmore and Gladys Gilmore, eds., *Readings in California History* (New York: T. Y. Crowell Co. 1966), 166, footnote 6. The figure of 346 claims made by non-Mexicans is from David J. Weber, *Foreigners in Their Native Land: Historical Roots of the Mexican Americans* (Albuquerque: University of New Mexico Press, 1973), 195.

13. Also see J. M. Guinn, "The Passing of the Rancho," *Annual Publication of The Historical Society of Southern California* 10, parts 1 and 2 (1915–16): 47.

14. John Hittell, "Mexican Land Claims in California," *California Controversies*, ed. Leonard Pitt (Atlanta: Scott, Foresman and Co., 1968), 93.

15. Paul W. Gates, "California Land Claims: A Modern Historian's View," *Readings in California History*, ed. N. Ray Gilmore and Gladys Gilmore (New York: T. Y. Crowell Co., 1966), 173.

16. Terry E. Stephenson, "Forster vs. Pico," *Quarterly Historical Society of Southern California* 18, no. 1 (March 1936): 22–30; in 18, no. 2 (June 1936): 30. Also see Martin Cole, "Foreword," in *Historical Narrative, 1877*, by Pío Pico (Glendale, Calif.: Arthur H. Clark Co., 1973), 14–15.

17. Henry D. Barrow, "Pío Pico: A Biographical and Character Sketch of the Last Mexican Governor of Alta California," *Historical Society of Southern California Publication* 2, part 1 (1891–96): 63.

18. "cuando ya su dueño primitivo había sido arruinado" (Alvarado, 5:218).

19. From a letter written by M. G. Vallejo, reprinted in Madie Brown Emparán, *The Vallejos of California* (San Francisco: The Gleeson Library Associates, University of San Francisco, 1968), 139.

20. Mario T. García, "Merchants and Dons: San Diego's Attempt at Modernization, 1850–1860," *Journal of San Diego History* 21, no. 1 (Winter 1975): 56, 71.

21. "con el cambio de bandera, la mayoría ha ganado" (Alvarado, 1: iii–iv).

22. Unable to restock their ranges, the *rancheros*, even wealthy land and cattle capitalists like Stearns, would be forced to subdivide the land, creating small land tracts of about forty acres, at prices ranging from two to ten dollars per acre (Guinn, 47). This first land boom in the south created new spaces of small land holdings for settlers from the north and from the eastern states.

The transcontinental railroad in 1869 and later the establishment of the Southern Pacific would bring additional waves of immigrants and numerous tourists to California, and lead to the establishment of new residential areas or townsites along the Southern

Pacific rail line or near cities. Also see Joseph Netz, "The Great Los Angeles Real Estate Boom of 1887," *Annual Publication of the Historical Society of Southern California* 10, parts 1 and 2 (1915–16): 57.

23. María Amparo Ruiz de Burton, *The Squatter and the Don,* eds. Rosaura Sánchez and Beatrice Pita (Houston: Arte Público Press, 1993), 352.

24. Antonio Ríos-Bustamante and Pedro Castillo, *An Illustrated History of Mexican Los Angeles, 1781–1985* (Los Angeles: UCLA Chicano Studies Research Center, 1986), 98, 105.

25. Pacheco, nephew of Benicia Vallejo, would serve as assemblyman, state senator, county judge, lieutenant governor, acting governor, and congressman; see Ronald Genini and Richard Hitchman, *Romvaldo Pacheco: A Californio in Two Eras* (San Francisco: The Book Club of California, 1985), 158.

26. Leonard Pitt, *The Decline of the Californios: A Social History of Spanish-Speaking Californians, 1846–1890* (Berkeley: University of California Press, 1966), 272–73.

27. Karl Marx, "The Communist Manifesto," *Selected Works of Karl Marx and Frederick Engels* (New York: International Publishers, 1968), 38.

28. Fredric Jameson, *Postmodernism; or, The Cultural Logic of Late Capitalism* (Durham: Duke University Press, 1991), 314–15.

29. Stuart Hall, "Race, Culture and Communications: Looking Backward and Forward at Cultural Studies," *Rethinking Marxism* 5, no. 1 (Spring 1992): 14.

30. Peter Skerry, *Mexican Americans: The Ambivalent Minority* (New York: The Free Press/Macmillan Inc., 1993).

31. Albert K. Weinberg, *Manifest Destiny: A Study of Nationalist Expansionism in American History* (Baltimore: Johns Hopkins University Press, 1935), 177.

32. John Hittell et al., *The Discovery of Gold in California, 1891* (Palo Alto: Lewis Osborne, 1968), 31.

33. See Sarah Royce, *A Frontier Lady* (New Haven: Yale University Press, 1932).

34. "los Californios eran considerados lo mismo que los demás americanos" (Coronel, 178).

35. Even in twentieth-century hegemonic essays on the bandits, the tendency is to portray those lynched as murderers. See Phillip J. Rasch, "The Story of Hangman's Tree," *Quarterly of the Historical Society of Southern California* 39, no. 1 (March 1957): 59–64.

36. Joseph Henry Jackson, "Introduction," *Joaquín Murieta,* by John (Yellow Bird) Rollin Ridge (Norman, Okla.: University of Oklahoma Press, 1986), xxi.

37. Antonio Gramsci, *Selections from the Prison Notebooks* (New York: International Publishers, 1978), 108.

38. Joshua Fishman and Gary Keller, *Bilingual Education for Hispanic Students* (New York: Columbia University Press, 1982), 13.

39. Michael C. Neri, "A Journalistic Portrait of the Spanish-Speaking People of California, 1868–1925," *Quarterly of the Historical Society of Southern California* 55, no. 2 (Summer 1973): 196.

40. David Levin, *History as Romantic Art* (New York: Harcourt, Brace & World, 1959), 107.

41. Ronald Genini and Richard Hitchman, *Romualdo Pacheco: A Californio in Two Eras* (San Francisco: The Book Club of California, 1985), 98.

42. See note 47 of chapter 2.

43. J. M. Guinn, "Los Angeles in the Later Sixties and Early Seventies," in *Quarterly of the Historical Society of Southern California* 3 (1893): 67.

Testimonial References

Unpublished Testimonials, Manuscripts, Letters, and Documents (from the Collection of the Bancroft Library, University of California at Berkeley)

Alvarado, Juan Bautista. *Historia de California.* 1876. (BANC MSS C-D 1, 2, 3, 4, and 5)

Argüello, Luis Antonio. *Diario formado en la expedición emprendida el diez y siete de octubre de 1821 de los acontecimientos ocurridos en ella desde su principio hasta su conclusión.* 1821. (BANC MSS C-C 230)

Avila de Ríos, Catarina. *Recuerdos.* 1877. (BANC MSS C-D 35)

Berreyesa, Antonio. *Relación.* 1877. (BANC MSS C-D 44)

Botello, Narciso. *Anales del sur de la California, 1833–1844. 1878. (BANC MSS C-D 49)*

Carrillo de Fitch, Josefa. *Dictation of Mrs. Captain Henry D. Fitch.* 1875. (BANC MSS C-E 67:10)

Carrillo de Vallejo, Benicia Francisca. Carta a Juan Frisbie (27 de septiembre de 1873). Vallejo family papers. (BANC C-B 441)

———. Carta a Platón Vallejo (5 de marzo de 1877).

———. Carta a Platón Vallejo (abril de 1877).

———. Carta a Platón Vallejo (12 de noviembre de 1878).

Castro, Manuel. *Informe de los principales acontecimientos políticos, militares y eclesiásticos de la Alta California.* 1876. (BANC MSS C-D 9)

Cerruti, Henry (Enrique). *Ramblings in California.* 1874. (BANC MSS)

Coronel, Antonio Franco. *Cosas de California.* 1877. (BANC MSS C-D 61)

de la Guerra de Hartnell, Teresa. *Narrativa de la distinguida matrona californiana Doña Teresa de la Guerra de Hartnell.* 1875. (BANC MSS C-E 67:2)

de la Torre, Estevan. *Reminiscencias.* 1877. (BANC MSS C-D 163)

Estudillo, José María. *Expedición 1819 a los Tulares por cimarrones.* 1819. (BANC MSS C-C 72)

Estudillo, José María (hijo). *Datos históricos sobre la Alta California.* 1878. (BANC MSS C-D 76)

Fernández, José. *Cosas de California.* 1874. (BANC MSS C-D 10)

González, Mauricio. *Memorias.* 1877. (BANC MSS C-D 91)

Isidora, viuda del príncipe Solano. *Relación de la entrevista que tuve con Isidora.* 1874. Entrevista de Enrique Cerruti. (BANC MSS C-E 65:12)

Larios, Estolario. *Vida y aventuras de mi padre Don Manuel Larios, vecino de San Juan Bautista.* 1878. (BANC MSS C-B 71)

Lorenzana, Apolinaria. *Memorias.* 1878. (BANC MSS C-D 116)
Machado de Ridington (Wrightington), Juana. *Los tiempos pasados de la Alta California.* 1878. (BANC MSS C-D 119)
Ord, María Angustias de la Guerra. *Ocurrencias en California.* 1878. (BANC MSS C-D 134)
Osuna de Marrón, Felipa. *Recuerdos.* 1878. (BANC MSS C-D 120)
Pérez, Eulalia. *Una vieja y sus recuerdos.* 1877. (BANC MSS C-D 139)
Pico, Pío. *Narración histórica.* 1877. (Microfilm X31 534)
Pico de Avila, María Inocenta. *Cosas de California.* 1878. (BANC MSS C-D 34)
Requena, Manuel. Carta a Eustaquio Barrón (5 de junio de 1841). Savage documents.
————. Carta a Antonio María Osío (enero de 1842). Savage documents.
Ruiz de Burton, María Amparo. Carta a Hubert Howe Bancroft (15 de julio de 1878). Savage documents, 2:121–23.
————. Carta a H. H. Bancroft (5 de agosto de 1878). Savage documents, 2:124–25.
————. *Biographical Sketch of Don José Manuel Ruiz.* 1878. Savage documents, 2:129–41.
Valdez, Dorotea. *Reminiscences of Dorotea Valdez.* 1874. (BANC MSS C-E 65:8)
Vallejo, José de Jesús. *Reminiscencias históricas de California.* 1874. (BANC MSS C-D 16)
Vallejo, Mariano Guadalupe. Carta a John Dwinelle (24 de septiembre de 1866). Vallejo documents.
————. Carta a Juan Bautista Alvarado (24 de agosto de 1874). Vallejo documents.
————. Carta a Juan G. Warner (29 de agosto de 1874). Vallejo documents.
————. Carta a Juan Bautista Alvarado (24 de diciembre de 1875). Vallejo documents.
————. Carta a Juan Bautista Alvarado (27 de diciembre de 1875). Vallejo documents.
————. Carta a Juan Bautista Alvarado (17 de marzo de 1876). Vallejo documents.
————. Carta a Juan Bautista Alvarado (17 de junio de 1876). Vallejo documents.
————. Carta a Platón Vallejo (abril de 1877). Vallejo family papers. (BANC MSS C-B 441)
————. Carta a Platón Vallejo (4 de marzo de 1885). Vallejo family papers. (BANC MSS C-B 441)
————. *Discurso histórico.* 8 de octubre de 1876. Vallejo documents.
————. *Documentos para la historia de la Alta California.* 1874. Vallejo documents.
————. *Recuerdos históricos y personales tocante a la Alta California.* 1874. (BANC MSS C-D 17, 18, 19, 20, 21)
————. *Vida de William B. Ide.* 1879. Savage documents, vol. 2.
Vallejo, Platón. Carta a su padre M. G. Vallejo (18 de septiembre de 1874). Vallejo family papers. (BANC MSS C-B 441)
————. Letter to his father M. G. Vallejo (14 July 1875). Vallejo family papers. (BANC MSS C-B 441)
————. *Memoirs of the Vallejos.* 1914. (BANC MSS C-D 5063)
Vallejo, Salvador. *Datos sobre el señor Sutter.* 1874. Vallejo documents.
————. *Notas históricas sobre California.* 1874. (BANC MSS C-D 22)
Vallejo de Leese, Rosalía. *History of the Bear Party.* 1874. (BANC MSS C-E 65:10).

Published Testimonials, Reports, and Essays

Alvarado, Juan Bautista. *Vignettes of Early California.* (n.d.) San Francisco: The Book Club, 1982.
Argüello, Luis Antonio. *The Diary of Captain Luis Antonio Argüello: October 17 to November 17, 1821.* Trans. V. Fisher. Berkeley, Calif.: Friends of the Bancroft Library, 1992.
Briones, Brígida. "A Glimpse of Domestic Life in 1827" and "A Carnival Ball at Monterey in 1829." *The Century Illustrated Monthly Magazine* 41, no. 62 (November 1890–April 1891): 468, 470.

Carrillo, Adolfo. *Cuentos californianos*. Los Angeles: *La Prensa*. n.d. (ca. 1922).

Carrillo, Carlos Antonio. *Exposition Addressed to the Chamber of Deputies of the Congress of the Union, 1831*. Trans. Herbert Ingram Priestley. San Francisco: John Henry Nash, 1938.

Castañares, Manuel. *Colección de documentos relativos al departamento de Californias*. México: Imprenta de *La Voz del Pueblo*. 1845.

"*El Clamor Público*, 1857. Letter to the Editor." In *Foreigners in Their Native Land*. Ed. David J. Weber. Albuquerque: University of New Mexico Press, 1973. 174–76.

Coronel, Antonio Franco. "A Mexican in the Mines: Translation of the Mining Experiences of Antonio F. Coronel as Related in his Memoirs." In Richard Morefield, *The Mexican Adaptation in American California, 1846–1875*. Berkeley, Calif.: University of California Press, 1955. 75–96.

———. "Letter to Father J. Adam on the Founding of the Pueblo of Los Angeles and the Building of the Church of Our Lady of the Angels, with a Translation and Correction." *Southern California Quarterly* 10 (1915–17): 124–27.

de la Guerra, Pablo. *Speech in the Senate of California on the 17th of April, 1855*. Sacramento: State Tribune Office, 1855.

Escobar, Agustín. "The Campaign of '46 against the American." In Carlos Hijar, Eulalia Pérez, and Agustín Escobar, *Three Memoirs of Mexican California*. Trans. V. Fisher et al. Berkeley, Calif.: Friends of the Bancroft Library, 1988. 107–12.

Fages, Pedro. "Repartición de solares y suertes de tierra de regadío y secadal." *Annual Publication of the Historical Society of Southern California* 15, part 1 (1931): 218–54.

Forster, Juan. "Pioneer Data from 1832." *Quarterly of the Historical Society of Southern California* 52, no. 3 (September 1970): 195–230.

Higuera, Prudencia. "Trading with the Americans." *The Century Illustrated Monthly Magazine* 41, no. 26 (November 1890–April 1891): 89–90.

Hijar, Carlos, Eulalia Pérez, and Agustín Escobar. *Three Memoirs of Mexican California*. Trans. V. Fisher et al. Berkeley, Calif.: Friends of the Bancroft Library, 1988.

Junta de Fomento de Californias. "Principal Actions of the California Junta de Fomento, 1825–1827." Trans. and ed. Keld J. Reynolds, *California Historical Society Quarterly* 24, no. 4 (1945): 289–320, and no. 5 (1946): 268–79.

Lugo, José del Carmen. "Life of a Rancher, 1877." Trans. by Mrs. G. W. Beattie in *Quarterly of the Historical Society of Southern California* 32, no. 3 (September 1950): 185–236.

Machado de Ridington (Wrightington), Juana. "Recollections, 1878." Trans. Raymond S. Brandes. *Quarterly of the Historical Society of Southern California* 41, no. 3 (September 1959): 195–240.

Ord, María Angustias de la Guerra. *Occurrences in Hispanic California, 1878*. Trans. Francis Price and W. H. Ellison. Washington, D.C.: Academy of Franciscan History, 1956.

Pico, Antonio María et al. "Petition of Antonio María Pico et al., to the Senate and House of Representatives of the United States." In *Foreigners in Their Native Land*. Ed. David J. Weber. Albuquerque: University of New Mexico Press, 1973. 195–99.

Pico, Pío. *Historical Narrative, 1877*. Trans. Arthur P. Botello, 1877. Glendale, Calif.: Arthur H. Clark Co., 1973.

Requena, Manuel, et al. "Petition to Congress against Forcing Statehood on South California, March 3, 1850." *Annual Publication of the Historical Society of Southern California* 10, parts 1 and 2 (1915–16): 75–76.

Rezanov, Count Nikolai Petrovich. *Rezanov Reconnoiters California, 1806*. Ed. Richard A. Pierce. San Francisco: Book Club of California, 1972.

Seguín, John N. *Personal Memoirs of John N. Seguín from the Year 1834 to the Retreat of General Woll from the City of San Antonio, 1842*. San Antonio: Ledger Book and Job Office, 1858.

"Treaty of Guadalupe-Hidalgo, 1848." In *Foreigners in Their Native Land*. Ed. David J. Weber. Albuquerque: University of New Mexico Press, 1973. 162–68.

Vallejo, Guadalupe. "Ranch and Mission Days in Alta California." *The Century Illustrated Monthly Magazine* 41, no. 2 (November 1890–April 1891): 183, 184, 189, 191–92. Reprinted in *Sketches of Early California*. San Francisco: Chronicle Books, 1971, 3–32.

Vallejo, Mariano Guadalupe, et al. "In the Matter of the Claim of M. G. Vallejo, Víctor Castro, and Agustín Alviso against the Republic of Mexico. Petition to the Secretary of State of the United States of North America." San Francisco: n.p., March 17, 1870.

Vásquez, Tiburcio. "Revenge Took Possession of Me. 1874." In *Foreigners in Their Native Land*. Ed. David J. Weber. Albuquerque: University of New Mexico Press, 1973. 226–28.

Zalvidea, Fr. José María de. "Preguntas y Respuestas: Mission San Gabriel in 1814." Trans. and ed. Maynard Geiger, O. F. M. *Quarterly of the Historical Society of Southern California* 53, no. 3 (September 1971): 235–50.

Index

Rosaura Sánchez is a professor in the Department of Literature at the University of California, San Diego. Her work in critical theory, literary analysis, and sociolinguistics has appeared in numerous literary journals and anthologies. Her fiction has also been published in a variety of Chicano journals. She is the author of *Chicano Discourse* and recently coedited the republication of *The Squatter and the Don,* a novel written by M. A. Ruiz de Burton in 1885.